Key Words, Concepts and Methods for Information Age Instruction:

A Guide to Teaching Information Inquiry

By Daniel Callison

ISBN 0-9742537-0-7

LMS Associates, LLC
17 East Henrietta Street
Baltimore, Maryland 21230-3910
http://www.schoollibrarymedia.com

Part II, pgs. 93-360 originally published in *School Library Media Activities Monthly*, 1996-2002, © LMS Associates, LLC

Table of Contents

continues on page iv

Table of Contents continued from page iii

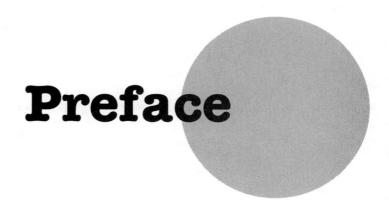

Preface

My goal for writing the regular column on "Key Words in Instruction" and this first book concerning "Information Inquiry" is to broaden the application of information literacy. Over the past ten years, much has been defined in terms of the "information literate student," but very little concerning the "information literate teacher" or "information literate librarian." Just because one holds the title "school library media specialist" does not mean that person knows how to teach and evaluate information literacy skills. Just because one holds the title "teacher" does not mean that person is well versed in inquiry-based and constructivist theory in order to fully engage their students in meaningful investigations.

Information inquiry is, therefore, at least a dual-path process. First, information inquiry provides an agenda for helping library media specialists and other teachers, from all disciplines, to become "instructional media specialists". Some have advanced these ideas before, only in different packaging and under different terms, "teacher-librarian" or "accomplished teacher." Second, information inquiry is based on the premise that one does not become a skilled teacher of information literacy unless he or she has first mastered both the content of information literacy and related literacies, and has mastered effective teaching techniques for modeling the learning process as well as for evaluating student information use performance.

There may be other paths. There is so much more to explore and so many more instructional terms and techniques to consider in relationship to information inquiry. But for now, let this book build beyond just the student as the only or central subject for becoming information literate. Let us, as educators, include ourselves in this educational process and use information inquiry as a way to model, collaborate, inspire, and learn with our students.

This is a huge task. It is a very complex and demanding undertaking. Most library media specialists and classroom teachers can work at these skills for the duration of their professional lives and not masters all elements. Many educators will never become information fluent, able to move from one discipline's research method to another, from one set of investigative skills to another depending on the need and demands of the situation. But, they must engage in the information inquiry process and strive to grow and mature to reasonable levels that will support them in efforts to teach young learners. Information inquiry, therefore is both a learning and a teaching process. The five elements (questioning, exploring, assimilation, inference, and reflection) interact among themselves and interact between teacher and student. This is an extremely dynamic process and this book provides only an introduction to key models, terms, concepts and techniques. The reader will find more depth of discussion among the resources associated with each chapter and each key instructional word.

It takes information literate teachers to implement and manage a curriculum for information inquiry. Jerry Harste, former NCTE President and Indiana University Professor, often tells language arts teachers that "curriculum is more than a series of prescribed activities to keep students and teachers busy." Information inquiry is a process, which provides the foundation for "inquiry as curriculum." Information literacy must be more than a set of skills that are mastered to help students show short-term gains on standardized tests. Information inquiry is a dynamic teaching and learning process of value to all, regardless of academic discipline, who value a progressive education for life-long learning.

Some models presented in this text will help to visualize the inquiry process. Some models have been sold as the grand formula to meet any information problem. While there are common elements found across these models for learning, teaching and problem-solving, to fit all tasks to a simple formula narrows the abilities of the human mind to fully explore possibilities, limits both creative and critical thinking, and ultimately places inquiry learning back within the confines of a textbook structure where the teacher dictates learning tasks, rather than engaging the learner in self-motivation and self-reflection. Information inquiry looks across many models to find common elements and provides a framework to apply these elements to a wide variety of learning situations across academic disciplines.

The instructional media specialist, teacher of information literacy, or teacher of inquiry described in this text is the master teacher who has moved into serious attempts to apply information inquiry to the teaching-learning processes. This instructional media specialist may come from any teaching background. He or she is not just one from a resources specialization such as school librarian, or just from a subject content such as history, science, or language arts teacher. The instructional media specialist strives to become resourceful in selection of information, use of multiple resources and media, and applies the princi-

ples of information literacy, media literacy, creative thinking, and critical thinking to the development and delivery of curriculum. At this level, all teachers become interchangeable parts ready to help students advance in their information skills. At this level, any teacher as instructional media specialist is able to introduce students to quality resources, give information advisory for meaningful information selection and use, and judge student application of information as evidence to make an argument, draw a conclusion, or elaborate on an event or issue.

Does this eliminate the need for teachers with special subject expertise or reduce the need for "teacher-librarians" as information specialists? NO. Information inquiry defines a teaching-learning level toward which all educators strive so that there can be a new level for collaboration in delivery of meaningful, perhaps for the first time truly authentic, learning environments. The instructional media specialist is an information scientist and the information library media resource center is a learning laboratory. Students become cognitive apprentices and the cycles of inquiry become the curriculum. Under this process teaching positions and school librarians do not disappear. They do, however, increase the level of their educational roles and combine in their efforts to model and enhance inquiry.

Many of the teaching roles and techniques described in the pages of this text are parallel to the national teacher of library media standards which recommend that educators in information literacy and library media:
- have knowledge of different learning styles and can analyze learner needs
- know how to engage students in active, more authentic learning
- can plan, implement, and assess learning and student performance
- can involve the school and its community members in learning
- can document teaching and learning as a reflective professional

Acknowledgments

My thanks to the following people who, collectively, have been a key influence on this work.

Paula Montgomery, founding editor of School Library Media Activities Monthly, told me clearly in an interview in Indianapolis in 1994 that she was seeing change in "library instruction", finally. There was movement away from simple orientations which introduced a single lesson or a small cluster of information tools toward units of instruction, integrated with classroom content, and centered on not so much location of resources, but finding meaning in the information found. Some school library media specialists were actually becoming educators as they modeled information use and application to information problem-solving. She has provided the forum for Key Words in Instruction and over the past six years, and we have explored dozens of concepts that provide the foundation for information inquiry. This book is a compilation to date, but, hopefully, not the end. There is much more to explore and more key words to define in relation to information inquiry.

Mike Printz and Patty Callison, my wife, both implemented extensive student inquiry projects at Topeka West High School in the 1970s, long before "information literacy" was a part of the librarian's standard vocabulary. Oral history multimedia reports developed by their students were projects that truly introduced information inquiry at higher levels than the basic information problem-solving we still see today as library "research" exercises. Their inventiveness and commitment to student learning served as a model and inspiration for what I have written for the pages of this text.

Carol Collier Kuhlthau, whose high level of research should be a goal for all of us in higher education and school media, has given me comments and has written the key documents that serve as a backbone to information inquiry. Kuhlthau defined for our field a process approach to library skills instruction and tied us closer to meaningful educational theory.

Edward Victor, a science educator who turned me on to the principles of inquiry learning and teaching. I first applied his ideas to free inquiry learning in children's museums and later, in the mid-1980s, to school library media programs. My article in School Library Journal, February 1986, included a warning that if school library media specialists did not increase their role as teachers and specifically apply principles of inquiry learning over traditional lock-step teaching techniques, that such would help justify the continuing decline in school media collection investments and continued lack of interest in such library programs. The elements of free inquiry I drew from Victor are:

- cooperative learning helps students manage complex tasks
- objectives for inquiry evolve as the student explores and gains background
- students can document the inquiry learning process to teach themselves and others
- content for inquiry is driven by questions and formulating or revising questions so that they are operational, realistic, and answerable; inquiry is the process of generating questions and not be satisfied with simple answers
- teachers provide direction and guidance, but students must be encouraged to take initiatives; motivation can come from such freedom
- time for inquiry units must be flexible; on-task may mean over several weeks or semesters
- peer tutoring, from students who have experienced inquiry, is valuable for students who are being introduced to inquiry
- projects become more valued by the student and others when they are shared with peers and parents
- inquiry will continue beyond the project as some students will choose to extend their learning beyond the academic exercise

Carol Tilley, who has provided a much more intelligent approach to literature reviews and educational theory than I have. I hope she will take much of what she has written and taught for us at Indiana University with her as she continues in her higher education teaching and research profession. Carol is one of many students I have had the pleasure of learning from as well as teaching. Hundreds of students have made the course we introduced in 1992, "Information Inquiry for School Teachers", one of the most useful classes for teacher education.

Cheryl McCarthy shared her excellent lists of resources for this publication.

And thanks to a cadre of Indiana school media specialists, several responsible for integrating the AASL information literacy standards into the new Indiana standards for student achievement, have given a great deal of guidance and feedback to me on the Key Words in Instruction. Julia Robinson, Kym Kramer, Sharon Roualet, Melissa Altman, Christine Somers, Nocha Flick, Ed Jurewicz, Ann Sheehan, Karen Sprunger, Shirley Ross, Monica Greene, Linda Cornwell, Leslie Preddy, Nancy McGriff, Catherine Trinkle, and Linda Mills are each Hoosier educators who have written or taught in some manner to influence the content of this book.

Danny Callison
Bloomington, IN

Part 1

Information

Chapter 1

Concepts and Components of Information Inquiry

This book contains a discussion of concepts, components, and methods for the most exciting and natural form of learning and teaching — inquiry. Questions posed to oneself or by others drive the learning and teaching processes.

Seeking one answer is never enough. Raising additional questions is always a goal. Learning there are multiple answers or a spectrum of possibilities, although one or two seem to have the strongest potential to be "right", is mind-opening, humanistic, euphoric.

Information abounds. It surrounds us without a single request on our part. With little effort, however, we can call upon much more information. How we determine meaningful ways to manage the information that flows to us and fit it to the questions we have determined to be most important, requires skills that are complex and demanding.

The instruction words defined in this collection are based on an ageless method for teaching and for learning, inquiry. Placed within the context of the Information Age, the Socratic Method takes on a new dynamic form. Through discussion of words related to progressive educational trends over the past two decades, information inquiry becomes a way to think and teach in the Information Age.

The components of information inquiry tie together the essential methods which must be practiced by both teacher and learner in order to meet basic information and media literacy skills. In its most dynamic application by those who have matured in their abilities to master these new skills, information fluency is possible across nearly any problem or project.

When integrated with academic content areas across the curriculum, information inquiry, supported by the knowledgeable use of modern information technologies can result in learners who are fluent in selection and application of methods to address their information needs. These learners are fluent in that they have mastered the concepts and components of information literacy to the degree they can adjust and address future changes as the Information Age continues to evolve.

The Five Components of Information Inquiry

A component represents a part of a compound or complex whole. The components described here are based on the essential concepts for information inquiry, those ideas for actions to be taken by the learner to acquire and apply knowledge. Elements of inquiry, especially in the learning process associated with the scientific method, are further defined in the key word "Inquiry."

Questioning. This component rests on natural curiosity held by most humans from birth. Who? What? Where? When? How? But most of all, Why? This component, as it interacts with the other four, becomes a more refined skill set. The result is the ability to ask more refined, focused, relevant, and insightful questions.

Questions trigger the interactions that can eventually lead to greater understanding of an environment, a situation, a problem, an issue, actions of a person or group. Today, these questions are raised in an environment dominated by a flood of information, often unorganized, misleading, and overpowering. Understanding, meaning, and solution are the indicators of the end products of the inquiry process. Conclusions are also the basis for a beginning to another set of questions. Information inquiry is based on a continuous questioning cycle, the essence of lifelong learning.

Exploration. Closely tied to questioning, exploration is the action taken to seek answers to the questions. In many cases, no specific questions are on the agenda, but the drive to satisfy coursity moves the learner to reading, viewing, listening to, and searching through information. As the information inquiry components interact and the abilities of the explorer mature, exploration becomes the action to gain information related to specific questions. Exploration becomes a systematic search for and examination of resources and information.

Sources of information, in whatever format the learner can gain access, are examined, accepted and disguarded based on gaining satisfaction. Over time and through many cycles of these components, information needs and tasks become more focused. As a result, exploration involves a more discriminating process to seek and select information. Mature abilities gained through practice and experience result in more efficient use of time to search, examine and reflect.

Assimilation. This component involves the actions to absorb and fit information to that which is already known, believed or assumed by the learner. In some cases, assimilation means reinforcing or confirming what is known. In other cases, assimilation involves an altering of what has been accepted as knowledge by the individual learner or group of learners.

Inquiry turns learning into more than a gathering of facts. Assimilation through inquiry leads to consideration of a wider range of perceptions and options. As the inquirer matures, assimilation involves linking a host of diverse information to that previously known and applying that information to meet different future situations. Assimilation involves accumulation of knowledge, alteration of accepted

knowledge, and constant consideration of alternatives.

New information assimilated with previously held information is accepted as knowledge, new knowledge on the part of the individual learner even if not new to many others. Such is also accepted as knowledge whether the information is right or wrong. The learner assimilates or comprehends a meaning and thus the information is retained as knowledge, not just a fact without relevance.

Inference. This component involves the actions or processes for deriving a conclusion from facts and premises. Inference may involve personal choice and actions taken based on conclusions which seem most relevant and meaningful for the situation. On a personal basis, inference is usually an internal message to the self, and not one that is conveyed in a formal manner to others.

In other cases, inference may involve a wider communication of conclusions. The inference is either shared among members of a group working on the same tasks in a cooperative effort, or the inference is presented to those who might need a recommendation for action, or need to evaluate the learner's ability to address a problem and communicate a solution.

A sharing of the conclusions may lead to further assimilation of more information for both the presenter and the audience. Presentation of inferences often refines the meaning of the conclusions and may be delivered to an audience to both inform them and often to persuade them. In nearly all cases, inference will raise new questions for exploration.

Information within the inference component is most useful when it becomes evidence. The information may come from observation, literature review, expert or witness interview, data from survey or experimental study, and range in levels from slight association to clear cause and effect. Evidence is necessary to support a claim, notion, plan for change or hypothesis. Without evidence, inference leading to conclusions and recommendations can not be made. Evidence may be necessary to justify the status quo or accepted norm.

Evidence is always necessary to justify change.

Reflection. This component raises the question which brings the interactions of the elements to a complete cycle, "Have I been successful in answering my question?"

Further, other questions which involve assessment of the information inquiry process extend from reflection. Where the resources used the best possible? What new questions have resulted and how should they be explored? Is what has been accepted as new knowledge meaningful to me, to others? Has this knowledge been understood to the extend that the communication process is complete? What evaluation of the application of this cycle in information inquiry do others have to offer?

As the learner matures in his or her ability, reflection will be used more and more within each component as well as an overall action. Reflections to assess exploration, assimilation, and inference are formative in that the the leaner is aware of the consequences of actions in one component on the limitations or opportunities in other components. Reflection that is summative in nature allows the learner and teacher to consider decisions connected across the entire project.

The learner who masters self-reflection

**The Information
Inquiry Interaction(s)**

becomes more likely to be not only a true independent learner, but also one who can help others master the information inquiry interactions. The teacher who masters both formative and summative assessment processes will provide more clarity to their guidance and feedback in judgment of learner actions. The teacher as a model of reflective behavior will serve as a mentor who learns from mistakes as well as success.

Information Issues:
Abundance, Access, Ability

We are just entering a new millennium. Our society continues on a projectory based on unpresentiented changes in economic, social and political structures over the past century. Now over two decades into the "Information Revolution" each citizen, nearly regardless of age or status, faces an abundance of information.

Greater access to the essentials for life was the purpose and was the result of the Agrarian and Industrial Revolutions. While information access is not new, its abundance and massive distribution to a large portion of the population are.

The challenges to manage food and materials production, distribution and consumption of the previous revolutions are similar to those for the Information Age. Clearly the information explosion has increased the need for a broader portion of the population to understand ethical, economic and information use issues. Consumer education of the 1960s had objectives similar to those found in information and media literacy education today. Over the past decade many of the educational reform efforts have centered on an understanding and wise use of information skills as a cornerstone for preparing children and young adults to learn in school and to enter the intellectual workforce.

The divide between those who have and those who have-not in the Information Age involves at least two major divisions. First is the gap between those who have access to information and those who do not. Despite continued growth in the information technologies, the expanding information base, and greater availability of information to the masses, access to the most valuable information remains with those who also have the economic resources.

This book does not deal with the access gap, but concentrates on the second, the ability gap. This gap pertains to the division between those who know how to deal with and learn from information and those who do not. To reduce this gap, instructional strategies and methods are presented in these pages which have provided opportunities for students, kindergarten to college, to master the skills relevant to their age group fundamental to survival in the Information Age.

These instructional terms, concepts, processes, and methods, based on inquiry components, are intended to help both teachers and students become more information literate. At the highest levels of information literacy mastery, teachers and students become learners who are fluent in their understanding, application, and communication of information. They know how to discern the best information available to them for various situations and how to communicate their findings.

Higher ability levels are reached with guided practice and measured intellectual growth. The maturity level to search for and use information is relative to different age groups and different environments. Therefore methods and skills will be presented for different grade levels and across different disciplines. The key components for information inquiry, however, remain basically the same. When these methods are applied in order to increase ability levels, the understanding of how to increase access to more information and to manage such increases as well. Therefore reducing the ability gap should lead to reducing the access gap as well.

In many cases, the skill sets associated with information inquiry learning will seem demanding and beyond the norm. This is probably true. Wise use of information is not an easy task. The abilities, patience, and institutional support to make these skill sets and methods part of the normal curriculum are all likely to be less than sufficient in most corners of our public schools. The conclusion should not be that these more challenging skills and methods should not be adopted.

Evidence increasingly shows that the information skills which have been validated by many national associations are essential to helping our teachers and students to be effective learners. The conclusion should be that we all need to try harder to make the changes necessary for information literacy to be a widely mastered skill set.

Inquiry

Inquiry is a learning method which has survived the ages and has served as an instructional tool enabling humans to survive and prosper. Inquiry is based on techniques similar to the scientific method involving systematic observation and documentation to draw a conclusion. It is the practice of these techniques which constitute teaching methods for the Information Age.

Teaching is the opportunity to provide meaningful situations for learners to experiment and deal with information problems. Teachers, whether classroom instructors, library media specialists, student peers, or parents will best instill inquiry skills when they are seen as model users of the process. It is essential, therefore, that current and future teachers master the information inquiry process and information literacy skills outlined in this book.

Not every information problem requires the use of the inquiry method in order to derive a solution. Certainly we learn from observation, example, and directions. Often by trial and error we sift through solutions that seem to best fit the problem and often transfer that solution to similar problems. Many important skills and facts are mastered through routine practice. Memorization and meaningful application of these skills and facts makes for efficient learning in many situations.

Raising questions which challenge the norm or which involve some new area not included in the prescribed knowledge base requires inquiry methods which will take the teacher and the student on a systematic learning path. The components of information inquiry help to define this path. Methods associated with inquiry serve to provide practice in question formulation, information exploration, assimilation of new information with previously understood information, inference of solutions or conclusions, and reflection on what was learned and how.

Depending on the ability and maturity of the learner, the complexity and importance of the problem, and other factors such as time and resources, meeting the information need may need to be very quick and direct or may take a life time. Information inquiry is the companion to lifelong learning, while experience and common sense combine to address many short term problems. Application of information inquiry methods are likely to add value to experiences and add wisdom to common sense.

Information Environments

Everyone faces problems related to information, and nearly every problem faced is related to information. Often associated with the need to answer a question, information problems are as varied as the tasks we attempt to complete and needs we face every day. These problems are common in three environments most of us find outselves at some stage in life: academic, personal, and workplace.

The academic environment, involving tasks in typical school situations is the main one used in this book to illustrate information problems and the techniques to address those problems. In some cases these techniques are steps the student can take on his or her own while many others require interventions and guidance on the part of the teacher.

In the academic setting problems can be real or contrived. Real information problems may be personal needs concerning how to enroll in a course, or how to prepare for an exam. Other information problems may be simulations or exercises assigned as learning experiences. Typical are term papers and reports which involve the use of multiple resources beyond the textbook.

Best practices would suggest that these resource-based information problems are stronger learning situations when they are as authentic as possible. Typical report assignments at any grade and across disciplines leave a lot to be desired in terms of challenging students and teachers to use multiple resources effectively and efficiently. Awareness of new resources, their location, and some practice in an exercise to extract and organize facts are often the only results.

A major purpose of this book is to provide descriptions of method and activities through defining the key words in instruction which are most likely to illustrate effective means to raise the level of typical academic report projects.

As the student leaves the academic environment and enters the workplace, authentic takes on new meaning. While simulations and perhaps even field experiences in school took the student closer and closer to the "real world", on-the-job information problems soon convince most people that not everything necessary for job survival was taught in school.

At its best, however, information inquiry can establish a foundation for trouble-shooting strategies that transfer from the academic to professional job and into personal information need environments. While the details of the problems may differ, methods to address the information problems in real life are similar enough to support initial success in the real world. The former student soon finds information decisions may need to be made come faster, may actually effect the personal lives of many others, and repeated wrong decisions lead to termination of the job, not just a corrected paper.

Personal information needs are present through out our lives. The components of information inquiry are reflected in the constant questions raised by preschoolers. Information preferences are often displayed as well as the child may seek out information sources they find to be safe, reliable and which reenforce what they want to hear. These are habits learners carry with them as they explore the information world in more detail through academic situations. Learning to be critical and open-minded is a combination of skills often difficult for even the best students to master.

Information Problems

Information problems range from simple with quick answers to complex questions without any hope of answers. Building on experiences with locating and extracting information to address questions leads to a fundamental ability to match resources to information need.

Starting in elementary grades, students can formulate questions that can be addressed through basic reference materials, simple Internet searches, further examination of the content of their textbooks, even phone calls to local experts on the topic if necessary. Question posed. Resource located. Acceptable response found. Such exercises can instill awareness of the value of different resources as well as confidence in information location if the student is successful.

Most students will gain even more confidence by taking command of raising their own questions. Thus, beyond the worksheets and set reference questions for practice, students at an early age should be encouraged to branch out form the standard questions posed and begin to personalize what they seek to learn. These are the first steps in inquiry, stating one's own questions and determining valid resources.

While much of what will help introduce the novice to information resources will include practice with questions answered with a single resource, inquiry does not really blossom until multiple resources are used to check and verify facts or perspectives.

The range of information problems can be seen in the range of information literacy skills given in the pages that follow. Each skill reflects how the average student at a given stage in intellectual development is expected to address a problem or set of problems.

As the novice enters the more complex information inquiry tasks, he or she is likely to raise the following types of questions:

- What must I do? How much and how soon?
- What must I use? How many resources and where are they?

- How will my answer be evaluated?

Other questions, such as those listed below, illustrate information problems expressed at higher levels of consideration. Although most students may not phrase their information need in the exact terms that follow, those who mature in the information inquiry process will explore ways to address not only these questions but many more. The mature inquirer expands questions to include:

- What is my need? What questions must be addressed? What do I know know and what do I want to find out?
- How do I locate the information I need? Where is the information most likely to be found and who might help me locate it?
- What methods will help me search effectively so I can locate the most useful information? What methods help me work efficiently so I can save time in searching and have more time to read, interpret the information and fit it with what I already know?
- How much information do I need? How complete should my answer be? Who must I satisfy with the information — me, my teacher, my classmates, my parents, my boss?
- How much time to I have to determine an answer? To what extent might I seek additional resources if time is available? Does the information I have located give me any leads or links to additional information? When do I have enough information?
- What is the acceptable level of evidence? Is one document, website, or article enough? Should the information be current and from an accepted expert? Do I need a second source to confirm the first?
- How do I apply this information to solve my problem? Should I gain opinions from others as to the usefulness and validity of the information?
- Is the information for me personally and to meet my own interests or needs, or must I also communicate the infor-

mation to others? Who are these others? Teachers? Classmates? Employers? Do I present my interpretation of the information in different ways to different audiences? Do I know their understanding of the problem and their likely understanding, acceptance or rejection of my conclusions?

- If an abundance of information is found, how do I decide what to select and what to exclude? If very little or no relevant information is found, and the questions are ones I must or want to address, how to I go about gathering original data?
- After finding information which seemingly supports my belief and information which seemingly counters what I believe, how do I determine which to accept and use? How do my own perceptions and biases fit agains the perceptions and biases found in the information I have located?
- Based on all possible information, primary and secondary, it is not possible to come to a conclusion. What can be learned from this and what might be done differently next time I try to answer these or similar questions?

These questions illustrate a wide range of information problems. They suggest challenging tasks. All the more reason students should be introduced to efficient ways to search for information as early in their lives as possible.

Literacy and Fluency

Information literacy is a set of skills through which the student demonstrates the ability to recognize when information is needed and to take steps that lead to location and selection of information that can be used effectively to address the need. The resourcefulness to move through this process with confidence and the abilities to adjust to different databases, and to deal with a variety of technology-based information systems are signs of information fluency.

While information literacy represents command over those skills which are needed at a given age level to function in academic settings of the Information Age, information fluency represents the ability to move beyond to levels of independent skill acquisition. Well versed in the use of information technologies, those who are information fluent are able to express themsleves creatively, to reformulate knowledge, and to synthesize new information.

Jamie McKenzie describes the student who has moved to the fluent stage as one who has the ability to "move across a menu of strategies until one works. [These students] do not allow themselves to get stuck in one place trying the same wrong tool or strategy over and over again, harder and harder. They are toolmakers and tool-shapers [they can formulate their own strategies when necessary] as well as tool-users." (p. 51)

The interactive processes that take place through information inquiry are the methods and techniques to help the student become information literate and to eventually strive for and achieve fluency.

For Further Reading and Viewing

Please note: This is the first of many lists for further reading or viewing. The hope is that the reader will do just that. While these items have been listed as references in association with the chapter or term they follow, more importantly they are links to additional examples and details. The books, articles, websites, and video programs that are found among these lists should result in establishment of quality professional development resource collections. Those who take the time to access and assemble these titles, promote them among the teaching and administative staff, and apply the exercises and methods detailed in these materials will find they will become leaders in inquiry learning and resource-based education.

Association of College and Research Libraries. "Information Literacy Competency Standards for Higher Education." Viewed June 1, 2001. http://www.ala.org/acrl/ilintro.html

Breivik, Patricia and J. A. Senn. <u>Information Literacy: Educating Children for the 21st Century</u>. New York: Scholastic, 1994.

Kuhlthau, Carol Collier. <u>Seeking Meaning: A Process Approach to Library and Information Services</u>. Norwood, NJ: Ablex, 1993.

McKenzie, Jamie. <u>Beyond Technology: Questioning, Research and the Information Literate School</u>. Bellingham, WA: FNO Press. 2000. http://fno.org   http://questioning.org

Neuman, Delia. "Beyond the Chip: A Model for Fostering Equity." <u>School Library Media Quarterly</u>. 18:3. 1990. Viewed June 4, 2001. http://www.ala.org/aasl/SLMR/slmr_resources/select_neuman.html

Schement, Jorge Reina and Terry Curtis. <u>Tendencies and Tensions of the Information Age</u>. New Brunswick, NJ: Transaction Publications, 1995.

Spitzer, Kathleen L., Michael B. Eisenberg, and Carrie A. Lowe (Editors). <u>Information Literacy: Essential Skills for the Information Age</u>. Syracuse, NY: ERIC Clearinghouse on Information & Technology, 1998.

Toffler, Alvin. <u>The Third Wave</u>. New York: Morrow, 1980.

Tyner, Kathleen. <u>Literacy in a Digital World: Teaching and Learning in the Age of Information</u>. Mahwah, NJ: Lawrence Erlbaum Associates, 1998.

Wurman, Richard Saul. <u>Information Anxiety</u>. New York: Bantam Books, 1989.

Chapter 2

The Instructional Media Specialist

The educator who is most likely to succeed in establishing information inquiry as a key method for teaching and learning is the instructional media specialist. Do such people exist in our schools today? Are they likely to increase in number in the future? From what teaching areas should they come and what training background should they have mastered? Is the instructional media specialist role one that can be played by several educators who come together as a collaborative team to change the learning and teaching environment within their school?

The potential role of the instructional media specialist has been described in several ways over the past few decades. There are practicing educators, usually found as library media resource or educational technology specialists, who practice several of the basic competencies of this role. A majority, however, do not, nor did many enter the school library media profession to accept instructional leadership responsibilities.

Is this instructional leader one who comes from the ranks of the computer technology specialists? Some would agree and yet others often find that these educators hold strong technical skills without the curriculum planning and instruction design skills. Too often individuals from this area, just as too often those from the library media area, stand to serve only as support staff who move to help when asked, but seldom take initiative to create means to integrate technologies and move local educational programs forward.

Are classroom teachers from various subject areas good candidates? Do we limit our field to only those successful in the teaching of reading, or those who teach science, social studies and language arts? Should we look for teachers with a wide subject background, including humanities as well as science interest? Should they have strong technical skills as well?

Perhaps the human interactive skills should be most important to consider. Often teachers who enjoy complex projects and collaboration with others in a team situation will demonstrate the skills and attitudes needed to fill the role of instructional media specialist. They often possess creativity, a vision for meaningful instructional activities and have practice in fair methods for evaluation and guidance of student work. They often lack the knowledge of a broad resource base and a wide understanding of many disciplines of study outside of their own, but these content areas can be understood quickly by those who have talents in collaborative teaching.

In nearly all cases, the educator who displays interest and ability for the role of instructional media specialist tends to not relish the administrative responsibilities that go with management of a resource center. Skills in budgeting and resource acquisition, however, prove to be extremely beneficial to those who center their work on curriculum development. Knowing how to draw in funding as well as an understanding of how to deal with vendors so that the best resources can be acquired are management skills that will enhance the instructional media specialist. Organization of materials, bibliographic resource control, inventory tasks on the other hand, each tend to take away from the instructional focus. Qualified staff support is necessary for these tasks.

The puzzle is a difficult one to fit together. In many cases there is not a complete instructional media specialist model in action for administrators to understand.

A Leader and Master of Teaching

Most of the current higher education preparation programs for school library media specialists accredited by the American Library Association are at the graduate level. A common expectation is successful teaching experience as a core part of the expertise for the profession. This is a shift from just three decades earlier when many school librarians were prepared for the field with "teaching credentials" but lacked evidence of teaching ability, innovation, and leadership. Often granted at the undergraduate level, the school librarian from training programs in the 1970s was usually one with an undergraduate degree and no advanced graduate study in instructional design.

Carol Tilley and Daniel Callison of Indiana University have found a shift in the content emphasized in school librarianship education from 1990 to 1999:

- From audiovisual to multimedia and telecommunications;
- From library skills to information literacy;
- From resource acquisition to needs assessment;
- From isolation to collaborative teaching;
- From resource-centered to learner-centered programming; and
- From meeting general learning needs to diversified needs.

Delia Neuman, from the University of Maryland and principal writer of the 1998 AASL/AECT national guidelines for school library programs (Information Power: Building Partnerships for Learning), conducted a forum for leading educators in 2000. Based on analysis of comments gathered through decision-support software, observations from these participants framed the following issues that must be addressed in current and future higher education programs if school librarians are to master the role of instructional media specialist:

- more emphasis on indepth teaching and learning experiences;
- continued emphasis on information access and delivery, including ethical issues related to information use and understanding how to critically evaluate information;
- new emphasis on learning theory, information literacy, curriculum/instructional design, use of technology for instruction, teaching skills, reading/literacy, assessment of student performance, and attention to special needs/diversity.
- greater emphasis in the administrative roles for public relations, budget development, staff development; and
- much stronger emphasis on leadership skills, collaboration across disciplinary areas, provision of local professional development (including ability to work closely with pre-service teachers), and application of technology for instructional purposes.

This is a very demanding skill set. These skills are relevant to many educators and reach beyond simply the school library media specialist to include many in the teaching ranks who also want to function as instructional media specialists in the Information Age.

The School Library Media Standards and Instruction

The American Association of School Librarians (AASL) and the Association for Educational Communications Technology (AECT) have issued joint national standards/guidelines three times since 1975 in which the position of school library media specialist has been defined. With each revision, the role has moved closer to that of instructional media specialist.

In 1975, with many school librarians resisting the change in their title to school library media specialist, responsibilities defined by the national guidelines included:

- works as a member of curriculum committees;
- is involved with instructional groups; and
- provides staff development programs for teachers in the evaluation, selection, and use of instructional materials.

In 1988, the library media specialist was defined as information specialist, teacher, and instructional consultant. In 1998, the library media specialist was further defined as a leader of curriculum with emphasis on information skills for student learning. To implement fully this leadership role, the national guidelines emphasized a collaborative role in association with as many other teachers as possible in the integration of information literacy across the curriculum.

In philosophy and in terms of best practice, AASL and AECT have progressed to descriptions that are very close to that of an educator who holds master level teaching experiences and skills, is committed to increasing the quality of teaching and challenges for learning, and invites fellow teachers to explore the best application of methods and technologies to the learning environment. Educators who hold these abilities and attitudes are instructional media specialists. They are potential members and leaders of instructional teams that can take the learning program to the high levels necessary for meaningful information inquiry.

The instructional media specialist may come from the school library media ranks, those of instructional computer technology, or gifted teachers from the classroom. What is added through this book, are the components of an information inquiry method which, with the understanding and application of key concepts in education, help these instructional media leaders emerge with confidence to improve instruction in the Information Age.

From Teaching Library Skills to Facilitating Information Literacy

Kathleen Craver's exhaustive literature review on the changing instructional role of the high school library media specialist lead her to conclude there was, from 1950 to 1984, a clear pattern of progressive development of the instructional role. The changes in the library media specialist's role from study hall monitor to curriculum designer can be termed substantive.

Craver, however, also concluded that there was a time lag between the practiced instructional role and the one espoused in the professional literature and standards. Nearly two to three decades are likely to pass before national standard roles are widely adopted and practiced. Much of the adoption of innovation in roles has more to do with development of a new generation of educators as they enter the field than with a complete retooling of educators on the job.

While one can find excellent examples of school media specialists who have given tremendous amounts of time and energy in retooling for the challenges of the Information Age, the full evolution to instructional media specialist over the next decade rests more with attitudes and skills held by those who are entering the schools as teachers of library media and information technologies now. Fresh ideas, combined with new technology skills and successful teaching experiences seem to be the right mix.

A majority of practicing school library media specialists today see themselves in a supportive instructional role at most. Many at the elementary level find it difficult to engage in instructional development because of the lack of media staff support. Others cite limited instructional programming because of regimented schedules that either take them to many schools, or lock them in to routine reading times for children and prevent meaningful contact with teachers. While time is often cited as the major barrier, often those practicing as school librarians do not have the desire or ability to take the instructional roles described here. In too many cases, even when given the time and staff necessary, many holding the role of school librarian would not move forward on instructional activities.

The role of the school library media specialist as instructor seems to also be influenced by the expectations of the principal as well as other teachers in the building. Most studies since 1975 have indicated higher expectations on the part of principals than school media specialists for participation in instructional activities. Neither group, however have shown exceeding high expectations for instructional leadership on the part of the school library media specialist.

There are indications of change, however. Over recent years some studies have indicated when the school library media specialist plays an instructional role in teaching and evaluating students in the use of strategies for information search and use, students seem to also show higher academic achievement. In addition, more and more new library media specialists are seeking out and demonstrating their instructional value.

Studies lead by Keith Lance in Colorado and Pennsylvania indicate a high relationship between the instructional role of the school media specialist and higher performance by students in critical thinking and reading skills for information searching and use. His findings have been validated and confirmed through the use of even more rigorous statistical analysis in a 2001 Texas study completed by Ester Smith. Cause and effect is rightfully never claimed in these correlation studies, but the emerging instructional role of the library media specialist seems to be very strongly associated with higher student achievement. Smith found strong associations with higher student achievement at secondary school levels when school library media specialists

- collaborated to develop instructional units with teachers, and
- provided leadership in professional staff development for teachers.

In order to be successful in the instructional role, the library media specialist must demonstrate more than the skill to teach online search techniques. They must be knowledgeable about new national curriculum standards across all disciplines, aware of new instructional materials in a variety of formats, understand instructional design and its application for teaching information literacy, and be welcoming to classroom teachers and students through the practice of clear interactive communication skills.

Defining the Instructional Role: An Evolution and Revolution

Margaret Chisholm, then at the University of Washington, and Donald Ely, from Syracuse University, proposed instructional design and teaching competencies for future school library media professionals in 1975. Chisholm and Ely visualized media programs organized under the guidance of a complete staff. Personnel would include several individuals. Some with expertise in specific instructional design and production functions. Others would manage information access.

In the instructional role, the library media professional would conduct in-service media training for teachers and develop learning programs that would assist all individuals in the access to and use of materials found in the school's collection. Instructional design tasks would involve clarification of learning objectives with teachers, analysis of learner characteristics in order to determine suitable teaching strategies, to provide alternative formats for presentation or use of information. Thus, more learners benefit from the resources regardless of learning abilities.

Chisholm and Ely placed the school media generalist in charge of all staff, including other professionals who held specializations in different information formats and services. The generalist would have department level chair status and coordinate overall planning for the media program. Specialists would provide support expertise in reference services, reading advisory, and media production. Such staffing is still held as ideal, and remains out of reach in most school environments because of limited funds and because of lack of vision for such programs.

The message from Chisholm and Ely nearly 30 years ago is that the primary task role held by the leader of the media program is to initiate curriculum planning and to involve the media center staff in supporting new curricular initiatives.

In 1980, Callison listed areas in which the school library media specialist can serve as a key instructional and should document these actions in an annual report:

- serving on or chairing committees for course content and learning objectives review;
- designing and conducting workshops for professional development;
- facilitating the sharing of lesson plans;
- helping instructors not only plan, but also evaluate instruction; and
- providing supervision of independent study for students with advanced research needs.

Margaret Hayes Grazier, then a professor in education at Wayne State University, provided one of the earliest and most clear models for the instructional role in 1976. Her model called for the media specialist to be involved at all stages of curriculum development, not just at the implementation stage. Grazier saw the role included in curriculum planning, implementation, and evaluation; the full cycle.

Writing over two decades before publication of the current national standards for school media programs, Grazier gave emphasis to a new collaborative role for instruction as she illustrated the changes which must take place. Although many of her references to material formats are now out of date, she describes the collaborative instructional role in the following manner:

"The traditional media specialist offers storytelling, book talks, recreational reading, viewing, or listening.

He teaches library skills. He supervises classes when teachers need planning periods or respite from classroom chores. His collections are resources for students engaging in independent study.

Teachers envy the load of the traditional media specialist — no lessons to plan, no papers to correct. Whereas teachers must instill knowledge in immature minds, the media specialist appears to worry about maintaining order on the shelves and quiet in the room.

In the *new role the media specialist* is an integral part of the teaching and learning functions. He collaborates in the selection of all learning resources — texts, workbooks, paperbacks, films, community people and agencies. He indexes all materials by curriculum objectives and level of difficulty.

He disseminates information about new materials based on user need profiles. Using a variety of strategies he instructs about locating 'and' evaluating resources, handling of equipment [for] production of materials [to support presentations]. He helps in the design of instructional strategies and content, adapting to the needs of teachers and working from task-centered orientation or from child-centered orientation [whichever is determined most suitable].

He offers in-service programs to help teachers produce and use materials [effectively]... .

Teachers perceive the new media specialist in the light of the many kinds of active collaboration in which they have engaged." (p. 201)

Nearly three decades later, Grazier's scenario has come to life in countless national and state standards/guidelines for school media programs and has sparked to action across thousands of school library media centers. As Craver has suggested, the instructional role is evolving, and now moving into its third generation, the instructional media specialist is emerging.

In 1991, Carol-Ann Haycock, then President of the Human Resources Development Group, issued a statement concerning the changing role and the emerging teacher librarian. Her vision, shared by many others reflected in the readings listed for further study at the end of this chapter, places the responsibility for demonstrating the potential of the instructional media specialist on those who educate "teacher-librarians" as well as those who strive to practice the instructional role in public school throughout the United States and Canada:

"It does no good to blame or to complain. What we must do is provide information about and demonstrate that role. We must create the knowledge base and experiential base that will lead to understanding and support. And in doing so, we would do well to take note of some lessons from advertising and sales and from what we know about human learning.

First, we must realize that we are involved in selling. What we are selling is potential; we must sell a vision of what could or should be. And that means we have to have a vision, preferably one that is commonly shared. Second, we must realize that people don't usually buy or learn on the basis of their first exposure. Think of how we are bombarded with advertising in our daily lives. Remember that it can take up to 35 repetitions for learning to occur. To present a case or say something once is not enough. It is necessary to create the vision, put the message out, and to keep it out there. Third, we must realize that information or talk alone is not enough. We also need to prove intent. We need to demonstrate, to the best of our ability, in the context of our own circumstances, the potential (i.e., the vision) of the role we want others to understand and support." (p. 62)

More Recent Definitions for Instructional Roles

Kay Vandergrift, professor at Rutgers The State University of New Jersey, has provided many insightful studies and comments on the school media specialist profession. Her 1994 list of library media specialist instructional responsibilities illustrates a more refined expectation nearly 20 years after Grazier, Chisholm and Ely:

- Provides assistance in identifying, locating, and interpreting information housed in and outside of the library media center.
- Uses a variety of instructional methods to meet the needs of different user groups.
- Teaches the structure of various media and the distinctive uses of compositional elements in media such as film, video, computer graphics.
- Demonstrates the effective use of newer media and technologies.
- Teaches the information curriculum as an integral part of the content and objectives of the school's curriculum.
- Includes instruction in accessing, evaluating, and communicating information.

- Integrates systematic learning activities with library media resources to emphasize higher-order cognitive strategies (critical thinking skills) for selecting, retrieving, analyzing, synthesizing, and evaluating information.
- Teaches the steps of research processes.
- Teaches students to articulate alternative responses to a particular work of art, literature, social/political issue.
- Participates in school, district, and departmental curriculum design and assessment.
- Analyzes learner characteristics as a part of the instructional design process. (p. 165)

These instructional tasks are exemplary and progressive. They take on an even more powerful mode when combined with understanding and application of the constructive process of learning outlined by Carol Kuhlthau, also of Rutgers University. Although she cites constructivist methods from many education theorists, Kuhlthau draws on Jerome Bruner's ideas to outline the components that follow. These are essential for the instructional media specialist to understand so that instructional interventions become methods to facilitate student learning. Learning reaches near maximum when it is meaningful to both teacher and student.

"...[Bruner] emphasized the individual's deep thinking, what he called interpretation, is central to the learning process. Bruner noted that it is not enough merely to gather information. If the individual is to understand it and learn from it, there is an essential, interpretative task. Interpretation is based on personal constructs built from past experience that enable students to go beyond the information they locate to create something uniquely their own. Bruner describes the interpretive task as occurring in five phases:

- perception (encountering new information)
- selection (recognizing patterns)
- inference (joining clusters and categories)
- prediction (going beyond the

information given)
- action (creating products of the mind)

The concept of going beyond the information given to form a personal understanding is central to constructive theory." (p. 12)

First and foremost in successful guiding of this learning process, the instructional media specialist initiates the process through open-ended problems, questions, or topics that need to be addressed by using a number of sources over a period of time. Kulthau informs us that these open-ended issues arise directly from the curriculum to initiate problem-directed research, rather than artificially imposed research assignments that only peripherally relate to the context, content, and objectives of the course of study.

Collaboration to Enable Content Integration Across the Curriculum

The instructional media specialist has a new role definition based on guiding students through challenging information selection and application tasks. Tasks which are demanding, but rewarding and motivating if they are personal and meaningful to the student.

Influence on learning styles, teaching methods and student achievement are more likely when the instructional media specialist collaborates with other teachers in the integration of information skills and the curriculum.

Kuhlthau has identified four basic enablers that must be in place for instructional media specialists (library media special specialists and other teachers) to successfully implement a process approach for information skills instruction:

1. A team approach to teaching with administrators, teachers, and library media specialists playing essential [not just auxiliary] roles in the instructional team.
2. A mutually held constructivist view of learning compatible with the process approach that provides the foundation for actively engaging students in problem-driven inquiry.

3. A shared commitment to teaching skills for lifelong learning and for motivating students to take a responsibility for their own learning.
4. Competence in designing activities and strategies to improve learning. (p. 16)

Communication with the Chief Instructional Officer: The Principal as CIO

In order to convey the instructional potential for school media professionals, some practical steps in communication are very important.

Although most studies on the perception of the role for school media specialists in instruction tend to show principals as well as classroom teachers have held higher expectations than library media specialists, those who would try to move the instructional role to the forefront will find that further educating the school principal will lead to positive results. Although expressed by many previous practicing media specialists, Carol Kearney, who has served as a media specialist at all levels in the Buffalo, NY public schools, has generated the most current and comprehensive list (synthesized and paraphrased from pages 24-31).

The instructional media specialist should:
- Bring to the principal's attention key concepts from national standards and association position statements, especially those issued by AASL and AECT.
- Share articles and ideas from professional journals which promote collaborative teaching and inquiry learning (often based on constructivist methods) and which are centered on resource-based exploration through the media center.
- Lead in-service sessions which reflect the higher levels of Loertscher's Taxonomy for Library Media Specialist in Instruction and Turner's Model for Collaborative Instructional Design (see For Further Reading at the end of this chapter and key word "Assignment).
- Take field trips with the principal and

key teachers to visit exemplary school library media programs in action.

- Schedule time to conference with the principal on the potential media center program goals and how they related to student learning, standards in across the curriculum, and may tie to local community library programs for school children.
- Compare notes on key issues with the principal; do your agree or disagree the instructional services of the school library program are understood and used effectively?
- Invite the principal to be a key player in several instructional activities as a speaker, one who responds to projects produced by students, one who attends to give praise to student presentations.
- Along with an advisory committee, discuss potential short-range and long-range goals for instructional services and evaluate using such instruments as A Planning Guide for Information Power.
- Present a semi-annual report to the principal that is concise, easy to read, relevant and highlights instructional engagements:
  1. curricular projects
  2. attempts at authentic learning activities
  3. lesson plans with new teachers
  4. resources selected in cooperation with teachers in direct support of a theme or unit
  5. statistics on frequency of instructional engagements such as booktalks, media production, information literacy instruction, introduction of new software or evaluation of websites
- Take an active role on curriculum planning committees and seek out a leadership role during accreditation review cycles.
- Provide the most recent information on instructional trends through a professional collection; promote at faculty meetings and teacher workrooms.
- Demonstrate the value of team planning

and the need for flexible scheduling to broaden access to resources and facilities, both in school and in the community; and show how such flexibility results in more challenging instructional units which are not limited by routine, fragmented class schedules.
- Plan in-service training for teachers on various instructional strategies or new technologies; seek collaboration with other teachers to plan and present in-service sessions.
- Compliment the principal on any signs of support for the school media program, especially when it is clear that the principal has provided additional time or resources in the investment for resource-based activities.

These same communication steps lead to greater instructional engagements among the instructional media specialist and other teachers.

Beyond one-to-one media specialist and teacher collaboration, the instructional media specialist seeks to build teams for collaborative action. These teams function to take a long-range view on the methods involved in information inquiry. They consider multi-disciplinary and multi-grade approaches. Teams, based on successful steps in building units of study, will find that they grow stronger as they involve community educators, such as local public and academic librarians, as well as parents and other community members who hold special expertise.

Eventually inquiry methods become a way of thinking and impact nearly all learning situations in both elementary and secondary schools.

New Guidelines and New Positions

Over the past decade new position statements and refined national guidelines for building partnerships for learning have been issued by the American Association of School Librarians. AASL has supported development of the school library media program as one that is not only integral to and supportive of the school curriculum, but also a program that provides a mechanism for choice and exploration beyond the prescribed course of study. The school library media center is a place where student may explore more fully classroom subjects that interest them, expand their imagination, delve into areas of personal interest, and develop the ability to think clearly, critically, and creatively about the resources they have chosen to read, hear, or view.

Beyond this, many in the profession believe the school library media program to be not just a place, but a concept, a way of thinking and exploring. Thus, the student and teacher are not limited by walls or by a few information formats. The library media program, when guided by those with instructional expertise, is a pathway to the human conversations concerning historical, present and future facts, events, people, issues, and ideas.

The AASL Position Statement on the Value of Library Media Programs in Education states, "School library media specialists are an integral part of the total educational team which pre-pares students to become responsible citizens in a changing global society. In today's information society, an individual's success, even existence, depends largely on the ability to access, evaluate and utilize information. Library media specialists are leaders in carrying out the school's instructional program through their separate but overlapping roles of information specialist, teacher and instructional consultant."

In the 1988 and 1998 national guidelines for school library media programs, as well as the most recent AASL Position Statement on the Role of the Library Media Specialist in Outcomes-Based Education, the characteristics of the instructional role are defined.

As information specialist, the library media specialist working collaboratively with teachers, administrators, and parents:
- provides knowledge of availability and suitability of information resources to support curriculum initiatives.
- engages in the developmental process with the planning team, using knowl-

Figure
Education of the IMS

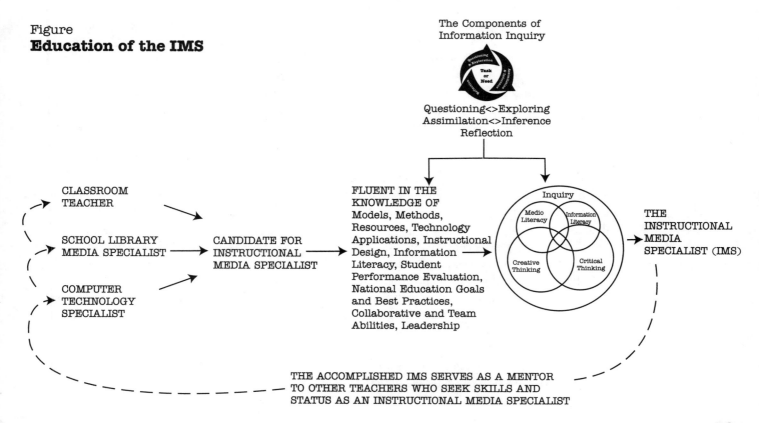

edge of the school curriculum and professional resources.

- facilitates the use of presentation tools in print, technology, and media for dissemination efforts;
- serves as an expert in organizing, synthesizing, and communicating information.

As teacher:
- determines learning outcome, including those in information literacy, for all students in the school and/or system.
- plans, implements, and evaluates resource-based learning.
- integrates information literacy into all curriculum outcomes.
- develops on-going performance-based assessments for determining the achievement of outcomes.

As instructional consultant:
- facilitates development of teachers' understanding and implementation of outcome-based education.
- plans for learning environments supportive of curricular integration.
- previews and selects resources and technology to accommodate the learning styles and multiple intelligences of students.
- designs and implements a variety of instructional strategies and experiences that engage each student in successful learning.

In order to implement fully resource-based education, along with enhancement of reading development as a key skill for learning, AASL takes the following position:
- The library media center is flexibly scheduled so that students and teachers have unlimited physical and intellectual access to a wide range of materials. Students are not limited to using only commercially prescribed or teacher-selected materials.
- Students choose from a varied, non-graded collection of materials which reflect their personal interests.

- Students learn to identify, analyze, and synthesize information by using a variety of materials in a variety of formats.
- Multi-disciplinary approaches to teaching and learning are encouraged.
- Teachers and library media specialists cooperatively select materials and collaboratively plan activities.
- Teachers and library media specialists share responsibility for reading and information literacy instruction. They plan and teach collaboratively based on the needs of the student.
- Continual staff development is critical to reading instruction.

Instructional Collaboration at the College Level

Information literacy models and skill sets for the college student are presented in this book in order to provide a full context for information inquiry. Instructional words, methods and concepts will be defined within the elementary and secondary school settings, but in nearly all cases these will transfer to the college setting as well. The library is a learning laboratory, tied closely to the academic lessons of the college, and serving as the learning environment for most of the course content. Collaboration between academic librarian and professor are also part of a similar instructional role sharing on the college campus that has been described above for the lower school setting.

Patricia Knapp's application of the library-college concept at Monteith College in the early 1960s was an experiment to integrate fully library instruction with the local liberal arts college curriculum. The project failed in a large part because faculty members were unwilling to or did not understand how to cooperate with librarians in the instructional process. In general teaching modes based mostly on lecture and textbook did not match the inquiry process that emersed the student in multiple resources. Knapp concluded:

"Our original notion that the ineffectiveness of traditional library instruction is due to its isolation from content courses was reinforced by our experience with the pilot project. But we are no longer content with the simple goal of getting the library somehow or other built into such courses. The relationship is more complicated than we thought. If it is to be effective, the library program must be not merely presented in the context of content courses, but truly consistent in goals and methods, in tone and style, with the overall education program in which it occurs." (p. 51)

Evan Ira Farber, famed advocate for library instruction and innovator of many techniques in bibliographic instruction at Earlham College in Indiana, has always argued that the role of the library on the college campus is to enhance the teaching/learning process. College librarians are agents of this process and design facilities, organize collections, provide information access, and collaborate in teaching the use of information sources in order to deliver on this role.

Farber, as many others in the academic library field today, advocated decades ago that these elements must be in place:

- library and information use instruction is best presented at point of need and is more likely to be effective when integrated with specific course content;
- both the professor and the librarian have educational goals and should share and build from both in development of library-based projects so that students learn both subject content as well as information process skills;
- library and information instruction should be constructed on analysis of student need and ability to determine what the student knows and brings to the situation, along with the expectations of the professor, before formal instruction begins;
- in the emerging Information Age, technologies will increasing both cover and create basic instructional needs; while more and more students will benefit from computer-assisted tutorials, keeping up-to-date with the vastly expanding information options and search engines will still require guidance from the librarian;

- the Information Age moves the librarian into the role of information advisor or information counselor, more demanding than the role of reading advisor; as reader advisor one informs the reader of the classic titles and sources, but as information advisor the librarian models and provides guidance in the selection, analysis, and application of the most relevant information possible for the student to access.

Collaboration is also viewed by some academic librarians as a process that should be used to enhance peer learning. Students should experience a "community of inquirers" and through interaction learn to help each other. Janice Sauer, of the University of Alabama Library, wrote in her 1995 award-winning essay,

"Librarians cannot expect to encourage any sense of complexity and multiplicity by using library assignments that expect single right answers. Nor can they encourage critical thinking by expecting students to learn tools without a larger view of context and diversity. No one can expect undergraduates to understand that they are to learn to participate in the construction of understanding and knowledge unless we actually encourage the practice of construction." (p. 135)

What better way is there to teach how knowledge is constructed than by using the same collaborative method used to construct knowledge?

As Barbara Fister states, "Group inquiry gives the students a working model of a scholarly community in the microcosm of the classroom. Before a person is able to think, they must first experience direct social exchanges with others. ...

Collaborative learning requires the establishment of an environment in which the teacher does not have the answer. The questions asked must be so complex [for the given learner] as to require analysis, debate, negotiation, and consensus before an answer can be suggested." (p. 147)

As the instructional words, concepts and methods defined in this book will demonstrate, information inquiry lays the foundation for both critical and creative thinking through strategies, modeled by instructional media specialists and other teachers beginning in the very early grades and continuing through higher education environments.

For Further Reading

American Association of School Librarians. A Planning Guide for Information Power Building Partnerships for Learning with School Library Media Program Assessment Rubric for the 21st Century. Chicago: ALA, 1999.

American Association of School Librarians. AASL Position Statements. www.ala.org/aasl/positions/index.html. Viewed June 6, 2001.

American Association of School Librarians and Association for Educational Communications Technology. Information Power: Building Partnerships for Learning. Chicago: ALA, 1998.

Brottman, May and Mary Loe. The LIRT Library Instruction Handbook. Englewood, CO: Libraries Unlimited, 1990.

Callison, Daniel. "Evaluator and Educator: The School Media Specialist." Tech Trends. October 1987. 24-29.

Callison, Daniel. History of the Research on Issues Related to School Library Media Programs and Services 1925-1995. In The Emerging School Library Media Center: Historical Issues and Perspectives, edited by Kathy Howard Latrobe. Englewood, CO: Libraries Unlimited, 1998. 91-136.

Callison, Daniel. "You Too Are an Important Resource." Instructional Innovator. October 1980. 24-25.

Chisholm, Margaret E. and Donald P. Ely. Media Personnel in Education: A Competency Approach. Englewood Cliffs, NJ: Prentice-Hall, 1976

Cleaver, Betty P. and William Taylor. Involving the School Library Media Specialist in Curriculum Development. Chicago: ALA, 1983.

Craver, Kathleen W. The Changing Instructional Role of High School Librarians. Champaign, IL: University of Illinois, 1986.

Dewey, Barbara I. Library User Education: Powerful Learning, Powerful Partnerships. Lanham, MD: Scarecrow Press, 2001.

Farber, Evan Ira. Bibliographic Instruction at Earlham College. In Bibliographic Instruction in Practice, edited by Larry Hardesty, Jamie Hastreiter, and David Henderson. Ann Arbor, MI: Pierian Press, 1993. 1-14.

Fister, Barbara. Teaching Research as a Social Act: Collaborative Learning and the Library. RQ. Summer 1990. 506.

Grazier, Margaret Hayes. "The Role for Media Specialists in the Curriculum Development Process." School Media Quarterly. Spring 1976. 199-204.

Haycock, Carol-Ann. "The Changing Role: From Theory to Reality". In School Library Media Annual Volume 9, edited by Jane Bandy Smith and J. Gordon Coleman. Englewood, CO: Libraries Unlimited, 1991. 61-67.

Haycock, Ken. "Role of the School Librarian as a Professional Teacher." Emergency Librarian. May/June 1981. 4-11.

Haycock, Ken. What Works: Research About Teaching and Learning Through the School's Library Resource Center. Seattle, WA: Rockland Press, 1992.

Kearney, Carol A. Curriculum Partner: Redefining the Role of the Library Media Specialist. Westport, CT: Greenwood Press, 2000.

Knapp, Patricia. The Monteith College Library Experiment. New York: Scarecrow Press, 1966.

Kuhlthau, Carol C. "Implementing a Process Approach to Information Skills: A Study Identifying Indicators of Success in Library Media Programs". School Library Media Quarterly. Fall 1993. 11-18.

Lance, Keith Curry, Marcia J. Rodney and Christine Hamilton-Pennell. Measuring Up to the Standards: The Impact of School Library Programs and Information Literacy in Pennsylvania Schools. Greensburg, PA: Pennyslvania Citizens for Better Libraries, 2000.

Loertscher, David V. Taxonomies of the School Library Media Program. 2nd edition. San Jose, CA: Hi Willow Research, 2000.

McCracken, Anne. "School Library Media Specialists' Perceptions of Practice and Importance of Roles as Described in Information Power." School Library Media Research. 4. 2001. http://www.ala.org/aasl/SLMR

Neuman, Delia. "Re-Visioning School Library Media Programs for the Future." Journal of Education for Library and Information Science. 42:2. Spring 2001. 96-115.

Rossoff, Martin. The School Library and Educational Change. Littleton, CO: Libraries Unlimited, 1971.

Sauer, Janice A. "Conversation 101: Process, Development and Collaboration." In Information for a New Age. Englewood, CO: Libraries Unlimited, 1995. 135-170.

Smith, Ester G. Texas School Libraries: Standards, Resources, Services, and Students' Performance. Austin: Texas State Library and Archives Commission, 2001. http://www.tsl.state.tx.us/ld/pubs/schlibsur-vey/index.html

Tilley, Carol L. and Daniel Callison. "Preparing School Library Media Specialists for the New Century: Results of a Survey." Journal of Education for Library and Information Science. 42:3. Summer 2001. 220-227. Based on The KALIPER Project for the University of Michigan, 1999-2001.

Turner, Philip M. Helping Teachers Teach: A School Library Media Specialist's Role. 2nd edition. Englewood, CO: Libraries Unlimited, 1993.

Vandergrift, Kay E. Power Teaching: A Primary Role of the School Library Media Specialist. Chicago: American Library Association, 1994.

Chapter 3

Models and Processes Related to Information Inquiry

A model provides a visual example of the whole, although often the full dynamics of the process, or actions within a model, are not possible to represent. Therefore, in some cases, the model may constitute a subset of the whole and illustrate the relationship among some specific tasks, skills, steps or objectives. A common model is a taxonomy or a classification of abilities, attitudes, or actions according to some organized structure, usually working from the lowest and most simple to the highest and most complex.

The term model implies something or someone of exemplar status worthy of imitation. Factors from various situations, however, lead to modification of models in order for reasonable goals to be accomplished. The ability to see, understand, and adjust for these factors is a key skill of the instructional media specialist.

A process is a series of actions that lead toward a result or conclusion. The conclusion in the learning process is often the student's report or response to his or her questions or those questions assigned by others. This product is often the only item evaluated, when the processes involved may hold evidence of student performance which are as valuable to evaluate. Thus, models may be presented at a way to identify the components of a process so that interventions to help students learn at point of need can be accomplished in an effective and efficient manner.

The models presented in this chapter are based on notions from individuals who have created such as an ideal or best practice. Some are based on observation of student and teacher behavior in their search for and use of information. Others are based on practices of model teachers who design and present lessons. Other models illustrate specific learning processes or sub-tasks the student experiences as he or she encounters new information and needs to assimilate it.

In all cases, these models are constructed of the basic components for Information Inquiry:

Questioning > raising the information need

Exploration > reading, viewing, listening

Assimilation > accepting, incorporating or rejecting

Inference > application for solution and meaning

Reflection > adjustment for additional questioning

In nearly all cases, these models, although linear in presentation, assume interaction among the elements or steps described. The cycles are both internal or within the process as well as a representation of the external whole. The processes of learning are often similar, although each model will represent a slightly different application of these processes.

The task of the instructional media specialist is to study these models, and to consider situations in which the given model may best suit the needs of the teacher and learner. The result may be use of the model to better construct, organize and manage the information environment so that adjustments can be made to search, access and use to meet the user's abilities as well as information needs. Models provide illustration of search, learning, and teaching approaches which are likely to provide a high level of success if they are applied by thoughtful instructional media specialists.

The models are presented below under citations to key resources in which the model has been explained in more detail. Nancy Pickering Thomas of Emporia State University has written an informative comparison of many of the library skills and information literacy models in her book Information Literacy Skills Instruction, Libraries Unlimited, 1999. Her insights are extremely valuable and should be examined along with the sketches of the models provided here.

Information Search Models

Pathfinder
Borne, Barbara Wood. <u>100 Research Topic Guides for Students</u>. Westport, CT: Greenwood Press, 1996.

The Internet Public Library. http://www.ipl.org/ Pathfinders. http://www.ipl.org/ref/QUE/PF/ The School of Information, Michigan University. Viewed June 28, 2001.

Kapoun, Jim M. "Re-Thinking the Library Pathfinder." <u>College and Undergraduate Libraries</u>. 2:1. 1995. 93-105.

The Pathfinder model evolved in the 1970s from the use of annotated bibliographies. The intention, however, was to give more than a list of selected resources organized by format, date, or author. Use of the Pathfinder outlined an approach to the library collection, a way to think about how to trace information on a given subject. The Pathfinder provided a visual connection of resources, working from general background resources to provide a beginning for understanding the topic before tracing the more specific resources. Not all possible resources are given, but key items along with key words for online searching and key classification numbers for browsing.

The Pathfinder provides a map of key resources and access points on a given topic, across all formats, and, in some cases, to resources beyond the local library collection. The structure of the Pathfinder, or research guide, can give the student a sense of organization and a rich picture of potential resource options. An assumption, often false, is that the user will not only locate necessary information on the topic, but that he or she will grasp the layout of the Pathfinder as a search strategy that can be used for nearly any topic to be investigated. While some students make this leap, others require guidance and strong coaching in order to understand how to apply this search strategy to other situations.

While the Pathfinder may help the student explore the resource options, this method does little to aid the student in formulation of specific questions and seeking precise information. On the other hand, Pathfinders can, if they are easily available and cover a wide spectrum of topics relevant to the needs of the student, provide encouragement to the novice that these topics of interest are valid ones to explore.

The Internet Public Library, developed and managed through the Michigan University School of Information, as developed a collection of online Pathfinders, each rich with links to websites as well as local print, association, and human resources. The extent of online access seems to depend on the topic of the Pathfinder. Their guide to mutual funds contains many links to basic investment sites while the guide to Greek mythology is based on more standard print resources. Regardless of topic area, the general framework for a Pathfinder provides a search strategy structure or model for exploring information organized in a library and beyond.

The Pathfinder Model
Background - Identify a few selected and key reference sources or websites, which will provide general overview on the topic including definition of important terms, events, and people. The student should be encouraged to compile terms and names from these sources as potential subject tracings later. In addition,

these background sources may contain bibliographies, which lead to other useful resources the student should obtain.

Browse - List the key classification numbers, either Dewey or Library of Congress, which will lead the user to groups of books to examine. An overview of several shelves may provide some idea of the range of related topics, while skimming of the table of contents and indexes may lead to identification of some initial areas of interest and may also begin to give focus to a potential topic.

Subject Tracings - What are the specific subject headings that will lead to accessing information on this topic through the use of the online catalog and other databases? Are there key terms that may work best on Internet searching?

Ephemeral Items - Depending on the topic area, special vertical files may contain clippings, which pertain to the topic, especially on a local basis. What topic headings should be considered?

Nonprint - Are there video programs relevant to this topic which provide an overview of the issues or illustrate specific related events?

Fiction - In some cases there may be young adult or classic fiction titles, which are important to read and gain a broader perspective while also refining questions to explore in more detail.

Associations - Some associations, national and local, will respond to requests for additional information and may even have an expert who can be interviewed. Websites of associations and organizations relevant to the given topic should be listed here.

Suggested Questions - Questions which might help the student begin to focus on a problem area might be provided here and trigger the more refined search for information.

Conceptual Frameworks
Ohio State University Gateway to Information Search Strategy Format See "Gateway Subjects" linked from http://www.lib.ohio-state.edu/gateway/. Viewed August 16, 2001.

Reichel, Mary and Mary Ann Ramey. Conceptual Frameworks for Bibliographic Education. Littleton, CO: Libraries Unlimited, 1987.

The conceptual frameworks approach allows identification of the key resources in a discipline area of study. Ohio State University has used this approach to provide useful subject outlines that identify the key reference tools, journals, review guides and other tools. In some cases, these frameworks, much like pathfinders, will also identify key authors and researchers.

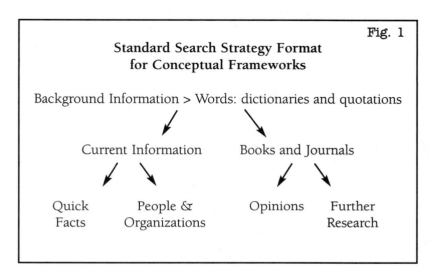

Fig. 1

Standard Search Strategy Format for Conceptual Frameworks

Background Information > Words: dictionaries and quotations

Current Information   Books and Journals

Quick Facts   People & Organizations   Opinions   Further Research

The Information Search Process (ISP)
Kuhlthau, Carol C. "Emerging Theory of Library Instruction." School Library Media Quarterly. 16:1. 1987. 23-27.

Kuhlthau, Carol C. "The Process Approach to Bibliographic Instruction." In Judging the Validity of Information Sources, edited by Linda Shirato. Ann Arbor, MI: Pierian Press, 1991. 7-14.

Kuhlthau, Carol Collier. Teaching the Library Research Process. 2nd edition. Metuchen, NJ: Scarecrow Press, 1994.

Applied in a wide variety of settings from elementary schools to colleges and professional work settings, and tested more extensively than any of the other models offered in this chapter, the Information Search Process (ISP) developed by Carol Kuhlthau of Rutgers

University provides the framework which has changed how many librarians now present the library research process. Kuhlthau's work has substantially changed the typical approach given in most grammar and composition texts prior to 1990. That standard term paper outline given below assumes the student has assimilated the necessary knowledge about the topic and has reached a comfort level with multiple resources to complete a rather complex set of tasks.

Typical Term Paper Outline
1. Select and limit the subject [often based on limits of time and resources without taking into account ideas, background and interests of the student]
2. Prepare a working bibliography - a list of available sources [often restricted to one library, without consideration of alternative ways to gather information such as interviews]
3. Prepare a preliminary outline [before potential research questions are raised]
4. Read and take notes [without exploring the texts for options that might help to focus the project and support student interests and abilities]
5. Assemble notes, write the final outline [without reflection on quality of resources and validity of evidence gathered]
6. Write the first draft [little if any peer review and interaction]
7. Write the revised draft [usually based on feedback from the teacher alone] and add footnotes and bibliography [without time to self-evaluate or to reflect on the process]

These steps clearly represent emphasis on the product, moving from one step to the next to efficiently complete the composition. Time, exercises, and instructor interventions were not provided to enrich and improve the student's ability to search for and to consider the merits of multiple resources prior to moving into the composition. More than any other feature, Kuhlthau's work has moved the exploration stage into the information search process. Understanding that there are phases of student adjustment, both in terms of feel-ings about the process and in assimilation of new information, new interactions between teacher and learner become critical. Through the early stages of exploration, information search modeling and use on the part of the instructional media specialist and others teachers is very important. Time for the student to explore, raise questions, and gain a foundation on which to seek focus is extremely beneficial. But all too often, time is a resource which many teachers continue to not provide.

Kuhlthau process relies heavily on library resources and individual student actions to complete the composition. Her work reflects use of library resources prior to full emergence of modern electronic information resources and more extensive access to resources beyond the local library. Stronger emphasis on cooperative learning over the past decade by many educators has highlighted the possibilities for students to work effectively through collaboration in research and writing. Still, her early ideas have provided one of the most important models in the information skill searching and use arenas. Her work has moved many instructional media specialists to increase the value placed on the processes of search and use, rather than concentrate evaluation of student performance on the product alone.

Kuhlthau's Prewriting Information Search Process

INITIATION

Task: prepare for the decision of selecting a topic.

Thoughts: contemplate assignment, prior learning, consider options

Feelings: apprehension and uncertainty

Actions: converse with others, browse, write out questions

Strategies: brainstorm, discuss, tolerate uncertainty

SELECTION

Task: decide on topic

Thoughts: compare topic criteria to personal interests, information available, time allotted;

predict outcome of possible choices

Feelings: confusion, anxiety, brief elation after selection, anticipation

Actions: consult with others; read for overview

Strategies: discuss options, read widely

EXPLORING INFORMATION

Task: investigate information with intent to find focus

Thoughts: unable to always express precise information needed; identify several focus possibilities

Feelings: confusion, doubt, uncertainty

Actions: locate relevant information; list interesting facts, ideas, names, and events; maintain bibliographic citations of useful sources and potential leads

Strategies: tolerate inconsistency and incompatibility of information encountered both within the information and with own assumptions; intentionally seek and frame several focus possibilities; maintain list of descriptors; read to learn more about topic.

FORMING FOCUS

Task: formulate a focus based from information encountered

Thoughts: predict outcome; consider again personal interest, requirements of the assignment, availability of materials and time.

Feelings: optimism, confidence in ability to complete task

Actions: consider project themes

Strategies: choose a particular focus and discard others or combine several themes to form one focus

COLLECTING INFORMATION

Task: gather information that defines, extends, and supports the focus

Thoughts: define, extend and elaborate on focus; select most pertinent information, organize information from notes

Feelings: realize extensive work is completed and gain confidence that the project can be managed; with assimilated knowledge on focus, interest will increase

Actions: seek out specific resources in libraries or other information collections; take detailed notes relevant to focus and research questions

Strategies: use descriptors to refine search and locate most pertinent information; be comprehensive in search of all options regardless of format; seek guidance to meet specific information needs

PREPARE TO PRESENT OR WRITE

Task: conclude search for information

Thoughts: identify any additional information for specific gaps; also notice most of additional information is redundant and resources options are nearly exhausted

Feelings: relief, satisfaction, but disappointment if some information needs are not met

Actions: recheck sources for information overlooked in first review; confirm information and bibliographic citations; organize notes, write outline

Strategy: return to library to make a summary search to assure all information leads have been exhausted

ASSESSING THE INFORMATION SEARCH PROCESS

Task: to evaluate the library research process

Thoughts: an increase in self-awareness; identify problems and successes; understand and plan research strategy for future assignments

Feelings: sense of accomplishment; perhaps also some disappointment

Actions: evaluate evidence of meeting focus, use of time, use of resources, use of library and librarian

Strategies: visualize the process in time line or flow chart; write an evaluative summary statement; discuss process with teacher and librarian

Information Use Models

Information Skills
Irving, Ann. Study and Information Skills Across the Curriculum. London: Heinemann Educational Books, 1985.

An early advocate of a complete information skills process, Irving gave detail to the skills needed to practice use of library resources. Key to her thinking, however, was the challenge to information users to apply higher order analysis and synthesis skills. Her outline laid the foundation for many that were to follow.

Irving's Study of Information Skills
1. Formulation and analysis of information need
2. Identification and appraisal of likely sources
3. Tracing and locating resources
4. Examining, selecting, and rejecting individual resources
5. Interrogating individual resources
6. Recording and storing information
7. Interpretation, analysis, synthesis and evaluation of information
8. Organize, shape, present or communicate information
9. Evaluation of the assignment

The REACTS Model
Stripling, Barbara K. and Judy M. Pitts. Brainstorms and Blueprints: Library Research as a Thinking Process. Englewood, CO: Libraries Unlimited, 1988.

As secondary school library media specialists, Barbara Stripling and Judy Pitts were greatly influenced by their close work with David Loertscher in Arkansas in the 1980s. Based on Loertscher's Taxonomy for involvement of the media specialist in instruction and Bloom's Taxonomy for learning skills, Stripling and Pitts developed the REACTS model which shows a progression of cognitive tasks for the student researcher. Lower level skills involve location and recall of facts or explaining the application of answers to who, what and where questions. Higher level skills are more challenging and require the student to analyze and synthesize information.

REACTS
A Taxonomy for Thoughtful Research

Recalling - Fact-finding: reporting on the information

Explaining - Asking and searching: posing who, what, where, and when questions and finding the answers

Analyzing - Examining and organizing: posing why and how problems and organizing information to fit the project

Challenging - Evaluating and deliberating: judging information on the basis of authority, significance, bias, and other factors

Transforming - Integrating and concluding: drawing conclusions and creating a personal perspective based on information obtained

Synthesizing - Conceptualizing: creating original solutions to problems posed

Information Problem-Solving (The Big Six Skills)
Eisenberg, Michael B. and Robert E. Berkowitz. Curriculum Initiative: An Agenda and Strategy for Library Media Programs. Norwood, NJ: Ablex, 1988.

Eisenberg, Michael B. and Robert E. Berkowitz. Information Problem-Solving: The Big Six Skills Approach to Library and Information Skills Instruction. Norwood, NJ: Ablex. 1990. http://www.big6.com/

The Big Six is one of the most popular models because of tremendous promotion of the process by the creators, and because in nearly any information problem situation, the model provides an effective way to think through what is needed to address the situation. The six steps in this model, as well as other similar models, provide a framework for a mental picture that helps the learner visualize the problem-solving process. Young learners gain confidence because they "see" the task can be managed.

Eisenberg and Berkowitz have also shown how information skills can be effectively integrated with many areas of the standard curriculum. Compact and efficient, the following six steps make for an understandable agenda for instructional collaboration between media specialist and teacher. More important, their model can be understood and therefore more likely to be applied by learners in elementary as well as secondary school situations.

Information Problem-Solving
1. Task Definition
    1.1 Define the problem
    1.2 Identify information requirements
2. Information Seeking Strategies
    2.1 Determine range of sources
    2.2 Prioritize sources
3. Location and Access
    3.1 Locate sources
    3.2 Find information
4. Information Use
    4.1 Engage with information (read, view, listen)
    4.2 Extract information
5. Synthesis
    5.1 Organize information
    5.2 Present information
6. Evaluation
    6.1 Judge the product
    6.2 Judge the process

A Portfolio of Information Skills
Callison, Daniel. "The Potential for Portfolio Assessment." In School Library Media Annual, Volume Eleven. Englewood, CO: Libraries Unlimited, 1993. 30-39.

Marland, Michael. Information Skills in the Secondary Curriculum. London: Methuen, 1981.

Spitzer, Kathleen L., Michael B. Eisenberg and Carrie A. Lowe. Information Literacy: Essential Skills for the Information Age. Syracuse, NY: Clearinghouse on Information and Technology, 1998.

Discussion has increased over the past decade concerning the best ways to document student progress in the application of information skills. With the new emphasis on valuing the process as much as the product, suggestions have been made as to what should be evaluated and documented during the process. Specific exercises for students to document steps in the library research process are given in such publications as Carol Collier Kuhlthau's Teaching the Library Research Process and Virginia Rankin's The Reflective Researcher. A series of questions associated with the process can serve as an outline or model for the contents of a student's information skill portfolio. The specific exercises that might address these skills would, of course, be modified to meet the grade level of the student. Portfolios constructed over several years, provide evidence of the student's maturation in the information selection and use processes.

Information Skill Portfolio Questions
What do I need to do?
The student should demonstrate the ability to:
- analyze the information task
- analyze the audience's information need or demand
- describe a plan of operation
- select important or useful questions and narrow or define the focus of the assignment
- describe possible issues to be investigated

Where could I go?
The student should demonstrate the ability to:
- determine the best initial leads to relevant information;
- determine possible immediate access to background information (gaining the larger picture)
- consider information sources within and beyond the library

How do I get to the information?
The student should demonstrate the ability to:
- identify relevant materials
- sense relationships between information items (supporting or countering each other; one leading to others based on sources cited)
- determine which resources are most

likely to be authoritative and reliable
- consider and state the advantages and disadvantages of bias
- present in resources
- consider discovered facts and search for counterfacts
- consider stated and personal opinions and search for counter opinions
- determine extent of need for historical perspective

How shall I use the resources?
The student should demonstrate the ability to:
- determine if the information is pertinent to the topic
- estimate the adequacy of the information
- test validity of the information
- focus on specific issues within the boundaries of the information obtained group data in categories according to appropriate criteria
- determine the advantages and disadvantages of different information formats and intellectual levels

Of what should I make a record?
The student should demonstrate the ability to:
- extract significant ideas and summarize supporting, illustrative details
- define a systematic method to gather, sort, and retrieve data
- combine critical concepts into a statement of conclusions
- restate major ideas of a complex topic in concise form
- separate a topic into major components according to appropriate criteria
- sequence information and data in order to emphasize specific arguments or issues

Have I got the information I need?
The student should demonstrate the ability to:
- recognize instances in which more than one interpretation of material is valid and necessary
- demonstrate that the information obtained is relevant to the issues of importance if necessary, state a hypoth-

esis or theme and match evidence to the focused goal of the paper or project
- reflect, edit, revise, and determine if previous information search and analysis steps should be repeated

How should I present it?
The student should demonstrate the ability to:
- place data in tabular form using charts, graphs, or illustrations
- match illustrations and verbal descriptions for best impact
- note relationships between or among data, opinions, or other forms of information
- propose a new plan, create a new system, interpret historical events, and/or predict likely future happenings
- analyze the background and potential for reception of ideas and arguments by the intended audience
- communicate orally and in writing to teachers and peers

What have I achieved?
The student should demonstrate the ability to:
- accept and give constructive criticism
- reflect and revise again, and again if necessary
- describe the most valuable sources of information
- estimate the adequacy of the information acquired and judge the need for additional resources
- state future questions or themes for investigation
- seek feedback from a variety of audiences

Pathways to Knowledge
Harada, Violet and Ann Tepe. "Information Literacy: Pathways to Knowledge." Teacher-Librarian. 26:2. Nov-Dec 1998. 9-15.

Pappas, Marjorie L. Introduction to the Pathways to Knowledge. Follett's Information Skills Model. McHenry, IL: Follett Software, 1997. http://www.fsc.follett.com and http://www.pathwaysmodel.com

Pappas, Marjorie L. "Pathways to Inquiry." School Library Media Activities Monthly. 16:9. May 2000. 23-27.

Pappas, Marjorie L. and Ann Tepe. Pathways to Knowledge and Inquiry Learning. Libraries Unlimited, 2002.

Majorie Pappas and Ann Tepe developed the Pathways to Knowledge model for Follette Software as a means to show how students and teachers can manage knowledge in the Information Age. Their model is constructed on the premise that the learning environment of today's student is no longer set within the walls of the school, but rather is everywhere, home, school, the community, libraries and the Internet. The Follett Information Skills Model shows an expanding field of skills and options for the learner. Students gather information from many formats and they are encouraged to use multiple presentation formats to share their discoveries. A unique feature of this model is the assumption that students will best find interest and focus for their investigations when they first gain appreciation for reading, viewing, and writing skills.

Pathways to Knowledge: Follett's Information Skills Model

APPRECIATION
Sensing, Viewing, Listening, Reading, Curiosity, Enjoyment

PRESEARCH

Establish a Focus

Develop an Overview: brainstorm, formulate initial questions, build background, identify key words, relate to prior knowledge, explore general sources

Explore Relationships: define questions, cluster, outline, webbing, listing, and narrowing and broadening

SEARCH

Planning and Implementing Search Strategy

Identify Information Providers: home and computer resources, museums, zoos, histori-cal sites, community agencies, libraries, etc.

Select Information Resources and Tools: indexes, people, Internet, media, reference resources, etc.

Seek Relevant Information: skim and scan, interview, confirm information and sources, record information, determine relevancy of information, explore and browse widely

INTERPRETATION

Assessing Usefulness of Information

Reflecting to Develop Personal Meaning

Interpret Information: compare and contrast, integrate concepts, determine patterns and themes, infer meaning, analyze, synthesize, classify, filter, organize, and classify

COMMUNICATION

Construct and Present New Knowledge

Apply Information: choose appropriate communication format, solve a problem, answer a question, and respect intellectual property

Share New Knowledge: compose, design, edit, revise, use most effective medium such as video, report, mural, portfolio, and animation

EVALUATION

Think about the Process and Product

Evaluate: end product, effective communication, redefining new questions, use of resources, meeting personal information needs

Instructional Models

ASSURE

Gagne, Robert. The Conditions of Learning. New York: Holt, Rinehart and Winston, 1985.

Heinich, Robert, Michael Molenda, James D. Russell, and Sharon Smaldino. Instructional Media and the Technologies for Learning. Englewood Cliffs, NJ: Merrill, 1996. 34-35. http://www.indiana.edu/~mmweb98/imtl.html

Careful planning will increase the effectiveness of instruction. The authors describe the ASSURE model as a procedural guide for planning and conducting instruction that incorporates media.

Robert Gagne, a major theorist in instructional design, revealed through his research that well-designed lessons begin with the arousal of the students' interests and then move to the presentation of new material. These stages or events of instruction involve students in practice, assessment of their understanding, and follow-up activities. The Heinich and Molenda AASURE model incorporates these instructional events.

AASURE

Analyze Learners - analyze in terms of general characteristics, specific entry competencies, and learning styles.

State Objectives - a statement of what the student will be able to do as a result of the instruction.

Select Methods, Media, and Materials - select from available materials, modify existing materials, design new materials.

Utilize Media and Materials - preview materials, practice implementation, make final choices in order to conduct instruction.

Require Learner Participation - require active mental engagement of learners so that performance can be observed, evaluated, modified, or praised through feedback.

Evaluate and Revise - evaluate the impact of the instruction and to what degree did learners meet the objectives; revise for future lessons.

The Learning Cycle

Biological Sciences Curriculum Study. Developing Biological Literacy. Dubuque: Kendall and Hunt, 1993

Colburn, Alan and M. Clough. "Implementing the Learning Cycle." The Science Teacher. 64:5. 1997. 30-33.

Alan Colburn, an assistant professor of science education at California State, illustrates the learning cycle based on a five-step

approach similar to ASSURE.

The 5E Model for the Learning Cycle

Engage - motive and gain student attention

Explore - activity for learning

Explain - reflect on experiment or learning experience

Expand - apply new knowledge to new situations

Evaluate - reflect on total experience

Abilities

Davies, Ivor K. Instructional Technique. New York: McGraw-Hill, 1981.

Gardner, Howard. Frames of Mind: the Theory of Multiple Intelligences. New York: Basic Books, 1993.

Gardner, Howard. Intelligence Reframed: Multiple Intelligences for the 21st Century. New York: Basic Books, 1999.

Ivor Davies reminds us that people are different and these differences lead to different learning styles and abilities. Howard Gardner has written extensively on multiple types of intelligence and how these multiple learning styles effect not only lesson plans but the total educational environment. Davies illustrates these differences with the following model of organization of abilities:

Fig. 2 Organization of Abilities

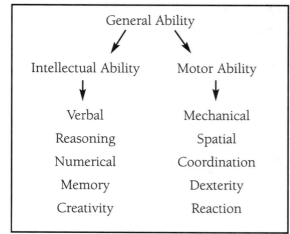

The Turner Helping, Instructional Design Model

Turner, Philip M. Helping Teachers Teach: A School Library Media Specialist's Role. Englewood, CO: Libraries Unlimited, 1993.

Philip Turner, an early advocate for the role of the school media specialist as an instructional player, gives emphasis to learner analysis in his model for instructional design. Needs assessment in terms of the teacher understanding the potential and limitations of the learning environment, resource availability, and learner ability all proceed the development of activities and materials selection. (Fig. 3)

Fig. 3. Instructional Design Model

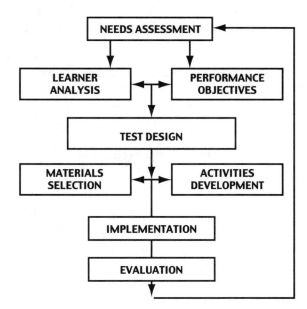

Integrated Model for Teaching Library Skills

Walker, H. Thomas and Paula Kay Montgomery. Teaching Library Media Skills. 2nd edition. Littleton, CO: Libraries Unlimited, 1983.

Few library media specialists prior to the 1988 and 1998 national guidelines considered full integration of library information skills with the curriculum, and even fewer practiced any form of collaborative instruction. Publications written and edited by Thomas and Montgomery were among the first to illustrate the difference between library skills planned in relation to but separate from the classroom and a more integrated approach to library information skills instruction. (Fig. 4 and 5)

Fig. 4. Integrated Model of Library Media Skills Instruction

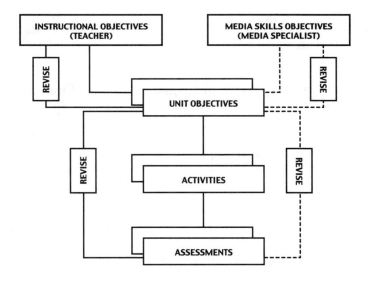

Fig. 5. Related Model of Library Media Skills Instruction

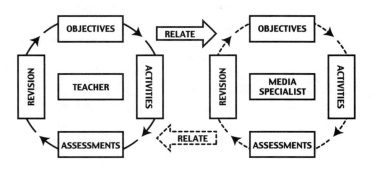

Evolution of Program and Skills and Program Evolution

Callison, Daniel. "Restructuring Pre-Service Education." In School Library Media Annual 1995, edited by Betty J. Morris. Englewood, CO: Libraries Unlimited, 1995. 100-112.

The evolution of the school librarian to school media specialist for information skills to instructional specialist in communication skills can be summarized as follows:

Fig. 6. Evolution Toward Instructional Specialist

The Instructional Media Specialist Evolution

Then	Now	Future
Library	Information	Literacy
Librarian	Media Specialist	Instructional Specialist
ITEMS	NETWORKS	IDEAS
Place and organizational skills	Program and materials use skills	Personal interaction and communication skills

Skills in Materials Organization

Gather resources locally, in systematic manner for common access	Map collection to curriculum, enhance units through collaborative planning; guided access to resources beyond school and electronic	Facilitate student-centered information needs and learning; collaborate in analysis of learner and evaluation of performance; access to resources is based on meeting those needs and is not restricted to local collection

Skills in Communication and Instruction

Respond to requests, provide reading advisory	Teach information skills integrated with curriculum	Develop and model instructional techniques to best position information inquiry and literacy as a dominate teaching method in all areas of the curriculum

---

Thinking Models

WebQuest

Dodge, Bernie. The WebQuest Page at San Diego State University. http://edweb.sdsu.edu/webquest/webquest.html. Viewed June 28, 2001.

Marzano, Robert J. A Different Kind of Classroom: Teaching with Dimensions of Learning. Alexandria, VA: Association for Supervision and Curriculum Development, 1992.

Marzano, Robert J. and others. Dimensions of Thinking: A Framework for Curriculum and Instruction. Alexandria, VA: Association for Supervision and Curriculum Development, 1988.

Bernie Dodge has defined WebQuest as an inquiry-oriented activity in which some or all of the information that learners interact with comes from resources on the internet, optionally supplemented with video-conferencing. He states there are two levels of WebQuests, based on Marzano's dimensions of learning.

For Short Term WebQuests the goal is knowledge acquisition and integration. At the end of the WebQuest, a learner will have grappled with a significant amount of new information and made sense of it. A short-term WebQuest is designed to be completed in one to three class periods.

For a Longer Term WebQuest, the goals include extending and refining knowledge. As a result of this learning experience, the student has analyzed a body of knowledge deeply, transformed it in some way, and demonstrated an understanding of the material by creating something that others can respond to. This experience will typically require a week to a month in a classroom setting.

The templates for development of a WebQuest have grown to be more complex over years of experimentation by thousands of students and teachers. The basic idea remains, however, each WebQuest site provides

- A clear task description
- Links to resources needed to address the problem
- Examples of the process to accomplish the task
- Guidance on how to sort and display information gathered
- Conclusion and summary of what the learner accomplished.
- Encouragement to move to higher learning domains

Dodge favors WebQuests which draw on the following thinking skills defined by Marzano in order to extend and refine knowledge:

Comparing - Identifying and articulating similarities and differences between or among things.

Classifying - Grouping things into definable categories on the basis of their attributes.

Inducing - Inferring unknown generalizations or principles from observations or analysis.

Deducing - Inferring unstated consequences and conditions from given principles and generalizations.

Analyzing Errors - Identifying and articulat-ing errors in one's own or others' thinking.

Constructing support - Constructing a system of support or proof for an assertion.

Abstraction - Identifying and articulating the underlying theme or general pattern of information.

Analyzing Perspectives - Identifying and articulating personal perspectives about issues.

Manzano identifies two more dimensions of learning:

Using Knowledge Meaningfully - The application of knowledge in order to complete a meaningful and constructive task during which skills of decision-making, problem-solving, invention, investigation and experimental inquiry are applied.

Productive Habits of Mind - This is the highest dimension of learning according to Manzano as the learner has matured in development of habits which regulate his or her behavior and approach to new tasks.

Critical thinking:
   be accurate and seek accuracy
   be clear and seek clarity
   maintain an open mind
   restrain impulsivity
   take a position when the situation
      warrants it
   respond appropriately to others' feelings
      and level of knowledge

Creative thinking:
   persevere
   push the limits of your knowledge and
      abilities
   generate trust and maintain your own
      standards of evaluation
   generate new ways of viewing a situation

Self-regulated thinking:
   monitor your own thinking
   plan appropriately
   identify and use necessary resources
   respond appropriately to feedback
   evaluate the effectiveness of your actions

Inquiry Process
Callison, Daniel. "School Library Media

MODELS AND PROCESSES RELATED TO INFORMATION INQUIRY

Programs and Free Inquiry Learning." <u>School Library Journal</u>. 32:6. 1986. 20-24.

Dalbotten, Mary S. "Inquiry in the National Content Standards." In <u>Instructional Interventions for Information Use</u>, edited by Callison, McGregor and Small. San Jose, CA: Hi Willow Research, 1998. 30-82.

Donham, Jean, Kay Bishop, Carol Collier Kuhlthau, and Dianne Oberg. <u>Inquiry-Based Learning: Lessons from Library Power.</u> Linworth Publishing, 2001.

Loertscher, David V. and Blanche Woolls. <u>Information Literacy: A Review of the Research</u>. Hi Willow Research and Publishing, 2002.

Preddy, Leslie. "Student Inquiry in the Research Process." http://pmms.msdpt.k12.in.us/imc/Inquiry/index.htm   Viewed April 1, 2003

Tilley, Carol and Daniel Callison. "Information and Media Literacies: Towards a Common Core." In <u>Instructional Interventions for Information Use</u>. San Hose: Hi Willow Research 1998 110-116.

The Elements in Callison's 1986 Free-Inquiry Model for Teaching and Learning
- Cooperative learning
- Objectives for the lesson are evolutionary and negotiated between student and teacher
- Students document the processes of learning and share them with others
- Content is driven by questions that students raise and answer (leading to more questions) by exploring resources in the library and beyond, and through interviews
- The teacher provides direction for learning, but students are encouraged to take initiatives and work independently in small groups
- Time for the learning is flexible and may run over a full semester or year
- Peer tutoring is encouraged
- Peer interaction and teaming is supported and rewarded; students share discovery of information and evidence
- Projects are shared with peers and parents in celebrations
- Students may choose to extend their learning beyond the project and develop more expertise as they continue through their schooling

Dalbotten and her staff at the Minnesota Department of Children, Families and Learning applied the model for information problem-solving developed by Eisenberg and Berkowitz to the Learning Profile for Inquiry portion of the state's curriculum. Across all areas of the curriculum, the inquiry process was applied to as one of ten strands for student learning. The other strands involved reading, writing, the arts, mathematics, science, cultures, decision making, managing resources, and languages. In all areas of the curriculum, Dalbotten found there were standards and learning activities for students to raise questions and apply data analysis which would imply possible answers. Data is broadly defined to include narrative or testimonial evidence as well as quantitative evidence.

Minnesota's Inquiry Process
1. Generate Questions: pose significant questions.
2. Determine Feasibility: identify strategy and method to address questions.
3. Collect Data: apply method to locate or generate new data.
4. Reduce and Organize Data: select data which is more relevant, organize to meet questions.
5. Display Data: present data in visual form to summarize and communicate findings.
6. Compile Conclusions and More Questions: what new questions come from this process?

Carol Tilley and Daniel Callison illustrated how the inquiry process includes all other approaches to critical and creative thinking found in information literacy or media literacy.

Fig. 7

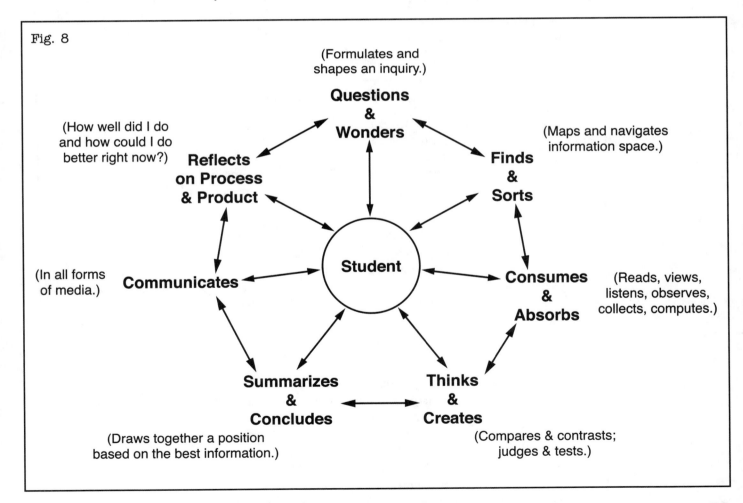

INQUIRY

MEDIA LITERACY

INFORMATION LITERACY

CREATIVE THINKING

CRITICAL THINKING

Loertscher and Woolls have created the following model to illustrate the inquiry process based on recent studies concerning the definitions of information literacy:

Constructivist Learning Environment

Carey, James O. "Library Skills, Information Skills, and Information Literacy: Implications for Teaching and Learning." School Library Media Quarterly Online. Volume 1. 1998. http://www.ala.org/aasl/SLMQ/skills.html

Jonassen, David H. Computers as Mindtools for Schools: Engaging Critical Thinking. New York: Prentice Hall, 1999.

Jonassen, David H. "Evaluating Constructivist Learning." In Constructivism and the Technology of Instruction, edited by T. M. Duffy and D. H. Jonassen. Hilsdale, NJ: Lawrence Erlbaum Associates, 1992.

Jonassen, David H., Kyle L. Peck, and Brent G. Wilson. Learning with Technology: A Constructivist Perspective. Upper Saddle River, NJ: Merrill, 1999.

Fig. 8

(Formulates and shapes an inquiry.)

Questions & Wonders

(How well did I do and how could I do better right now?)

Reflects on Process & Product

(Maps and navigates information space.)

Finds & Sorts

(In all forms of media.)

Communicates

Student

Consumes & Absorbs

(Reads, views, listens, observes, collects, computes.)

Summarizes & Concludes

Thinks & Creates

(Draws together a position based on the best information.)

(Compares & contrasts; judges & tests.)

David Jonassen, professor of instructional systems at Pennsylvania State University, is one of a growing number of instructional design theorists who believes that learning environments for effective advanced knowledge acquisition are best developed on the principles of constructivist learning theory. Although usually placed within higher education, his viewpoint has implications for secondary and elementary school settings as well.

Writing in 1992, Jonassen stated:

"Constructivism holds that the mind is instrumental and essential in interpreting events, objects, and perspectives on the real world, and that those interpretations comprise a knowledge base that is personal and individualistic. The mind filters input from the world in making those interpretations. An important conclusion from constructivistic beliefs is that we all conceive of the external world somewhat differently, based on our unique set of experiences with that world and our beliefs about those experiences." (p. 139)

A model that represents the attributes of meaningful learning under constructivist theory includes:

Active - manipulative, observant, interactive experiences and engagement in the activities to experience and learn by doing.

Constructive - articulative, reflective so learners try to deal with new experiences which present new ideas, information or methods than they have previously experienced.

Intentional - reflective and regulatory to meet a goal, and the learner articulates what goals are to be or have been reached.

Authentic - complex and contextual so that the learning tasks are challenging, and not overly simplified.

Cooperative - the learning tested, refined and shaped through collaboration and conversation as the learner shares ideas with others in order to receive and give constructive feedback.

James Carey, professor of library and information science at South Florida University, has applied the constructivist approach (Fig. 9 and

Fig. 9

Carey: Taxonomy for Teaching Problem-Solving Skills in the School Media Center Context		
Skills	Teacher Role	Student Outcomes
Library	[Explain] sets of tools for accessing, manipulating, creating, and reporting information in a variety of formats.	Find information from multiple resources and use it in preparing reports or presentations.
Information	Teach library skills and a process by which students can be guided in their solution of information problems.	Apply a generic solution strategy to a variety of information problems, and construct new meaning through the interaction between what they know and the new information that they encounter.
Information Literacy	Create learning environments and cooperative group structures in which the natural outgrowth of curiosity is the collaborative construction among students of effective information problem solving strategies	Construct personal solution strategies for information problems, and generalize, test, and adapt those strategies in new problem situations.

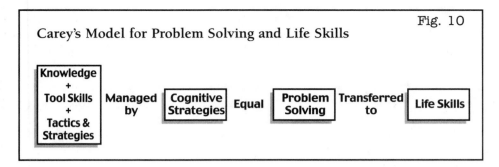

Fig. 10

Carey's Model for Problem Solving and Life Skills

Knowledge + Tool Skills + Tactics & Strategies | Managed by | Cognitive Strategies | Equal | Problem Solving | Transferred to | Life Skills

10) to instructional design for facilitating the education of students in information literacy.

Carey also applies principles of the constructivist learning approach to more the more traditional instructional model.

Comparing Traditional Instructional Design with Constructivist Learning

1. Traditional:
   Teacher provides a motivational introduction.
   Constructivist:
   - Foster motivation through ownership by giving students choices in the content they explore and methods they use for exploration.
   - Situate the problem in a meaningful (authentic) context that is rich in content and interest.

2. Traditional:
   Teacher states what is expected, remind students of what students should know.
   Constructivist:
   - Problem scenarios should emphasize constructing process over finding answers.
   - Scenarios should require reflective thought, looking back to incorporate foundational knowledge into new knowledge.

3. Traditional:
   Teacher presents the new content with examples that will help the students recall for application.
   Constructivist:
   - Use cooperative learning so that students can negotiate the meaning of

what they are learning.
   - Design problem scenarios of high complexity requiring use of multiple process strategies and knowledge skills.
   - Encourage multiple perspectives and interpretations of the same knowledge.
   - Situate the problem in authentic contexts.

4. Traditional:
   Provide students with opportunity to practice new skills.
   Constructivist:
   - Problem scenarios must be generative rather than prescriptive; that is, students construct their own investigation and knowledge acquisition rather than following steps of a prescribed process.
   - Encourage group participation for trying out and negotiating new knowledge and process

5. Traditional:
   Provide student with information about how well they are doing in their practice.
   Constructivist:
   - Balance the potential frustration of aimless exploration with just enough facilitation to ensure progress; facilitation techniques include modeling, scaffolding, coaching, collaborating, but fade as students become more skillful.
   - Facilitate group interaction as needed to ensure peer review of knowledge and process.

6. Traditional:
   Teacher provides a review and relates new skills to real-world applications and upcoming lessons.

Constructivist:

- Students should have opportunities to explore multiple, parallel problem scenarios where they will apply to a new scenario of information [need] processes they have previously constructed.

7. Traditional:
   Teacher provides tests, performance checklists, rating scales, attitude scales, or some other means of measuring mastery of new skills.
   Constructivist:

   - Suggest tools that students can use to monitor their own construction of knowledge and processes; students should be reflective and critically review previous learning and newly constructed positions.
   - Standards for evaluation cannot be absolute; but must be referenced to the student's unique goals, knowledge, and past achievement.
   - The ultimate measure of success is transfer of learning to new, authentic environments.

Instructional Intervention
Instructional Interventions for Information Use: Research Papers of the Sixth Treasure Mountain Research Retreat. Edited by Daniel Callison, Joy H. McGregor, and Ruth V. Small. San Jose, CA: Hi Willow Research, 1998.

Kuhlthau, Carol C. Seeking Meaning. Norwood, NJ: Ablex, 1993.

Kuhlthau, Carol Collier. "The Process of Learning from Information." School Libraries Worldwide. 1:1. January 1995. 1-12.

Instruction serves different purposes depending on the learners' needs and abilities. Those who must plan and delivery instruction in the search for and use of information are often limited to general presentations to a group of students without the opportunity to meet individual needs. Kuhlthau and others have explored the more effective methods for instruction which allow for instructional media specialists and others responsible for bibliographic instruction to not only introduce tools, skills and search strategies, but to intervene at point of need for more constructive and personalized guidance in the selection and use of information. Kuhlathu has defined the intervention role of the library media specialist or academic library instructor at five levels.

Levels of Intervention
ORGANIZER
The information skills instructor arranges, and manages resources; creates a user-friendly, self-service environment; and establishes policies that maximize opportunities for student access to information resources in anticipation or in advance of information needs.

LECTURER
The information skills instructor provides tours and orientation sessions focusing on location of collections and departments to acquaint students with organizational schemes and specific reference tools to increase student interest and use of the library and its resources.

INSTRUCTOR
The information skills instructor provides one or a series of cooperatively planned lessons on specific references and types of sources related to needs arising from classroom activities and tailored to the students' cognitive levels.

TUTOR
The information skills instructor presents informational resources in ways that show the relationships among different kinds of resources and recommends a sequence for their use.

Sessions are provided when student needs dictate and are based on collaborative planning and active teaching by both teachers and librarians.

COUNSELOR
The information skills instructor actively participates in the students' information search process, assists, and provides cognitive,

behavioral, and emotional support for students related to their tasks at initiation, selection, exploration, formulation, collection, presentation and evaluation.

The Research Cycle

McKenzie, Jamie. <u>Beyond Technology: Questioning, Research and The Information Literate School</u>. Bellingham, WA: FNO Press, 2000. See also http://fno.org and http://questioning.org. Viewed June 28, 2001.

McKenzie opens his book Beyond Technology with these statements: "Questions and questioning may be the most powerful technologies of all. How might this be so? Questions allow us to make sense of the world. They are the most powerful tools we have for making decisions and solving problems, for inventing, changing and improving our lives as well as the lives of others.

Questioning is central to learning and growing. An unquestioning mind is one condemned to 'feeding' on the ideas and solutions of others.

An unquestioning mind may have little defense against the data smog so typical of life in this Information Age." (p. 1)

McKenzie's message in central to the inquiry process. Too often students are asked to use resources to "find out" or "cut and paste" without the challenge to raise and answer their own questions. Learning to formulate questions both as an individual and with groups is the most essential skill in the research cycle. He sees students in a more productive mode when they move through the Research Cycle several times before they begin to determine what they will report.

McKenzie's Research Cycle

Determine the essential questions

Determine subsidiary questions

Develop a research plan - what sources are needed?

Gather information - skim and select

Synthesize and evaluate findings

Revise questions

Revise plan and [revisit or locate more sources]

Gather information again

Sort and sift information again

Synthesize [to invision, propose or invent] and evaluate again

Revise questions [and focus]

Revise plan [for access to most relevant sources]

Gather [more precise information]

Sort and sift [to show meaning]

Synthesize to [infer and evaluate]

Report findings

Information Inquiry Model
Daniel Callison. 2001.

Fig. 11

Composition Models

The Authoring Cycle
Harste, Jerome C. "Visions of Literacy." <u>Indiana Media Journal</u>. 17:1. Fall 1994. 27-33.

Short, Kathy G. Jerome C. Harste, Carolyn Burke. <u>Creating Classrooms for Authors and Inquirers</u>. 2nd edition. Portsmouth, NH: Heinemann, 1996.

Short, Kathy G. <u>Learning Together Through Inquiry</u>. York, ME: Stenhouse Publishers, 1996.

The Authoring Cycle is a process used by the whole language advocate team of Harste, Burke, and Short in a variety of curricular areas including introduction to writing and reading

Fig. 12

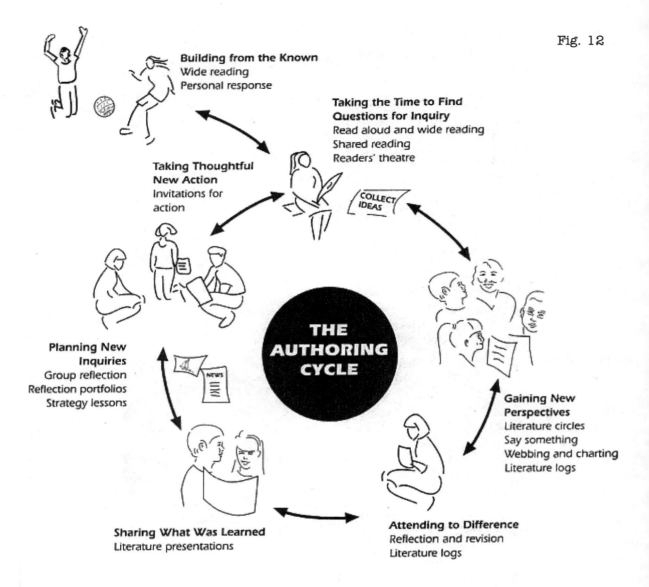

Building from the Known
Wide reading
Personal response

Taking the Time to Find Questions for Inquiry
Read aloud and wide reading
Shared reading
Readers' theatre

Taking Thoughtful New Action
Invitations for action

COLLECT IDEAS

THE AUTHORING CYCLE

Planning New Inquiries
Group reflection
Reflection portfolios
Strategy lessons

Gaining New Perspectives
Literature circles
Say something
Webbing and charting
Literature logs

Sharing What Was Learned
Literature presentations

Attending to Difference
Reflection and revision
Literature logs

in elementary schools. Their cycles reflect the inquiry process. Inquiry, to this team, is what education is about. Teaching reading as inquiry is quite different than teaching reading as comprehension. Writing as inquiry is quite different than writing as transmission or even expression. Problems are not something to be avoided but opportunities to inquire. The very act of teaching itself becomes a process of inquiry. Both teachers and students are learners. The elements for classroom inquiry are:

Voice - all children bring language of their experiences and should be encouraged to recontextualize what they bring to the learning situation.

Connection - students should be invited to make connections between what they bring to learning and what others bring. These connections provide a window for both error and expectations for the teacher.

Perspective - knowledge is open rather than fixed. Knowledge changes over time as well as by how we look at it.

Tension - difference, not consensus, propels the learning process. Learners have nothing to learn by concentrating on what they already know. Focusing on the new, the anomaly, the surprise is more efficient. When the surprise makes sense, according to Harste, learning has occurred.

Reflection - learners take time to think about

what they have learned as well as what implications it has for how they think and act in the world. The key to understanding reflection is thoughtfulness. Thoughtfulness means that new ideas force learners to adjust old ideas as well as how they act and interact with the world. Learners literally reposition themselves both mentally and physically in the world as a result of learning.

I-Search

Duncan, Donna and Laura Lockhart. <u>I-Search, You Search, We All Learn to Research</u>. New York: Neal-Schuman, 2000.

Joyce, Marilyn Z. and Julie I. Tallman. <u>Making the Writing and Research Connection with the I-Search Process</u>. New York: Neal-Schuman, 1997.

Macrorie, Ken. <u>The I-Search Paper</u>. Portsmouth, NH: Heinemann, 1988.

Moulton, Margaret R. "The Multigenre Paper: Increading Interest, Motivation, and Functionality in Research." <u>Journal of Adolescent & Adult Literacy</u>. April 1999. 528-539.

Joyce and Tallman, after field-testing the I-Search process, concluded "I-Search is an approach to research that uses the power of student interests, builds on personal understanding of the research process, and encourages stronger student writing. Originally developed by a college professor for his freshmen composition students, the I-Search is adaptable for use as a beginning research experience at the third grade or a sophisticated search at the graduate level." (p. vii)

Frustrated with student papers which dealt with topics of little interest to the students or to him, Ken Macrorie moved the typical research paper into a personalized learning experience. He shifted many of the assignment parameters normally established by the instructor over to the responsibility of the student. The key task for the student became topic selection. More than thinking of a topic, the student had to think through a topic in an informed manner. This involves more time and effort by the student to complete background reading, drafting portions of a report and sharing ideas with others, as well as seeking out experts to interview about the potential of a topic. Through this process, the "topic chooses the student" in that eventually the student discovers a set of questions which are personally interesting, so much so that they are motivated to give the time that is needed to explore the resources necessary to investigate the topic. Moulton has labeled this approach "the multigenre paper" and encourages students to explore a wide variety of presentation formats (posters, poems, video and multimedia productions, drama, and more) in order to express themselves and their findings in a variety of ways. Some messages and some audiences just do not fit the traditional approach of just words printed on paper.

Macrorie also allows a personal first person writing style rather than a cold or journalist third person. Students seemed to express more personal perspectives under this style. Journals seem to help them document personal observations concerning the issues related to the topic. Joyce and Tallman found value in students also making journal entries to discuss the value of the information sources used and for students to think through alternative ways to gain information. Journaling served to map a reflective pathway for the student as he or she faced the rather complex task of making many content and resources selections normally predetermined by the instructor.

The I-Search Steps
  I. Free-write - give 30 to 45 minutes to write freely and/or openly discuss what you know and find to be of interest about an issue or topic.
  II. Want to Know - begin to classify what you know and what you really want to know about a set of issues or topic.
  III. Expert Knowledge - extend your basic knowledge about the issues through wide reading of materials associated with the topic, but gain indepth perspectives through interviewing an expert.

IV. Tell a Story - share what you know and what you would still like to learn with your classmates through a summary or story of what you have learned and how you gained the information.

V. Refine - make some choices as to what are the most meaningful things learned for both yourself as well as for audiences to whom you may report your findings.

VI. Specific Research - seek out the information to address remaining questions in a specific manner.

VII. Composition Mechanics - revise and edit the paper for clarity, correct spelling, and to acknowledge the sources of information.

Joyce and Tallman have summarized the application of the I-Search process with the following outline which includes interventions on the part of the teacher to help provide guidance to the learner as they work through information selection and use.

The I-Search Process
I. Topic Selection [Brainstorming]
  A. Webbing
  B. Skimming Resources
  C. Intervening and Conferencing
  D. Sharing
II. Finding Information
  A. Generating Research Questions
  B. Key Words and Names
  C. Background Reading without Notetaking
  D. Using Pre-notetaking Sheets and Preparing Bibliographies
  E. Reading Indepth
  F. Interviewing
III. Using Information
  A. Highlighting Texts
  B. Double-entry Drafting
  C. Reflecting and Conferencing
  D. Using Learning Logs
IV. Preparing the I-Search Product
  A. Using First Person
  B. Telling about Search
  C. Using Learning Logs
  D. Editing by Peers

V. Transferring the Research Process [to Future Tasks]

Cultural Celebration
Miller, Lynda, Theresa Steinlage, Mike Printz. Cultural Cobblestones: Teaching Cultural Diversity. Mctuchen, NJ: Scarecrow Press, 1994.

Wigginton, Eliot and his students. Foxfire: 25 Years. New York: Anchor Books, 1991.

Wigginton, Eliot. Sometimes a Shining Moment: The Foxfire Experience. Garden City, NY: Anchor Press Doubleday, 1985.

The local student reporting and journal writing approach developed by Eliot Wigginton in Georgia in the 1970s demonstrated that secondary school students could explore their own heritage through their local culture. The final product included a locally produced magazine with illustrations on a wide range of topics, from hog butchering to log cabin construction. Nationally, the result has included nearly a dozen best-selling books. The foxfire method was based on finding that one spark that would ignite student interest and then supporting that exploration through the basic journalistic model of discovering and reporting on "who, what, where, when, why and how."

Mike Printz, a national figure in young adult literature promotion and whose name is now carried on an annual award for young adult authors, was intrigued by Wigginton's methods and adapted them to his projects in Topeka, Kansas. He and his co-librarians and teaching staff guided hundreds of senior high school students through oral history products of local personalities. His philosophy for learning was based on first, being a personal model for inquiry by reading extensively himself. Everything interested Mr. Printz. And second, to guide the student researcher in exploring the culture around the student and to find personal meaning in that personal heritage. In his last few years as a school librarian, Printz moved more into celebration of diverse cultures through art and literature.

Lynda Miller, art teacher, and Theresa Steinlage, language arts teacher, helped to document these celebrations in Cultural Cobblestones.

Celebration of student learning, based on the Printz philosophy, was to establish through the school library an environment for the entire learning community to engage in a topic or theme. For a month to six weeks, he would concentrate on the theme to the extent that everyone in the school including principal, counselors, secretaries, and nearly all parents would be engaged in the stories, films, books and displays related to the topic at hand. Dozens of assignments around the school would be associated with the theme. Special student forums would run on numerous evenings in which students would make special presentations, guest speakers would respond to in-depth questions from students and parents, and student multi-media products were kept for future use by other students. Thus, student research became a means to provide documents for future learners. Student research, writing, and artwork were valued as much as similar products from the professional ranks. Many of these student-produced programs became documents now housed with the local state historical society.

A Model for Cultural Celebration
READ - For Enjoyment, Discovery and Ideas

Identify Personal Interest Related to Local History

Explore Primary and Secondary Sources for Background

Seek and Record Interview for Oral History

Document through Photographs, Original Drawings, Original Poetry

Organize Student Products with Other Events for Celebration

Maintain Student Work in a Format for Future Use

Lab Report - Technical Writing
Nearly all models which have been designed to represent information literacy skills have come from social studies or the humanities. This is not surprising as the creators come from those disciplines. Records of clear observation and precision of documentation actually have a stronger model in the sciences. Inquiry, after all, is basically the application of the Scientific Method to observe, document, and infer. The model for composition of the lab report reflects key elements that should be considered for any investigation.

The Lab Report Format Model
Purpose - Statement of the reason for conducting the experiment. Purposes can be stated as questions.

Hypothesis - The hypothesis is stated as an if...then...statement. The "if" part of the statement is based on related facts that one know to be true. The "then" part of the statement is an educated guess on the outcome of the experiment.

Materials - This is a list of all equipment and chemicals needed to do the experiment. Exact amounts are to be noted.

Procedure - The procedure describes exactly what was done in terms of steps, time, amount, and method. The procedure may affect the results and should be detailed in narrative format. This documentation makes it possible for others to duplicate the experiment to validate or challenge results, or to move the experiment into a different setting with control of factors to help isolate causes and to transfer findings.

Observations - The observation tells exactly what happened. An observation is measurable information and can include experimental data in the form of labeled tables, graphs, drawings, and other visuals.

Conclusions - What conclusions are drawn and explained. Is the hypothesis supported or rejected based on the data and observations. Part of the conclusion may be a new hypothesis and further questions for future experiments.

Chapter 4

Selected Key Documents on Information Inquiry and Information Literacy

Over the past three decades, many educators have attempted to define the key skills students should be taught, encouraged to demonstrate, and to explore more fully on their own in order to survive in the Information Age. Many of these skills derive from curricula designed for practice of critical thinking, while others represent information skills associated closely with specific discipline areas of study. Selected documents illustrate the proposed evolution from a narrow library skill base to a more open and demanding critical inquiry process. These documents also call for a leadership role on the part of new instructional library media specialists.

1906 A Great Awakening

Kenneth Pray of the University of Wisconsin and W. F. Rocheleau of the Illinois Normal Academy wrote in their series on "Home Study of History" in 1906, "within recent years a new element has been made prominent in history courses ... so prominent that wide-awake and progressive teachers find it necessary to recognize its utility and value. This is the use by teacher and pupil of other books and materials besides the text." (p. ii)

As they continued in their introduction these two educators defined the textbook as a summary, an item of brevity, but containing an outline to provide a larger picture and relationships. Other resources, however, reproduce historical scenes; create personalities; explain motives; raise and suggest answers to the "why" questions; instill reading habits if the teacher is also an appreciative user of literature. The up-to-date teacher, concluded Pray and Rocheleau, looks upon the library as an "essential" part of the school. That teacher realizes that the lifeblood of the subject flows through books [and other resources], while the text alone can furnish but the dry bones of information.

1955 A Laboratory-Workshop

Martin Rossoff served as the librarian for James Madison High School in Brooklyn. Rossoff authored several books decades prior to discussions on what the school media field now terms information literacy. His concept of the school library as a laboratory in which to debate issues and find evidence to support arguments was not new, but he is certainly one of the early practicing school librarians to place critical inquiry in the center of the school media program. A list of the questions from Rossoff which illustrate how his students were expected to explore their library and eventually debate positions illustrates his approach. Although his issues reflect a specific time period, the method to raise additional questions and propose resolutions to these questions remains the same today.

- McCarthy - menace or savior of democracy?
- Are our civil rights in danger?
- Should Hawaii and Alaska be admitted to statehood?
- Is mercy killing justifiable?
- Should the government censor comic books?
- Should 18 year-olds be allowed to vote?

In the early 1970s, Rossoff wrote of his views concerning the need for educational change:

"...teachers continue to require students to memorize large doses of information, extracted from inadequate textbooks, most of which is obsolete and most of which is forgotten once the test papers have been graded. This practice was inherited from an earlier stable period in history, when there were comparatively few facts to be learned. The question is now: Can this method succeed in an environment characterized by an unprecedented social and technological change, bursting accumulations of knowledge, and a disturbing uncertainty about the facts themselves?" (p. 21)

Rossoff described the "new education" in terms of a curriculum based on broad concepts and development of the student's ability to reason. He saw application of new technological inventions to classroom instruction. A third consideration, he wrote, "in the readjustment of education was a theory of learning which holds that there was more to the process of education than mere stimulus and response or trial and error. While our knowledge of how people actually learn is still dim, there is general agreement that no learning took place unless motivation existed. Students have to be convinced that learning was worthwhile." (p. 30)

Students can learn a great deal by themselves, with guidance, and they can learn a great deal from each other, with facilitation. Rossoff envisioned the school library as a center for exchange of ideas. This interaction among learners was the major purpose and books, magazines, and equipment gathered in or near the library were all artifacts to support this process. The inquiry/discovery method, according to Rossoff, has merit but it is unquestionably impossible in schools that are without libraries and laboratories.

1985 Educating Students to Think

In the summer of 1985, a small group of educators gathered in Chicago at the invitation of Tony Carbo Bearman, then Executive Director of the National Commission on Libraries and Information Science. Bearman's charge to the group was to explore alternative ways school library media programs could move beyond just support of simple skills for location of library resources to playing a stronger role in preparing young people for the demands of the Information Age. These discussions took place prior to the concepts envisioned for Information Power, the national guidelines for instructional roles of the school library media program.

Three individuals agreed to draft a position statement for the group: Jacqueline Mancall, then associate professor at Drexel University; Shirley Aaron, then professor at Florida State University, and Sue Walker, then program coordinator for library media services with the Lancaster, PA schools. This team combined years of professional experience, knowledge of the research record in school library media management, and most of all, knowledge of emerging educational theory on metacognition and national school performance review.

The final report from this group is one of the key foundational documents which defines the shift away for teaching library skills based on tools and location toward instruction in critical thinking based on selection, use, analysis and synthesis of information to meet the intellectual needs of individual students. The contribution Mancall, Aaron and Walker made with this paper to move the instructional role of the school library media specialist in a new direction is beyond measure.

"Educating Students to Think" identified, among other current problems in public education, the following aspects with which school library media specialists as instructors as well as other educators, must be concerned and change. Studies indicated:

- Our educational system focuses primarily on teaching youth "what" to think rather than "how" to think.

- Failure to help students develop higher-order skills has seriously limited their ability to cope adequately in an increasingly complex society.
- Students are often satisfied with their initial interpretations of what they had read and seemed satisfied with their initial efforts to explain or defend their points of view. Few students could provide more than superficial responses to [information comprehension and interpretation] tasks, and even the better responses showed little evidence of well-developed problem-solving critical thinking skills.

Mancall, Aaron, and Walker called for the current school library media programs which were library-centered, concentrating on physical objects collected and organized, to move toward programs which should be information-centered. These programs would be directed at greater understanding of student and teacher learning needs as well as the intellectual content of the resources held or accessed through the media center. Meeting the needs for knowledge and learning should drive the program, not just what has been placed on the shelves. When the school librarian plans lessons, the target is meeting the learning and teaching needs, not just the needs of how to access what is on the shelf.

Among other new aspects for the school library media program, their position paper supported the information guidance service role proposed by James Liesener, Professor at the University of Maryland.

He proposed that information guidance services are provided by knowledgeable intermediaries who offer assistance to students as they attempt to find, interpret, and evaluate materials, information, and/or ideas. This is key role for both teachers and school library media specialist who function as information advisors in an increasingly complex information world.

This information advising and teaching role should concentrate on establishing learning situations and interactions among teachers and learners on the following critical

thinking skills:
- distinguishing between verifiable facts and value claims;
- determining the reliability of a source;
- determining the factual accuracy of a statement;
- distinguishing relevant from irrelevant information, claims, or reasons;
- detecting bias;
- identifying unstated assumptions;
- identifying ambiguous or equivocal claims or argument;
- recognizing logical inconsistencies or fallacies in a line of reasoning;
- distinguishing between warranted or unwarranted claims; and
- determining the strength of an argument.

Other Documents from the 1980s

Several other articles were written at the time of the Mancall, Aaron, and Walker publication. These also added to the emerging definition of information skills and serve as a foundation for greater use of inquiry methods to teach and explore these skills k-12.

In 1984, Michael Eisenberg, then assistant professor at Syracuse, introduced his ideas on mapping the curriculum for integration of library media skills. This approach was to assure that library skills at the elementary school level would not be left in isolation and seen to be without value.

In 1986, Daniel Callison, then assistant professor at Indiana University, outlined elements of free inquiry learning for the school library environment. He used principles from science education to illustrate how the discovery method also applies to teaching of library information skills. He recommended that students work in teams, explore and share their findings about information sources rather than simply listening to library tool orientations, and that the school media center environment needed to be open for support of personal inquiry that would continue beyond assigned library research projects.

In 1987, Carol Kuhlthau, then assistant

professor at Rutgers, summarized an emerging theory of library instruction. She attempted to move beyond simple introduction of resources and tools for information location, to teaching skills, which help students seek meaning from the information they use. Information gains meaning when it becomes evidence. The task, therefore, is to build on the student's experiences and knowledge so that information encountered can be discerned as either useful evidence or discarded as quickly as possible if it has no relevance. Kulthau provided the first clear ties to Constructivist Theory for effective teaching of information skills.

A speech by Karen Sheingold to the American Library Association Annual Conference in New York in 1986 was printed in School Library Media Quarterly in 1987. Then Director of the Center for Children and Technology at Bank Street College, Sheingold illustrated how inquiry is key to keeping children's knowledge active and vital. Her examples of critical inquiry associated with environmental education served to provide tangible activities for moving inquiry beyond just the books and walls of the library.

Barbara Stripling, who was later to become President of the American Association of School Librarians, summarized the impressions of one who has both practiced the techniques for inquiry instruction and managed the demanding operations of a school media program. Written while serving as editor of School Library Media Quarterly and a library media specialist at the Fayetteville Public Schools in Arkansas, Stripling raised these questions and issues for future information literacy instruction:

Challenge 1

To provide intellectual and physical access to information and ideas for a diverse population whose needs are rapidly changing.
- How can we tell if students are understanding the information they find and are using it well?
- What thinking skills can we teach effectively in the library. How do they improve the students' abilities to understand, evaluate, and use information?

- How can we build a client/professional relationship with students that will enhance our credibility and encourage them to involve us while they search for and use information?

Challenge 2

To ensure equity and freedom of access to information and ideas, unimpeded by social, cultural, economic, geographical, or technological constraints.
- How does availability of computers at home affect students' online database searching skills?
- Do low-income students make less voluntary use of technology that is available in the school?
- Are there gender issues which pertain to extent of technology and information access and use?

Challenge 3

To promote literacy and enjoyment of reading, viewing, and listening for young people at all ages and stages of development.
- What programs have been most successful in engaging both student and teachers to read, for pleasure and for information?
- What can be done to foster reading interest among low-achieving students?
- What is the appropriate role of library media services in whole language education?

Challenge 4

To provide leadership and expertise in the use of information and instructional technologies.
- How can we shift the emphasis of library instruction from location to information use?
- What methods are successful in helping teachers to incorporate new technologies into their classrooms?
- How does the use of the new technologies improve teaching and learning?

Challenge 5

To participate in networks that enhance

access to resources located outside of the school.

- What impact does electronic networking [telecommunications] have on the learning environment of the school; the community?
- When students are provided access to resources beyond the school, what effect does this have on their motivation and quality of learning?

1987 ALA and Information Literacy

In 1987, the President of the American Library Association Margaret Chisholm appointed a special committee to define information literacy, to identify models of information literacy development which seem appropriate for informal learning environments, and to determine implications of information literacy in education. Patricia Senn Breivik, long advocate for information literacy standards in higher education, served as chair of the committee.

Ultimately, the committee stated, information literate people are those who have learned how to learn. They know how to learn because they know how knowledge is organized, how to find information, and how to use information in such a way that others can learn from them. They are people prepared for lifelong learning, because they can always find the information needed for any task or decision at hand.

Information literacy, concluded the committee, is a means of personal empowerment. It allows people to verify or refute expert opinion and to become independent seekers of truth. It provides them with the ability to build their own arguments and to experience the excitement of the search for knowledge.

The ALA Presidential Committee on Information Literacy went on to describe situations in which people use information skills to address problems in business, citizenship, and personal needs as well as in school environments. From this report, one can conclude that information literacy, or information

Figure.
The Relationship among Workplace, Personal, and Academic Information Problem Sets and Authentic Learning. 2001. Daniel Callison

inquiry as a broader set of concepts presented this book, impacts all areas of life, personal, professional, and academic. This can be illustrated with the intersections of information problems shown below

As the Figure above implies, information problems from these three domains can easily overlap, similar in origin and in solution. Although not illustrated in this manner by the ALA Presidential Committee, such a diagram helps us understand the purpose of establishing authentic and learner-centered inquiry problems within the academic setting. The closer educators can come to creating information problem experiences which involve aspects all three areas, the closer educators come to placing the student in situations in which they must explore and apply solutions to authentic, real world problems. Understanding of information problems from each of the three domains and how they interrelate moves us toward authentic instruction and authentic assessment.

1989 Information Literacy and Higher Education

Two leaders in higher education in Colorado, one an administrator for library and information services and the other an administrator for faculty development and leadership, co-authored an extensive discussion of the role of the academic library in developing lifelong learners.

Patricia Senn Breivik, then Director of

Academic Libraries and E. Gordon Gee, then President of the University of Colorado, jointly called information literacy the survival skills in the Information Age. They wrote: "Instead of drowning in the abundance of information that floods their lives, information-literate people know how to find, evaluate, and use information effectively to solve a particular problem or make a decision, whether the information they select comes from a computer, a book, a government agency, a film, or any of a number of other possible resources. Students have long relied on the knowledge of teachers and the information skills of librarians. In fact, when the volume of information was modest, they could often manage without becoming information literate themselves. What the information explosion has done is turn an old problem, functional literacy, into a new crisis. To address this crisis, we need a new educational philosophy based on a fuller understanding of the information explosion and a redefinition of literacy that includes information skills." (p. 12)

Breivik and Gee also called for more collaborative communication between college librarians and secondary schools in order to help prepare high school graduates better for the college library information search complexities. They recommended implementation of less lecture for "library instruction" and adoption of better teaching practices for the library-based curriculum. Academic experiences are better, they suggested, when the learning activity:

- imitates reality [is Authentic]
- is active and students have opportunities to learn by discovery
- is individualized
- is responsive to a variety of learning styles
- accommodates constantly changing information
- is provided in an environment that is least threatening.

1992 The Information Literate Person

Christina Doyle conducted a Delphi Study among dozens of educators versed in educa-

tion for information and technology instruction. Her study was concluded in the early 1990s as the Information Age was beginning to burst on the world with access to personal computerized communication as never before experienced. Published in 1994 by the ERIC Clearinghouse on Information and Technology, the following characteristics of an information literate person have proven to be a benchmark in defining core information literacy skills:

- recognizes that accurate and complete knowledge is the basis for intelligent decision-making;
- recognizes the need for information;
- formulates questions based on information needs;
- identifies potential sources of information;
- develops successful search strategies;
- accesses sources of information including computer-based and other technologies;
- evaluates information;
- organizes information for practical application;
- integrates new information into an existing body of knowledge; and
- uses information in critical thinking and problem-solving.

1993 A Position on Information Literacy Standards

In 1993, The Wisconsin Educational Media Association established an outline of the key skills for information literacy. These were endorsed by the Wisconsin Department of Education and became the basis for the "AASL Position Statement on Information Literacy and School Library Media Programs." Several other states developed similar information skill statements which served as models to integrate these skills across the curriculum. Leading examples included Colorado, North Carolina, Michigan, and Washington.

Recently revised and expanded, this AASL Position Paper now provides one of the best outlines for methods and skills leading to information literacy education based on collaboration between the school library media specialists and other teachers. This paper has received the endorsement of the National Forum on Information Literacy, a group representing sixty educational associations.

The AASL Position Paper provides further definition of some important elements related to inquiry. The first stage is paraphrased below:

I. Defining the Need for Information
- recognize different [needs for and] uses of information (occupational, intellectual, recreational)
- [establish] a frame of reference for the information need (consider who, what, where, when, how, and why)
- relate the information need to prior knowledge
- [initiate a strategy] to solve the problem through consideration of a variety of questioning skills (yes and no for facts; open for working hypothesis)

Additional stages are defined for search strategy, resource location, interpreting the information, communicating information and evaluation of the product and process. An element which is defined in detail for the AASL paper involves the task to consider new information and how to analyze it to determine its usefulness and potential for assimilation to the learner's knowledge base. These skills are outlined in the fourth stage, and are critical to the inquiry process:

IV. Assessing and Comprehending the Information
A. Skim and scan for major ideas and keywords to identify relevant information.
B. Differentiate between primary and secondary sources.
C. Determine the authoritativeness, currentness, and reliability of the information.
D. Differentiate among fact, opinion, propaganda, point of view, and bias.
E. Recognize errors in logic.
F. Recognize omissions, if any, in information.
G. Classify, group or label the information.
H. Recognize interrelationships among concepts.
I. Differentiate between cause and effect.
J. Identify points of agreement and disagreement among sources.
K. Select information in formats most appropriate to the student's individual learning style.
L. Revise and redefine the information problem if necessary.

In 1999, several scenarios were added to the position paper to illustrate the educational environment in which students (as well as media specialists and other teachers, along with local experts and citizens of the community) would best be able to demonstrate information literacy skills. Examples of these scenarios are:

Elementary Setting
Elementary students who are setting up a fresh-water aquarium in their classroom during a study of aquatic life, plan their class time with the teacher before they consult and work with the school library media specialist to locate and use print and nonprint resources. They collect the materials, plants, and animals based on their completed research. The teacher and library media specialist locate biological data through the Internet and students confer with the local experts via telephone and e-mail.

Middle School Setting
A team of middle school teachers and the library media specialist plan a study of life in the middle ages that will involve a special mock celebration. They group students, identify projects that will be completed, and suggest resources necessary. [Information inquiry skills are essential for educators who develop meaningful instructional resource plans.] They also determine the best information access points for each group to get started and experience some immediate success, and settle on a schedule for efficient use of time.

High School Setting

In the high school library media center students are preparing to produce a video news report set in the Civil War. They are searching the school district online catalog, a database of statewide library resources and online historical magazine indexes and a laserdisc of resources from the Library of Congress. They also have access to several new digital library collections that provide photographs from the time period. Among the resources selected by one student are primary source newspapers, a videotaped documentary, an audio recording of folk songs, along with books and magazine articles. Electronic mail is used to request some of the items through interlibrary loan, as well as to contact the state historical society and history content experts at several universities.

1994 Model Information Literacy Guidelines

Sponsored by the Colorado State Library and often coordinated by Dian Walster of the University of Colorado at Denver, a group of forward thinking school library media specialists drafted any early version of learning standards for information literacy. Their model served as one of the key documents for later development of standards for student learning by the American Association of School Librarians. The philosophy, guidelines, and statements of student performance written by this Colorado group have helped to define the characteristics of the mature student information user.

Philosophy: Information literate students are competent, independent learners. They know their information needs and actively engage in the world of ideas.

They display confidence in their ability to access information and to communicate. They operate comfortably in situations where there are multiple answers, as well as those with no answers. They hold high standards for their work and create quality products. Information literate students are flexible, can adapt to change, and are able to function independently and in groups.

Guidelines for Student Performance:

1. The Student as Knowledge Seeker. The student constructs meaning from information.
   - Determines information needs
     - states the purpose
     - explores options
     - defines a manageable focus
   - Develops information-seeking strategies and locates information
     - frames appropriate questions
     - identifies likely resources
     - uses a variety of strategies
     - builds a reasonable timeline
     - makes ethical decisions (see guideline 5)
     - records bibliographic information
   - Acquires information
     - questions others
     - listens actively
     - queries electronic resources
     - reads for significant details and concepts
     - views for significant details and concepts
     - extracts appropriate details and concepts
   - Analyzes information relative to need
     - identifies criteria in terms of authoritativeness, completeness, format, point of view, reliability, and timeliness
     - applies criteria to information
     - retains only appropriate material
   - Organizes information
     - creates outlines, storyboards or graphic organizers
     - assembles material to meet information need
     - credits appropriate sources
   - Processes information
     - integrates information from a variety of sources
     - makes inferences
     - draws conclusions
     - constructs meaning
     - builds connections to prior knowledge
   - Acts on information
     - answers a questions

- satisfies a curiosity
- takes informed action
- develops a product
- solves a problem
- presents information
- Evaluates process and product
  - determines level of product success (see guideline 2)
  - identifies process strengths and weaknesses
  - develops a plan to continuously improve the process

2. The Student as Quality Producer. The student creates a quality product.
   - Recognizes quality and craftsmanship
     - uses existing models and criteria as a guide
     - critically evaluates those models
     - develops personal criteria for quality product(s)
   - Plans the quality product
     - establishes a clear purpose
     - considers the audience
     - determines product content
     - chooses format
     - develops process
     - identifies necessary resources
   - Creates a quality product
     - uses resources and technology (see guideline 1)
     - reflects knowledge of learning styles
     - integrates appropriate media (see guideline 5)
   - Presents a quality product
     - communicates clearly
     - reflects established criteria
     - demonstrates effective presentation skills
   - Evaluates quality product
     - evaluates the process and the product continuously
     - measures product against models and criteria
     - revises and refines as necessary
     - determines if product has achieved its purpose
     - decides if product has reached its desired audience
     - reflects on personal satisfaction with

the product (see guideline 3)

3. The Student as Self-directed Learner. The student learns independently.
   - Voluntarily establishes clear information goals and manages progress toward achieving them (see guidelines 1 & 2)
     - realizes that not all problems have a solution
     - makes choice to pursue or modify the search
   - Voluntarily consults media sources [and media specialist]
     - reads for pleasure, to learn to solve problems
     - uses media sources for information and personal needs
     - seeks answers to questions
     - considers alternative perspectives
     - evaluates differing points of view
   - Explores topics of interest
     - uses the library media center, public library and other information sources (e.g. electronic information, bookstores, directories, experts)
     - asks for help
     - recognizes organization and structure of information centers and resources
   - Identifies and applies personal performance guidelines
     - engages in reflective analysis
     - internalizes the model and process of inquiry (see guidelines 1 & 2)
     - balances internal and external performance demands
     - reflects on personal satisfaction

4. Student as Group Contributor. The student participates effectively as a group member.
   - Helps group determine information needs (see guideline 1)
     - works with group to define project or problem parameters
     - collaborates to determine:
       common definitions
       questions
       processes [for action]
       information access [strategies]
   - Shares responsibility for planning and producing a quality group product (see

guideline 2)
- collaborates to define roles and divide responsibility
- completes tasks in a timely manner
- helps synthesize individual tasks into finished product
- Collaborates to determine relevant information
  - selects information using various resources and technologies
  - works with others to organize information
  - helps integrate information from a variety of sources
- Acknowledge diverse ideas and incorporates them when appropriate
  - shows respect for others' ideas, backgrounds, and learning [and communication] styles
  - discusses opposing viewpoints constructively
  - helps create projects that reflect differences among individuals
- Offers useful information to the group, defends that information when appropriate, and seeks consensus to achieve a stronger product
  - offers well thought-out evidence justifying information presented
  - moderates ideas of group toward consensus, while allowing individuals to maintain their own opinions
  - demonstrates effective interpersonal communication skills
- Clearly communicates ideas in presenting the group product
  - assimilates ideas of others into group presentation
  - helps ensure that all participants' contributions are represented
  - uses a variety of media effectively to communicate ideas
- Evaluates the product, the group process, and individual roles continuously
  - works with the group to set criteria for the product
  - uses the criteria to determine the success of the product

5. Student as Responsible Information User.

The student uses information [in a responsible and ethical manner]
- Practices ethical usage of information and information technologies
  - applies copyright guidelines
  - cites references in proper format
  - does not plagiarize
  - recognizes copyright as protection from the copyright holder
- Respects the principle of intellectual freedom
  - understands the concept of intellectual freedom
  - recognizes the importance of intellectual freedom
- Follows guidelines and etiquette using electronic information sources
  - utilizes electronic resources to locate, retrieve, and transfer information
  - applies time and access constraints when using electronic resources
- Maintains the physical integrity of information resources and facilities
  - follows policies and procedures
  - preserves integrity of print and non-print materials
  - acknowledges and respects the rights of others
- Recognizes the need for equal access to materials and resources

1995 Redefining the Librarian

The Library Instruction Round Table of the American Library Association published a collection of essays in 1995 which described the changing role of many librarians moving toward a much more involved educational responsibility. This seemed to be true for librarians in all institutions, school, public, academic, and special. Callison took the instructional role further than simply presentation or even co-planning to the level that defines the educator in the critical-thinking curriculum as an evaluator of student performance.

In reviewing the recommendations from the Association for Supervision and Curriculum Development (ASCD) as well as ideas from educators such as Kathleen Craver and Melvin Bowie, Callison defined the critical thinking curriculum and the school media specialist roles in the evaluation of students.

The thinking curriculum is not a course to be added to a crowded program when time permits. It is not a program that begins after basics have been mastered. Skills in reasoning, problem-solving, making judgments, stating inferences need to spread from the top of Bloom's cognitive domain to all levels associated with learning. Each fact, each event, each concept presented should have a context and be questioned to the extent that relationships to the learner's personal abilities and individual needs are acknowledged.

This is not to say that learning is without steps, levels, or that there are no prerequisites. It is necessary, however, that students become aware of such increments themselves and that they construct their intellectual webbing based on as many informational items, thoughts, or conclusions as can be made relevant to their intellectual schema and relevant to their own current and possible future social contexts.

1989 ASCD recommendations suggest that construction of any thinking curriculum should employ the following practices in what they term "cognitive apprenticeship."

Practice a real task. Writing an essay for an interested audience, not just the teacher who will give a grade; reading a text that takes some work (asking questions, discussion, comprehension, comparisons) to understand; exploring a physical phenomenon that is inadequately explained by a current concept.

Contextualize the practice. Students would not do exercises on separating facts from opinions, but they would take on tasks of analyzing arguments (and statistics) on particular topics or participating in debates, both of which might engage them in a contextualized version of figuring out reliable information in a communication.

Observe models. Students need plenty of opportunity to observe others doing the kind of work they are expected to learn or to do. This observation (reinforced with the challenge to evaluate or critique) gives them standards of effective performance against which they can judge their own efforts.

The Thinking Curriculum is based on students practicing the process of raising questions, testing a variety of possible answers, and eventually voicing, writing, constructing, sculpting, drawing, and arguing the meaning of those answers. This information inquiry process is founded on gathering information for the purpose of seeking various perspectives, not just a single conclusion. Most directly, it means that students must be engaged in a conversation of their own and with others.

Craver has given school library media specialists a superb summary of the implications from library and information science research related to new concepts in teaching critical thinking. Successful methods in placing students in the critical thinking mode include the expectation that the student generate his or her own analysis of a given text to identify, organize, and raise questions concerning issues presented.

Thoughtful discussion leaders and students reacting to peer opinions in groups tend to increase critical thinking. In a discussion situation, deliberate use of wait time conveys to students that they are expected to respond intelligently to posed questions. Open debate that results in capturing issues in written form followed by a cooling period in which students search for supportive or counter evidence may serve to raise the level of critical exchange.

Bowie has listed very tangible activities that the school library media specialist and the classroom teacher can employ in order to challenge students in the reasoning process. Some of these are paraphrased below:

- Ask a class to gather and sort opposing viewpoints on a social issue; use all possible sources; analyze merits of each opinion including questioning of the qualifications of "authorities."
- Compile a file of popular advertisements (record television and radio spots as well) and lead students in a discussion of how information is manipulated (spoken and visual).
- Students should construct infinite bibliographies (pathfinders or webographies) to show location of information through a variety of formats both in

and beyond the library, including human resources.

- Create activities that require comparison of maps, charts, census data over time and in relation to major events.

Bowie terms her activities intervention strategies. This term is important to note because intervention is a concept that must be broadened in the evaluation role of the instructional library media specialist and the classroom teacher. Self, peer, and mentor evaluations are considered at each stage of the inquiry process, not just at product conclusion.

Intervention represents an opening created by either the teacher or instructional media specialist in order to cue a point of instructional need (identification of the "teachable moment"). Intervention works best when collaboratively planned and implemented and classroom content-grounded.

Both the instructional media specialist and the classroom teacher need to be skilled, however, to handle interventions individually when necessary. The goal is to establish such critical thinking activities at the forefront of lesson planning to the extent that the adjective intervention can be dropped, and inquiry activities become the curriculum. Using varied resources, raising questions, presenting results of the information search and inference become the standard, not the exception. Inquiry and critical thinking become the curriculum, not simply a special process and set of skills added to lessons by a few teachers.

Above all, the teaching methods that work best to provide an environment for critical thinking should be used by the instructional library media specialist in teaching information use skills. Instead of always lecturing and saturating students with "how-to" methods and reference sources, actively involve them in learning. Let them raise problems and suggest solutions. Use cooperative learning teams whenever possible so peers teach, learn from, and motivate each other. Supplement the library resources with access to human expertise found in other teachers, parents, and community contacts. Interviews are conducted to gather more current information or to confirm facts found in often out of date print resources. To build activities within the limited confines of the school library is as undesirable as allowing a textbook to determine the parameters for learning.

In order to make inquiry units that are based on critical examination of information effective, Callison argued in his 1995 essay, that students must have access to an extensive amount of materials. This means that a variety of resources should be available in terms of format, date, reading level, and points of view. There is nothing new in the idea that school library media center collections provide a variety of materials. What must be different in order to create an environment for critical examination of information is the depth of the school's library collection and the extent to which students truly have access to as many information sources representing a wide spectrum of views. Three actions must be taken.

First, school library media collection development needs to take a sharp turn toward support of a few selected units. Build depth, not breath. For these units, acquisition of items and agreements for electronic access should be extensive. Use of fiction, historical and scientific, may all be necessary for some units in order to provide the student with a greater appreciation of the cultural context for the events being examined.

In some cases, collections of unique local resources may need to be gathered, boxed in special storage, added to over several years, and then controlled through a reserve system so that these difficult-to-obtain materials will be available to students when it comes time for the specific unit. Targeting a substantial portion of base collection funding, perhaps 25% or more, and seeking additional special funds will allow the resource pool to become rich with the various materials needed. Planning and mapping, as developed by David Loertscher, creates more chances that the school media specialist will say "yes" to inquiry units. Depth of ownership and access is constructed so inquiry can have the resource base for the exploration component to become operational.

Second, the collection compiled in support

of critical information units should not be sanitized and should come, as much as possible, in its "real world" packaging. For secondary school students this means that tabloids and other "supermarket checkout line materials" take a place beside the respected news magazines and newspapers usually recommended to students. It means that the extremes on both sides of an issue are easily available. Original documents are provided, not just some safe summary of opposing views. The spectrum of arguments should be full with right to left opinions. Access to factual (and perhaps not so factual) data from government, private, and even personal records is pursued. Contacts with local public, academic and historical libraries become part of the resource collection process.

Third, the long march to move materials to a centralized location called the school library media center will need to take an about-face. The school library becomes a clearinghouse, a dissemination center, and an often-used learning laboratory. It is a major access point for information, but widely disseminates to the classroom and to the student's home. It is a center for discussions, documenting the discussions, and providing access electronically to these discussions for students and teachers.

Classrooms will need to house and teachers will need to share information materials as never before. In some cases, special collections of materials, realia, and artifacts for a given unit will need to be boxed and moved from one building to another as the inquiry unit is implemented at several schools over the academic semester. Some of these artifacts may be captured as digital library collections, to be accessed by anyone in the learning community.

District level acquisition services may find they serve a central role in development of these special traveling and digital collections to support projects at different buildings and different grade levels. Centralized distribution for telecommunication access to the distance learning program, digital archives, and communication with experts beyond the local community will become a collection of services managed by school library media professionals.

1998 Library Power and

Information Literacy Standards for Student Learning

The power of collaborative teaching, infusion of new dollars to build collections to give depth to the curriculum, and the value of professional development of all educators in the meaning of information literacy was operational across several school districts in the DeWitt Wallace Reader's Digest Library Power Project. In cooperation with the American Asociation of School Librarians (AASL), this project involved dozens of school districts from 1988 to 1994. Documented by Doug Zweizig and Dianne Hopkins, both of Wisconsin University, the action research and evaluation evidence for the AASL national guidelines.

Nine information literacy standards were identified through a national review process. The AASL standards committee, lead by chief author Delia Neuman, associate professor of library and information science at the University of Maryland, agreed on the following list as the key skills for students k-12:

Information Literacy
- accesses information efficiently and effectively
- evaluates information critically and competently
- uses information accurately and creatively

Independent Learning
- pursues information related to personal interests
- appreciates literature and other creative expressions of information
- strives for excellence in information seeking and knowledge generation

Social Responsibility
- recognizes the importance of information to a democratic society
- practices ethical behavior in regard to information and information technology
- participates effectively in groups to pursue and generate information

While these nine statements provide concrete definitions of information literacy skills, depth has been given to these standards for student learning through:

- Indicators of student performance and levels of proficiency for each indicator
- Standards in action to illustrate potential learning situations which require practice in information literacy skills
- Examples of content-area standards to show a relationship across all academic disciplines with information literacy

An example of the depth behind each standard is illustrated below from Standard 2: The student who is information literate evaluates information critically and competently.

Indicator 1. Determines accuracy, relevance, and comprehensiveness.

Levels of Proficiency:
Basic — Defines or gives examples of the terms "accuracy," "relevance," and "comprehensiveness."
Proficient — "Compares and contrasts sources related to a topic to determine which are more accurate, relevant, and comprehensive.
Exemplary — Judges the accuracy, relevance, and completeness of sources of information in relation to a range of topics and information problems.

Standard in Action:
Students realize they will find conflicting facts in different sources, and they determine the accuracy and relevance of information before taking notes. They determine the adequacy of information gathered according to the complexity of the topic, the research questions, and the product that is expected.

Example of Content-Area Standard:
Civics. Knows how to use criteria such as logical validity, factual accuracy, emotional appeal, distorted evidence, and appeals to bias or prejudice in order to evaluate various forms of historical and contemporary political communication. (e.g., Lincoln's "House Divided," Sojourner Truth's "Ain't I a Woman?," Chief Joseph's "I Shall Fight No More Forever," Martin Luther King Jr.'s "I Have a Dream," as well as examples of campaign advertising and political cartoons.)

From just this one example it is clear that analysis and synthesis skills need to build from early learning environments up through school. Activities which place the student in information evaluation, problem-solving and decision-making situations are necessary across all areas of the curriculum so students understand information literacy and inquiry as process skills relevant to all learning. The complexities of many of these skills also indicates that there will be various levels of success and failure, and the role of the instructional media specialist and other teachers as information intermediaries is much greater than simply helping with access and location. Interpretation must be at the center of the learning objectives so teachers and students experience high level challenges through analysis, synthesis, and evaluation.

2002 Reviews of the Research Emerging Library Media Scholars, and a White House Conference

Based on their work with hundreds of practicing school Librarians and fellow researchers, David Loertscher and Blanche Woolls of San Jose State University published their revised review on information Literacy. A nearly comprehensive guide to models and studies, this collection is likely to be expanded even more through future Treasure Mountain Research Conferences.

In 2002, Callison published a review of the research pertaining to school library media programs in the Encyclopedia of Library and Information Science. His review concentrated on the studies from 1970 to 1999. Studies consistently gave emphasis to the need for strong instructional leadership on the part of new school library media specialists and how this has often been conflicted by lack of acceptance of this role by those in school librarian positions.

There was evidence, however, that during the last decade of the Twentieth Century this attitude was changing and more school library media specialists were seeking an instructional leadership role. This role, along with the relationship between school library media programs and student academic achievement were topics for a research retreat held at Excelsior Springs, Missouri in May 2002. At that retreat, a foundation was established for an Academy of Emerging Library Media Scholars. This Academy will serve to support new researchers who are concerned with the diverse learning issues pertaining to children and young adults and information use behaviors as well as advocating strong instructional roles for school library media specialists.

The First Lady of the United States, and former school librarian, Laura Bush hosted a White House Conference on School Libraries on June 4, 2002. Keith Curry Lance, Director of Library Research Services in Colorado and Gary Hartzell, Professor of School Administration at the University of Nebraska, Omaha were among the speakers. Comments from each are given below to illustrate the central message of the conference for the key school administrators who attended.

Lance reported:

Looking across the six studies we have completed most recently, three major sets of findings figure prominently.
- the level of development of the school library,
- the extent to which school librarians engage in leadership and collaboration activities that foster information literacy, and
- the extent to 3which instructional technology is utilized to extend the reach of the library program beyond the walls of the school library.

When school libraries have higher levels of professional and total staffing, larger collections of print and electronic resources, and more funding, students tend to earn higher scores on state reading tests.

In the aftermath of the original Colorado study, one of the more intriguing findings to many people was the one concerning the importance of the school librarians playing a strong instructional role. To the disappointment of many practitioners, the earlier report did not define what that means, so they were uncertain how to act differently on the job. In our recent studies, we have succeeded in elaborating just what that instructional role involves.

In order to play an instructional role successfully, school librarians must exercise leadership to create some sort of working environment they need to help students and teachers succeed. Specific activities which define such leadership include:
- meeting frequently with the principal,
- attending and participating in faculty meetings,
- serving on standards and curriculum committees, and
- meeting with library colleagues at building, district and higher (state, national) levels.

When school librarians demonstrate this kind of leadership in their daily activities, they can create an environment conducive to collaboration between themselves and classroom teachers. That, in turn, enables them to work with classroom teachers to instill a love of reading and information literacy skills in their students.

Collaboration activities in which school librarians should participate, according to our research, include:
- identifying useful materials and information for teachers,
- planning instruction cooperatively with teachers,
- providing in-service training to teachers, and
- teaching students both with classroom teachers and independently.

Hartzell reported:

Library programs that make a difference not only have a certified librarian in place, and adequate support staff, and up-to-date and large collections • all monetary investments •

they also have schedules that allow the librarian time to collaborate with other staff members. The librarian serves on curriculum committees, provides measures for staff development, and participates in a wide variety of school operations. None of this happens if the principal doesn't want it to. The research evidence also is clear that teachers collaborate more with other teachers and with the librarian when the principal openly encourages it and makes schedules that facilitate it. It works even better when assessments of collaborative activities become part of teacher evaluation. You might have the very best librarian you could every get on your staff, but being ready, willing, and able represents only three-quarters of what it takes to make significant contributions. The fourth part is opportunity, and opportunity rests in the principal's hands. The principal is an absolutely essential element in maximizing the return on library investment.

For Further Reading

American Association of School Librarians. Information Literacy: A Position Paper on Information Problem Solving. 1994. Bibliography revised in 1999. Scenarios added by Paula Montgomery. www.ala.org/aasl/positions/ps_infolit.html

American Association of School Librarians and the Association for Educational Communications and Technology. Information Literacy Standards for Student Learning. Chicago: ALA, 1998.

Beyer, Barry K. "Critical Thinking: What Is It?" Social Education. 49:4. April 1985. 270-276.

Bowie, Melvin M. "The Library Media Program and the Social Studies, Mathematics, and Science Curricula: Intervention Strategies for the Library Media Specialist." In The Research of School Library Media Centers, edited by B. Woolls. Castle Rock, CO: Hi Willow, 1990. 21-48.

Breivik, Patricia Senn and E. Gordon Gee. Information Literacy. New York: Macmillan, 1989.

Callison, Daniel. "Expanding the Evaluation Role in the Critical-Thinking Curriculum." In Information for a New Age: Redefining the Librarian. Englewood, CO: Libraries Unlimited, 1995. 153-169.

Callison, Daniel. "School Library Media Programs and Free Inquiry." School Library Journal. February 1986. 20-24. Also in School Library Journal's Best, edited by Lillian N. Gerhardt and compiled by Marilyn L. Miller, Neal Schuman Publishers, 1997.

Callison, Daniel. "The Twentieth-Century School Library Media Research Record." Encyclopedia of Library and Information Science. Vol. 71. 2002. 339-368.

Colorado Department of Education and the Colorado State Library. "Information Literacy Guidelines: Assessment for Information Literacy and Assessment of School Library Media Programs." Indiana Media Journal. 18:4. Summer 1996. 39-71.

Craver, Kathleen W. "Critical Thinking: Implications for Library Research." In The Research of School Library Media Centers, edited by B. Woolls. Castle Rock, CO: Hi Willow, 1990. 121-134.

Donham, Jean, Kay Bishop, Carol Collier Kuhlthau, and Dianne Oberg. Inquiry-Based Learning: Lessons from Library Power. Worthington, OH: Linworth Publishing, 2001.

Doyle, C. S. Information Literacy in an Information Society: A Concept for the Information Age. Syracuse, NY: ERIC Clearinghouse on Information and Technology, 1994.

Eisenberg, Michael. "Curriculum Mapping and Implementation of an Elementary School Library Media Skills Curriculum." School Library Media Quarterly. Fall 1984. 411-418.

Kuhlthau, carol Collier. "An Emerging Theory of Library Instruction". <u>School Library Media Quarterly</u>. 16:1. Fall 1987 23-8

Liesener, James W. "Learning at Risk: School Library Media Program in an Information World." In <u>Libraries and the Learning Society</u>. Chicago: ALA, 1984. 69-75.

Loertscher, David V. "Collection Mapping: An Evaluation Strategy for Collection Development." <u>Drexel Library Quarterly</u>. 21:2. Spring 1985. 9-21.

Loertscher, David V. and Blanche Woolls. <u>Information Literacy: review of the Research</u>. 2nd Edition. HiWillow Research and Publishing, 2002.

Mancall, Jacqueline C. "(Un)changing Factors in the Searching Environment: Collections, Collectors, and Users". <u>School Library Media Quarterly</u>. Winter 1991. 84-89.

Mancall, Jacqueline C., Shirley L. Aaron, and Sue A. Walker. "Educating Students to Think: The Role of the School Library Media Program." <u>School Library Media Quarterly</u>. 15:1. Fall 1986. http://www.ala.org/aasl/SLMR/slmr_resources/ select_mancall.html

National Forum on Information Literacy. Patricia Senn Breivik, Chair. http://www.infolit.org

Newmann, F. M., W. G. Secada, and G. G. Wehlage. <u>A Guide to Authentic Instruction and Assessment: Vision, Standards and Scoring</u>. Madison, WI: Wisconsin Center for Education Research, 1995.

Resnick, Lauren B., Leopold E. Klopfer and Laura Resnick eds. <u>Toward the Thinking Curriculum: Current Cognitive Research</u>. Washington, D. C.: Association for Supervision and Curriculum Development, 1989.

Rossoff, Martin. <u>The Library in High School Teaching</u>. New York: H. W. Wilson, 1955.

Rossoff, Martin. <u>The School Library and Educational Change</u>. Littleton, CO: Libraries Unlimited, 1971.

Sheingold, Karen. "Keeping Children's Knowledge Alive through Inquiry." <u>School Library Media Quarterly</u>. Winter 1987. 80-85.

Stripling, Barbara. "Rethinking the School Library: A Practitioner's Perspective." <u>School Library Media Quarterly</u>. Spring 1989. 136-139.

Thompson, Helen M. and Susan A. Henley. <u>Fostering Information Literacy: Connecting National Standards, Goals 2000, and the SCANS Report</u>. Littleton, CO: Libraries Unlimited, 2000.

Tyner, Kathleen R. <u>Literacy in a Digital World: Teaching and learning in the age of information</u>. Mahwah, NJ: Erlbaum Associates. 1998.

Walker, H. Thomas and Paula K. Montgomery. <u>Teaching Media Skills: An Instructional Program for Elementary and Middle School Students</u>. Littleton, CO: Libraries Unlimited, 1976.

White House Conference on School Libraries. The Institute of Museum and Library Services. http://www.imls.gov/pubs/white-house0602/whitehouse.htm Viewed July 17, 2002.

Zweizig, Douglas L. and Dianne McAfee Hopkins. <u>Lessons from Library Power: Enriching Teaching and Learning</u>. Englewood, CO: Libraries Unlimited and Teacher Ideas Press, 1999.

Chapter 5

Information Literacy and Inquiry Skills:
Scope and Sequence and Best Practices across the Curriculum

Scope and sequence are instructional terms that carry both positive and negative connotations. Positive in that such written outlines provide an overview or full picture of the skills , activities, and potential levels of student performance across all grade levels. Such a complete plan allows educators from elementary and secondary programs to identify areas in which they may cooperate and reduce duplication of instructional activities. Educators also can gain some reasonable entry skill expectations so they can build activities based on the assumption that most of the students coming into certain later grade levels have been introduced to or have mastered key skills on which to build new experiences. As new teachers join the educational environment, scope and sequence plans can serve to provide an efficient map for novice instructors to identify where their lessons fit in the school district's plan.

If communication is maintained through professional development forums, curriculum can be coordinated. If not, scope and sequence plans become time-consuming and frustrating efforts for a few ambitions educators and the results are simply long lists of skills on paper that are filled for no practical use.

From a negative pedology, sequencing can result in lock-step instruction determined on the needs of the many and ignoring the learning problems of or advanced opportunities for the few. Each student is manufactured to come out the same , with the same training, at the same time. While sequential learning plans can serve as a guide to the important steps necessary to lead to more complex skills, effective application of sequenced sets requires the wise observation and evaluation of the master teacher. The objective should not be to program learners, but to match skills to abilities and experience levels so the learner gains understanding as soon as possible. Thus, many of the skill sets presented here can easily overlap from one grade level to another, with remediation necessary for some learners and opportunities for quick advancement necessary for others.

A combination of skills from library orientation, information literacy, technology use, and media literacy can be combined to for a scope and sequence of skills for the information inquiry process.

Library Skills

Carol Kuhlthau, as she has in many other areas of study and application of information inquiry, documented her early thoughts and experiences with teaching the use of the library and its resources. Kuhlthau's first experiences involved elementary school children and proceeded her classic observations of high school student search behavior. Her application of educational theory provides a framework for scope and sequence of information and technology skills that are foundational to inquiry.

She constructed her sequential library skills program on Piaget's stages of cognitive development:

> Sensory Motor — Birth to Age 2
>   Learns through senses and movement.
> Pre-operational — Ages 2-7
>   Can use symbols to represent reality, such as language.
>   Has an egocentric point of view.
> Concrete Operational — Ages 7-11
>   Can perform mental operations on a concrete level.
>   Can categorize and use classification.
>   Is not capable of abstract thinking.
> Formal Operational — Ages 12-16
>   Can use abstract thought.
>   Can generalize.
>   Can form a hypothesis.

A sequential structure matched to the normal skill development of the learner is assumed to increase the chances the student will build his or her learning at the time of being able to understanding meaning and application. Thus skill mastery builds from one level to the next and exercises are designed to introduce skills based on previously demonstrated mastery.

Kuhlthau is quick to emphasize library and information skills are not separate school subjects. Like reading and writing, they are process skills — skills used to reach other learning goals. We read to derive meaning. We write to convey thoughts. We use library skills, according to Kuhlthau when she published many of her activities in 1981, to locate and interpret materials that expand our understanding and better enable us to make decisions and choices. When process skills are taught in isolation, learning problems, such as lack of motivation, retention, and transference, often result.

Kuhlthau built the elementary scope and sequence experiences toward skills involving inference. While location of information was a common part of her activities, the objectives involved information interpretation, appreciation, and application. These early exercises clearly were the basis for her later work with adults and young adults attempting to seek meaning and a deeper understanding of the library research process.

Levels of Learning

Few educators have made it through methods courses and graduate studies without a heavy dose of "Bloom's Taxonomy for Educational Objectives." Written by a committee of distinguished educators of the mid-Twentieth Century, the classification of cognitive skills has had a strong influence on cognitive skill performance and measurement. These skill levels, building from knowledge, comprehension, application, analysis, synthesis, and evaluation, served as the framework for a scope and sequence information skills curriculum guide issued by the Washington Library Media Association in 1987.

The Washington sequence has been republished dozens of times over the past decade and holds a reasonable outline for identification of when to introduce certain skills. The guide also gives reasonable indication of when key skills are likely to be mastered because of student ability levels, and reminds us that all skills must continue to be reinforced in association with subject content and student need throughout the academic experience.

Constructed from a pre-search set of skills for formulating questions as well as understanding how to search for resources, the Washington guide was one of the early scope and sequence plans to give emphasis to interpretation skills. These higher level skills include:
- Interpret, Infer, Analyze, and Paraphrase
  - identify main ideas, opinions and supporting facts
  - summarize important facts and details
  - relate to the central question
  - interpret graphic sources
  - derive valid inferences from information
- Organize Information for Applications
  - compare, summarize and generalize
  - select appropriate organizational style

(including chronological, argumenta-
tive, rank order of importance, prob-
lem-solution, or topical)
- determine most effective method of
presentation
- plan, practice, revise
- Apply Information for Intended Audience
  - clear, well-supported presentation, relevant to the audience
  - draw conclusions based on obtained
information
  - evaluate the project and search process

Technology Skills

In the Information Age, technology use
skills have become essential for efficient means
of search and retrieval. Technology tools can
also play an important role in effective analysis,
synthesis, and presentation of information.
The International Society for Technology in
Education (ISTE) has issued national educational technology standards for students. Tied
to subject content areas, constructed on new
learning environments which require application of inquiry skills, these student behaviors
are important to link to the library information
skills scope and sequence.

Media Literacy Skills

Media literacy skills also have a place within the mix of library skills, information skills,
and technology skills to make information
inquiry complete. Several sources, especially
those authored by David Considine and by
Kathleen Tyner in recent years provide ideas
for both these skills and for student performance levels in a k-12 scope and sequence.

Scope and Sequence for Information Inquiry

Elementary School
Before completion of elementary school,
the average student should be able to perform
the following skills through the information
inquiry process.
1. Evaluation and Selection Techniques
   a. can select books and other resources
   of personal interest
   b. understands there are various forms
of literature
   c. shows discrimination in selecting
books
2. Search and Reporting Techniques
   a. can look up information in a general
encyclopedia, print or nonprint
   b. can find nonfiction books on a specific topic
   c. is acquainted with bibliographies in
books
   d. can focus on a specific question for
which one may search for information to address the question
   e. can brainstorm ideas and information
about the central question by recalling previous personal experiences
   f. can summarize the main ideas regarding the central question
   g. can recognize the use of the library
media center resources, including the
consulting role of the library media
specialist
   h. can recognize that library materials
are indexed, and that this index
may be in a variety of forms (card,
computer)
3. Listening and Viewing
   a. is able to attend to the sights and
sounds of storytelling
   b. can participate in discussion following a story
   c. can recall, summarize, and paraphrase what is listened to and viewed
4. Literature Appreciation
   a. can draw the point of the story into
own experience
   b. is familiar with many different types
of literature
5. Technology Application Skills
   a. uses input devices (e.g. voice activation, mouse, keyboard, remote control) and output devices (e.g. monitor
and printer) to successfully operate
computers, VCRs, audiotapes, tele-
phones, and other technologies
   b. uses developmentally appropriate
multimedia resources (e.g. interactive
books, educational software, and ele-

mentary multimedia encyclopedias) to support learning

   c. works cooperatively and collaboratively with peers, family members, and others when using technology in theclassroom or at home

   d. practices responsible use of technology systems and software

   e. creates developmentally appropriate multimedia products with support from teachers, family members, and student partners

   f. uses technology resources (e.g. puzzles, logical thinking programs, writing tools, digital cameras, and drawing tools) for problem solving, communication, and illustration of thoughts, ideas, and stories

   g. gathers information and communicate with others using telecommunications, with support from teachers, family members, or student partners

6. **Media Literacy**

   a. identifies media forms; e.g. news, drama, cartoon, advertising, entertainment

   b. can define terms and techniques involved in media production such as edit, pan, close-up

   c. can discuss how stories occur in the media and compares these stories to types of stories he/she already knows

   d. identifies and describes different stereotypes depicted in the media

   e. identifies the difference between an event and the representation of that event in the media

   f. discusses the ways in which media can affect the individual and on their local environment

   g. views media deliberately and critically

   h. selects a medium and develops a simple theme for a story, and develops a story line

Middle School

Before entering high school, the average student should be able to perform the following skills through the information inquiry process:

1. **Evaluation and Selection Techniques**

   a. can use various parts of a book and other resources (website, video) to determine scope, format, timeliness, and document the information found

   b. is developing discrimination in selecting books and periodicals to read, films and television to view

   c. knows the different types of biographical materials and can locate information in each

   d. can distinguish the unique characteristics of various reference sources

   e. understands the difference between fiction and nonfiction

   f. is familiar with various magazines, newspapers and other serials and understands they are a source of recent information

   g. is familiar with various online databases and websites and is aware of selection criteria for acceptable electronic documents

   h. uses information from the general resource materials to identify major/significant sources of information regarding the central question

   i. recalls words, terms, methods. events, facts, concepts by using broad, general information resources

   j. understands the purpose and apply selection techniques for compiling bits and pieces of information for later use; identifies key words and phrases and locates major heading, skims and scans for major ideas

   k. locates and selects the most useful sources from among those available

   l. evaluates the currency of information; can identify copyright date and understands the significance between dated and current information

   m. distinguishes among fact, nonfact, opinion, and propaganda

2. **Search and Reporting Techniques**

   a. understands different classification systems, basic search techniques, and search engines

   b. can locate materials to discover what others have found out about a topic

c. can use ideas gained through different materials

d. can carry basic guided research through to a conclusion

e. can present information in a written report, illustration, or oral presentation

f. can make a bibliography of sources from various formats and understands the function of footnotes

g. can use the nonfiction collection as a source of information

h. understands how to extract information from television and film sources

i. understands how to extact information from human resources

j. understands the difference between primary and secondary resources

k. uses a variety of questioning skills (yes/no, open-ended, follow-up and probing)

l. brainstorms ideas and information about the central question by recalling previous personal learning experiences

m. understands that information can be used as evidence to support or reject a position

3. Listening and Viewing
   a. interprets what is heard and seen
   b. can recall, summarize, paraphrase and extend what is listened to and viewed

4. Literature Appreciation
   a. can interpret meaning from many forms of literature
   b. understands use of resources to determine quality literature

5. Technology Application
   a. applies strategies for identifying and solving routine hardware and software problems that occur during everyday use
   b. demonstrates knowledge of current changes in information technologies and the effect those changes have on common workplace environments and local society
   c. exhibits legal and ethical behaviors when using information and technol-

ogy, and discuss consequences of misuse

d. uses content-specific tools, software and simulations, including web-based tools, to support learning and basic information research

e. designs, develops, and presents products including web-based pages and short video programs, based on using technology resources that allow for demonstration of curriculum-related concepts to audiences in school and beyond

f. collaborates with peers, experts, and others using telecommunications and collaborative software to investigate curriculum-related problems, issues, and general information

g. evaluates the accuracy, relevance, appropriateness, authoritativeness, comprehensiveness, and bias of electronic and print information sources pertaining to real-world problems and issues

6. Media Literacy
   a. identifies some major genres or categories, e.g. soap opera, sitcom, action adventure
   b. identifies and uses media techniques such as camera angles, arrangement of people, different sound levels and mixing, shot transitions such as fade, dissolve, cut
   c. recognizes devices for controlling narrative, such as voice over
   d. follows multiple/parallel plots within a narrative
   e. asks questions about the intended message and states opinions about the content concerning accuracy, relevance, bias
   f. compares their own experiences with those attributed to their age group in the media
   g. identifies some stereotypes in media depictions of various children in their age group and explains how they imply judgments of various social, racial, and cultural groups
   h. identifies narrative patterns and how

A SCOPE AND SEQUENCE SKILLS SET FOR INFORMATION INQUIRY

they are used in the presentation of fictional and nonfictional material in the media

    i. considers how the same story can be adapted for different audiences and through the use of different media

    j. identifies and discusses differences between an event and the representation of the event in media

    k. produces own media to express opinion or view point, promote an item or activity, or to entertain

High School

Before graduation from high school, the average student should be able to perform the following skills through the information inquiry process:

1. Evaluation and Selection Techniques
   a. understands and is familiar with documents (journals, newspapers, websites) which have different purpose, scope, perspective, bias
   b. is tolerant to review of information which does not immediately fit personal perspective and seeks evidence from all perspectives before drawing a conclusion
   c. can discriminate between important and less important questions and resources
   d. explores information widely, and brings focus to the central problem based on background readings, personal experiences and interests, and identified need for further research
   e. can evaluate the process and project of self, peers, and experts

2. Research and Reporting Techniques
   a. can conduct advanced and refined key word searches in online catalogues and multiple databases
   b. can conduct extensive searches through various search engines to compare and contrast electronic documents
   c. can develop and define the terms in a question regarding a problem, or otherwise limit a topic
   d. can carry basic research through independently and to a conclusion
   e. can present information using a multiple number of formats and styles which best fit the message and the audience
   f. formulates a working hypothesis and supports the central question or thesis statement with relevant evidence and original discussion and conclusion
   g. knows the value of a literature review to set the context for the research project and can summarize the main ideas regarding the central question
   h. understands advantages and disadvantages, and application of various methods to gather original data including survey, interview, experiment, and case study
   i. understands a variety of modes to present findings and adjusts techniques and media to meet the best communication for a given audience or need

3. Listening and Viewing
   a. can derive key information for evidence from interviews and critical examination of events and perspectives as depicted in educational and popular media
   b. interprets graphic sources for information from all media formats including maps, charts, and other visuals or illustrations
   c. understands the potential for products to inform, persuade, and entertain

4. Literature Appreciation
   a. values the information and literature products of the human record and gives credit to thoseitems which have informed the inquiry process and product
   b. derives valid inferences from information and literature resources and understands potential for adding to and/or using this these conclusions to solve problems and possibly add to the human record

5. Technology Application
   a. identifies capabilities and limitations

of contemporary and emerging technology resources and assesses the potential of these systems and services to address personal, lifelong learning, academic and common workplace needs

b. analyzes advantages and disadvantages of widespread use and reliance on technology in the workplace and in society

c. demonstrates and advocates legal and ethical behaviors among peers, family, and community regarding the use of technology and information

d. uses technology tools and resources for managing and communicating personal and likely professional information

e. selects and applies technology tools for research, information analysis, problem solving, and decision making for personal, academic, and likely workplace needs

f. investigates and applies expert systems, intelligent agents, and simulations in real-world situations

g. collaborates with peers, experts, and others to contribute to a content-related knowledge base by using technology to compile, synthesize, produce, and disseminate information, ideas, models, conclusions and perceptions, and other creative works

6. Media Literacy

a. is widely knowledgeable in the terms which define the techniques and technologies of mass media

b. recognizes that all forms of media contain messages

c. has skills to decode and analyze media messages

d. gains an informed understanding of media through critical analysis

e. critically examines and interprets media messages in an historical, social, and cultural context; understands the relationship among audiences, media messages, and the world

f. is able to access and articulate personal media use and speculate on the media use of others

g. has knowledge of various media to solve problems, communicate, and produce self-selected and self-initiated projects as well as those assigned

The College Student

Over the past three decades, the Association of College and Research Libraries (ACRL) has issued several outlines for standards of student performance and bibliographic instruction. In 2001, ACRL revised several statements and issued a new outline for the information literate student in higher education as well as collaborative roles between the academic librarian and college professor in assuring the practice of these skills will be integrated with disciplines of study. Although some of the skills overlap with previous statements found in scope and sequence for the educational experience prior to college, other items take information literacy to a higher level. At the college level, inquiry becomes more discipline-focused. ACRL standards often refer to the need for the college student to begin to grasp the discourse and primary investigation methods of specific disciplines and to gain an understanding of how they differ.

A selected sample of the ACRL competancy standards for higher education illustrates these additional expectations.

Competency Standard One, Performance Indicator 2: The Information literate student identifies a variety of types and formats of potential sources of information.

1.2.a. Knows how information is formally and informally produced, organized, and disseminated.

• describes the publication cycle appropriate to the discipline of a research topic

• defines the "invisible college" (e.g., personal contacts, listservs specific to a discipline or subject) and describes its value

1.2.b. Recognizes that knowledge can be organized into disciplines that influence the way information is accessed.

• names the three major disciplines of

A SCOPE AND SEQUENCE SKILLS SET FOR INFORMATION INQUIRY

knowledge (humanities, social sciences, sciences) and some subject fields that comprise each discipline.

- finds sources that provide relevant subject field- and discipline-related terminology
- uses relevant subject- and discipline-related terminology in the information research process
- describes how the publication cycle in a particular discipline or subject field affects the researcher's access to information

1.2.d. Identifies the purpose and audience of potential resources (e.g. popular vs. scholarly, current vs. historical)

1.2.e. Differentiates between primary and secondary sources, recognizing how their use and importance vary with each discipline.

Competency Standard One, Performance Indicator 3: ...considers the costs and benefits of acquiring the needed information.

1.3.a. Determines the availability of needed information and makes decisions on broadening the information seeking process beyond local resources (e.g. interlibrary loan; using resources at other locations; obtaining images, videos, text, or sound

Competency Standard One, Performance Indicator 4:...reevaluates the nature and extent of the information need.

1.4.a. Reviews the initial information need to clarify, revise, or refine the question

1.4.b. Describes criteria used to make information decision and choices

- demonstrates how the intended audience influences information choices
- demonstrates how the desired end product influences choices

Competency Standard Two, Performance Indicator 1: ...selects the most appropriate investigative methods or information retrieval systems for accessing the needed information.

2.1.c. Investigates scope, content, and organization of information retrieval systems

2.2.d. Constructs a search strategy using appropriate commands for the information retrieval system selected (e.g. Boolean operators, truncation, and proximity for search engines, internal organizers such as indexes for books)

2.2.e. Implements the search strategy in various information retrieval systems using different user interfaces and search engines, with different command languages, protocols, and search parameters

2.2.f. Implements the search using investigative protocols appropriate to the discipline.

- locates major print bibliographic and reference sources appropriate to the discipline of a research topic

Competency Standard Two, Performance Indicator 4: ...refines the search strategy if necessary.

2.4.a. Assesses the quantity, quality, and relevance of the search results to determine whether alternative information retrieval systems or investigative methods should be utilized

- determines if the quantity of citations retrieved is adequate, too extensive, or insufficient for the information need
- evaluates the quality of the information retrieved using criteria such as authorship, point of view/bias, date written, citations, etc.
- assesses the relevance of information found by examining elements of the citation such as title, abstract, subject headings, source, and date of publication
- determines the relevance of an item to the information need in terms of its depth of coverage, language, and time frame

Competency Standard Three: Performance Indicator 2: ...articulates and applies initial criteria for evaluating both the information and its sources.

3.2.a. Examines and compares information from various sources in order to evaluate reliability, validity, accuracy, authority, timeliness, and point of view or bias

- locates and examines critical reviews of information sources using available resources and technologies
- investigates an author's qualifications and reputation through reviews or biographical sources
- investigates validity and accuracy by consulting sources identified through bibliographic references
- investigates qualifications and reputation of the publisher or issuing agency by consulting other information resources

3.3.c. Recognizes prejudice, deception, or manipulation

- demonstrates an understanding that information in any format reflects an author's, sponsor's, and/or publisher's point of view
- demonstrates an understanding that some information and information sources may present a one-sided view and may express opinions rather than facts
- demonstrates an understanding that some information and sources may be designed to trigger emotions, conjure stereotypes, or promote support for a particular viewpoint or group

Competency Standard Three, Performance Indicator 4:...compares new knowledge with prior knowledge to determine the value added, contradictions, or other unique characteristics of the information.

3.4.e. Determines probable accuracy by questioning the sources of the data, the limitations of the information gathering tools or strategies, and reasonableness of the conclusions

3.4.g. Selects information that provides evidence for the topic

College Level Critical Thinking Skills

In 1995, the final report on an assessment of communication and critical thinking skills necessary for the successful college student was released by the U. S. Department of Education's Office of Educational Research and Improvement. Ratings of skills were compared among groups of college educators, policymakers and employers. Although there were some differences commonly acceptable sets of these skills were identified as essential. They reflect many of the previously describe skills of the information literate college student.

These skill sets also place analysis, synthesis, and evaluation on a higher level. The student becomes a critical thinker based not so much on information location, but abilities in analysis of arguments, meaningful communication, and cultivation of an inquiring mind. Accomplished skills in critical thinking take information literacy and inquiry to the higher levels toward instruction should strive. We many not reach these levels in all information inquiry lessons nor at each grade, but these should be the standards toward which we construct any scope and sequence curriculum in the Information Age.

Critical Thinking in Communication and Inquiry Interpretation:

- categorize information
- classify data and make comparisons
- translate data from one medium to another
- clarify meaning of data
- recognize confusing, vague language
- ask relevant or penetrating questions
- identify and seek additional resources
- develop analogies or other forms of comparisons
- provide examples to explain ideas

Analysis:

- identify the explicit and implicit features of a communication
- examine ideas and purposes by assessing the constraints on the practical applications, as well as interests, attitudes, or views contained in those ideas

- identify stated, implied or undeclared purposes of a communication
- identify the main conclusion of an argument
- determine whether a communication expresses a reason(s) in support of or in opposition to some conclusion or point of view
- assess the credibility of a communication and evaluate the strengths of claims and arguments
- determine if arguments rest on false, biased, or doubtful assumptions
- assess the importance of an argument and determine if it merits attention
- evaluate an argument in terms of reasonability and practicality
- assess statistical information
- determine how new data may lead to further confirmation or questioning of a conclusion
- determine if conclusions are derived from sufficiently large and representative samples

Evaluation:
- assess bias, narrowness, and contradictions
- judge consistency of supporting reasons and evidence

Inference:
- collect and question evidence
- formulate a plan for locating information
- determine if sufficient evidence is present to form a conclusion
- judge what background information is most useful
- seek evidence to confirm or disconfirm alternatives
- seek opinions of others
- assess the risks and benefits of each option
- develop new alternatives when appropriate

Present Arguments:
- clear communication and justification of the results of one's reasoning
- present the crucial point of an issue
- evaluate key assumptions
- formulate accurately alternative

positions
- illustrate central concepts with examples that apply to real situations

Reflection:
- monitor one's comprehension
- correct one's process of thinking
- make revisions in one's own arguments, when self-examination reveals inadequacies
- apply the skills of analysis to one's own arguments

Dispositions or Behaviors [signs of the mature critical thinker and inquirer]:
- curious
- organized
- fair-minded
- open-minded
- flexible
- creative
- perseveres
- applies insight from other cultures
- willingly self-corrects
- learns from errors

In the practice and application of these critical thinking skills, college students should have the opportunity to find ways to collaborate with others to reach consensus, share testing of alternative approaches, and compare and contrast results in attempting to address problems and issues.

Information Inquiry Across Disciplines

Over the past few years most new standards for various areas of the curriculum in schools k-12 have included statements that pertain directly to the information literacy and inquiry. Examples from hundreds of such statements include:

Art: knows how visual, aural, oral, and kinetic elements are used in the various art forms.

Dance: improvises, creates, and performs dances based on personal ideas and concepts from other sources

Music: knows and appreciates songs representing genres and styles from diverse cultures

Theatre: assumes roles that exhibit concentration and contribute to the action of dramatizations based on personal experience and heritage, imagination, literature, and history

Visual Arts: use visual structures and functions of art to communicate ideas

Math: use models, known facts, properties, and relationships to explain thinking and justify answers or solutions

Science: use data to construct a reasonable explanation; communicate investigations and explanations

History: draw conclusions about roles in life from data gathered through photos, documents, primary sources

Civics: debate the issues pertaining to a proposed piece of legislation or plan to change the status quo

One can probably find the closest correlation to information inquiry skills to those required in the methods for scientific investigation: framing the question, testing the hypothesis, controlling experiments to isolate factors, comparison of findings to previous studies, providing the findings to others so conclusions can be validated, perhaps generalized, but always open for further discussion and often contested.

Examples from Language Arts

The modern language arts curriculum gives a very rich scope and sequence representation. A cadre of accomplished school media specialists in Indiana constructed a correlation between their state's new language arts standards and those standards issued by the American Association of School Librarians for student learning. Selected student standards from the language arts illustrate the grade-level scope and sequence for these skills and how information inquiry is associated with this subject content area:

Kindergarten
- connect the information and events in texts to life experience
- distinguish fantasy from reality
- identify favorite books and stories

- share information and ideas, speaking in complete and coherent sentences

First Grade
- classify categories of words
- respond to who, what, when, where, and how questions and discuss the main idea
- confirm predictions about what will happen next in a text by identifying key words
- describe the roles of authors and illustrators
- discuss ideas and select a focus for stories or writing
- listen attentively
- ask questions for clarification and understanding
- use visual aids such as pictures and objects to present oral information

Second Grade
- use title, table of contents, and chapter headings to locate information
- recognize cause and effect relationships in a text
- organize related ideas together to maintain a consistent focus
- review, evaluate, and revise writing for meaning and clarity
- paraphrase information that is shared orally by others
- report on a topic with supportive or illustrative facts and details
- report on a topic with facts and details, drawing from several sources of information

Third Grade
- use glossary and index to locate information
- distinguish the main idea and supporting details in expository (informational) text
- discuss ideas for writing stories and use diagrams and charts to develop ideas
- use computers to draft, revise, and share writing
- write descriptive pieces about people, places, things, experiences

- write for different purposes and to a specific audience or person
- organize ideas chronologically or around major points of information
- distinguish between the speaker's opinions and verifiable facts

Fourth Grade

- use organization of informational text to strengthen comprehension
- distinguish between cause and effect and between fact and opinion
- use multiple reference materials and online information sources
- understand the organization of information sources such as almanacs, newspapers, periodicals
- ask thoughtful questions
- use examples and analogies to explain or clarify events and information
- evaluate the role of the mass media in focusing people's attention on events and issues

Fifth Grade

- use features of informational texts such as graphics and diagrams
- analyze text that is organized in sequential or chronological order
- recognize main ideas presented in texts, including the identification and assessment of evidence
- draw inferences, conclusions, or generalizations about content in text and support arguments
- discuss ideas for writing, keep a list or notebook of ideas, use graphic organizers
- use note-taking skills
- review, evaluate, and revise writing for meaning and clarity
- edit and revise writing to improve meaning and focus
- write basic research reports about important ideas, issues, people, events
- ask questions that seek information not already discussed
- interpret a speaker's verbal and nonverbal messages, purposes and perspectives
- select a focus, organizational structure, and point of view from an oral

presentation
- clarify and support spoken ideas with evidence and examples
- analyze media as sources of information for entertainment, persuasion, interpretation

Sixth Grade

- identify and interpret figurative language and words with multiple meanings
- identify the structure features of popular media and use those features to obtain messages and meaning
- connect and clarify main ideas by identifying their relationship to multiple sources
- note instances of persuasion, propaganda, and faulty reasoning in text
- explain the effects of common literary devices, such as symbolism, imagery, analogy, metaphor
- choose the form of writing that best suites the intended audience
- write informational pieces of several paragraphs
- use a variety of effective organizational patterns, including comparison and contrast
- use organizational features of electronic text, such as bulletin boards and databases
- use a computer to compose documents with appropriate formatting and citations
- edit and proofread one's own writing, as well as others, and share ideas on information needs
- support opinions and perspectives with documented evidence with use of visual media
- identify persuasive and propaganda techniques used in electronic media and mass media
- deliver meaningful narrative and informative presentations
- deliver persuasive presentations
- deliver presentations which offer potential solutions to problems

Seventh Grade

- locate information by using a variety of consumer and public documents
- analyze text that uses the cause and effect organizational pattern
- use strategies of note-taking, outlining and summarizing to improve writing structure
- identify topics; ask and evaluate questions; and develop ideas leading to inquiry
- write biographical and autobiographical narratives
- write and present persuasive reports with supporting evidence and meaningful illustrations
- ask questions to elicit information from speakers, including evidence to support the speaker's claims
- arrange supporting details, reasons, descriptions, and examples effectively
- provide helpful feedback to speakers concerning the coherence and logic of the speaker's presentation
- analyze the effect on the viewer of images, text, and sound from educational and mass media

Eighth Grade

- compare and contrast features and elements of consumer materials
- compare the original text to a summary to determine if the summary is accurate; understand abstracting
- create compositions that have a clear message and coherent thesis
- support thesis or conclusion with analogies, paraphrases, quotations, opinions, data and understand when information becomes evidence
- plan and conduct multiple-step information searches by using computer-based databases
- achieve an effective balance between researched information and original ideas, giving proper credit
- match the message, vocabulary, voice modulation, expression, and tone to the audience
- evaluate the credibility of a speaker, author, and other communicators of ideas, arguments, perspectives, and plans for change or support of status quo

Ninth Grade

- distinguish between what words mean literally and what they imply
- prepare an annotated bibliography of reference materials for a report
- synthesis the content from several sources or works by a single author
- critique the logic of presented in functional documents
- evaluate an author's argument or defense of a claim
- discuss ideas for writing in collaboration with classmates, teachers and other writers and develop drafts which are shared and revised
- use writing to formulate clear research questions and to compile information from multiple sources
- develop the main ideas within the body of the composition through supporting evidence
- integrate quotations and citations (footnotes) into a written text while maintaining the flow of ideas
- write documents related to career development
- write technical documents such as a manual or rules of behavior for conflict resolution
- choose and practice appropriate techniques for developing the introduction and conclusion in a speech
- produce concise notes for extemporaneous speeches
- compare and contrast the ways in which media genres cover the same event
- assess how language and delivery affect the mood and tone of oral communication

Tenth Grade to Twelfth Grade

- use clear research questions and suitable research methods
- develop the main ideas within the body

A SCOPE AND SEQUENCE SKILLS SET FOR INFORMATION INQUIRY

of a composition through supporting evidence

- use appropriate conventions for documentation of text, notes, bibliographies, references
- use a computer to integrate databases, visuals, graphics, and other resources
- use precise technical or scientific language when appropriate for specific forms and topics
- identify logical fallacies used in oral addresses, written documents, and mass media
- use multimedia for communications, including historical investigations, technical reports, reflective and persuasive presentations
- critique the power, validity, and truthfulness of arguments set forth in public documents
- demonstrate an understanding of the elements of discourse and debate
- develop presentations by using clear research questions, based on creative and critical research methods
- use technology for all aspects of creating, revising, editing, and publishing (sharing and presenting)

Before Graduation from High School

This example from the 2001 Indiana Language Arts Standards illustrates a high degree of information literacy to be part of the student's proven skills before graduation.

Students formulate thoughtful judgments about oral communication. They deliver focused and coherent presentations that convey clear and distinct perspectives and demonstrate solid reasoning. Students deliver polished formal and extemporaneous presentations that combine traditional speech strategies of narration, exposition, persuasion, and description. They use gestures, tone, and vocabulary appropriate to the audience and purpose. Students use the same Standard English conventions for oral speech that they use in their writing.

Comprehension

- Summarize a speaker's purpose and point of view, discuss, and ask questions to draw interpretations of the speaker's content and attitude toward the subject.

Organization and Delivery of Oral Communication

- Use rhetorical questions (questions asked for the effect without an expected answer), parallel structure, concrete images, figurative language, characterization, irony, and dialogue to achieve clarity, force, and artistic effect.
- Distinguish between and use various forms of logical arguments, including:
  — inductive arguments
  — deductive arguments
  — syllogisms and analogies
- Use logical, ethical, and emotional appeals that enhance a specific tone and purpose
- Use appropriate rehearsal strategies to pay attention to performance details, achieve command of the text, and create skillful artistic staging.
- Use effective and interesting language, including information expressions for effect, Standard English for clarity, technical language for specificity.
- Use research and analysis to justify strategies for gesture, movement, and vocalization, including dialect, pronunciation, and enunciation.
- Evaluate when to use different kinds of effects (including visuals, music, sound, and graphics) to create effective productions.

Analysis and Evaluation of Oral and Media Communications

- Analyze strategies used by the media to inform, persuade, entertain, and transmit culture (including advertisements; perpetuation of stereotypes; and the use of visual representations, special effects, and language).
- Analyze the impact of the media on the democratic process (including exerting influence on elections, creating images of leaders, and shaping attitudes) at the local, state, and national levels.
- Interpret and evaluate the various ways in which events are presented and

information is communicated by visual image-makers (such as graphic artists, documentary filmmakers, illustrators, and news photographers).
- Critique a speaker's use of words and language in relation to the purpose of an oral communication and the impact the words may have on the audience.
- Analyze the four basic types of persuasive speech (propositions of fact, value, problem, and policy) and understand the similarities and differences in their patterns of organization and the use of the persuasive language, reasoning, and proof.
- Analyze the techniques used in media messages for a particular audience to evaluate effectiveness, and infer the speaker's character.

Speaking Applications
- Deliver reflective presentations that:
  — explore the significance of personal experiences, events, conditions, or concerns, using appropriate speech strategies, including narration, description, exposition, and persuasion
  — draw comparisons between the specific incident and broader themes and to illustrate beliefs or generalizations about life
  — maintain a balance between describing the incident and relating it to the more general, abstract ideas
- Deliver oral reports on historical investigations that:
  — use exposition, narration, description, persuasion, or some combination of those to support the thesis
  — analyze several historical records of a single event, examining each perspective on the event
  — describe similarities and differences between research sources, using information derived from primary and secondary sources to support the presentation
  — include information on all relevant perspectives and consider the validity (accuracy and truthfulness) and

reliability (consistency) of sources
- Deliver oral responses to literature that:
  — demonstrate a comprehensive understanding of the significant ideas of literary works and make assertions about the text that are reasonable and supportable
  — present an analysis of the imagery, language, universal themes, and unique aspects of the text through the use of speech strategies, including narration, description, persuasion, exposition, or a combination of those strategies
  — support important ideas and viewpoints through specific references to the text and to other works
  — demonstrate an awareness of the author's style and an appreciation of the effects created
  — identify and assess the impact of ambiguities, nuances, and complexities within the text
- Deliver multimedia presentations that:
  — combine text, imagers, and sound by incorporating information from a wide range of media, including films, newspapers, magazines, CD-ROMs, online information, television, videos, and electronic media-generated images
  — select an appropriate medium for each element of the presentation
  — use the selected media skillfully, editing appropriately, and monitoring for quality
  — test the audience's response and revise the presentation accordingly

Authentic Tasks

The skills of information inquiry are most meaningful for teacher and student when placed in an authentic context. It may not always be possible to tie directly with the real world. Tasks mastered in near real-world simulations have a better chance for transfering meaningful skills into the workplace. More importantly, learning experiences tied to local businesses, organizations, civic groups, and experts create a community of learners and teachers. Issues discussed and addressed in inquiry projects may be global in nature, but will have the greatest benefit to the learner when applied locally.

Standards for authentic tasks were identified in 1995 by the Wisconsin Center for Educational Research. In summary, the inquiry curriculum should be facilitated so that all learners have the opportunity to experience the following:

1. Organization of Information: The task asks students to organize, synthesize, interpret, explain, or evaluate complex information in addressing a concept, problem, or issue.

2. Consideration of Alternatives: The task asks students to consider alternative solutions, strategies, perspectives, points of view, experiences as concepts, problems, and issues are considered,

3. Disciplinary Content: The task asks students to show understanding and/or use of ideas, theories, or perspectives considered central to an academic or professional discipline.

4. Disciplinary Process: The task asks students to use methods of inquiry, research, or communication characteristic of an academic or professional discipline.

5. Elaborated Written Communication: The task asks students to elaborate on their understanding, explanations, or conclusions through extended writing.

6. Problems Connected to the World: The task asks students to address a concept, problem, or issue that is similar to one that they have encountered or are likely to encounter in life beyond the classroom.

7. Audience Beyond the School: The task asks students to communicate their knowledge, present a product or performance, or take some action for an audience beyond the teacher, classroom, and school building.

For Further Reading

Association of College and Research Libraries. Information Literacy Competency Standards for Higher Education, 2001. http://www.ala.org/acrl/ilcomstan.html

Association of College and Research Libraries. Objectives for Information Literacy Instruction: A Model Statement for Academic Librarians, 2001. http://www.ala.org/acrl/guides/objinfolit.html

Baltimore County Public Schools. "Roles of the Library Media Specialist" and "Scope and Sequence" http://www.bcps.org/offices/lis/office/teach.html Viewed November 1, 2001.

Bloom, Benjamin S., editor. Taxonomy of Educational Objectives: The Classification of Educational Goals. Handbook I: Cognitive Domain. New York: Logman, Green and Co., 1956.

Carlin, Diana B. and James Payne. Public Speaking Today. Chicago: NTC/Contemporary Publishing, 1998.

Considine, David. "An Introduction to Media Literacy: The What, Why, and How To's." Telemedium. 41:2. 1995. 1-8.

Indiana Department of Education School Library Media Specialist Leadership Cadre, Information Literacy Task Force Committee, Nancy McGriff, Chair. Correlation of the Library Information Literacy Standards and the English/language Arts Standards 2000 for Indiana Schools. 2000. http://ideanet.doe.state.in.us/standards/welcome.html

International Society for Technology in Education. National Educational Technology Standards for Students: Connecting Curriculum and Technology. 2000.

Jones, Elizabeth A. National Assessment of College Student Learning: Identifying College

Graduates' Essential Skills in Writing, Speech and Listening, and Critical Thinking. Washington, D. C.: U. S. Department of Education, Office of Educational Research and Improvement and the National Center for Education Statistics, 1995.

Kuhlthau, Carol Collier. School Librarian's Grade-by-Grade Activities Program: A Complete Sequential Skills Plan for Grades K-8. West Nyack, NY: The Center for Applied Research in Education, 1981.

Newmann, F. M., W. G. Secada, and G. G. Wehlage. A Guide to Authentic Instruction and Assessment: Vision, Standards and Scoring. Madison, WI: Wisconsin Center for Education Research, 1995.

Opper, Sylvia, Herbert P. Ginsburg, and Sylvia Opper Brandt. Piaget's Theory of Intellectual Development. Upper Saddle River, NJ: Prentice-Hall, 1987.

Payne, James. Communication for Personal and Professional Contexts. Topeka, KS: Clark Publishing, 2001.

Thompson, Helen M. and Susan A. Henley. Fostering Information Literacy: Connecting National Standards, Goals 2000, and the SCANS Report. Englewood, CO: Libraries Unlimited, 2000.

Tyner, Kathleen. Literacy in a Digital World: Teaching and Learning in the Age of Information. Mahwah, NJ: Lawrence Erlbaum Associates. 1998.

Washington Library Media Association. Information Skills Curriculum Guide: Process, Scope, and Sequence. 1987.

Zemelman, Steven, Harvey Daniels, and Arthur Hyde. Best Practice: New Standards for Teaching and Learning in America's Schools. Portsmouth, NH: Heinemann, 1998.

Chapter 6

Information Literacy and Media Literacy with Carol Tilley

When and under what circumstances does illiteracy become a social, indeed, a political "problem?" Answers to such questions will surely depend upon what we take "literacy" to be. Is it simply being able to ritually sign your name (as it was through so many years of American voting history), or should we require that a literate person not only decipher but comprehend what a piece of written text is about-grasp not simply what is written (heard or viewed), but what is meant? If we insist upon the latter criterion, then at what level of comprehension should we set the line? A commonsense, pragmatic approach to all issues of this order must obviously start with "It depends" (Bruner 1991).

In Changing Our Minds, Miles Myers (1996) describes the evolution of literacy in American society and education. For what he terms the new "translation/critical literacy," the primary literacy goal shifts from decontextualized parts (i.e., skills in isolation) to contextualized wholes (i.e., language experiences and communicative events). Within this framework, learners are actively aware of their own efforts to fashion themselves as thinkers. Because they influence how we think about and solve our problems, as well as communicate our answers, we must broaden our understanding of technologies and media.

Traditional print media, the news bite, the digital byte, and the pluralistic world of the Internet are all part of the communicative voice of this generation. Media merge to create multimedia where written, spoken, and visualized images bring both improved clarity and new complexities to the communication process. Tables, charts, and icons appear more frequently to summarize data, express conclusions, and depict ideologies. Messages can be targeted at, tailored for, and delivered to a variety of audiences with increased ease, speed, and precision. While data are highly accessible and pressed on us constantly, the ability to successfully identify meaningful information, create meaningful information, and convey meaningful information becomes more challenging each day.

Various associations and societies, as well as individual educators, have attempted to create heuristics to help students meet these challenges. Often these come in the guise of literacy movements — media, information, computer, numeracy, visual — that seek both to address the perceived short-comings of modern curricula and to create students who can negotiate the complex demands of the Information Age. By examining the two literacies, information literacy and media literacy, which seem to be most frequently prescribed, we hope to demonstrate that there is potential for dynamic interaction between them that can lead to a richer application of both approaches, and, ultimately, greater student success.

Media Literacy: Decoding for Reality

A common assumption of media literacy is that people are confronted with a barrage of messages from mass media, including newspapers, magazines, movies, and television, whether they want the messages or not. Therefore, the lessons in media literacy often help the learner confront and live with these messages, not by turning them off, but by understanding the various intentions of the messages' producers. Through understanding the concepts and constructs of mass media, students are better able to determine what is real and what is important about the messages they receive. Ultimately, the power of the media over students may be lessened if they understand how to decode and evaluate these messages (Robinson 1994).

According to the Ontario Ministry of Education (1989), a media literate person understands that

- All media are constructs. Although media appear to be a natural reflection of reality, they are rather a carefully constructed presentation of reality that reflects an intended message or point of view.
- All media construct reality. Media offer a message or point of view that becomes real to the audience if first-hand information is not available. The audience accepts this mediated information as reality and uses it to judge the world.

Activity: Show students the video spaghetti harvest "documentary" that was first aired on the BBC show Panorama on April 1, 1957. What are the documentary conventions used to make this film believable? Discuss the implications of people accepting the content of this film as truthful.

- Audiences negotiate meaning in media. Everyone filters meaning from media through their own personal experiences, beliefs, and knowledge. Not everyone receives a mediated message in the same way; neither do all audiences receive the same message intended by the producer.
- Media have commercial implications. The audience is the commodity being bought and sold. Content and format depend on whom is paying for contact with the audience. The audience is defined by demographics. The message, point of view, format, and marketing

are constructed to match the audience.

Activity: Have students collect advertising found on the main pages at Yahoo! (http://www.yahoo.com) or another popular World Wide Web directory. How do the advertisements seem to be targeted? For example, if you look at music listings, is there a banner advertisement for a music service on the page? Do the advertisers offer special deals to Internet users?

- Media contain ideological and value messages. Media sell a lifestyle, value, or belief to audiences in a palatable or subtle manner that often seeks to reinforce the dominant culture. Audiences tend to be aware of the messages with which they most disagree.
- Media have social and political implications. Most Americans get information about their world from the media. Family life, leisure activities, consumer patterns, politics, and government are all influenced by the media.

Activity: Have students work in groups to monitor at least one week's worth of national television news broadcasts and front page headlines from major local newspapers. Compare and contrast the amount and placement of coverage given to events across the different media. Discuss the implications this might have for people who get their news information from only one media outlet. The Television News Archive at Vanderbilt University (http://tvnews.vanderbilt.edu/) is a useful resource for this activity.

- Media have unique aesthetic forms that are closely related to content. The format both influences and limits the content. Information is tailored to the format and presented differently in different forms of media.

Activity: Compare descriptions and advertisements of movies as they appear in movie theater trailers, on television, on radio, in the newspaper, in magazines, and on the Internet. How does the depiction differ among formats? What are the predominant conventions of each medium?

The media literate person is in control of his or her media experiences because he or she understands the basic conventions of various media and enjoys their uses in a deliberately conscious manner. The media literate person understands the impact of music and special effects, for example, in heightening the drama of a television program or film. However, this recognition does not lessen the enjoyment of the action. Instead, it can prevent the viewer from being unduly credulous or becoming unnecessarily frightened.

Activity: Show a brief clip from a well-known movie such as Jaws or Raiders of the Lost Ark. The first time through, show the clip with the original soundtrack. Then turn off the sound and use several different varieties of music for the soundtrack as you show the clip again. How do different soundtracks affect viewers' perceptions about what is happening on screen?

Information Literacy: Problem Solving

"Information literacy" is the term being applied to the skills and attitudes required to master information problem solving. As in media literacy, the learner must understand how to decode messages. The information literate student is able to describe the need for more information and use it to counter bias and stereotypes and extend arguments. While the media literate student considers the same decoding tasks in relation to confronting the mass media, the information literate student seeks out and isolates the information problem regardless of setting-occupational, recreational, or intellectual (AASL 1993).

The information literate student has the ability to access and use information that is necessary to succeed in school, work, and personal life. Although similar to media literacy in skills of evaluating, comprehending, interpreting, and communicating information to convey a message with a purpose, the information literacy approach emphasizes problem identification and information search strategy skills.

The information literate student successfully:
- Defines the need for information. An information need is dependent on the person-prior knowledge and experience-who has the need as well as the context in which it is placed. Information needs can be established and clarified through questioning.
- Initiates an information search strategy. Search strategies are most successful when the information seeker is able to identify and categorize concepts relevant to an information need. In addition, successful search strategies require the information seeker to understand the search system (e.g., indexes, online catalogs, Boolean logic) as well as to assess the potential value of retrieved information.

Activity: Before a formal search strategy is initiated, students should brainstorm individually to identify and cluster the relevant prior knowledge they have about the topic. A convenient way to do this is through webbing. This activity provides students a basic map of the topic as well as potentially valuable search terms. The completed web also can serve as a useful conversation point between student and teacher to see where faulty understanding might lie or where students might need more direction.
- Knows a variety of access points for resources, data, and assistance in interpretation if necessary. The information seeker understands how to utilize a variety of information sources and agencies, as well as human resources, in order to gain useful information. In addition, he or she understands the value of consulting with resource specialists and critical peers to reframe and refine questions and inquiries if necessary.

Activity: At the beginning of a new unit or substantial project, work with students to identify potentially useful resources and contacts. These may be print or other media items as well as professionals, agencies, and businesses that can provide you and students with vital information about an area of interest. Build a database of resource and contact suggestions to use with classes or in the future.

Activity: When beginning research projects, assign students to pairs or small groups to act as critical friends in the information seeking and use process. Model for students how critical friends might be used to spot gaps in the information seeking process and to refine information needs. Allow students time each day in the research process to meet with their critical friends to discuss progress and pitfalls.

- Assesses and comprehends the information. The information seeker identifies information important to a need and assesses its reliability, bias, authority, and intent. He or she also organizes new information in meaningful ways to determine where gaps may exist and to formulate the central question or thesis that can be addressed (Doyle 1994).

The Critical Core

Central to both literacy movements is the set of intellectual abilities and skills students are expected to master. While the structure and discourse of this set may vary from one discipline to another, and even from one teacher's classroom to another, the key elements for student performance remain constant. Using Bloom's familiar <u>Taxonomy of Educational Objectives</u> (1956) as a framework, this set of skills and abilities can be described as follows:

Comprehension of messages, implicit and explicit
- Understanding the core message (hypothesis, argument, idea) being communicated
- Understanding non-literal statements such as metaphor, symbolism, irony, and exaggeration
- Interpreting various types of social data
- Dealing with conclusions, including predicting continuation of trends

Activity: Present students with an editorial

from a local newspaper or a mission statement from a national organization, such as the National Rifle Association (http://www.nra.org). Work with students to identify the core message as well as nonliteral statements that the writer uses. Is the message stated or implicit? The same mission statement or editorial can be used to discuss other pertinent elements such as biases, unstated assumptions, and persuasive devices.

Activity: Practice writing questions, generating issues, or creating proposals that can be managed for student research. Gaining the ability to identify what investigations are possible is key to becoming information literate. This skill should not be denied students through the use of topic lists generated by teacher selection.

Application of general ideas, rules of procedures, or generalized methods
- Applying established norms to phenomena described in written, oral, and visual communication, both personal and formal
- Identifying factors that cause change and predicting the probable effect of the change

Activity: Have students work in groups to stage videotaped mock news broadcasts. How did students organize and format their broadcasts? What conventions of televised news broadcasts did they incorporate? If students deviated from news broadcasts norms, why did they choose to do this and how did the audience (you and the other students) react? These conventions may range from the types of stories reported, the dress of the anchors and reporters, the sequencing of stories, or the broadcast sets. If staging broadcasts is too time-consuming, work with students to compare local or national news broadcasts to see what conventions can be identified.

Analysis of elements, relationships, and principles
- Recognizing unstated assumptions
- Distinguishing facts from hypotheses
- Examining the consistency of a hypoth-

esis, argument, or line of reasoning with given information and assumptions
- Recognizing form and pattern in literacy or artistic works as a method to understand their meaning
- Recognizing the general techniques used in persuasive materials, such as advertising and propaganda, as well as social structures, such as peer pressure and authority status

Activity: The Opposing Viewpoints book series from Greenhaven Press often includes exercises in their books for distinguishing fact from opinion. Make an overhead transparency from one of these exercises and work with students to determine relevant identifiers for factual and opinion or hypothesis statements. Demonstrate how to link facts and opinions that lead to establishing evidence to accept or reject a given proposal.

Synthesis of communication, action, or relationships.
- Selecting relevant parts and arranging or combining to form a meaningful whole conclusion or message
- Organizing ideas, statements, and evidence to create a written, spoken, or visual message
- Diagnosing actions that constitute a plan
- Formulating an appropriate hypothesis or argument based upon analysis of factors involved and modifying such in light of new evidence

Activity: Instead of having students present a group oral report for a project, ask students to create mock-ups (on poster board) for, or, if you have capable students, actual World Wide Web pages to present their findings. Stress the importance of proper page layout, good navigation, concise and coherent text, useful images, etc. Provide students with examples of both good and bad World Wide Web page design. Some examples and general guidance can be found at sites such as the Yale C/AIM Web Style Guide (http://info.med.yale.edu/caim/manu-

al/), Web Pages That Suck (http://www.webpagesthatsuck.com/), or Dzine Online Guide to Good Design (http://www.lcc.gatech.edu/gallery/dzine/).

Evaluation of internal evidence and external criteria
- Making judgments about the value of materials, methods, data, and various forms of evidence for given purposes
- Evaluating the accuracy of a communication from such evidence as logical reasoning, documented authority, and consistency
- Referencing established external criteria of excellence
- Posing revisions in evaluation criteria when warranted

Activity: Have students regularly evaluate their peers. Work together to create documents that can be used for evaluation purposes. Discuss why some criteria for evaluation may be more or less important than others. Count peer evaluation towards students' grades or give students credit for the evaluations they complete.

A worthwhile shorthand to condense these critical skills into more common language is as follows:

Today's information and media literate citizen (student or teacher, in academic, social, or workforce situations) should be able to:
- pose worthwhile questions;
- evaluate the adequacy of an argument;
- recognize facts, inferences, and opinions and use each appropriately;
- deal with quandaries and ill-formed problems that have no fixed or unique solutions;
- give and receive criticism constructively;
- agree or disagree in degrees measured against the merits of the issue and audience;
- extend a line of thought beyond the range of first impressions; and
- articulate a complex position without adding to its complexity.

The Two Literacies:

Working Together in the Classroom

While there are many commonalities shared between media and information literacies, one difference is the selection of the communicative channel, that is, how to present or convey information. Media literacy promoters tend to give preference to the visual and audio modes associated with television and motion pictures. Many educators who promote media literacy argue that the best way to understand media is to produce media. However, information literacy is not void of the application of media production skills and activities. Basic composition abilities are essential for scripting, editing, and expression of commands that lead to the production of media programming. The usual communicative channel in information literacy has been the essay or written term paper with video production gaining some application in recent years. New technologies that include advancements in group software and in multimedia authoring are changing communicative channels dramatically and moving the presentation mode of these two literacy sets closer than they have been before.

More and more students are practicing information literacy presentation skills through collaborative efforts staged in electronic groupware composition exercises. Merits of evidence, for example, once shared can now be examined through electronic sharing of student essays while they are in the writing phases. Peer editing in these situations has started to reach new levels of critical analysis of evidence posed, sources quoted, and data extracted and displayed. Argument and counter-argument can take place not only upon presentation of the final paper, video, or discussion panel, but can also take place very effectively within the construction of the script, outline, persuasive paper, advertising plan, speech, or debate strategy formulation. Students can move forward in information analysis by demanding of themselves and their peers: Do you have a second source to substantiate? Do you have a series of documents over time that can be linked together to support your conclusion? Can you validate this source through rea-sonable credentials of the author or the institution the author represents?

In addition to electronic group composition processes, final products from the standpoint of information and media literacy are beginning to look very similar because of the greater ease of multimedia authoring through platforms such as HyperStudio and the World Wide Web. Text, animation, graphics, tables, icons, voice, and video blur the differences between media literacy and information literacy as verbal, visual, and audio manipulations have become increasingly necessary to deliver the final product. Multimedia presentation design and production involves the same dynamics of group composition as participants bring unique talents to the process and play different roles. But all students share in the process of critically selecting text, visuals, and sounds to construct the message. Audience analysis has gained some recent emphasis in both approaches as composition groups and media production groups struggle with conveying a message that will be received. Analysis of the intended audience's information need and level of information reception (understandings and assumptions the audience brings to the text or visual) are critical skills regardless of communication format.

Scenario: In the high school media center, students are preparing to produce a video news report set in a scene from the American Civil War. In order to solve the problems of set design, costumes, story content, language or dialect of the time, and frame of reference to events as chronologically correct as possible, these students have accessed a wide variety of resources. Some have searched the online catalog including a database of historical materials available through their state's historical society. They have examined a website of visual resources from the U. S. Library of Congress. Some have interviewed Civil War experts over electronic mail. Others have gathered replicated Civil War songs and speeches from the local public library and from the nearby academic library through interlibrary loan. The students will be evaluated not only on the organization and presentation of the media event, but on how well they substantiate the authenticity of the information used for the production.

Information and Media Literacies Together:

Creating Critical Classrooms

In conclusion, we suggest that the most salient differences between media literacy and information literacy is the locus of intended influence. Media literacy involves the learner reacting to an external factor-learning how to decode messages sent to influence his or her thinking, feelings, and actions. Information literacy involves the learner reacting to an internal need to know more-to take systematic steps and to employ strategies in order to find meaningful evidence or information to solve a personal, academic, and workplace problem.

While we have strained to identify different characteristics of these two literacy sets, the proposal here is that both need to be in operation across the language arts curriculum (as well as other curricular areas). The recent Standards for English Language Arts (NCTE 1996) calls for instruction that makes productive use of the emerging literacy abilities that children bring to school. The combination of media and information literacies can drive the creation of new learning environments that demand the critical use of language in order to read, write, and communicate effectively to a variety of audiences. Within this framework, students can conduct research on issues and interests by generating ideas and questions and by posing problems. Students can also gather, evaluate, and synthesize data from a variety of sources to communicate their discoveries in ways that suit their purpose and audience. Based on these combined literacies, students also will have increased opportunities to use a variety of technological and informational resources to gather and synthesize information and to create and communicate knowledge.

For Further Reading

American Association of School Librarians. Information Literacy: A Position Paper on Information Problem Solving. Chicago: AASL, 1993.

Bruner, Jerome. Introduction to Literacy: An Overview of Fourteen Experts, edited by Stephen R. Graubard. New York: Hill and Wang Noonday Press, 1991.

Doyle, Christina S. Information Literacy in an Information Society: A Concept for the Information Age. Syracuse, NY: ERIC Clearinghouse on Information & Technology, Syracuse University, 1994.

Myers, Miles. Changing Our Minds: Negotiating English Literacy. Urbana, IL: National Council of Teachers of English, 1996. National Council of Teachers of English. Standards for English Language Arts. Urbana, IL: NCTE, 1996.

Ontario Ministry of Education. Media Literacy Resource Guide: Intermediate and Senior Division. Toronto: Ontario Ministry of Education, 1989.

Robinson, Julia. "Media Literacy: The School Library Media Center's New Curriculum Baby." Indiana Media Journal 16, no. 3 (1994): 66-72.

Taxonomy of Educational Objectives: The Classification of Educational Goals. New York: Longmans, Green, 1956.

Part 2
Key Words

Key Words
Achievement Testing

Achievement testing involves examinations designed for local specific lessons or on a common basis for standardized, national comparisons that attempt to measure student accomplishments following a period of study, training, or practice. Aptitude refers to the psychological characteristics of individuals that predispose and, thus, predict differences in later learning under specified instructional conditions. Aptitude exams attempt to measure the current skills of the learner with the assumption that mastery of such skills in turn will predict the potential for success in situations where those skills are essential.

Both types of examinations have relevance to information skills instruction. Achievement tests can be criterion-referenced to test how well the student can demonstrate a specific set of skills presented in a lesson or unit of study. Does the student demonstrate the ability to:

- use search terms most valid for a given index or database?
- select websites based on criteria for quality presented by the library media specialist?
- cite information properly within the text as well as reference documents for proper credit at the end of the paper or media presentation?

Each of the standards for student information literacy in Information Power: Building Partnerships for Learning leads to a set of indicators for testing student achievement. These indicators can be used to establish rubrics to measure the levels of student accomplishment. For example:

Indicator: The student seeks information from diverse sources, contexts, disciplines, and cultures.
Levels of Proficiency:
  Basic-The student identifies several appropriate sources for resolving an information problem or question.
  Proficient-The student uses a variety of sources covering diverse perspectives to resolve an information problem or question.
  Exemplary-The student seeks sources that represent a variety of contexts, disciplines, and cultures, and evaluates their usefulness for resolving an information problem or question.

Is it possible to predict the aptitude for a student to understand and apply the skills of information literacy? Probably, although such a specific aptitude exam has not been developed.

One might assume that strong verbal skills performance would indicate an aptitude for reading and comprehension skills. Strong math skills might indicate the ability to interpret and apply numerical data. Other aptitudes also might need to be present for the student to be successful in application of information skills and reaching high levels in the information inquiry process:

- Patience and organization skills to handle multiple resources often gathered over time and from a wide variety of formats.
- Ability to comprehend information, to not only draw conclusions, but to identify remaining questions and to see a wide spectrum of perspectives.

- Ability to understand personal information needs and/or the needs of the intended audience so that application of the information to solve a problem or to inform a group will be clealy applied and understood.

While such aptitudes are nearly impossible to measure through standardized examinations that are limited to multiple-choice responses, informed instructional media specialists and other teachers can identify such abilities through observation of student behavior. Such observations coupled with some pretesting of basic information search skills become very valuable in the planning process for resource-based activities. Specific skills that need to be introduced can be identified as well as a prediction as to the amount of time students will need to complete the assignment and the degree of information advisory that will be necessary along the way.

History of Student Achievement and Library Skills

Elaine Didier's review of research studies intended to identify association between school library media programs and student achievement provides a benchmark for this research area. She reviewed thirty-eight studies conducted between 1955 and 1980. Several of those studies suggest a moderate to strong relationship between high student academic achievement and the presence of, under definitions of the time, a centralized school library media program managed by a certified school library media specialist.

In the early 1960s, under thirty percent of the elementary schools in the United States housed a centralized school library media center, and even fewer were managed by a certified school library media specialist. Much of the growth in both the number of elementary school libraries and school librarians that was to take place through the 1960s was based on the support of federal funding to match and greatly expand local initiatives. Mary Gaver at Rutgers University issued two key findings in

1963 that also serve to set the stage for the studies that followed over the next thirty-five years:
- Educational gain, based on the difference between fourth- and sixth-grade test scores, indicated the higher educational gain is associated with schools that have school libraries;
- Provision of a school library does not depend on the socioeconomic level of the school, although the ranking for the total community may play a larger part in determining resources and attitudes related to the presence or absence of a school library.

Additional studies conducted through 1980 provided some support for these conclusions, although they were often limited to the local research study without a strong case to generalize across a wider population:
- The presence of a librarian and the guidance function [help and instruction in resource use] of the librarian appeared to exert [meaningful] influence on pupil achievement in information-gathering skills and in the reading of charts and graphs.
- Students taught by both teachers and librarians revealed that instruction by librarians contributed substantially to student [information] problem-solving abilities, as well as proficiency in note-taking skills and ability to express ideas effectively.

Although fully recognizing the need for more research, especially under controlled experimental methods, Didier concluded that there was evidence by 1980 to suggest:
- The nature and extent of the education of the library media specialist can be related to the number and quality of library media program services provided, as well as the amount and quality of curricular and instructional involvement [supported by the school library media program].
- The curricular and instructional roles of the library media specialist can be related to teacher and administrator expec-

tations, competency with media, and attitudes toward the use of library media services.

Reading Achievement

Findings reported in the mid-1950s suggested that children with access to a centralized school library read more books of high quality and greater variety than did students with access to classroom collections only. Dozens of studies conducted over the next four decades attempted to show the link between greater access to books (and other reading materials) leads to a greater amount of reading. More reading by students at any grade level and in nearly any environment leads to better reading achievement. Stephen Krashen of the University of Southern California reviewed dozens of studies and concluded that reading by students from materials of their choice and for pleasure is especially powerful in advancing vocabulary and generating interest in reading even more. His reviews also demonstrated that frequent and sustained independent reading opportunities, usually also involving teachers as reading models, leads to at least equal and often higher reading growth compared to standard, regimented, commercial reading and phonics programs.

Although Krashen found that more reading is academically healthy for students across all social and economic situations, he and others have concluded that some children in affluent families may have educational advantages based on access to more books in the home, parent models for reading with and to them, and may have a quiet and comfortable place that encourages reading. Krashen also found that the quality of the school library was a significant predictor of fourth-grade NAEP reading scores. While easy and extensive access to reading materials does not guarantee the student will become accomplished in reading skills, lack of access almost certainly leads to little or no academic performance gain.

Jeff McQuillan examined several factors in association with student scores on the verbal portion of the Scholastic Aptitude Test (SAT). He included data from all fifty states and the District of Columbia for 1987-88. He concluded that school library quality (the greater number of books per pupil the higher the quality of the library) and high public library book circulation were the most reliable predictors of reading achievement at the high school level, even when controlling for such factors as per pupil spending, classroom size, and amount of computer software available. Further, McQuillan associates most of the decline in reading scores and lower student achievement in California during the 1980s and early 1990s with the state's failure to invest in public and school libraries and California's decline in the number of school library media specialists.

The State Studies on Achievement Tests

McQuillan related many of his findings to conclusions drawn from studies conducted through the Colorado Department of Education. Keith Lance, Linda Welborn, and Christine Hamilton-Pennell examined data from 221 Colorado public schools during the 1988-89 school year. A detailed record of their study was published in 1993, and provided the first strong indication that, among other factors of the school library media program, the engagement of the school library media specialist in instructional activities could be linked to student achievement. Among the reported highlights of the Colorado study are:

- Where the library media center is better funded, academic achievement of students tends to be higher regardless of the economic status of the community and the educational status of the adults in the community.
- Better funding for library media centers fosters academic achievement by providing students with access to more library media staff, as well as larger and varied collections.
- Students whose library media specialists participate in the instructional process are higher academic achievers.

By the end of the 1990s, Lance had coordinated similar studies in Alaska and

Pennsylvania. Attempting to tie measures as closely as possible to the 1998 AASL/AECT national guidelines for school library media centers, Lance and his research team concluded that the more often students receive library/information literacy instruction in which the library media specialists are involved, the higher the test scores (California Achievement Tests for reading and language arts). They also concluded that the higher the number of professional library media staff available in a given public school in Alaska, the more frequently library/information literacy instruction would take place.

In Pennsylvania, the Lance team reported the success of any school library information program in promoting high academic achievement depends fundamentally on the presence of adequate staffing. Specifically, they recommended each school library media center should have at least one full-time, certified school library media specialist with at least one full-time aide or other support staff member. For all three tested grades (elementary, middle, high school), the relationship between such staffing and the Pennsylvania System of School Assessment (PSSA) reading scores was both positive and statistically significant. Higher achieving schools also tended to invest more in resources such as books, periodicals, and especially in computers, for the purpose of providing extensive access for students to online information.

Quality of the school library media center collection is becoming defined more and more in terms of access rather than ownership. Access through electronic online systems, as well as cooperative efforts through interlibrary loan, allow for a broader definition of reading and information materials that support student achievement. Depth of immediate access to reading materials for pleasure is now described more often in terms of classroom library collections associated with the central library collection.

The Lance team also found that higher and lower scoring elementary schools were distinguished by the amount of time school library staff spent in teaching students and teachers how to access and use print and electronic information sources. At higher achieving schools, library staff spent three days on such activities for every two by similar staff at low achieving schools. At higher achieving schools at all grade levels, library staff professionals were involved in committees and provided in-service training to teachers. Library staff members at lower achieving schools usually did not engage in these activities. From the Pennsylvania study came the following recommendations, supported not only by this one state study, but by conclusions reached in dozens of investigations over the previous four decades:

- School library programs should have funding for adequate professional and support staff, information resources, and information technology. Such conditions are necessary to generate higher levels of academic achievement.
- School library media specialists must assert themselves as leaders in their schools. It is their responsibility to take the initiative required for information literacy to become an integral part of the schoolsâ approaches to both standards and curriculum.
- Principals can do much to make integration of the library media specialist with teaching teams possible, including adoption of policies and practices and communication of expectations that encourage school library media specialists to act as professional educators and for classroom teachers to accept them as colleagues.
- The school library program cannot be limited to the library media center as a place. Just as school library media specialists must involve themselves in the design and delivery of instruction, information technology must be used to make information resources available to teachers and students wherever they may be in the school.
- While Internet access is important, the school library media specialist plays an important role in ensuring that teachers and students have access to high-quality licensed databases from which current, authoritative information may be obtained.

A Word of Caution

While the history of research aimed to find linkages between school library media programs and higher student achievement in reading and other skills is encouraging, one must remember that many of these studies are based on association at best. Although we can draw attention to these studies and show a long history of relatively strong correlation between school library media programs and student achievement, we must remember that strong cause-and-effect evidence remains difficult to establish.

We know that where we find high performing students and quality education programs, we also will find school library media programs rich in reading resources and technology. We also know that this string of studies on student achievement points more and more to the likely trigger for implementing actions leading to better student achievement, the instructional library media specialist. When the resources are available and combined with the collaborative actions of library media specialists and other teachers to support and enhance information skills, the strongest links to improving student performance may eventually be found.

Confirmation Findings in Texas 2001

Ester G. Smith completed a study on school library programs in Texas in 2001 for the Texas State Library. Her findings confirmed much of what Lance and other researchers found in similar state studies. The Texas study demonstrated higher Texas Assessment of Academic Skills (TAAS) performance at all educational levels in schools with librarians than in schools without librarians. Library variables found to be associated with stronger student academic performance were:

Elementary School Level
- Greater number of recent library books purchased per student
- More expenditures per student in library operation budget
- Greater number of computers with modems and new software packages per student

Middle/Junior High Level
- Media specialist took a stronger role in identification of materials for instructional purposes in cooperation with teachers
- Media specialist provided information skills instruction to individuals and groups

High School Level
- More library staff per 100 students
- More library hours of operation per 100 students
- More volumes of books per students
- Greater number of subscription to magazines and newspapers (print and electronic) per 100 students
- More time by library media specialist in planning instructional units with teachers
- More time and leadership invested by library media specialist in providing staff development to teachers

For Further Reading

ALA/AECT. Information Literacy Standards for Student Learning. Chicago: ALA, 1999.

Callison, Daniel. "The Twentieth-Century School Library Media Research Record." Encyclopedia of Library and Information Science. Vol. 71. New York: Marcel Dekker, 2002. 339-368.

Didier, Elaine K. "Research on the Impact of School Library Media Programs on Student Achievement-Implications for School Media Professionals." In School Library Media Annual 2, edited by S. L. Aaron and P. R. Scales, 343-361. Englewood, CO: Libraries Unlimited, 1984.

Gaver, Mary V. Effectiveness in Centralized Library Service in Elementary Schools.

Rutgers University Press, 1963.

Krashen, Stephen. The Power of Reading: Insights from the Research. Englewood, CO: Libraries Unlimited, 1993.

Lance, Keith Curry, Lynda Welborn, and Christine Hamilton-Pennell. The Impact of School Library Media Centers on Academic Achievement. Castle Rock, CO: Hi Willow Research and Publishing, 1993.

Lance, Keith Curry, Marchia J. Rodney, and Christine Hamilton-Pennell. Measuring Up to Standards: The Impact of School Library Programs and Information Literacy in Pennsylvania Schools. Pennsylvania Citizens for Better Libraries and the Pennsylvania Department of Education, 2000.

McQuillan, Jeff. The Literary Crisis: False Claims, Real Solutions. Portsmouth, NH: Heinemann, 1998.

Smith, Ester G. Texas School Libraries: Standards, Resources, Services, and Students' Performance. Texas State Library and Archives Commission. April 2001. http://www.tsl.state.tx.us/ld/pubs/schlibsurvey/index.html

Key Words

Analogy

Good teachers frequently use analogies to render unfamiliar matters comprehensible to their students. An "analogy" is a form of logical inference based on the assumption that if two things are known to be alike in some respects, then they must be alike in other respects as well. Stated in more common terms, an analogy is an illustrated likeness in some ways between things which are otherwise unlike. How a jet plane flies can be explained, to some extent, by showing an analogy with air escaping fast from a toy balloon. A "metaphor" is the use of a word or phrase in a way that is different from its usual use to show a likeness to something else. "The curtain of night" is a metaphor that likens night to a curtain that hides something.

An "instructional analogy" is an explicit, nonliteral comparison between two objects, or sets of objects, that describes their structural, functional, and causal similarities. An example is: A red blood cell is like a truck in that they both transport essential supplies from one place to another through a system of passageways. The purpose of analogies is to allow relational information to be mapped from a source known to the learner onto one that is unknown. The analogy or model that is established in the learner's mind is the "base domain" and the concept toward which the teacher wants to move the learner for acceptance and understanding of new knowledge is the "target domain."

Effective instructional analogies depend on several factors:
- The illustrated analogy fits the learner's previous experiences so that he or she can identify with the illustration.
- The illustrated analogy provides a concrete link to the new concept, notion, or process that is being introduced so that the learner can adapt or assimilate to held mental models.
- Although never truly authentic, analogies are most useful if there is likeness or similarity to "real-world" application of the target concepts.
- Analogies should be integrated into lessons and immediately related to practice of skills, steps, or techniques so that the learner understands more clearly the actual application rather than just the illustration provided.
- Upon completing the new experience, the learner should be encouraged to elaborate on the given analogy or to create his or her own in order to demonstrate understanding and new mental models.

Studies have indicated that analogies, presented in an effective manner, can improve understanding and depth of learning new concepts. However, analogies can, in themselves, result in the need for time and effort to explain the analogy itself and for some learners such analogies may not be an efficient way of learning. Thus, these variables may influence the degree to which an analogy is effective:
- students' level of understanding of the analogy;
- the amount of distance between the base and target domains;
- the amount of time available in which to understand and apply the analogy:

- use and timing of explanations and/or cues regarding the usefulness of the analogy; and
- the type of learning given in the instructional goal-learning facts quickly may not be worth the analogy exercises, but greater comprehension of a concept and its implications for future work may be worth the time for development, illustration, and discussion through a good analogy.

The Structure of Analogies

Jerry Galloway, an educational researcher from Indiana University Northwest, has summarized the structure of analogies. An "analogy" is a mapping between objects and relations in two domains. One domain must be familiar to the learner, and this serves as the vehicle for understanding the target domain. A common analogy is to use the solar system to explain the structure of an atom. If one knows nothing about a solar system, the analogy is useless. However, a possible alternative might be simply the swinging of a ball in a circular motion at the end of a string. Analogies vary in their usefulness in the learning process both because of the existing knowledge of the learner and because of the variation among analogies in the similarity of their relationships to the target concept.

According to Galloway, the distinction between a "literal similarity" and "shared relations between two domains" is critical in understanding what an analogy is. For example, the comparison between an atom and a solar system includes specific features that are obviously different, not the least of which are size, mass, and temperature. However, the focus of this analogy is on certain relationships, such as the orbital nature of the smaller object around a nucleus and the attraction between the objects.

Good teachers are well aware of the pragmatic importance of using analogies in matters that are familiar to their students. In science education, chemistry teachers particularly seem to be fond of making analogies to the everyday lives of students. For example, the chemical bonds that hold atoms together can be compared to the rope that holds two people together in a tug of war.

Technically, a "perfect" analogy does not exist, in the sense that two different domains cannot be completely identical. There are, therefore, limitations to any analogy. Recognizing both the similarities and differences with a fully developed analogy can be essential in developing a clearer and more complete understanding of the target domain.

Fishing for Information

Common analogies used to help younger learners become excited about the search for information in the library media center include the treasure hunt and solving a mystery. One analogy may be based on "nuggets of golden information" and the other on gathering evidence to solve a puzzle or even a crime. Another analogy used to help some novice library users is "fishing for information."

Marta Davis of Southern Illinois University Library explains the similarities between fishing and information searching as follows:

The successful angler studies fish and plans a strategy. He knows that catching the desired fish is related to the choice of lure or bait as well as the water being fished. For example, different kinds of fish are attracted to different lures; and the best lure for catching fish in a shallow, weedy cove may not be the best in deeper water. Thus the angler's tackle box contains a variety of lures, hooks, lines, and other resources. Moreover, results with a particular lure or bait will suggest whether the angler should continue with it or try a different one.

In this [analogy], the fish represent the information sought, the lures and baits represent keywords or other search terms, and the various waters represent the indexes and other sources to be searched. Thus the successful researcher analyzes the topic and plans a search strategy for finding particular information. He makes a studied choice of subject headings and keywords, and of where to use them. Through experience, the researcher learns that for ["catching"] specific information, the most productive search terms will differ from one index to another. The citations retrieved are like hooked fish.

A common proverb used in relation to this analogy is, "Give a child a fish and you feed him for a day; teach him how to fish and he is fed for a lifetime."

For Further Reading

Davis, Marta A. "Tackle Box Strategy: Using a Matrix to Facilitate Library Research Strategy." Research Strategies 14, no. 4 (1996): 205-213.

Galloway, Jerry P. "Teaching Educational Computing with Analogies." Journal of Research on Computing in Education 24, no. 4: 499-512.

Newby, Timothy J., Peggy A. Ertmer, and Donald A. Stepich. "Instructional Analogies and the Learning of Concepts." ETR&D 43, no. 1 (1995): 5-18.

Quaratiello, Arlene Rodda. The College Student's Research Companion. New York: Neal-Schuman Publishers, 1997.

Thagard, Paul. "Analogy, Explanation, and Education." Journal of Research in Science Teaching 29, no. 6 (1992): 537-544.

Key Words
Analysis

As defined in 1956 by a committee of college and university examiners, commonly known as Bloom's Taxonomy of Educational Objectives, "analysis" is a key category of skills at a somewhat more advanced level than the skills of comprehension and application. In "comprehension," the emphasis is on the grasp of the meaning and intent of the material. In "application," it is on remembering and bringing to bear upon given material the appropriate generalizations or principles.

Analysis emphasizes the breakdown of the material into its constituent or related parts and of the way those parts may be organized and relevant to each other. Analysis also may be directed at the techniques and devices used to convey the meaning or to establish the conclusion of a communication.

Analysis and Synthesis Contrasted

Analysis and synthesis differ in application and purpose. The information literate student uses analysis skills to critically review a document written by someone else or a task presented to the student by someone else in order to determine the merits of various elements and options. Although there is also self-analysis, primarily we analyze documents and evidence offered by others to help satisfy our information needs. The information literate student uses synthesis to create a new or different document that includes the student's selection of key arguments, evidence, or descriptions in order to convey his or her ideas and conclusions. Although this may include, to some degree, a synthesis of ideas and evidence from others, primarily synthesis is used to convey a new and personal reflection in terms and format that best communicate to the desired audience.

Often set aside as one stage or level in models for information use processes, it is important to remember that analysis includes skills that permeate the entire process and are needed at a variety of levels depending on the task, ability of the learner, and the expectations of the information literacy teacher. Analysis may range from the mundane, such as determining parameters of the assignment and what can be reasonably negotiated, to the complex and difficult challenge of giving fair attention to all arguments on an issue before weighing the merits of each.

Analysis: Prelude to Evaluation

Over four decades ago, Bloom's committee concluded that analysis is best considered as an aid to fuller comprehension or as a prelude to an evaluation of material or information and is less effectively considered as an isolated technique. The committee also noted that analysis may be found in any field of study including science, social studies, philosophy, and the arts. In summary, activities that involve analysis lead to student performance of abilities to:
- distinguish fact from hypothesis in a communication.
- identify conclusions and supporting statements.
- distinguish relevant from extraneous material.

- note how one idea relates to another.
- see what unstated assumptions are involved in what is said.
- distinguish dominant from subordinate ideas or themes.

Analysis involves both determining the meaning of an argument and determining the quality of the construction of the argument. Analysis skills help the mature information literate student to make wise judgments in task selection, information selection and application, and presentation of arguments to a variety of audiences. Ultimately, analysis skills are essential to determine the success or limitations of the completed communication project through self-evaluation.

Analysis involves some difficult and demanding tasks, but practice in this skill set across the curriculum and across the spectrum of the information research process should not be limited to just the gifted or advanced student groups. Practice in analysis is essential for both learners and teachers at all levels. Becoming cognizant of when analysis should take place, is taking place, and the limits or opportunities that result from analysis is a knowledge base toward which all learners must strive, from novice to expert.

An Analysis of Analysis

Analysis processes can be classified into three basic clusters or parts, each of which has a relationship to the other. Each has a subset of skills, all of which are relevant to the tasks that must be considered by the information literate student and the teacher of information literacy.

Analysis of Elements

A communication may be conceived as composed of a larger number of elements or several pieces of information. Some of these elements are explicitly stated or contained in the communication and can be recognized and classified easily. The communication is "taken at its face value." Conclusions may be stated along with evidence to show how one reached such conclusions.

However, there are many other elements in a communication or a document that are not so clearly labeled or identified by the author. The reader must analyze the document in terms of:

- Authority. What expertise or background does the author have to make such conclusions, or is the author simply reporting conclusions of others?
- Source. Are there any political, social, or economic agendas held by the institution, press, or agencies that provided the means for this communication to be distributed?
- Context. Relevant to what situations was this document developed? Are there issues concerning date of publication, related events, or economic or political gain for such a publication? Are conclusions of experiments reported in context of the findings of other similar experiments?
- Method. What methods were used by the author to gather information and were these methods reasonable for the investigation? What are the merits of various information resources such as primary sources, eye witnesses, observations, interviews, systematic experiment, and conclusions from accepted authorities?

Such questions, among others, may lead the information literate student to detect the nature and function of particular statements in a given communication or document. Statements, evidence, and conclusions must be judged on levels such as fact, value, and intent. Hidden assumptions along with unstated or misleading evidence often will lead to false conclusions. Analysis, therefore, also involves looking for what is not reported.

Some examples of educational objectives that help to illustrate the skills involved in analysis of elements include:

- Ability to distinguish factual from normative statements. Is conventional wisdom, majority, or common choice at this time on this issue correct, or is such simply one snapshot of opinion?

- Ability to determine the motives for the communication. Is it to inform, to pursue, to sell, to indoctrinate?
- Ability to distinguish a conclusion from the statements that support it. Is the evidence valid and comprehensive?

Analysis of Relationships

Having identified the different elements within a communication or document, the information literate student moves on to consider the relationships among the various parts of the document. Many of these judgments deal with questions of consistency and relevance from one piece of evidence to the next and in support of a stated position, conclusion, or hypothesis.

- Ability to recognize which facts or assumptions are essential to a main thesis of the document or central message of the communication. Are the most useful and valid pieces of evidence present to convey the desired message to the intended audience?
- Ability to distinguish relevant from irrelevant statements. Are there statements or items of evidence that detract from making a valid and well-informed conclusion?
- Ability to recognize the causal relationships and the important and unimportant details in a historical account or a current event description. Are the key points that focus the reader on the who, what, where, why, and how of an event present and constructed in an organized manner?

Analysis of Organizational Principles

While organization of evidence for arguments or events for historical description help to examine relationships among statements, organization principles also have to do with analysis of presentation mode or style for conveying the message. In order to analyze at this level, the information literate student must investigate the merits of different communica-

tion styles and patterns to consider if the arguments are best suited for the intended audience. In doing such analysis, the information literate student will consider the merits of such communication modes for his or her own final product. Analysis involves such questions as: Has the author found the best means by which to reach the intended audience? Would such a platform be useful to me as well?

Thus, documents for communication easily involve film, drama, poetry, dance, new reporting, flyers and pamphlets, advertising, and much, much more. What is the best medium to convey the message? At what level will my audience comprehend facts and/or emotions? Do I want to get my message across to a few selected individuals who may have a higher than average awareness of the issues, or is my target audience the general masses? At this level, analysis involves practice in the:

- ability to find, in a particular work of art, the relation of materials and means of production.
- ability to recognize form and pattern in literacy or artistic works.
- ability to infer the author's purpose, point of view, or trains of thought and feeling as exhibited in his or her work.
- ability to see the techniques used in persuasive materials such as advertising and propaganda.
- ability to recognize the point of view or bias of a writer and how such bias may have influenced the means or methods used to communicate.

Analysis Questions at Several Task Levels

Task Analysis Questions

Given the parameters of the assignment, on what personal abilities can I capitalize and with what personal weaknesses will I need help to correct?

Through questioning, mapping, and brainstorming, can I determine the wide variety of elements of the overall process and the options for exploring a topic or seeking information for which I want to invest my time and energies?

In what ways will I need to expend my time personally and independently and in what ways will I need to work with others?

Information Analysis Questions

What additional background information do I need in order to identify an area for concentration and focus for my investigation and how may that focus relate to similar investigations conducted by my classmates?

What are the best sources in terms of access, authority, and age-appropriateness for me to use in addressing my information needs?

Audience Analysis Questions

What is my audience's knowledge of the subject?

What is my audience's attitude toward the subject?

What do I expect my audience to understand, consider, or accept as a result of my communication?

What seems to be the most effective and most manageable means to convey my message?

Self-Evaluation Analysis Questions

In what manner was the communication successful?

In what manner could the communication be improved?

How would the communication change for other audiences?

What new areas of inquiry are of interest to explore as a result of this communication experience?

For Further Reading

Bloom, Benjamin S., ed. Taxonomy of Educational Objectives: The Classification of Educational Goals. New York: David McKay, 1956.

Callison, Daniel, "Synthesis" School Library media Activities Monthly. (June 1999): 39-41, 46

Eisenberg, Mike. "Task Definition: What Needs to Be Done." Emergency Librarian (September-October 1997): 25.

Eisenberg, Mike. "Use of Information: Where the Rubber Meets the Road." Emergency Librarian (March-April 1998): 43-44.

Elmhorst, Jeanne. "How Do They Know That? Teaching Students to Trace, Read and Critique Research Cited in Texts." ERIC Document ED363896. 1993.

Fortuna, Carolyn. "Creating Critical Media Analysis Skills." ERIC Document ED458669. 2001.

Grover, Robert. "A Proposed Model for Diagnosing Information Needs." School Library Media Quarterly (Winter 1993): 95-100.

Key Words
Anchored Instruction

In 1990, the Cognition and Technology Group at Vanderbilt began work on a series of videodisc programs that were intended to provide information-rich environments that encouraged students and teachers to pose and solve complex, realistic problems.

The success of these controlled and focused interactive programs, especially with students who have difficulty in dealing with multiple information sources, has gained the attention of the U. S. Department of Education's Office of Education Research and Improvement. Through a process called anchored instruction, children (many of them with learning disabilities) view video and animated adventures on CD-ROM discs. Teachers use these adventures to organize lessons that help students to select a challenging topic, discover what it means, and then communicate this information to their peers, other teachers, and their families.

This description is not very different from the common process now often accepted as directed inquiry or the library research process. Anchored instruction, however, seems to provide a more narrowly-focused center core for projects and involves more direct intervention in discussion of topics and direction of student tasks than in the wider-ranging information access and selection process intended to challenge the critical thinking skills of students who do not display learning disabilities. More controlled practice in such skills may be of great value for students, regardless of their intellectual abilities.

Essential in either situation is development of situations in which students must make resource choices within a situational context in order to make meaning out of the information selected for presentation. The Office of Educational Research and Improvement has also noted that teachers can improve students' ability to read informational texts critically by providing opportunities in which students actively compare their initial thoughts and conceptions against those found in new information. Using multiple texts written from different perspectives is an important method of helping students develop a critical stance while digging deeper into a subject.

This process becomes even stronger when students are placed in discussion situations and must confront varied audiences in order to express their thoughts. Student learning is increased by using group discussion to connect core or common readings from literature to personal experiences and prior knowledge. Discussion among students, at any age, in which they hear different points of view and collaborate to solve problems, serves as a catalyst for developing reasoning skills. Several current researchers have concluded that the more students work in groups or pairs, the more productive their discussions will become, especially as their social skills become more refined.

Emphasis on Visual Materials

Providing a central novel or essay from which the class spins a web of related research projects has become a fairly common technique to help students in the same class move out and into more narrow and yet interrelated topics for either individual or small group research projects. The Vanderbilt Group, which has refined anchored instruction, has added two important elements in order to engage a wider student audience, especially those with low reading skills.

First, there is an emphasis on situations which have a visual format for presentation. Students see issues raised, and specific situations can be isolated and replayed through the use of the videodisc format. Teachers who have used these programs have also commented that management of class attention and discussions tends to be easier and often more extensive when there is a visual situation for all in class to consider. Those teachers who learn the search procedures seem to be more comfortable moving from one situation to another from the disc than in attempting to manage their own resources gathered from a variety of documents and often in different formats requiring different equipment. Verbal information, displayed either on a handout, a common textbook, or on the computer screen, seems to be less manageable and less engaging.

Second, the Vanderbilt Group promotes visual anchors as effective ways to get things started, not as final endpoints of instruction. The Group wants to encourage student-generated projects and seeks to broaden the spectrum of students who will commit their attention to such activities. The video anchors often stimulate a wider array of student involvement by providing more concrete examples and practice in problem-solving, formulation of arguments and issues, and application of information to these issues before students branch out on their own to explore a wider range of resources.

Practice in such tasks as identifying and organizing issues, selecting specific information relevant to specific issues and discussing why, and synthesizing the information to draw a conclusion for a problem being addressed for a specific audience is a powerful learning opportunity to which teachers too often give very little instructional time. Anchored instruction, therefore, is more than just a set of visual cuing scenarios. It is best considered as a technique to engage students in shared analysis of a set of situations posed to the entire class. Use of visual materials may vary in degree according to the interests and abilities of the students; however the use of core or common situations for initiating discussion can lead to greater involvement and eventually greater understanding of issues by a greater number of students.

The Role of the Instructional Media Specialist

Anchored instruction is driven by the following steps that must be facilitated by instruction information specialists:

- noticing aspects of the video program that suggest relevant issues for further inquiry;
- identifying sources of information relevant to these issues (usually through the library media center and database searches);
- reading the relevant information and taking it back to one's work group;
- communicating the results from the work groups to other members of the class.

More refined information skills are also practiced:

- considering multiple possible solution plans;
- defining the sub-goals necessary to accomplish each plan;
- identifying relevant data and separating it from irrelevant data;
- calculating appropriate answers in order to evaluate various plans;
- communicating one's own reasoning with other members of one's work group and class.

For Further Reading

Applebee, A. N. Literature in Secondary School: Studies of Curriculum and Instruction in the United States. Urbana, IL: National Council of Teachers of English, 1993.

Cognition and Technology Group at Vanderbilt. "Anchored Instruction and Situated Cognition Revisited." Educational Technology (March 1993): 52-77.

Montgomery, A., and R. Rossi. Educational Reforms and Students at Risk: A Review of the Current State of the Art. Washington, DC: U. S. Department of Education, 1994.

Key Words
Assignment

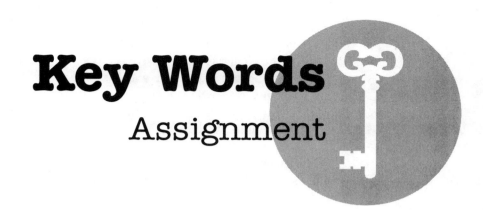

The assignment dictates the task for the student. The assignment will define parameters and identify what will be valued. Students, some more successful than others, will analyze the assignment so they can determine what should be accomplished and by when to satisfy the charge.

An assignment is a very powerful item in the education puzzle. The assignment can determine the limitations or the opportunities in use of multiple resources. The lack of vision and inexperience with information resources on the teacher's part often result in an assignment tailored for quick application, quick return, quick evaluation, and little, if any, learning for the student.

Information research models that call for task analysis also should include the option to question the value of the task. If the given assignment is not much more than "drive-through research" based on straightforward ready reference efforts, the question has to be raised, "Is this a valid information inquiry assignment?"

The teacher of information literacy, whether from the classroom or from the library media center, recognizes that assignments in the Information Age are most effective when students must make choices and justify those choices. Coming up with "something" is not a challenge in our information-rich world. Coming up with information that is relevant, precise, and authoritative can be very challenging.

The need to shift emphasis from information location to information use became very apparent during the late 1980s when new online databases and electronic reference tools were first being introduced to the schools. Daniel Callison and Ann Daniels concluded the following after their experiences in Indiana to experiment with the first introductions of H. W. Wilson online databases with high school students in 1986:

> It may be that the value of the online search experience is not only the ground-level introduction for the high schooler with future technologies he or she will experience [in college and chosen profession], but the challenge to make information-use decisions based on facts, relevancy, recency, and authority. Such a challenge requires a great deal more be added to library instruction in the schools than "how to search online." The cost for use of online systems will need to be justified not in terms of "x" number of additional articles located, but in terms of truly challenging assignments to be placed before the student.

> If the objective of the term paper is to "learn how to take notes, organize notes, write a logical and readable paper, and footnote the facts," then modules that have the materials pulled and ready for student examination will meet the assignment. Such a process might be very healthy for the first experience, and common topics would allow the teacher to find a more equal base on which to evaluate the product. If the intent is to provide the student with the challenge to seek all avenues for location of information to meet a student-identified information need and to determine the quality of a document compared to other documents (to be a wise consumer of information), then the library media specialists and teachers must be prepared to expand the current typical research paper assignment at the high school level. Two major problems that prevent such a curricular change are: (1) too many

school teachers and school library media specialists have not experienced for themselves the challenge of extensive information seeking and evaluation; and (2) uncertainty as to who is going to teach these skills and where they fit in the typical curriculum. (p. 180-181)

Following the pilot evaluation of the new online systems, assignments that required a certain number of references and also required use of several different information formats began to seem more unreasonable and unrealistic. Requiring students to find something from all formats (a magazine, a newspaper, a book, an audiovisual item, and a file) seemed to be counterproductive. Students were seeing an information explosion around them. Information could always be gained from many different resources, but the expansion over the past two decades has caused us to realize that information can be valid from any format. Only the efficiency with which information is gathered may be format dependent.

David Loertscher, professor of school library media at San Jose State, provides this view of the multi-resource assignment:

> In the information world and the world of multimedia, we often advocate that more is better. While we have been preaching, the information pool has increased exponentially; suddenly, the information age has come upon many schools. Thus, a few years ago where students were able to wrest only a few tidbits of information from our collections, now they are flooded. Students accustomed to mud-puddle libraries now have Olympic size pool LMCs. Lots of young people are being thrown into the deep end of these new pools without any swimming lessons. ...[We should] construct product assignments that require students to think rather than just cut, clip, and copy. In other words, students won't be able to find "the answer" in any source. (p. 21)

Encyclopedic Trivia

Assignments that are encyclopedic in nature and ask the student to simply gather and report some facts will result in very limited engagement with information. Location of facts to answer given questions in reference resources around the library media center may give some practice in searching both print and electronic resources. Such trivial pursuits or treasure hunts are a stronger introduction to the information world when the students also are expected to:

- discuss other ways to find the answers.
- compare resources as to which are most current, easy to use, and available at other libraries or at home.
- think about how the information found could be of real use.
- suggest what additional information is needed in order to make what was found even more useful.
- understand why different answers may be found in different sources for the same question.

Matching the assignment content to the learner's skills, needs, and interests are the complex portions of the assignment construction. Such requires a skilled observer of the student's previous performances and regular conversations between teacher and learner. The rest of the formula, however, is simpler. Assignments that will demand greater information-use skills and lead naturally to learning how and where to seek information should involve these characteristics:

Comparison: Information is used to compare and contrast events, items, or people. Who were the best major league pitchers of the past century? What were the three most important battles of the Civil War? What are the most critical steps in child care? What are the most important things to consider when purchasing a car? What ten photographs best illustrate the changing youth culture in America since 1950?

Process: Describe and reflect on the process you completed to gather and use the information. Information assignments should include a companion piece in which the student describes his or her choices and which were wise and which were a waste. This aspect also includes the process of seeking original information through surveys, interviews, and observations.

Justification: Support the information as the most useful evidence possible given the time and resources available. Is this justification built on selection from several information sources? Has the justification been confirmed by others who may have expertise to help you judge? Have you defined the important keys in your research question?

Solve a Problem: Based on questions designed to address information needs, the student attempts to solve a problem. Problems may include addressing information gaps for description of an event or biography; a literature review to speculate on an experiment and the documentation of the results of the experiment; and interviews and other evidence to determine perspectives and actions that might help meet the needs raised from a current social issue or conflict.

Personalize: What would you do if __? This is what the evidence from the literature and from your interview and observations leads one to conclude; however, do you agree or disagree? With all or some of the conclusions? Make the situation local. Who are the best leaders in school? Why? Can you construct a method to determine an answer to this that is similar to how you and others have determined the best U. S. Presidents? Criteria might include popularity, wisdom, and/or being the right person for the situation at hand.

Thoughtful Research Projects

Barbara Stripling has supplied our profession with many valuable insights concerning how library-based assignments can be made more meaningful. Her best assignment ideas follow a progression similar to the skill development outlined by Bloom's Taxonomy for Learning. Some of these are paraphrased here:

Level 1: Recalling
- Select five accomplishments of the person you have researched and produce a "Hall of Fame" poster based on those accomplishments.
- List five dos and don'ts about a social or health issue that you have researched.

Level 2: Explaining
- Illustrate the events of your research on a map and explain the importance of each event.
- Dramatize a particularly exciting event that was part of the time period you researched. Explain why this event is the best one of those possible to dramatize. Is your choice influenced by your interests and skills, the likely audience, resources, time, and location? Is your choice of an event based on its importance to other events and therefore makes your choice the milestone or most important? How can this presentation best be accomplished? Newscast? Dramatic reading? Dance? A play? In addition to writing and staging, be ready to explain your choices.

Level 3: Analyzing
- Create a timeline for the social events you have researched and correlate these to other important political, economic, and religious events.
- Rewrite a given historical event from two different points of view. After considering all sides, which do you tend to favor, and why?
- Compare your lifestyle and neighborhood to those of people living in the time period you have researched.

Level 4: Challenging
- Act as an attorney and argue to punish or acquit a given historical character for a crime or misdeed.
- Create an editorial cartoon that reflects your judgment of the key issues in a given historical event.

Level 5: Transforming
- Invite three famous scientists to dinner and predict what they are likely to discuss over the meal. Transform the conversation from the original historical context to a modern context.

Level 6: Synthesizing
- Describe either the possible evolution of or extension of an animal species and

predict what effect that might have on other animals, including humans.

- Propose an ethical code for political campaigning and finance.

Pitfalls of Library Assignments

George Merrill, a high school library media specialist from Santa Rosa, California, has summarized many of the problems in assignments that are intended to engage students in the use of the library in middle and high schools. His list, adapted from Carol Kuhlthau's guide to teaching the library research process and outlined in the Horace Newsletter in 1995, is rephrased here.

Form over Function. The teacher overemphasizes form, especially when explaining the assignment. Discussions on length, number of sources, margins, date due, and final point value often get more time and attention than sessions to help students raise questions, consider access to resources beyond the school, or discuss research methods that may involve collection of original data.

Product over Process. Evaluation of student work is placed entirely on the final product. Little, if any, reward is based on the process or evidence that the student understood the process. Teachers fail to give value to framing a reasonable set of questions, or placing those questions within a context for the student's work and those of his or her peers. Nor is value given to selection of sources and determination from possible choices of the most useful evidence. Students often are not challenged to determine the best mode of presentation for a given audience and to consider who might read, hear, or view the product.

Information Gathering and Processing. Students often lack the skills for a full range of gathering information. Students often do not understand basic browsing skills for print and electronic collections, or potential use of indexes and abstracts. Nor do they understand the need to identify key terms and to match a controlled vocabulary that may change from one information pool to the next. Processing information from resources is also a skill that requires modeling and practice. Extracting the facts, opinions, arguments, and examples that eventually build into evidence often are not required as many library assignments can be satisfied with use of a few basic resources.

Little Interest. Students are not engaged by the subject matter of the assignment. A good research project creates a question in the student's mind that he or she wants to answer. Library media specialists and other teachers, along with the student's peers can help the student generate possible options and increase the chances that something will be of interest. Proponents of the I-Search Process would argue that student interest is the key to a successful project. Without interest and relevance, the student is simply going through the steps. With interest and relevance come challenge and self-determination.

Associated not Integrated. The assignment is seen as something peripheral to the central concerns of the course. Ideally a research project should be integral-one of the ways students explore the essential question(s) of the course's content and objectives. Further, the assignment should require the use of multiple resources and critical choices in information selection to be integral with the library research process. Assignments should challenge the scope of information access and push the demands for more resources beyond those in the school. This, in turn, helps to drive the demand to increase school library resources and services and reduces the use of the library media center as simply a large textbook with some additional chapters. Library research projects should lead teachers and students to, what is for them, the new and unexplored, not just more of the same common ground found in most classroom texts.

Overly Emotional. A topic may be so emotional that students begin not with investigation and reflection but with simplistic conclusions that they attempt to "prove." They make no attempt to evaluate the resources found. In such cases, changing the topics may not be the problem, but giving greater emphasis to several stages in information gathering and frequent class discussions of resources and evidence can help the student to be more open to different opinions.

Students should be placed in positions to voice and defend a variety of perspectives along the way. For some, this process, practiced prior to completion of the final product, will open minds to a wider spectrum of resources.

Lengthy Assignments. Students lack the skills to manage a lengthy assignment. They often procrastinate, then slap together a mush of undigested material from a few obvious sources. Library media specialists and teachers should provide graded "checkpoints" designed to bring students along in the process. Frequent practice should be relevant and rewarded. Products from these steps should be shared and displayed. Students thus will have greater opportunity to learn from each other. Students should see "good questions;" "meaningful notes;" "clear arguments;" "examples and analogies that communicate;" and "the best websites, reference books, and local experts for personal interviews." Calendars should be used to plan time and to allow time for students to gain resources from beyond the school. Students need guidance, models, encouragement, and feedback at several points of intervention in order to survive and "thrive" a demanding project.

Split Roles. Without sufficient planning time, the teacher falls into the accustomed role of assigner and the library media specialist becomes the resource finder. Worse still, the assignment is made without consulting the school library media specialist at all. Sometimes, even with enough lead time, these roles don't change. The library media specialist should have a great deal to offer in the way of being an instructional specialist who recommends points of intervention, practice, and evaluation. Teachers can be powerful advocates of specific resources, and when teamed with the library media specialist to review and recommend resources together, a more meaningful research orientation will result.

Little Time for Guidance. Students receive too little time and guidance. A class is often brought to the library media center with minimal or no preparation, usually at the exploratory phase of the research process. Teachers often do not value or are not aware of the need for students to explore resources and gain a context for the possible research problems. Students should be encouraged to read background materials, both common to all and relevant to their special interests so that they build a pool of knowledge to draw on in discussions leading to topic selection and research questions. Such exploration helps to broaden experiences and to refine notions they might raise as potential topics are considered.

Up-Front Library Media Center Orientation. Students are instructed in "using the library" before beginning the research process and seldom engaged in follow-up lessons or practice. Extended lessons prior to entering the project often do not match to the "point of need" and are better broken into several mini-lessons spread across the project. A fifteen-minute session, given every other day for library visit and research, to introduce, review, and answer problems in front of all class members is worth much more than the traditional sixty-minute heavy frontload. These brief introductions can serve to help the teaching team as well as the students to focus on teachable moments.

Final Product Not Seen by Library Media Specialist. The students' final products are often not shared beyond the classroom teacher. Some library media specialists and teachers debrief after a team lesson effort to determine different approaches for next time. These sessions should include examination of papers by the library media specialist, especially to determine what resources were used. Are there items that proved to be useful that are new to the library media specialist, and perhaps should be added to the collection? Are there items used correctly based on introduction to the resources in the school library media center? Were sources not used correctly or did the student not challenge him or herself to use a wide variety of resources?

Audience. Often there is no audience beyond the classroom teacher. Students need feedback from peers, other faculty, community representatives, and subject experts in some cases. Such may not be the case for all library-based projects, but the wider the audience possibilities, the more challenging the assignment will be for the student.

A New Prescription

Carol Gordon, head of the Educational Resources Library at Boston University, has studied the attitudes and abilities of ninth and tenth grade students concerning the assignment to complete a research project.

She has found that guidance focused through instructional sessions across the project, usually presented by the library media specialist, greatly helps students to become more authentic researchers as they collect data through interviews, questionnaires, and content analysis that will be displayed and analyzed as evidence. These sessions are based on the following questions, with the introduction of specific resources and search skills woven in as examples. Lessons focus on the questions, with information sources playing a secondary role.

1. What is research and how is it different from reporting?
2. What is a researchable question?
3. How do I prepare a proposal for my research?
4. How can we evaluate our own success as authentic researchers?
5. Where do I go for information?
6. How do I get data from a primary source?
7. How do I display and analyze data?
8. How do I present my paper using a style sheet?
9. How do we edit and revise our papers using the writing process?
10. How can we evaluate the success of this unit?

For Further Reading

Callison, Daniel. "Introducing End-User Software for Enhancing Student Online Searching." School Library Media Quarterly 16, no. 3 (Spring 1988): 173-181.

Callison, Daniel, Jim O'Brien, and Judy Carnal. "Introducing the Electronic Encyclopedia across the Curriculum at the Perry Township Schools." Indiana Media Journal 12, no. 1 (Fall 1989): 18-26.

Cushman, Kathleen. "Information, Literacy, and The Essential School Library." Horace 12, no. 1 (1995): 1-8.

Dalbotten, Mary S. "Dalbotten's Correlation of Inquiry Skills to National Content Standards." In Information Literacy, edited by Kathleen L. Spitzer, 285-295. ERIC, 1998. http://mecr.state.mn.us/lalist

Gordon, Carol. "Students as Authentic Researchers: A New Prescription for the High School Research Assignment." School Library Media Research. Vol. 2. ALA, 1999. http://www.ala.org/aasl/SLMR/authentic.html HistoryChannel.Com. http://www.historychannel.com/

Inquiry: Thoughts, Views, and Strategies for the K-5 Classroom. The Institute for Inquiry and the Exploratorium. San Francisco. http://www.exploratorium. edu.IFI/index.html

Loertscher, David. "All that Glitters May Not Be Gold." Emergency Librarian 24, no. 2 (November-December 1996): 21-27. Parker-Gibson, Necia. "Library Assignments." College Teaching. Vol. 49, no. 2 (2001): 65-71.

Stripling, Barbara K. "Practicing Authentic Assessment in the School Library." In School Library Media Annual, edited by Carol Collier Kuhlthau, 40-55. Vol. 11. Libraries Unlimited, 1993.

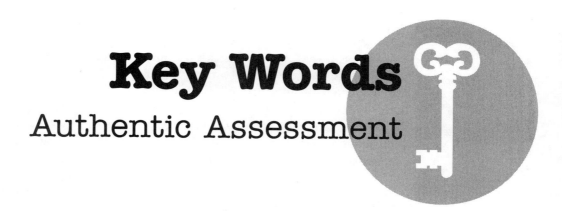

Key Words
Authentic Assessment

Authentic assessment is an evaluation process that involves multiple forms of performance measurement reflecting the student's learning, achievement, motivation, and attitudes on instructionally-relevant activities. Examples of authentic assessment techniques include performance assessment, portfolios, and self-assessment.

Performance assessment consists of any form of assessment in which the student constructs a response orally or in writing. Portfolio assessment is a systematic collection of student work that is analyzed to show progress over time with regard to instructional objectives. Student self-assessment offers opportunities for the student to self-regulate learning, and the responsibility of appraising his or her own progress. Integrated assessment refers to evaluation of multiple skills or assessment of language and content within the same activity. A written science report, for example, might include assessment of language skills, information selection and use skills, reasoning skills, as well as scientific content knowledge.

Other terms help to define the meaning of authentic assessment. In a broader sense, assessment is any systematic approach for collecting information on student learning and performance, usually based on different sources of evidence. Alternative assessment involves approaches for finding out what students know or can do other than or in addition to the use of multiple-choice testing. Authentic assessment, therefore, is a subset of these alternative evaluation processes, and is based on the assumption that there is a much wider spectrum of student performance that can be displayed than that limited by short-answer, standardized tests. This wider spectrum should include real-life learning situations and meaningful problems of a complex nature not solved with simple answers selected from a menu of choices.

Moving toward Authentic Assessment

The increased interest in authentic assessment is based on two major issues: current assessment procedures do not assess the full range of essential student outcomes and teachers have difficulty using the information gained for instructional planning. Multiple-choice examinations, for example, have emphasized the assessment of discrete skills and do not contain authentic representations of classroom activities, social interactions, use of multiple resources, or real-life situations.

In their classrooms, students read interesting literature, write creative papers, integrate resource information with personal viewpoints, work on projects in teams or other cooperative settings, share information while summarizing their conclusions, and use information from one content area (such as science or math) to solve problems and integrate information in other content areas (such as history or economics). The ability to select accurately one of a number of options to brief questions does not reflect what students will be expected to do in solving complex problems, communicating constructive ideas, persuading others on important positions, organizing information and managing human resources, and working cooperatively with others in the workforce.

J. Michael O'Malley, Supervisor of Assessment at the Prince William County Public Schools of Virginia, and Lorraine Valdez Pierce, of the Graduate School of Education at George Mason University, have listed characteristics of student performance that should be considered in authentic assessment.

- Constructed Response: The student constructs responses based on experiences he or she brings to the situation and new multiple resources are explored in order to create a product.
- Higher-Order Thinking: Responses are made to open-ended questions that require skills in analysis, synthesis, and evaluation.
- Authenticity: Tasks are meaningful, challenging, and engaging activities that mirror good instruction often relevant to a real-world context.
- Integrative: Tasks call for a combination of skills that integrate language arts with other content across the curriculum with all skills and content open to assessment.
- Process and Product: Procedures and strategies for deriving potential responses and exploring multiple solutions to complex problems are often assessed in addition to or in place of a final product or single-correct-response.
- Depth in Place of Breath: Performance assessments build over time with varied activities to reflect growth, maturity, and depth, leading to mastery of strategies and processes for solving problems in specific areas with the assumption that these skills will transfer to solving other problems.

Types of Authentic Assessment

O'Malley and Pierce have also categorized common types of authentic assessment and the student actions that should be observed and documented. Their examples include the following:

- Oral Interviews: teacher asks student questions about personal background, activities, readings, and other interests.
- Story or Text Retelling: student retells main ideas or selected details of text experienced through listening or reading.
- Writing Samples: student generates narrative, expository, persuasive, or reference paper.
- Projects/Exhibitions: student works with other students as a team to create a project that often involves multimedia production, oral and written presentations, and a display.
- Experiments/Demonstrations: student documents a series of experiments, illustrates a procedure, performs the necessary steps to complete a task, and documents the results of the actions.
- Constructed-Response Items: student responds in writing to open-ended questions.
- Teacher Observations: teacher observes and documents the student's attention and interaction in class, response to instructional materials, and cooperative work with other students.
- Portfolios: a focused collection of student work to show progress over time.

Rubric: A Scoring Scale

Assessment requires teacher evaluation of student performance. To aid in making such judgments accurate and valid (teachers measure what is intended to be measured), and reliable (performances tend to be measured in the same manner from one situation to the next), a scoring scale or rubric should be established. Often the levels of evaluation in a rubric are classified as 1=basic, 2=proficient, and 3=advanced. The criteria for each performance level must be precisely defined in terms of what the student actually does to demonstrate skill or proficiency at that level.

Examples of rubric scales which reflect student progression in the use of information are as follows:

- Demonstrated indicator of student performance: integrates new information

into one's own knowledge.
- Basic: puts information together without processing it.
- Proficient: integrates information from a variety of sources to create meaning that is relevant to own prior knowledge and draws conclusions.
- Advanced: integrates information to create meaning that connects with prior personal knowledge, draws conclusions, and provides details and supportive evidence.
- Demonstrated indicator of student performance: distinguishes among fact, point of view, and opinion.
- Basic: copies information as given and tends to give equal weight to fact and opinion as being evidence.
- Proficient: uses both facts and opinions, but labels them within a paraphrased use of the evidence.
- Advanced: links current, documented facts and qualified opinion to create a chain of evidence to support or reject an argument.

Role of the Instructional Library Media Specialist

Barbara Stripling, past president of the American Association of School Librarians, has stated that there are several roles for the school library media specialist in the development and implementation of authentic assessment. The library media specialist is in an ideal position to help teachers shift from textbook and multiple-choice exams to alternative techniques such as projects, exhibits, and multimedia productions.

The library media specialist works with teachers in the co-role of expanding the assignment and creating a learning environment that allows authentic learning activities to become possible. Secondly, the library media specialist facilitates the activity with the teacher so that many learning environments can be made available to students including different locations for information gathering and use outside of the school beyond regular school hours. Third, the library media specialist is versed in the authentic assessment process so that, as a professional teacher, the library media specialist provides an additional perspective to the judgment of student performance. The library media specialist provides input and evidence in the evaluation of the student's ability to process information into meaningful communication.

Making Academic Experiences More Authentic

An additional key role of the instructional library media specialist is that of curriculum consultant. In this role the library media specialist, in collaboration with other teachers, examines the curriculum and the activities that compose it to expand typical academic exercises into more authentic or real-life situations. Moving from basic textbook exercises and multiple-choice exams toward more team projects is one step, but creating challenging activities which involve authentic resources should be the goal.

Authentic exercises place the student in simulations in which he or she must seek and obtain relevant information to purchase a used car; finance a college education; plan a vacation for the family; invest in the stock market; care independently for a pet; determine key resources needed to start a small business; plan a reception for visiting officials; make a proposal for new state legislation; determine which health management organization to select; and more...much more. These authentic activities require extensive use of resources that are up-to-date and often only accessible beyond the school library media center. A key message to instructional library media specialists in the implementation of authentic activities is that they must look, with their teachers, beyond locally-housed resources and into the community for access to information resources which will support real-life decision-making assignments.

For Further Reading

Biondi, Linda A. "Authentic Assessment Strategies in Fourth Grade." ERIC Document ED460165, 2001.

Borowski, Maureen Coursey, Carol Thompson, and Karen Zaccaria. "Portfolios; Authentic Assessment." ERIC Document ED457189, 2001.

Griffin, Patrick, Patricia Smith and Noel Ridge. The Literacy Profiles in Practice. Portsmouth, NH: Heinemann, 2001.

Hart, Diane. Authentic Assessment: A Handbook for Educators. Dale Seymour Publications, 1993.

Klein, Davina, Louise Yarnall and Christina Glaubke. "Using Technology to Assess Students' Web Expertise." CSE Technical Report 544. Washington, D.C.:Office of Educational Research and Improvement, 2001.

Newman, Delia. "Alternative Assessment: Promises and Pitfalls." In School Library Media Annual, Volume Eleven, edited by Carol Collier Kuhlthau, 13-20. Englewood, CO: Libraries Unlimited, 1993.

O'Malley, J. Michael, and Lorraine Valdez Pierce. Authentic Assessment for English Language Learning: Practical Approaches for Teachers. New York: Addison-Wesley Publishing, 1996.

Ratcliff, Nancy J. "Using Authentic Assessment to Determine the Emerging Literacy Skills of Young Children." Childhood Education 78, no. 2 (2001/2002), 66-71.

Stripling, Barbara K. "Practicing Authentic Assessment in the School Library." In School Library Media Annual, Volume Eleven, edited by Carol Collier Kuhlthau, 40-56. Englewood, CO: Libraries Unlimited. 1993.

Tanner, David E. "Authentic Assessment: A Solution or Part of the Problem?" High School Journal, 85, no. 1 (2001), 24-30.

Key Words
The Brain

Jane M. Healy and Eric Jensen are two experienced teachers who have gained popular attention over the past decade. Both have lectured, written, and consulted widely concerning new research about the human brain. Their practical suggestions for changes in current schools which might enhance student learning are often obvious, but probably will continue to be met with lack of action as schedules, curriculum routines, and teaching behaviors are very difficult to change. Understanding some basic facts about the brain and awareness of new research findings concerning growth and development of the brain may help us reconsider how information literacy skills are best introduced and enhanced.

The Human Brain

The brain has four areas called lobes:
- Occipital-in the middle back of the brain; primarily responsible for vision.
- Frontal-around the forehead; involved with purposeful acts such as judgment, creativity, problem solving, and planning.
- Parietal-on the top back area; processing higher sensory and language functions.
- Temporal-left and right sides above the ears; responsible for hearing, memory, meaning, and language.

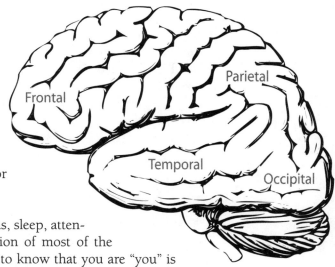

The mid-brain area, limbic system, is responsible for emotions, sleep, attention, body regulation, hormones, sexuality, smell, and production of most of the brain's chemicals. The location of the brain area that allows you to know that you are "you" is disputed. The lower back area of the brain, the cerebellum, seems to be responsible for holding long-term memory for motor or physical movement learning.

What supplies the energy for these brain parts to function? Blood provides glucose, protein, trace elements, and oxygen. The brain gets about eight gallons of blood each hour, nearly 200 gallons per day. Water provides the electrolytic balance for proper functioning. Some scientists estimate the brain needs up to a dozen glasses of water a day for optimal functioning. Dehydration is a common problem in school classrooms, leading to lethargy and impaired learning.

Oxygen is also critical to proper brain function. Higher levels of attention, mental functioning, and healing are linked to better quality air-less carbon dioxide, more oxygen. Some educators feel that nearly two-thirds of K-12 students do not receive the daily physical exercise to assure the oxygen-rich blood needed for highest academic performance. Rest is also a major factor. Physical exercise along with intellectual challenges can lead to sleep that is more likely to recharge the mind.

Is the conclusion, then, that we need more water fountains and exercise mats in the school library media center? While such might be important factors in the enhanced learning equation, there are other elements that are involved as well. Being aware that each of these factors has a role in the overall learning environment can increase the chances that students will function better when employing information search and use strategies. It means that the learning environment is a complex series of many activities and the student should be involved in all aspects. Those who have good physical exercise experiences, good nutritional habits, and who have gained emotional stability from having their basic needs met are more likely to engage fully in the intellectual challenges of literacy.

Learning and memory are two sides of a coin to neuroscientists. We cannot consider one without the other. After something is learned, the only evidence of the learning is memory. Jensen reminds us that the mind is not a thing, but a process. Our brain is quite a miracle. The brain is what we have and the mind is what it does. Nurturing one is necessary to open demanding processes that challenge and lead to intellectual maturation.

Challenging the Brain from Birth

Both Healy and Jensen conclude that too much of what and how we teach and test is superficial and passive. At all grade levels, teachers tend not to ask students to synthesize information, solve problems, or think independently. Too often we measure only what students recognize and not how they might use information. Applications of information, or the processes for use, are the skills of the Information Age, not a checklist of facts. Information Age jobs do not involve multiple choice responses, but an analysis and synthesis of the options. Without the student practicing such, rather than the teacher always stating the task, the ability to formulate their own tasks will not evolve.

Neurobiologists now tell us that much of our vision and thought processes develop in the first six months after birth, and most agree that along with proper nutrition, the mother has a great deal of influence on the child's intellectual development during the last months prior to birth. More and more studies indicate babies listen to words even though they cannot yet speak. Children need a flood of interactive information engagements including music, being read to, spoken to, and even hearing questions. Handling objects, learning shapes and movements, and hearing sounds all contribute to that important foundation for future developments.

A role that information literacy educators should consider is that of advocate of community programming for expectant mothers and preschool age children. Instructional library media specialists can do a great deal to support and encourage parents, daycare staff, and public librarians who frequently conduct preschool reading and information programming. Exploration centers for children in both the formal settings of the public library and informally at home can involve games, tasks, questions, and conversations, as well as reading aloud. The challenge is to reverse what we know to be currently true- a majority of our nation's parents do not read frequently, if at all, to their children, while a majority also allow, even model, passive use of television and video games.

Today, most scientists who consider the mix of heredity and environment agree that both have a great deal of influence. Some argue that environment may carry as high as 70% of the cause for development of a human's learning. Understanding of the individual characteristics inherited by the child may help parents and teachers better predict the most effective timing for instructional interventions. Differences among learners may span several years. The frequency of repetition and reinforcement may vary as well. Repetition is important, but so are novelty, variety, and challenge so the learner will gain more interest in the task. All children and, eventually, all students benefit from such enhancements, not just the gifted and talented.

Students also benefit from reinforcement of their strengths as well as challenges to address their weaknesses. Some great scientists have promoted for others what they have found to be true for themselves, the value of integration of imagination into the scientific pursuit. Enriched learning environments, therefore, include classrooms, school library media centers, hallways, and homes filled with posters, maps, illustrations, and other objects that invite questions. Most importantly, these items are a mixture of models from what our culture values as exceptional along with the products of the students themselves. Walls covered with evidence of student-generated questions, student-designed maps to find information, student-composed reviews of readings and viewings, and student products from the information use experience are signs of the learning processes at work. In-school video monitors that are limited to showing a list of school events and the cafeteria menus for the week are a waste of effort if they do not also contain great visuals produced by the learners of that school. These video systems can provide a continuous display of student illustrations, photographs of field trips, and even brief book recommendations composed by students.

Jensen concludes that, surprisingly, it doesn't matter to the brain whether it ever comes up with an answer. Neural growth happens because of the process, not the solution. A student could go to school for twelve years, rarely get right answers, and still have a well-developed brain. This should not mean, however, that we do not give our energy and ideas as educators to the creation of learning situations in which our students can succeed. Variety, experimentation, and challenge help our minds grow as much as the students'.

Time to absorb and reflect is also important. Maturation in information seeking and use evolves and builds over time. Too often, information skills, even when integrated with the classroom subject areas, is a rushed, drive-by, fast-food delivery experience. Much of what we learn cannot be processed consciously-it happens too fast. We need time to process and reflect. In order to create new personal meaning, we need internal think time. Meaning, most scientists in this area now the-

orize, is generated from within, not externally. After new learning experiences, we (students and teachers, all learners) need time for the learning to "imprint."

Kovalik's Integrated Thematic Instruction Model

Recognized nationally as a leading educator, Susan Kovalik initiated her Integrated Thematic Instruction (ITI) Model in a series of field applications in the early 1980s. Based on the theory that effective thematic instruction takes place when the educator takes into account brain research when developing curriculum and implementing teaching strategies, Kovalik proposes that enrichment for one theme should involve as many of the teachers in a given school as possible and be tied to relevant activities for the entire school year.

Common themes focus on concepts, topics, or categories. Typical conceptual approaches are "change," "honor," "imagination," "community," "survival," "ecology," "habitat," or "liberty." Topics with nearly endless related categories might be more concrete, such as "islands," "flight," "sun," or "water." Kovalik's school teaching background is anchored in science and many of the projects she has inspired have been centered on scientific inquiry, with systematic methods tied to discovery learning. The approach, however, quickly flows across the curriculum. While much of the ITI experimentation has been in elementary schools, the model has strong implications for secondary schools as well if the desire is to tie several disciplines together for a semester. Several elementary schools have reported that over time, student performance on thinking and reading skills is boosted if the school is immersed in the ITI model.

Kovalik bases the approach on assuming eight brain-compatible elements that must be understood, appreciated, and reflected by all teachers:
- Absence of Threat. Students are free from anxiety about their physical safety and have a sense of well-being.
- Meaningful Content. Teachers select topics that address standards and

engage students.

- **Student Choices.** Students have the opportunity to select assignments that meet individual learning needs.
- **Adequate Time.** The schedule provides ample and flexible time for thorough exploration.
- **Enriched Environment.** The school offers an interesting and inviting setting with emphasis on real world objects for students to see and touch.
- **Collaboration.** Students work together to enhance achievement and build social skills.
- **Immediate Feedback.** Students receive accurate feedback as they are learning.
- **Mastery of Application.** Students internalize deeply what they learn and apply it to real world situations.

This is a demanding agenda for any educational environment and has merit for school library media environments as well as the classroom. Often, physical description of a classroom in the discovery mode similar to the ITI model sounds as if it is a library media center in that it is well stocked with books and other materials, lots of hands-on items are present, kids may explore realia and online information, and kids are encouraged to raise questions and seek answers with peers. Free inquiry is the goal and should not change from classroom to school library media center and visa versa.

A Year to Plan, A Year to Implement

The year-long approach may seem a barrier, but in reality it is an opportunity. A concept or theme can be selected by the school (administrators, instructional library media specialist and other teachers, and students) a year in advance of study. Given in September of one year that "inventions" will be the theme for the coming year, curricular planning sessions, identification of local speakers and field trips, and acquisition of library media center resources take on a new focus for the school months and through the summer. The parent newsletter and school website designed to open the next school year takes on an exciting new look. Parents and teachers become more sensitive to the learning possibilities as everyone is engaged in possible ties to the theme. The theme, therefore, provides common direction while encouraging innovation and exploration. In how many ways can we think about "inventions?" The processes for any theme or concept remain the same:

- Define the possibilities.
- Identify resources.
- Identify roles and responsibilities.
- Engage students in exploration.
- Gather information and share results widely.

When one school completes a year with a theme, some resources and ideas may be packaged and sent on to another school that is considering the same theme for the following year. The package, of course, will not be complete or localized, but can serve as a primer for the next school as they begin to add their own flavoring.

The theme or concept does not take away time for the "regular curriculum," but provides instead some excitement and freshness to standard content areas. Brain fluids and brain waves have a chance to flow in taking new perspectives on old content. In this sense, instructional library media specialists and other teachers may not necessarily make curriculum, they "make curriculum better."

With this much time given to the topic, there is a greater chance that teachers and students will move up the ladder of learning based on human experience. The common sense Chinese proverb becomes a definition for learning engagement: "Tell me, I forget; show me, I remember; involve me, I understand." Engagement and learning may increase when time is given to move toward levels where students become teachers of themselves and others. We learn and retain, suggests Kovalik:

- 10% of what we hear,
- 15% of what we see,
- 20% of what we both hear and see,
- 40% of what we discuss,
- 80% of what we experience directly or practice, and

- 90% of what we attempt to teach others.

Of course, "results vary," but the progression remains the same. Supporting the learner with an increased role at each stage as eventual teacher or peer expert in some aspect of the topic area can have powerful results.

Kovalik combines the learning stages of Bloom's Taxonomy with the seven types of intelligence proposed by Howard Gardner to produce an "Inquiry Builder Chart." At the highest level of performance, skills represent creative and critical thinking:

- Linquistic: compose, propose;
- Spatial: formulate, design, plan;
- Musical: compose;
- Bodily-Kinesthetic: assemble, construct, design; and
- Logical-Mathematical: predict, solve, formulate.

Renate and Geoffrey Caine, educational researchers and consultants from California State University, contend that the key to transforming education successfully so that students guide their own learning lies in educators' ability to transform themselves. Unlike a computer, human learning involves questions such as, Do I want to learn this? Have I ever wondered about that? Is this related to what I already know? How does this make sense? What do I get when I learn this? Such questions define the human learner who also is seeking purpose for the processes, making the mindful considerations that are not artificial.

In addition to changes in behavior and perception, learning has a physiological component. The brain itself is physically altered by experiences, according to the Caines, a phenomenon called "plasticity." Research they review tends to show that many of the body and brain main systems develop concurrently. But they caution that the brain's capacity to learn so exuberantly is not a justification for force-feeding young children with drills and memorization. The young brain learns best from the way that it is engaged in social, emotional, and sensory experiences. What shapes the brain is the type of experience that it has,

not only the type of information that is packaged and presented to it.

For Further Reading

Brandt, Ron. Powerful Learning. Alexandria, VA: Association for Supervision and Curriculum Development, 1998.

Caine, Renate Nummela, and Geoffrey Caine. Making Connections: Teaching and the Human Brain. New York: Addison-Wesley, 1994.

Freed, Jeffrey, Laurie Parsons, and Jeffery Freed. Right-Brained Children in the Left-Brained World: Unlocking the Potential of Your ADD Child. Fireside, 1998.

Gardner, Howard. Frames of Mind. New York: BasicBooks, 1983.

Goleman, Daniel. Emotional Intelligence. New York: Bantam Books, 1995.

Healy, Jane M. Endangered Minds. New York: Touchstone/ Simon and Schuster, 1990.

Jensen, Eric. Brain-Based Learning. Del Mar, CA: Turning Point, 1996.

Jensen, Eric. Teaching with the Brain in Mind. Alexandria, VA: Association for Supervision and Curriculum Development, 1998.

Kovalik, Susan. Integrated Thematic Instruction: The Model. Kent, WA: Kovalik & Associates/Books for Educators, 1994.

Nelson, Kristen. Teaching in the Cyberage: Linking the Internet and Brain Theory. Arlington Heights, IL: SkyLight Professional Development, 2001.

Key Words

Cognitive Apprenticeship

(by Carol Tilley)

"Apprenticeship" is a traditional mode of teaching and learning in which the skills and knowledge of a trade, such as tailoring or healing, are passed from master to apprentice. In an apprenticeship, the apprentice spends time observing the master in action and practicing increasingly complex components of the skill being observed. The master guides the apprentice throughout the learning process by offering hints, suggestions, and critiques, until the apprentice demonstrates competency and is ready to go out on his or her own.

In the past two decades, educational theorists and researchers have proposed and tested a similar method of apprenticing the mind: cognitive apprenticeship. Like traditional apprenticeship, cognitive apprenticeship works by providing students with the opportunity to observe experts and practice skills while receiving expert guidance. Unlike traditional apprenticeship, however, cognitive apprenticeship is focused largely on teaching and learning tacit skills and knowledge.

Information problem solving and information literacy are examples of complex sets of skills and knowledge that are amenable to teaching and learning through cognitive apprenticeship. In both instances, the knowledge (e.g., the difference between fact and opinion), strategies (e.g., when to use a magazine index instead of the OPAC), and processes (e.g., how to use a bibliography to identify additional resources) required to be competent and literate are implicit, hidden in the minds of the teacher and student. The cognitive apprenticeship approach provides a model for making this knowledge visible and, as a result, making teaching and learning more successful.

Cognitive Apprenticeship

Collins, Brown, and Newman proposed one of the best-known frameworks for cognitive apprenticeship. In their model, content in the form of knowledge (conceptual, factual, and procedural) and strategies (heuristic, control, and learning) are taught in an environment that emphasizes situated learning within a culture of expert practice. Teaching and learning occurs through interactions similar in form to traditional apprenticeship with teachers modeling, coaching, scaffolding, and fading knowledge and strategies in a specific sequence for students.

"Modeling" is the process of demonstrating behavior in order to provide a model for imitation and learning. In cognitive apprenticeship, modeling is thinking made visible. By having teachers (N.B. library media specialists are considered to be teachers throughout this article) demonstrate a task, students develop a rich, conceptual model of the task to be performed. This model allows students to see what expert performance looks like and provides a guide for feedback. Modeling is more than making available a finished product, such as a sample composition or multimedia presentation. Modeling requires that teachers allow students to witness the mental wrangling that goes into creating an end product.

"Coaching" is the process of guiding behavior through incremental skills practice in the form of scaffolding as well as through giving feedback. Scaffolding involves breaking a skill into its components and then supporting students-just as scaffolding supports construction workers-as they practice the components. As students become more competent, scaffolding decreases, and students are empowered to do more on their own. Coaching requires knowing what support is necessary for each student and when each student's needs change, so that coaching, like scaffolding, lessens (this is "fading"). Coaching also compels teachers to assist students in understanding how their performance differs from the expert model and to provide strategies or guidance so that the students' performance becomes more expert.

Cognitive apprenticeship also encourages students to improve their metacognition, the act of thinking about thinking. By providing students with opportunities to articulate, reflect, and explore what they are learning, they gain better control over the knowledge, strategies, and processes that comprise expert practice. As a result, they may be better able to monitor their own progress and performance. Dialogue between teacher and student is one way to promote metacognition, but cooperative and competitive student group learning activities are equally useful.

One of the key ideas underlying cognitive apprenticeship is the notion that learning occurs primarily through social interaction. The work of Vygotsky and others suggests that knowledge, strategies, and processes are "learned" only after students have opportunities to try them out and/or talk about them. Just as young children mimic language long before they understand what the words and patterns mean, students of all ages try out ideas and actions before true understanding occurs. Dialogue between teacher and student and interactions between and among students provide a means of testing out ideas and actions.

A second key idea underlying cognitive apprenticeship is the importance of placing learning in an authentic context with authentic activities. Lave and Wenger, among others, refer to this as situated learning and it allows students to become acculturated to real-life expertise. Although schooling invariably has artificial elements, the more authentic the task, the audience, the tools, and the practice, the

better. If expert practice does not include worksheets and tests of recall or recognition, then ideally activities for students should not include them either.

Information Literacy and Cognitive Apprenticeship

Studies of students' information seeking and use suggest that students could benefit greatly from a cognitive apprenticeship approach to teaching and learning information problem solving and information literacy. For example, McGregor found that students focus on the final product of information seeking, often to the exclusion of the process that goes into creating it. A possible reason for this is that students lack an explicit model for the knowledge, strategies, and processes that information seeking and use requires; the product is something tangible on which to focus. Research by Pitts upholds this supposition. The students in her study not only lacked models to guide their information seeking and use, but when they asked their teachers for guidance, the help they received never extended beyond directional assistance in using the library media center.

When students lack expert models, they flounder in their attempts at information seeking and use. The result is often that they produce (and often are rewarded for) products that are little more than the result of cut-and-paste strategies. In these instances, the inquiry or research assignment becomes an activity in which incidental items such as bibliographic form, preliminary outline, and internal citation receive higher value than the ability to demonstrate expertise in information seeking and use. Ultimately, it is the apprenticeship of form instead of function.

Several authors have suggested implicitly and explicitly the utility of a cognitive apprenticeship approach to teaching information problem solving and encouraging information literacy. Kuhlthau writes about the importance of teachers mentoring students' information seeking through mediation and guidance in a way that meets the needs of individual students. This tactic is similar to coaching in cognitive apprenticeship. Sheingold also suggests that features of cognitive apprenticeship such as modeling and scaffolding are valuable techniques to develop inquiry skills. Callison suggests that features of cognitive apprenticeship provide a useful structure for developing any program of instruction that works to improve students' thinking and critical information use skills, while Mancall, Aaron, and Walker similarly emphasize the role of metacognition.

Practicing Cognitive Apprenticeship

Joy McGregor associate professor at Texas Woman's University, suggests that teachers and library media specialists have the enrichment and extension of students' thinking skills as a central goal of their jobs. While teachers typically encourage students to think about information as argument, library media specialists emphasize thinking about information as artifact. Cognitive apprenticeship calls for a more fluid definition of labor between teachers and library media specialists with regard to teaching thinking. A full-scale cognitive apprenticeship approach to teaching information problem solving and information literacy takes time and support to develop. Most teachers, though, can begin to implement some aspects of apprenticeship with minimal effort combined with basic cooperation and collaboration.

Some ideas to begin implementing an apprenticeship approach in the library media center include:

- Strive toward authentic tasks and contexts. Knowledge, strategies, and processes need to be taught as they pertain to specific tasks in progress, not as isolated entities. Worksheets, games, and tests seldom fit the definition of "authentic" and therefore are of questionable benefit.
- Practice modeling your own thinking (metacognition) about information problem solving and information literacy in both group and individual teaching opportunities. If trying this in front of an audience initially makes you nervous, practice alone. Pose an information problem and start talking aloud as you work to solve it. Becoming fluent and comfortable with verbalizing one's mental processes takes time and repetition. You likely will learn something about your own thinking and problem solving that surprises you.
- Divide big tasks into authentic and manageable components for students. Two important considerations here: first, not everyone goes about solving information problems in the same way, so be open to alternatives; second, not everyone works on the same timetable, so be flexible in providing students with support and guidance.
- Provide students with tools and strategies for developing their own metacognitive skills. For example, webs (or similar graphic organizers) may be useful for helping students refine information needs, planning a course of action, or visualizing the relationships among pieces of information. Double-entry note-taking in which students elaborate or reflect directly on the notes they take may help them evaluate and integrate information. Also, teaching students how to summarize or paraphrase may encourage them to go beyond directly copying information as well as serve to improve their comprehension.
- Allow time for students to learn from each other. Recognizing the social nature of learning does not automatically require the development of group projects. Instead, give students opportunities to talk to each other about their projects, both to share and to evaluate other's work. Peer conferencing may help students evaluate information, determine a course of action, or even identify information needs.

For Further Reading

Callison, Daniel. "Expanding the Evaluation Role in the Critical-Thinking Curriculum." In Assessment and the School Library Media Center, edited by Carol Collier Kuhlthau, 43-57. Englewood, CO: Libraries Unlimited, 1994.

Collins, Allen, John Seely Brown, and Susan E. Newman. "Cognitive Apprenticeship: Teaching the Crafts of Reading, Writing, and Mathematics." In Knowing, Learning, and Instruction: Essays in the Honor of Robert Glaser, edited by Lauren Resnick, 453-494. Hillsdale, NJ: Erlbaum, 1989.

Hockly, Nicky. "Modeling and Cognitive Apprenticeship in Teacher Education." English Language Teachers Journal, 54, no. 2 (2000), 118-126.

Kuhlthau, Carol Collier. Seeking Meaning: A Process Approach to Library and Information Science Service. Norwood, NJ: Ablex, 1993.

Lave, Jean, and Etienne Wenger. Situated Learning: Legitimate Peripheral Participation. Cambridge, UK: Cambridge University Press, 1991.

Mancall, Jacqueline C., Shirley L. Aaron, and Sue A. Walker. "Educating Students to Think: The Role of the School Library Media Program." School Library Media Quarterly 15, no. 1 (1986): 18-27.

McGregor, Joy. "Cognitive Processes and the Use of Information: A Qualitative Study of Higher-Order Thinking Skills Used in the Research Process by Students in a Gifted Program." School Library Media Annual 11 (1993): 124-133.

Pitts, Judy. "The 1993-1994 AASL/Highsmith Research Award Study: Mental Models of Information." School Library Media Annual 13 (1995): 187-200.

Sheingold, Karen. "Keeping Children's Knowledge Alive through Inquiry." School Library Media Quarterly 15, no. 2 (1987): 80-85.

Steuck, Kurt and Todd M. Miller. "Evaluation of an Authentic Learning Environment for Teaching Scientific Inquiry Skills." ERIC Document ED409217, 1997.

Tilley, Carol L., and Daniel Callison. "The Cognitive Apprenticeship Model and Adolescent Information Use." In Instructional Interventions for Information Use: Proceedings of Treasure Mountain VI, edited by Daniel Callison, Joy H. McGregor, and Ruth V. Small, 393-409. San Jose, CA: Hi Willow Research and Publishing, 1998.

Vygotsky, Lev. Mind in Society: The Development of Higher Psychological Processes. Cambridge, MA: Harvard University Press, 1978.

Key Words
Collaboration

"Collaboration" is one of the most frequently used words in the 1998 revision of the national guidelines for school library media programs, Information Power: Building Partnerships for Learning. The term appears over sixty times-three dozen times alone in Chapter 4 "Learning and Teaching." Therefore, collaboration must be an important instructional term.

Collaboration is defined very briefly, however, as "working with others" and a key theme in building partnerships for learning. While a three-word definition serves as a beginning, there must be more to the meaning of "collaboration." The authors of Information Power do provide several word associations to extend the context for instructional actions: collaborative inquiry, collaborative planning, and collaborative teaching.

While examples and guiding principles are clearly given in the new national guidelines, collaboration will be given a wider context here in order to extend its meaning and application. Collaboration should involve a broad range of partnerships, from various planning levels and across the many groups who comprise the learning community.

At its entry or beginning levels, collaboration may represent at least a willingness to converse and discuss possibilities. At its highest and most effective levels, collaboration should involve interactive trust and support. Collaboration at the interactive levels means that while members of instructional teams may have some specific unique tasks, they serve equally in many areas of teaching and evaluation, and share in leadership roles with their common shared focus always being on improving the learning environment.

At the highest levels of collaboration, there are few distinctive differences between the school library media specialist and the classroom teacher. Both possess and practice curriculum development-information literacy integrated across the curriculum-and both possess extensive knowledge of information and literature resources. Collaboration does not take place because one educator needs the other's expertise as much as the collaboration is built on shared goals and knowledge that are enriched by a partnership for instruction. Yes, there will be different levels of expertise in some subject content areas. But in terms of instructional strategies and implementation of information literacy, all collaborative educators carry a similar focus and skill base to the tasks of teaching students to be effective users of information.

Collaboration can be related to various roles of the instructional library media specialist. Cooperation with the local public library, for example, may involve routine borrowing and returning of materials and the courtesy to inform public library staff of upcoming student projects that will demand use of local materials beyond those of the school library media center. Collaboration levels, however, imply joint long-range collection development between school and public librarians and coordination of efforts to be certain that the institutions reduce duplication of titles whenever possible and together provide local students a wider array of materials. Levels of planning and extent of interactivity best define collaboration in the instructional arena as well.

Meeting in the Middle

Barbara Herrin, AASL Director of Professional Development, brought teams of teachers, administrators, and library media specialists together to develop teaching plans based on collaborative efforts. The gathering in the nation's center, Kansas City, was sponsored by the U. S. Department of Education and titled "Meeting in the Middle." Geographically and pedagogically, educators found consensus and enthusiasm through collaboration.

The lesson planning at Kansas City was based on the premise that collaboration is essential for successful integration of information skills instruction into curriculum subject areas. But collaboration is often used to mean cooperation or coordinating, and there's a big difference among the three terms. Reporting on lessons learned from the project, Robert Grover of Emporia State University edited and AASL summary with the following definitions in 1996:

Cooperation is informal, with no commonly defined goals or planning effort: information is shared as needed. A library media specialist and teacher in a cooperative relationship work loosely together. Each works independently, but they come together briefly for mutual benefit.

[Coordination] suggests a more formal working relationship and the understanding of missions. Some planning is required and more communication channels are established. In a library media program, the teacher and the library media specialist make arrangements to plan and teach a lesson or unit, and a closer relationship is [therefore] required.

Collaboration is a much more prolonged and interdependent [interactive] effort. Collaboration [results from the following shifts in actions on the part of all involved]:
- Competing to building consensus.
- Working alone to including others from different fields and backgrounds.
- Thinking mostly about activities and programs to thinking about larger results and strategies.
- Focusing on short-term accomplishments to requiring long-term results.

In summary, collaboration is a working relationship over a relatively long period of time. Collaboration requires shared goals, derived during the partnership. Roles are carefully defined, and more comprehensive planning is required. Communication is conducted at many levels to ensure success. Leadership, resources, risk, control, and results are shared. As a result of collaboration, there is substantial benefit [in that] more is accomplished jointly than could have been individually.

Cognitive Styles Influence Collaboration

Several years prior to the "Meeting in the Middle" conference, Paula Montgomery presented her dissertation findings to the AASL Research Forum. Her work established the thesis that differences in cognitive styles of library media specialists are related to perceived levels of cooperation (between teachers and library media specialists) when planning and teaching library media skills.

Montgomery's study was based on, among other factors, a working definition of the difference between cognitive styles of field-independent and field-dependent individuals. Field-independent individuals perceive objects as separate from the field, abstract figures from a field, impose personal structures on the environment, state self-defined goals, work alone, choose to deal with abstract subject matter, are socially detached and rely on their own values, and are self-reinforcing.

In contrast, field-dependent people tend to rely on the field for clues about an object, prefer a structure provided by the environment, experience the environment more globally, are interested in people, use externally defined goals, receive reinforcement from others, focus on socially-oriented subject matter, and prefer to work with others.

Montgomery's data showed that library media specialists who perceived their roles based on field-dependent characteristics were more social in their cooperative actions and tended to engage more frequently in collaborative efforts with classroom teachers. Such social interaction may tend to take place more frequently by those who are field-dependent regardless of commonly raised limitations of time, resources, and classroom teacher resistance to team efforts.

Montgomery relates her findings to a comprehensive research literature that tends to support the notion that socially interactive people-those who are willing and enjoy sharing ideas and responsibilities including the leadership role when necessary-are likely to be more successful in collaborative efforts.

Certainly subject content expertise for the school library media specialist should include a wide knowledge of resources and literature, an understanding of curriculum development, and use and application of technologies for instruction and information access. However, moving school library media professionals into a more interactive mode is dependent on development and practice of effective social skills. Beyond "love of books," those entering the profession should possess the ability to diagnose information and instructional needs and comprehend the value of helping people. For some, such skills are natural, but the opportunity to practice and enhance such skills should be given a more formal place in pre-service education and professional development.

Schedules and Collaboration

Julie I. Tallman and Jean Donham van Deusen reported in 1994 that in elementary school settings, a flexible schedule allowed for a substantial amount of additional time to be devoted to team planning and such resulted in over twice the number of collaborative teaching efforts between classroom teachers and school library media specialists.

They found that library media specialists managing flexible schedules were able to devote substantially more time to the collaborative planning process than those on fixed schedules. That extensive increase in time spent allowed the library media specialist to contribute considerably more to the planning process, and provide access to more resources. In situations where there was a combination of flexible time management available to the library media specialist and team planning was

frequent, the number of collaborative units was five times that of situations in which the library media specialist had to meet a fixed schedule of meeting classes without any level of cooperation with classroom teachers.

Strategies for Successful Collaboration

Linda Lachance Wolcott, from the Department of Instructional Systems Technology at Utah State University, has outlined several useful strategies leading to a greater chance that instructional partnerships will be successful.

- Together, reflect on teaching and learning. Let the commonalities of experience and mutual concerns serve as the basis for an ongoing dialogue. Occasions for such conversations can be formal or informal. The key is to establish such engagement as high priority.
- Approach the planning process from the teachers' perspective. Planning, as prescribed by numerous instructional design models, is not the same as the manner in which most teachers plan. While design models may be prescriptive and will likely provide some framework for some discussions, they are not representative of how many classroom teachers approach planning. Written lesson plans will help to clarify communication and planning based on prescribed instructional stages may help to monitor progress, but be flexible and ready to engage in planning on a recursive basis. Engage successful teachers at their point of reference and elaborate from there.
- Accommodate various types and styles of planning. Planning is often a solitary activity for teachers and many may not welcome or be familiar with partnership approaches. Identify both comprehensive and incremental planners among the faculty and approach them accordingly.
- Provide the leadership. Library media specialists need to be active in raising

expectations about their involvement in the development of curriculum and instruction. Don't wait to be asked. Assume partnership and look for opportunities to plan with teachers. Openly model the process whenever possible.

Diagnosis for Collaboration

Phil Turner, dean of library and information science at North Texas University, has been a long-time leader in systematic development of instructional planning. His research and models have served as a key basis for methods to help teachers teach. Recently, Turner has proposed communication techniques that help teachers of information literacy (classroom teachers and instructional library media specialists) identify areas for close collaboration efforts.

Turner recognizes that some team efforts may be met at lower levels of cooperation. Initial levels may include exchanging lesson plan ideas or collecting possible instructional materials for examination by teachers. Such cooperative efforts may or may not lead to more extensive collaboration.

Information to diagnose instructional needs can be gathered through brief written surveys (managed easily today with e-mail), interviews (with student assistants possibly helping to make contact with all teachers), or brainstorm sessions as a portion of regular teacher meetings. Results given in Turner's experience include the following areas in need of in-depth collaboration:

- In-service training in use of the newest multimedia;
- Workshops on the latest instructional techniques, especially model teaching and critical thinking; and
- Workshops on motivational strategies.

For Further Reading

American Association of School Librarians. Collaboration. Edited by Robert Grover. Lessons Learned Series. Chicago: ALA, Fall 1996.

American Association of School Librarians and Association for Educational Communications and Technology. Information Power: Building Partnerships for Learning. Chicago: ALA, 1998.

Asper, Vicki. "Ladders of Collaboration." Library Talk 15, no. 2 (2002), 10-12.

Callison, Daniel. "Evaluator and Educator: The School Library Media Specialist." Tech Trends 32, no. 5 (October 1987): 24-29.

Callison, Daniel. "Restructuring Pre-Service Education." In School Library Media Annual 1995, edited by Betty J. Morris, 100-112. Englewood, CO: Libraries Unlimited, 1995.

Cook, Lynne, and Marilyn Penovich Friend. Interactions: Collaboration Skills for School Professionals. Addison-Wesley, 1999.

Grover, Robert, et al. "Planning and Assessing Learning Across the Curriculum." Knowledge Quest 28, no. 1 (1999), 10-16.

Grover, Robert and Janet Carabell. "Diagnosing Information Needs in a School Library Media Center." School Library Media Activities Monthly 11, no. 5 (1995), 32-36, 48.

Harvey, Carol. "It Takes Two: Collaboration, Media, and You!" School Library Media Activities Monthly 18, no. 7 (2002), 27.

Montgomery, Paula. "Cognitive Style and the Level of Cooperation between the Library Media Specialist and Classroom Teacher." School Library Media Quarterly 19, no. 3 (1991): 185-191.

Tallman, Julie I., and Jean Donham van Deusen. "Collaborative Unit Planning-Schedule, Time, and Participants: Part Three." School Library Media Quarterly 23, no. 1 (1994): 33-37.

Turner, Philip M. Helping Teachers Teach: A School Library Media Specialist's Role. Englewood, CO: Libraries Unlimited, 1993.

Turner, Philip M. "What Help Do Teachers Want, and What Will They Do to Get It?" School Library Media Quarterly 24, no. 4 (1996): 208-212.

Wolcott, Linda Lachance. "Understanding How Teachers Plan: Strategies for Successful Instructional Partnerships." School Library Media Quarterly 22, no. 3 (1994): 161-165.

Key Words
Concept Mapping

Concept mapping is a heuristic device that has proven to be useful in helping learners to visualize the relationships or connections between and among ideas. Of equal usefulness, mapping of term relationships helps to demonstrate to the teacher what the learner is constructing or assimilating. Thus, while mapping is a method to organize the pieces taken from a new piece of information (article, chapter, lecture, etc.), it presents a visual for the learner and teacher to further discuss the merits of what the learner believes to be the new knowledge gained.

Advance (in advance of lesson or project, not necessarily of high complexity) organizers, help to visualize a connection of ideas offered during brainstorming. This visual map may be constructed by the individual as he or she considers all possible associated terms, events, people, or questions related to a central theme. Such becomes a visual web and can represent shared ideas when produced by a small group or the entire class. Concept mapping serves the purpose of helping the learner clarify what he or she has just read or heard. Concept mapping involves a short-hand or visual sketching of key terms around a central idea or concept.

The learner visually maps what he or she believes best represents the message from the new information and may place such within a visual context of what he or she already

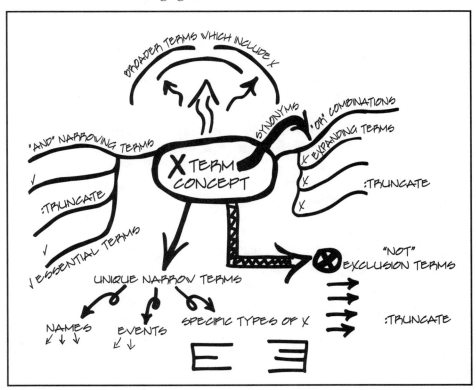

knew about the concept. The concept map thus will focus on those points and relationships that are most important and can most likely be retained for a longer duration than other items.

Because the process involves choices and a focus, along with some organization of terms, the learner becomes engaged with the content derived from the reading or lecture. Through the process, the learner gains some ownership. As a result, the student creates visual notes that are more meaningful than attempts to compose lengthy notes. Focus, selection, relationships, and visual representation strengthen the image for the new mental model.

How to Begin a Map

Select a term that represents the main idea of a reading, book, or lecture. Often this comes from the title. On a clean sheet of paper, preferably without lines, write the term in the center. Quickly, without pausing, write terms and phrases that come from the new information and are associated with the central concept. Do so without analyzing, judging, or editing.

Concept mapping, at this point, may seem very much like brainstorming. Both mapping and brainstorming may be used to encourage the generation of new material, different interpretations, and viewpoints. Mapping, however, relies less on intentionally random input. Brainstorming attempts to encourage highly divergent lateral thinking. Mapping, by the structure that will be imposed, provides opportunity for convergent thinking, i.e., fitting ideas together.

After the sheet is filled or there are no more terms that come to mind to write on the sheet, examine the content and begin to link or organize the terms. Group similar terms together through similar colors or connecting with lines or arrows. Those items that seem to be very clearly associated may be rewritten as lists and others may look more like a series of branches that grow from the central concept.

Advantages of this mapping process include:

- Helps to define the central idea and give it perspective.
- Helps visualize relationships and subsets.
- Key or essential concepts emerge and become trigger words or phrases that are remembered, and later will serve to help the learner recall the minor or detailed points that emerge from these major ones.
- Gaps will become apparent, which will lead to new questions that will guide what to read next or lead to new questions.

Map Applications

The concept mapping process can be applied to document or information summaries as described. Some advocate the use of this method as a more focused, yet free-thinking, way to take notes during a lecture. Others find the process more powerful when used to summarize the lecture content over several class sessions in a way to find areas of emphasis and association.

Some writing instructors encourage concept mapping as a way to generate an essay layout or plan. Following background reading and discussion of possible essay themes, students may find they move much faster into the construction of the essay if they spread the pieces out through terms and phrases on one sheet. Allowing the ideas to get out and on paper will open the opportunity to grouping and clustering as a foundation to the working outline for the essay.

Carol Gordon at Boston University has documented how a small group of high school students that were engaged in concept mapping of terms related to their term paper topic were more likely to focus on their project in an efficient manner than those students who did not construct such maps. The most dramatic differences seem to show during electronic searching for information, as those who had practiced concept mapping:

- spent less time searching;
- searched for fewer and shorter sessions;
- preferred subject heading to key word searching; and
- performed a larger percentage of depth searches rather than breadth or exploratory searches.

Mind Mapping Strengthens Note-Taking

Mind mapping is a process developed by Tony Buzan. As president of the Brain Foundation, Buzan has authored books and produced tapes on his method for corporate training. Much of his research has concerned how students take notes in lectures. Buzan has concluded there are four major disadvantages of standard notes.

- They obscure the key words. Important ideas are conveyed by key words. In standard notes, these key words often appear on different pages, obscured by the mass of less important words. These factors prevent the brain from making appropriate associations between the key concepts.

- They make it difficult to remember. Monotonous (usually single color) notes are visually boring. As such, they will be forgotten. Standard notes often take the form of endless similar-looking lists.

- They waste time. Standard note-taking systems waste time at all stages:
  - by encouraging unnecessary noting,
  - by requiring the reading of unnecessary notes,
  - by requiring the re-reading of unnecessary notes, and
  - by requiring the searching for key words.

- They fail to stimulate the brain creatively. By its very nature, the linear presentation of standard notes prevents the brain from making associations, thus counteracting creativity and memory. In addition, especially when faced with list-style notes, the brain constantly has the sense that it has "come to the end" or "finished." This false sense of completion, according to Buzan, acts almost like a mental narcotic, slowing and stifling our thought process.

Buzan proposes "radiant thinking" or a more organic process for note-taking. The emphasis is on letting the key elements grow and connect and to be highlighted in some manner either through color, size, position, or relation to other items. Unlike the structured organizers with boxes and circles positioned for students to fill in for purposes of comparing terms or listing terms without discriminating as to which are more valuable than others, Buzan calls for conscious effort to give visual weight to that which is most important. This is

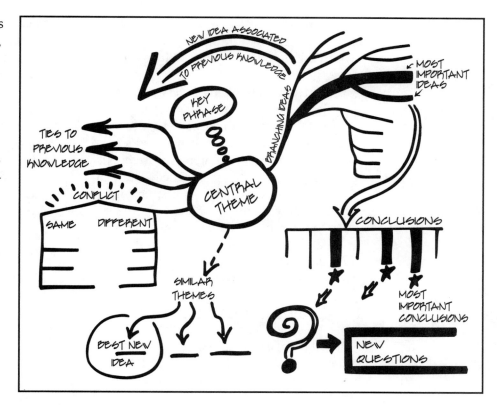

necessary in order to pull to the forefront that which must be remembered and assimilated.

Some of Buzan's guiding principles for mind mapping are:

- Use emphasis-highlight or bold the most important.
- Use one central image.
- Use several colors per central image.
- Use dimension in images.
- Use variations of size of printing and line.
- Make associations with arrows and other connectors.
- Print all words.
- Print key words on lines.
- Make central or more important lines thicker and organic.
- Develop a personal style with signals you immediately understand for skimming at quick revisits-the more personal, the better the information retention.

Research Conclusions on Note-Taking

Note-taking and mapping are forms of summarizing. Both are attempts to capture in a few words that which is most important to retain. Studies have shown these conclusions concerning the value of note-taking and mapping:

- Verbatim note-taking is very likely the least effective way to take notes.
- Notes should be considered a work in progress and should be revisited so that the most important items are highlighted and other items discarded. Through review and revision of notes, new information patterns are found.
- Notes that have been redrawn and visually mapped will serve to help the student concentrate on the essential items for tests and essays.

For Further Reading

Buzan, Tony. The Mind Map Book. New York: Plume, 1993. (Mind Map is a registered trademark of the Buzan Organization, 1990.)

Gordon, Carol A. "The Effects of Concept Mapping on the Searching Behavior of Tenth Grade Students." School Library Media Research 3 (2000). http://www.ala.org/aasl/SLMR/mapping/mapping.main.html.

Gordon, Carol A. Information Literacy in Action. European Council of International Schools. Suffolk: Catt Educational, 2000.

Gordon, Carol A. "Methods for Measuring the Influence of Concept Mapping on Student Information Literacy." In Proceedings of Treasure Mountain Ten and the ELMS Academy, 2002.

Hyerle, David. Visual Tools for Constructing Knowledge. Alexandria: Association for Supervision and Curriculum Development, 1996.

Kinchin, Ian M. "If Concept Mapping is so Helpful to Learning Biology, Why Aren't We All Doing It?" International Journal of Science Education 23, no. 12 (2001), 1257-69.

Marzano, Robert J., Debra J. Pickering, and Jane E. Pollock. Classroom Instruction that Works: Research-Based Strategies for Increasing Student Achievement. Alexandria, VA: Association for Supervision and Curriculum Development, 2001.

Key Words

Constructivism

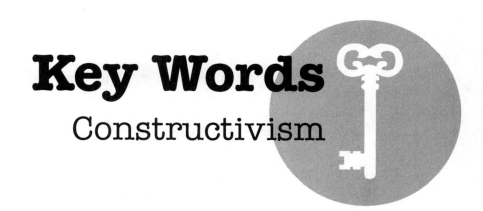

Constructivism is a theory about the nature of reality and how people understand the world around them. Constructivists argue that humans make or construct their own knowledge based on their experiences. Ideas are not held to be absolutely true or false. Instead, ideas explain and predict in ways that are better or worse than other ideas. Therefore, some ideas are more viable than others. Solutions to problems will depend on the situation and the factors involved.

The extent to which the learner moves forward in considering ideas and the potential for solutions to problems depends on what experiences the learner brings to the situation. The potential for learning is relative to the factors involved in the given learning environment and those experiences and expectations brought to the situation by both the learner and the teacher.

Constructivist teaching is one form of "discovery learning," a term generally applied to any learning environment in which the student is actively involved in problem solving.

The dominant learning theory for the past century has been behaviorism, or the learner as a passive reactor to the teacher. Learning, especially simple skills, can be effectively and efficiently managed through control of stimulus and response. The learner is more or less helpless and whatever he or she learns and does is a function of his or her environment.

Behaviorist theory fails to explain more complex learning behaviors and does not provide a meaningful framework for how learners can and should be engaged in development of higher-order thinking skills. Constructivism seems to offer a theory to move in the direction of learning processes that center on such skills as analysis, synthesis, and evaluation.

Although defined in several different ways, according to Tom Duffy and Don Cunningham of Indiana University, the definition of constructivism usually includes:

- learning is an active process of constructing rather than acquiring knowledge; and
- instruction is a process of supporting that construction rather than simply communicating knowledge.

John Zahorik, professor of curriculum at the University of Wisconsin, writes "Knowledge is constructed by humans. Knowledge is not a set of facts, concepts, or laws waiting to be discovered. It is not something that exists independent of a knower. Humans create or construct knowledge as they attempt to bring meaning to their experience. Everything we know, we have made." (p. 2)

Constructivist Assumptions about Learning

David Jonassen, a leader in instructional design from Pennsylvania State University, has offered several assumptions about learning that are made by those who accept constructivist theory. The process of making meaning, as theorist Jerome Bruner has called it, assumes that we learn from experiencing phenomena (objects, activities, events, interactions, conversations, processes); interpreting those experiences based on what we already know; reasoning about them; and reflecting on the experiences and the reasoning in order to assimilate those experiences as new knowledge.

1. Constructivists believe that knowledge is constructed, not transmitted.

Knowledge construction, according to Jonassen, is a natural process. Whenever humans encounter something they do not know but need to understand, their natural inclination is to attempt to reconcile it with what they already know in order to determine what it means. Constructivists believe that knowledge-the richness and fullness of knowing-cannot be simply transmitted by the teacher to the student. Portions of lower levels of knowledge can be transmitted so that the student becomes aware or comprehends meaning as conveyed by the perspective given from the teacher.

Transmission of knowledge is never pure. The teacher's personal context is always different from that of the student. Because of those differences, the fullness of what the teacher knows cannot be transmitted completely to the student. The greater the understanding between teacher and learner of their experiences and abilities, the higher the potential for more meaning that can be communicated. The initiative to learn more about what the student brings to the learning situation is clearly the responsibility of the teacher. In the constructivist approach, creating situations so that the teacher can gain more understanding of the learner is essential. Although there are some common behaviors among most students, the teacher resists application of general assumptions to the student group and finds ways to explore for individuality. Construction of knowledge, therefore, will differ with each learner, and will certainly differ for that of the teacher.

2. Knowledge construction results from activity, so knowledge is embedded in activity.

Facts about a state capital will have more meaning when the student has been guided to apply his or her personal knowledge to that gained from a well-planned and implemented field trip to the capital. Construction of meaning, however, will vary from student to student and from student to teacher as each has a different experience level on which to build or construct knowledge.

3. Knowledge is anchored in and indexed by the context in which the learning activity occurs.

Knowledge construction consists of not only the ideas, but also the context in which the ideas or content is experienced. Rules and formulas are more likely to make sense when applied to concrete problems or real situations with which the learner identifies.

4. Meaning is in the mind of the knower.

Knowledge is not an external item or object to be gained, but an internal process that evolves based on the interactions with the outside world and the interactions within the mind.

5. Therefore, there are multiple perspectives on the world.

Jonassen and other constructivists conclude, since no two people can possibly have the same set of experiences and perceptions of those experiences, each of us constructs our own knowledge, which in turn affects the perceptions of the experiences that we have and those we share.

6. Meaning making is prompted by a problem, question, confusion, disagreement, or dissonance (a need or desire to know) and so involves personal ownership of that problem.

The degree to which the learner constructs meaning based on higher-level skills depends on the challenge and extent of authentic problem solving in which the learner is engaged for his or her ability level.

Problem solving at its lowest level may simply be an exercise and the learner is guided through the process. Practice or drill situations may be useful, but do not take the student into higher-order learning. A good teacher should be able to model problem-solving methods, and such examples are essential to help the student create a vision for his or her own approach.

At higher levels of problem solving, emphasis is on student application of the skills to address a problem-to "enter the game and play," rather than simply to practice the shots.

Common sense suggests that all experience levels, including basic skills practice, are needed. But the constructivist would argue that too much of what we call teaching today never goes beyond that basic level, and we must move into more authentic situations without fear for student or teacher as both are able to learn new problem-solving techniques.

7. Knowledge building requires articulation, expression, or representation of what is learned (meaning that is constructed).

In order to evaluate or reflect on learning, it must have some tangible form. The learner demonstrates or shows what he has learned through speaking, writing, or doing some observable act. Those who support management of learning through objectives would argue that learning is not present until there is an observable, measurable change in the direction defined by the teacher.

More important to the constructivist, however, is the notion that processes of learning, as well as the products of learning, should be gathered in concrete form for the learner to analyze. Reflection by the student on what he or she has learned is more powerful than the reflections of the teacher. More powerful, in that self-reflection can result in internal as well as external change in terms of attitude and motivation. Ability often is limited by the lack of motivation.

Self-reflection is also a key element for sustained or transfer knowledge. It can serve to help the student retain a greater portion of the new knowledge and also may serve to help the student approach new problems on his or her own without teacher guidance.

8. Meaning also may be shared with others, so meaning making also can result from conversation.

Learning is formed when the individual is placed in the position to communicate to others. Learning is reformed by the feedback from or conversations with others.

9. Meaning making and thinking are distrib-uted throughout our tools, culture, and community.

Meaning, as it develops over time and experiences, influences what groups with which we communicate, what discourse in which we engage, what tools for communication we use, and in what culture and community we decide to mix. In most cases, this is a process of finding a position that is comfortable and low in conflict. In other cases, the learner finds that in order to continue to learn, he must challenge himself and place himself in contexts that are alien.

10. Not all meaning is created equally.

Although a common constructive approach to engage the learner is through brainstorming exercises in order to help identify what the learner brings to the situation, not all learning is equal. Even though brainstorming often includes no value judgments in order to encourage all to share in the process, ultimately learners will progress at different paces from different places and reach different levels. Evaluation, therefore, must include measurement of these differences for each individual. Learning becomes not just reaching a goal or an objective set for all, but also the degree and level of individual growth and development.

The Constructivist Teacher

The Association for Supervision and Curriculum Development (ASCD) has endorsed the following actions that define the constructivist teacher:

1. Constructivist teachers encourage and accept student autonomy and initiative.

The student is encouraged to be a "problem finder" as well as to be a "problem solver." Looking beyond the given task, to find questions of personal interest that are challenging and relevant to the subject content, is a student behavior valued by the constructivist teacher. Robert Marzano states for ASCD, "Robbing students of the opportunity to discern for themselves importance from trivia can evoke the conditions of a well-managed classroom at the expense of a transformation-seeking classroom."

2. Constructivist teachers use raw data and primary sources, along with manipulative, interactive, and physical materials.

Collaboration between the classroom teacher and the resourceful instructional library media specialist is very important in this area. Use of multiple resources, access to primary and local documents, and activities that require the student to gather information through survey, observation, or tests take learning to authentic levels.

3. When framing tasks, constructivist teachers use cognitive terminology such as "classify," "analyze," "predict," and "create."

Marzano writes for ASCD, "The teacher who asks students to select a story's main idea from a list of four possibilities on a multiple-choice test is presenting to the students a very different task than the teacher who asks students to analyze the relationships among three of the story's characters or predict how the story might have proceeded had certain events in the story not occurred." School library media specialists who promote a heavy dose of computerized reading tests, accelerated or not, should ask if such exercises are really of merit. Do we allow such routine, computerized book reviews to take the place of more valuable, but more time-consuming, book discussion groups and reading circles?

4. Constructivist teachers allow student responses to drive lessons, shift instructional strategies, and alter content.

This does not mean that students and their opinions alone determine course content. It means that their questions, and what they do and do not bring to a learning situation, influence the content. Effective teachers use this analysis of their students to identify quickly "a series of teaching moments" and move to address them so that student interest can be captured. Successful interactions on these moments can result in further motivation of students and deeper content understanding based on a common teacher-student learning experience. The teachable moment does not take place when just "the student is ready to listen," but occurs when teacher and student are both ready to listen.

5. Constructivist teachers inquire about students' understandings of concepts before sharing their own understandings of those concepts.

Too many inquiry opportunities are cut short by teachers who deliver what students tend to accept as the dominate perspective or accepted conclusion. The opportunity to freely explore then becomes a challenge to authority and difficult to initiate by most students. An open opportunity to question and consider alternatives should come very early in the lesson. Frequently teachers do have the "correct answer" and often neither teacher nor student want to "waste time." The constructivist teacher looks for opportunities to open inquiry from the beginning, and recognizes that not all engagements are meant for full inquiry. In some cases, delivery of basic facts or background become necessary in order to establish the groundwork for more meaningful inquiry to follow.

6. Constructivist teachers encourage students to engage in dialogue with the teacher and with one another.

Learning involves not only reading and doing, but talking about what is read, heard, and performed, or is in the process of being performed. Talking provides a shared communication so the teacher may respond, and peers also may provide suggestions. Most of all, the student "hears" himself/herself and often learns by thinking through what needs to be said as well as thinking about the responses received. Conversations initiate nearly all demonstrations of learning performance. These conversations must take place in an active manner in all learning environments, including libraries once thought to be quiet reading coves only.

7. Constructivist teachers encourage student inquiry by asking thoughtful, open-ended questions and encouraging students to ask questions of each other.

As models for inquiry learning, teachers must be ready and willing to accept questions from students that lead to open discussion and often no quick solution, if there is a solution at all. Instructional specialists who also manage information centers need to model reference services that are beyond "ready reference" and help students move beyond just the facts found in almanacs, encyclopedias, and handbooks.

Practice exercises that place students in the position of seeking answers through the use of library media center materials should be developed by students asking each other questions rather than a school library media specialists who alone always formulates a "trivia treasure hunt." Turn a set of encyclopedias over to a group of fifth graders and instead of dictating questions, ask them to raise all the questions they can come up with that can be answered in the set. Ask that they also list as many questions as they can that probably can't be answered, and why. After one hour of such activity, the instructional library media specialist will have a full agenda to discuss with students concerning what they should and should not expect from the encyclopedia and where to go for leads to other information resources.

8. Constructivist teachers seek elaboration of students' initial responses.

Initial responses should be verbalized and shared. They serve as the foundation from which we can raise additional questions. Elaboration means reading more, listening more, exploring multiple resources, and building on and revising the original response. Learning is a constant process of elaboration. Typical library-based research projects are more effective when the student can demonstrate growth from the initial idea to more complex findings that are shared with the class.

9. Constructivist teachers engage students in experiences that might engender contradictions to their initial hypotheses and then encourage discussion.

The student is challenged to defend or reject his or her personally-held assumption or belief. This is an important process as the student searches and examines information for facts or evidence to accept or reject. Too often,

the student determines relevance or authority based on content that agrees with his or her original assumptions. Acceptance of opinions or statements that come from individuals the student accepts as an authority on all matters, regardless of expertise, is a sign of novice information selection. A constant pattern of accepting or rejecting evidence based on assumed authority without question usually will lead to false conclusions. Such action certainly will not broaden the student's perspective on the issues.

10. Constructivist teachers allow wait time after posing questions.

Allow students to think about the posed situation. In some cases, teachers have given a great deal of thought to asking the question and have probably asked the questions dozens of times before. Suddenly students are supposed to be ready with a response within a few seconds. Complex questions may need some small group discussion time so that students may talk among themselves and test out possibilities before presenting responses before the entire class.

11. Constructivist teachers provide time for students to construct relationships and create metaphors.

Metaphor and analogies allow for creative expressions and lead to new visions on an event or problem. Marzano writes, "Metaphors help people to understand complex issues in a holistic way and to tinker mentally with the parts of the whole to determine whether the metaphor works." Formulation of potential cause-and-effect and other patterns or relationships require several attempts. Any of these require time for the student to write or state possibilities and to place them side by side for comparison and analysis.

12. Constructivist teachers nurture students' natural curiosity through frequent use of a learning cycle model.

The first step is discovery through the interaction with purposefully selected materials in order to raise questions and hypotheses. In the second step, the teacher facilitates concept introduction aimed to focus the students' questions and to give meaning to new terms or vocabulary needed for the lesson. The third step is concept application, a series of attempts to apply solutions to the problem or test the hypothesis. From this third step, new questions arise and the cycle begins again.

Student discovery at its first level may be guided by the teacher so that basic concepts often are gained from what the teacher already holds and understands. Higher-level discovery is not uncovering what the teacher "has hidden" or knows and hopes the student will find out for himself. Ultimately, discovery at its highest levels will involve new learning for both the student and the teacher as collaborative learners.

For Further Reading

Brooks, Jacqueline Grennon. In Search of Understanding: The Case for Constructivist Classrooms. Alexandria, VA: Association for Supervision and Curriculum Development, 1999.

Bruner, Jerome. Acts of Meaning. Cambridge: Harvard University Press, 1990.

Bruner, Jerome. "The Act of Discovery." Harvard Educational Review 31 (1961): 21-31.

Colburn, Alan. Constructivism and Science Teaching. Bloomington, IN: Phi Delta Kappa Educational Foundation, 1998.

DeVries, Rheta. Developing Constructivist Early Childhood Curriculum: Practical Principles and Activities. New York: Teachers College Press, 2002.

Duffy, Thomas M., and Donald J. Cunningham. "Constructivism: Implications for the Design and Delivery of Instruction." In Handbook of Research for Educational Communications and Technology, edited by David H. Jonassen, 170-198. New York: Simon & Schuster, Macmillan Library Reference, 1996.

Green, Susan K. and Margaret E. Gredler. "A Review and Analysis of Constructivism for School-Based Practice." School Psychology Review 31, no. 1 (2002), 53-71.

Jonassen, David H., Kyle L. Peck, and Brent G. Wilson. Learning with Technology: A Constructivist Perspective. Upper Saddle River, NJ: Merrill, 1999.

Marlowe, Bruce A., and Marilyn L. Page. Creating and Sustaining the Constructivist Classroom. Corwin Press, 1998.

Marzano, Robert J. A Different Kind of Classroom: Teaching with Dimensions of Learning. Alexandria, VA: Association for Supervison and Curriculum Development, 1992.

Tomlinson, Carol Ann. The Differentiated Classroom: Responding to the Needs of All Learners. Association for Supervision & Curriculum Development, 1999.

Zahorik, John A. Constructivist Teaching. Bloomington, IN: Phi Delta Kappa Educational Foundation, 1995.

Key Words
Content Literacy

Anthony and Ula Manzo introduce their ideas for interactive teaching strategies and content area literacy with the assumption that acquisition of large amounts of information is less important than the acquisition of effective strategies for accessing and evaluating information. The movement to place learners in educational environments that challenge students to analyze, reflect, communicate, create, and critically review has parallel strands in reading education and information literacy education.

Content literacy seems to imply integration of strategies and experiences in at least two ways. First, effective strategies for reading, writing, speaking, listening, and thinking are more likely to develop more naturally and easily when tasks are integrated than when isolated. Second, meaning is enriched across subjects and experiences when content literacy embraces discourse and text from several distinct disciplines.

Ultimately, the student who is content literate has a heightened awareness and use of the organization and structure of distinct texts in diverse fields of study and knows how to read in strategic ways to obtain important knowledge from them. The strategic reader knows, for example, the value of doing an initial preview of a research article in order to become familiar with the focus, scope, general findings, length, and level of complexity of the materials before doing a more thorough analytical reading of the text.

A less informed and strategic reader, on the contrary, is apt to approach diverse texts in a generic fashion, covering the assigned pages once, with limited comprehension and recall, perhaps highlighting but failing to consolidate the information in some form of manageable and meaningful study notes. This underprepared reader is also likely to cling to a single inefficient and ineffective method of chapter previewing or reviewing, regardless of the actual assignment demands or subject area.

Furthermore, students who lack content literacy skills frequently exhibit passive and dependent learner behavior, avoid assigned readings, and rely upon peer tutors or class lectures to access needed information from texts. Students who lack content literacy skills or who are in educational environments that fail to provide such opportunities across the curriculum may gain general reading proficiency but will not function well on tasks required of the independent information-literate learner.

Manzo and Manzo contend that the basic approach to content literacy is based on interactive methods for teaching reading-thinking concurrently with subject area knowledge and application. Regular use of such methods from grade to grade and across subject areas supports student development of independent reading-learning strategies and empowers even relatively poor readers to read and learn from materials that they otherwise would find difficult.

Content Literacy Expertise

Reading comprehension is enhanced greatly, according to those who support content literacy, when students strive to obtain the expert level strategies. These techniques also serve the student striving for more meaningful levels of information literacy. Expertise is refined by analyzing purpose, questioning content and experiences brought to the text or new information, and reflecting on what is found in order to assimilate new information for new understanding. This is illustrated by Manzo and Manzo in three phases and one of the thinking strategy sets practiced by proficient readers:

- Before reading, expert readers activate schema and set a purpose for reading. This involves:
  - looking for organizing concepts
  - recalling related information, experiences, attitudes, and feelings
  - deciding how easy or difficult the reading selection is likely to be
  - setting a purpose for reading
  - trying to develop a personal interest
- During silent reading, readers continuously monitor comprehension and use fix-up strategies as needed. Doing this involves:
  - translating ideas into own words, and ideas to personal experience
  - trying to identify main ideas, and stop and question when this is unclear
  - noting important details
  - rereading whenever necessary for clarification
  - consolidating ideas into meaningful groups
  - noticing unfamiliar vocabulary
  - forming mental pictures
  - evaluating the author's purpose, motive, or authority when appropriate
  - inventing study strategies as needed
  - managing time to sustain concentration
- Following reading, expert readers check basic comprehension, build schema, and decide on relevant applications of the new information. Elements of this process include:
  - checking basic comprehension by reciting or recall, "What did I learn?"
  - organizing information into chunks of manageable size, "How can I remember it?"
  - deciding what is important, "How much should I understand of this?"
  - evaluating new information in terms of previous knowledge and experience, "Does this make sense?"
  - developing study strategies according to class demands or personal purposes, "What should I do to remember this?"
  - reviewing material periodically, "How much do I remember now?"

Thematic Approach to Content Literacy

Marian Tonjes, Ray Wolpow, and Miles Zintz, a research/teaching team from Washington and New Mexico, have promoted integrated content literacy for years. Their approach to reading and use of new information for making meaning, reflecting, and remembering is based on this philosophy:

- Strive for integrating knowledge-blurring borders between subjects, rising above our individual content area ruts, and bringing a fresh perspective to learning.
- Reading, thinking, writing, and studying are not separate subjects or entities but flow across the entire curriculum.
- Support cooperative teaching and learning and allow for freedom of choice when feasible.
- Everyone has the potential for creativity, but for many it has been downplayed in early years. To flourish it must be encouraged and practiced often.
- Create a nonthreatening, stimulating classroom environment in which students feel free to risk, experiment, and make mistakes without ridicule.
- Believe in the innate dignity and worth of every student, no matter what the student's background, culture, or ability.

- The process, or keys to opening avenues of learning, is as important or even more so than the product or knowledge gained. When we feel comfortable with how and when to perform the process, we will be more apt to continue learning on our own, and then the knowledge gained will be more personally meaningful.
- Teach through modeling and guided practice of what you preach and use exemplars when possible. To best teach information literacy, practice and converse about information literate habits of your own.
- Because we organize, store, and retrieve information by categorizing data into patterns, we should make it a common practice to construct a cognitive map of our learning.
- Teaching is not just telling, nor is it an easy task if performed properly. Teaching takes continuous effort, study, and willingness to try the unknown-a combination of curiosity and a caring heart.

Thematic approaches to reading and information research projects may create the most options leading to integration of content literacy across the curriculum. Montgomery has reminded library media specialists and other teachers that they must be sensitive to the students and what they may bring to the thematic literature approach. The approach assumes that the student can easily comprehend general information when reading; most prevalent is the ability to generalize. The student must be adept at and probably enjoy examining bits of information, rearranging those information bits, and drawing general conclusions about the information. The student's experience base or prior knowledge is extremely important, according to Montgomery, and the student must be able to advance in practice of skills to summarize and analyze both the concrete examples and the more abstract ideas provided in a variety of texts.

Advantages of the thematic approach to techniques and strategies in practice of content literacy include the opportunity to introduce different literary forms that are centered on the same idea so that students can compare and contrast the presentation of the same theme. Montgomery also suggests that thematic approaches naturally promote instruction across curriculum areas. Thinking, speaking, listening, reading, and writing may be incorporated into a meaningful context. Such may increase the chance that the content of the work becomes key to the motivation for reading and students increasingly may feel, as the varied projects are initiated and they return to the original text, more emotion and personal involvement. Options across the curriculum in the thematic approach create opportunities for self-identification.

A Content Literacy Cross-Curriculum Sample

Content literacy exercises may involve reading and selection of relevant information from different disciplines. Meaning may be found through narrative, graphs, tables, charts, or illustrations depending on the subject content and the manner in which data, opinion, or emotions are best displayed for that subject. Information may be displayed differently by literature genre as well and students extract meaning from poetry, diaries, and dramatic scripts, along with novels and short stories.

A basic approach to constructing a content literacy experience may be similar to the following content literature web or outline proposed by Tonjes, Wolpow, and Zintz:

Central piece of literature and (theme):
Island of the Blue Dolphins (Survival)

Related student activities to engage content literacy might include:

- Literature-Compare and contrast to Swiss Family Robinson.
- Geography-Describe a good choice for the location of this island.
- Music-Compose or select music that would serve to set the theme or mood for different chapters.
- Health-What would be the most healthy diet possible on the island?

- Science-Chart and classify the wildlife likely on the island.
- Social Studies-Who are the Aleuts and what are their customs?
- Mathematics-What are the dimensions for a typical shelter, and what would be a sketch for a basic plan?
- History-Explore the history of how wild dogs eventually became pets.

For Further Reading

Atwell, Nancie. In the Middle: New Understandings about Writing, Reading, and Learning. 2nd ed. Portsmouth, NH: Boynton/Cook, 1998.

Brown, Jean E., and Elaine C. Stephens. Handbook of Content Literacy Strategies: 75 Practical Reading and Writing Ideas. Christopher-Gordon, 1999.

Fountas, Irene C. and Gay Su Pinnell. Guiding Readers and Writers, Grades 3-6: Teaching Comprehension, Genre, and Content Literacy. Westport, CT: Heinemann, 2001.

Manzo, Anthony V., and Ula C. Manzo. Content Area Literacy: Interactive Teaching for Active Learning. Upper Saddle River, NJ: Merrill, 1997.

McEneaney, John E. "Learning on the Web: A Content Literacy Perspective." ERIC Document ED443098, 2000.

Montgomery, Paula Kay. Approaches to Literature through Theme. Phoenix: Oryx, 1992.

Stephens, Elaine C. and Jean E. Brown. A Handbook of Content Literacy Strategies: 75 Practical Reading and Writing Ideas. Norwood, MA: Christopher-Gordon Publishers, 2000.

Key Words
Cooperative Learning

Cooperative learning refers to instructional situations in which students work together in small groups and receive rewards or recognition based on their group's performance. This has been the standard definition since the 1980s, with recent linkage of associated terms. Over the past decade, these concepts have been related in theory and practice to cooperative learning: activity units, group dynamics, interpersonal relationship, peer teaching, social integration, and teamwork.

Many educators who believe that they are using cooperative learning are, in fact, missing its essence. There is a critical difference between simply putting students in groups to learn and structuring cooperation among students. Cooperation is also more than a student being physically near other students, discussing material with other students, helping other students, or sharing materials among students, although each of these aspects is important in cooperative learning.

No single method for structuring the learning environment should be awarded the prize as the most effective in all situations; however, there is much to be said for the positive aspects of cooperative learning applied to library and information literacy activities. Cooperative learning receives more discussion and consideration than actual application in classroom settings. Effective teachers of library and information skills, however, will be quick to note that there is a growing awareness of the merits of cooperative learning in situations where students are to deal with multiple resources, address a variety of issues and perspectives, and present information using a variety of formats. Put simply, assignments that require multiple resources tend to result in richer processes and products from groups of individuals who share a variety of skills than from most students who face such assignments on an individual basis. Beyond the academic activity, students are placed in situations in which they must participate in effective interpersonal communication in order to be successful. The process, the product, and social skills all benefit from cooperative interactions.

Beyond Bloom

Bloom's Taxonomy of Instructional Objectives has been the predominant influence on identification of cognitive, affective, and motor skills for the past three decades. The cognitive domain is the root for the skill stages often listed for current information problem-solving activities. Knowledge, comprehension, application, analysis, synthesis, and evaluation have provided the standard pattern since the mid-1950s for a wide array of instructional objectives across all areas of the curriculum. A fourth skills set, extending from overlaps within the cognitive and affective domains, is gaining attention. The emerging interpersonal domain is foundational to the student skills that can be observed and measured in cooperative learning.
Interpersonal skills can be classified in six categories:
1. Seeking/giving information. Asking for/offering facts, opinions, or clarification from/to another individual or individuals.

2. Proposing. Putting forward a new concept, suggestion, or course of action; providing evidence of support.
3. Building and supporting. Extending, developing, enhancing another person, his or her proposal, or concepts.
4. Including. Involving another group member in a conversation, discussion, or action.
5. Disagreeing. Providing a conscious, direct declaration of difference of opinion, or criticism of another person's concepts; providing counter evidence.
6. Summarizing. Restating in a concise and clear form the important items from the content of previous discussions or considerations.

Circles of Learning

David and Roger Johnson, brothers, co-researchers and the most prolific writers on cooperative learning have identified five essential components that must be in place for "circles of learning" to be successful. These are not easy components for the teacher to implement, and even if we assume that humans are naturally social creatures, the components are not easy for students to practice. These components must be modeled, structured, and rewarded by teachers and by peers. As with other instructional approaches, cooperative learning groups may be challenged by parents who want to be certain that their child receives justified credit for excellent academic performance without being "brought down" by student group members who do not excel. These critical components are:

1. Positive interdependence. Group members must perceive that they are linked with each other so that one cannot succeed unless everyone succeeds. Students must realize that each other's achievement results from sharing resources, assisting each other's efforts, providing mutual support, and celebrating their joint success.
2. Promotive interaction. Time and reward must be provided for students to communicate. Activities should be based on

orally explaining to other students how to solve problems, discussing what information has been gathered or concepts learned, sharing gained personal knowledge with classmates, and expressing how new knowledge connects with past assumptions.
3. Individual accountability. Evaluation can be facilitated by the teacher and/or group peers, with the goal being to provide some level of individual accountability for each group member. Evaluations are shared, adjustments are made so that an individual is not allowed to "hitchhike" on the work of others.
4. Interpersonal and small-group skills. Cooperative learning provides an environment in which social skills can be demonstrated, observed, and corrected. Strategies for teaching constructive social skills must be employed along with those for teaching the academic task. Leadership, trust-building, and conflict management are taught just as purposefully and precisely as academic skills.
5. Group processing. Group members discuss how well they are achieving their goals and determine what actions are helpful to improve future cooperative efforts.

Meaningful-Use Tasks

One of the major decisions in planning for the meaningful use of knowledge (beyond memorization and reciting of facts) is whether students will work in cooperative groups. The meaningful-use tasks (decision making, investigation, experimental inquiry, problem solving, and invention) are probably completed more efficiently by a cooperative group than by an individual. Meaningful-use tasks require gathering a lot of information, and a cooperative group can naturally gather more information than an individual can. A long project can easily exhaust the energy and resources of one person, whereas the energy and resources of a properly trained and supported cooperative group can "go the distance."

When meaningful-use tasks are performed in cooperative groups, two special aspects evolve: group reward and task specialization. Group rewards based on every group member's performance increase instructional effectiveness because such rewards are likely to motivate students to do whatever is necessary to make it possible for the group to succeed. No individual can succeed unless the group succeeds.

Task specialization inherently enhances the quality of the meaningful-use tasks because it maximizes the knowledge, ability, resources, and energy available for each component of the task. Where one student might not have the knowledge necessary to complete a component of an experimental inquiry task, another would. Where one student might not have the ability to set up an experiment, or conduct a complex electronic search for information, others in the group may be able to initiate such tasks and are likely to be key instructors, teaching peers in their group.

Applications to Library Information Projects

Several strategies used by language arts teachers have direct application to increasing cooperative activities that are based on school library media center projects. The strategies outlined here are intended to help one consider greater cooperative learning during the process of library information research. Frequently, there is cooperative effort in such activities as producing a video news program, constructing a hypercard database, giving oral reports on world religions, and so forth. Students are placed in groups, territories and responsibilities are sorted out, and eventually, in most cases, a role is identified for each student to play.

Listed below are suggestions of cooperative activities that are matched to the interpersonal skill domain. Activities have been suggested that lead to observable behavior, and therefore such student actions could be included in performance criteria to be graded by teachers of information literacy.

1. Seeking/giving information. While it may be more and more common for students to be encouraged to help each other seek information, openly giving information within a structured manner that can be rewarded is not so common. In fact, conventional wisdom suggests that exercises in library information skills should lead to developing students who can search well on an independent basis and to become self-sufficient. Modern technologies applied to cooperative efforts, however, allow for students to gather evidence, classify it, reference it, and submit it to a database established for the student's group or for the entire class. Thus, "electronic note cards" are shared with everyone in the group, and gaps showing information needs are easier for the group to detect and discuss. At the very least, even without the advantages of computerized storage, members of a group should be given time and direction to describe their success and failures in information searching so that other group members can provide suggestions as well as be sensitive to such information needs for others while they browse for their own sources. Such discussions can be initiated if the group has a deadline for each member for presenting to the rest of the group all of the note cards compiled to date and describing the story or argument their evidence justifies to date.

2. Proposing. One of the most difficult tasks for students in the information search and use process is to define focus and to eventually state the hypothesis, purpose, or main message of the product. Oral sessions in which group members are expected to verbalize to other members the state of their focus and related issues that may shift that focus should be placed in the list of regular tasks, perhaps as frequently as a twenty-minute focusing session for each four-member group every third day. One specialized task may be for one member of the group to compile and

map a record of these sessions so that the group can visualize progress as well as problems.

3. Building and supporting. A student who offers his or her talent to assist others has a high-level interpersonal skill. Although students live and learn in an interactive social environment, they may not know all of the skills held by members. Each member who is strongest in grammar, spelling, argument construction, evidence linkage, editing, illustrating, or conceptualizing story lines has a talent that should be applied for the purpose of teaching other members and raising the overall ability level of group. Evidence of shared expertise may be gathered in student journals if students are encouraged to document occasions in which they felt they received special assistance from another group member.

4. Including. Seeking out hidden talents or making progress in respecting talents of an individual who is not normally accepted into group situations should be encouraged and rewarded. This skill may be the most difficult to activate-even painful for some to demonstrate-and yet may be the most intrinsically rewarding. Again, through compiling a journal in order to reflect on the investigative experience, students may be encouraged to write about situations in which their talents were valued by others who had not known of or noticed these skills before. Journals might also include entries in which the student describes observing talents of another student. It may be necessary for the teacher to interview younger student groups in order to obtain an impression of the practice of this skill.

5. Disagreeing. It is unlikely that there will be any difficulty in members of the group to disagree on something, but such conflict can be counterproductive. Disagreeing in constructive, measured ways can be managed. Learning how to make a motion, submit discussion, and

vote is a common method to settle group disagreements. Learning that there are degrees of disagreement also helps, in that many arguments become cooler once parties understand that there are also areas of agreement. While applying library information activities, learning how to identify constructively group opinions on the issues related to the academic content at hand will be necessary as well. The attention of the group should be directed toward identification of the major content issues related to their topic and demonstration of how to categorize those issues with supporting and counter evidence. Practice sessions in which they make such cases within their group obviously help to polish what the group will present to the class or some other audience.

6. Summarizing. Can each member of the group state what they learned from others during the process of constructing the project? While each member would also be expected to state or write what they knew or assumed prior to the project compared to their knowledge at the close of the project, they should also be expected to identify and summarize any changes in the impressions they hold about members of their group. In addition, academic measurement can be taken in this skill area as well. Based on the cognitive skills of analysis and synthesis, can the student extract from a group's discussion for the day the key issues, related evidence, and what needs to be done over the short term to fill information gaps? An end-of-the-week summary check, written in 100 words or less, will provide teachers a snapshot of this skill and may help teachers of library information skills identify groups that need special attention during the week ahead.

Group cooperative projects can be enhanced if students are placed in specific roles to match either their skill strengths or placed in roles for which they need to practice specific interpersonal skills in order to improve their cooperative behaviors and improve their communication. In an authoring cycle mode, for example, students can role play the tasks of managing editor, copy editor, illustrator or layout designer, reviewer, or publisher. These roles easily transfer to webmastering. In production of video programs, roles include story board consultant, script writer, producer, director, and even promoter of the final student product.

Regardless of the cooperative processes and final product, a major concept to govern such projects is that school library media centers are not only places for information, but one of several places for constructive conversations. Moving the student within an isolated and narrow environment in which he or she concentrates on only his or her content and talent alone limits the possibilities of the student gaining a wider and richer perspective of the issues, arguments, and alternatives for communication. Interpersonal skills, practiced through cooperative learning, can greatly deepen the meaning of information literacy.

For Further Reading and Viewing

Gardner, Howard. Frames of Mind: The Theory of Multiple Intelligences. New York: Basic Books, 1983.

Goleman, Daniel. Emotional Intelligence. New York: Bantam Books, 1995.

Golub, Jeffrey N. Activities for an Interactive Classroom. Urbana, IL: National Council of Teachers of English, 1994.

Heinich, Robert, Michael Molenda, and James D. Russell. Instructional Media and the New Technologies of Instruction. New York: Macmillan, 1993.

Hilke, Eileen Veronica. Cooperative Learning. Bloomington, IN: Phi Delta Kappa, 1990.

Jacobs, George and Patrick Gallo. "Reading Alone and Reading Together." Reading Online (Feb, 2002), 16-26.

Jensen, Murray, Randy Moore, and Jay Hatch. "Cooperative Group Activities for the First Week of Class: Setting the Tone with Group Web Pages." American Biology Teacher 64, no. 2 (2002), 118-120.

Johnson, David W., and Roger T. Johnson. Learning Together and Alone: Cooperative, Competitive, and Individualistic Learning. Allyn & Bacon, 1998.

Johnson, David W., Roger T. Johnson, and Edythe Johnson Holubec. The New Circles of Learning: Cooperation in the Classroom and School. Alexandria, VA: Association for Supervision and Curriculum, 1994.

Kagan, Spencer, and Celso Rodriguez. Cooperative Learning. Kagan Cooperative, 1997.

Kassner, Kirk. "Cooperative Learning Revisited: A Way to Address the Standards." Music Educators Journal 88, no. 4 (2002), 17-22.

Katz, Lilian G. "On How Children Learn Through Cooperation." Early Childhood Today 16, no. 6 (2002), 42.

Libraries Are for Conversations. 30 min. Heinemann Video Distributions, 1994. Videocassette.

Lunsford, Suzanne. "In-service Inquiry." Science Teacher 69, no. 2 (2002), 54-57.

Marzano, Robert J. A Different Kind of Classroom: Teaching with Dimensions of Learning. Alexandria, VA: Association for Supervision and Curriculum, 1992.

Napier, Rodney W., and Matti K. Gershenfeld. Making Groups Work: A Guide for Group Leaders. Boston: Houghton Mifflin, 1983.

Palladino, Lucy Jo. The Edison Trait: Saving the Spirit of Your Nonconforming Child. Times Books, 1997.

Reid, Jo-Anne, Peter Forrestal, and Jonathan Cook. Small Group Learning in the Classroom. Portsmouth, NH: Heinemann, 1989.

Short, Kathy G., and Carolyn Burke. Creating Curriculum: Teachers and Students as a Community of Learners. Portsmouth, NH: Heinemann, 1991.

Slavin, Robert E. Cooperative Learning. New York: Longman, 1983.

Key Words
Creative Thinking

John Chaffee, director of the Center for Critical Thinking and Language Learning at the City University of New York, offers two useful and contrasting definitions:
- Thinking creatively is the cognitive process we use to develop ideas that are unique, useful, and worthy of further elaboration.
- Thinking critically is the cognitive process we use to carefully examine our thinking (and the thinking of others) in order to clarify and improve our understanding.

Creative thinking will be discussed here in relation to modern instructional programs and information literacy with some comparison to critical thinking. In last month's column, emphasis was given to critical thinking and defined in terms of skills rated as extremely important by educators, employers, and policy makers.

The Artist in Each of Us

People often confuse being creative with only being artistic-skilled at art, music, poetry, creative writing, drama, or dance. Although artistic people are certainly creative, there are many ways to be creative that are not artistic. Chaffee suggests that we each consider all of the activities we enjoy doing-cooking, creating a wardrobe, raising children, playing sports, or cutting or braiding hair. Whenever you are investing your own personal ideas or putting on your own personal stamp, you are being creative.

Howard Gardner, in his examination of selected prominent creative minds, concludes that creators differ from one another not only in terms of the dominant intelligence but also in terms of breadth and combination of intelligences. Sigmund Freud and T. S. Eliot had strong scholastic abilities, reflecting linguistic and logical aspects of intelligence, and they presumably could have made contributions in many academic areas. Pablo Picasso, on the other hand, was weak in the scholastic area, while exhibiting quite strongly targeted strengths in spatial, bodily, and personal intelligence spheres. Igor Stravinsky and Mahatma Gandhi were indifferent students, but one senses that their lackluster performances arose more out of lack of interest in school than out of any fundamental intellectual flaw. Stravinsky, while weak in scholastic aspects had strengths in musical aspects. Gandhi, while weak in artistic aspects, was creative through personal and linguistic intelligences. Martha Graham had broad intellectual strengths-weak in logical-mathematical aspects, she was never fully engaged in the creative process until she encountered the world of dance.

Chaffee concludes that thinking critically enables humans to identify and accept a given problem. When humans generate alternatives for solving a problem, they are using creative thinking abilities. When they evaluate the various alternatives and select one or more to pursue, humans are thinking critically. Developing ideas for implementing solutions and alternative approaches, if necessary, involves thinking creatively. Constructing a practical plan of action and evaluating the results depends on critical thinking.

Teaching for Thinking

Good creative and critical thinking take place in a context of questioning and open inquiry that requires a certain spirit of thought manifested in certain attitudes and dispositions like being open-minded and considering points of view other than one's own. Creating a classroom or establishing the school library media center as an information laboratory, rather than teaching for specific skills, is the most difficult aspect of teaching to generate thinking. Development of such learning environments requires continual experimentation and self-monitoring.

Robert J. Swartz of the Critical and Creative Program at the University of Massachusetts summarizes a brief taxonomy for creative thinking skills:

- Fluency of thought: generating ideas in a multitude of different categories.
- Originality of thought: coming up with new ideas.
- Elaboration of thought: generating as many details as possible. (p. 107)

These skills are typically viewed as non-judgmental and therefore different from critical thinking skills, which are based on evaluative judgments and choices. These creative attributes or dispositions are basic to inventiveness. Thomas Edison explored thousands of alternatives for filament fiber before creating a workable light bulb. Hundreds of lab technicians and a competitive marketplace have served to refine Edison's invention to increase its durability and to adjust its composition to meet specific needs.

There is a danger, Swartz warns, in separating critical thinking from creative thinking, separating each into sets of skills, and then structuring lessons that involve students in using these skills piecemeal. In developing good thinking skills, students also must develop a sense of when and where they can be used most appropriately and effectively. Creative alternatives and critical selections work best in tandem.

Common Techniques to Spark Creativity

It seems that as learners grow older, there is greater need for encouraging creative thinking. Techniques which help to "grant a license to question authority" include the following:

- Fractionation: An established pattern is usually taken for granted. To create new patterns, it is necessary to separate the whole into the smallest parts possible and then reconnect the pieces in a different manner. Consider breaking apart a model of a school and creating a structure for future facilities with more ties to the community and technology; evolution of future automobiles; the common structure of a reference book in print moving to electronic format; or rewriting the United States' Constitution for 2001.
- Reversal: In the reversal method, one takes things as they are and then turns them around, inside out, upside down, back to front. Then one sees what happens. How does this painting sound? How does this song look?
- Suspended judgment: The need to be right all the time is the biggest barrier there is to new ideas. To explore new ideas, one needs to delay judgment, avoid making summary evaluation of an idea, and consider even an obviously wrong idea to see why it is wrong. This technique is necessary in brainstorming. Some group discussion leaders use "po" to respond to most ideas. Po is a linguistic tool to counteract the most powerful and limiting word in our language, "no." Po is neither yes or no, but is a wildcard and stands for nothing and everything.
- Analogy: This often involves translating a problem into an analogy and then relating similarities back to renewed consideration of the original problem.

Consider folk tales and legends as models for new stories created by students. Ask learners to compose a scenario that describes an event for a future school, or describe how one might approach homework differently if a proposed technology plan is funded. Analogies allow the creative thinker to illustrate, elaborate, and eventually sooth or excite an audience. (see keyword Analogy)

Activities to Create the Mind's Museum

The critical thinker moves through a museum to consider factual information presented. How relevant? How authoritative.? The critical thinker will tend to review and evaluate the evidence displayed. The creative thinker will see what is not displayed and raise questions that lead to new exhibit ideas. John B. Bunch of the Curry School of Education at Virginia University has collected several sets of questions related to creative and critical thinking activities that can serve to prime students for constructive field trips. (Visit "Going to the Museum" on the World Wide Web at http://curry.edschool.virginia.edu/curry/class/ Museums/ Teacher_Guide/.)

- Compare and Contrast: the ability to see similarities and differences between two or more concepts. How is this artifact like a puzzle? How is this painting like a party, a song, or a mathematical formula? In what ways are the visuals produced by Mathew Brady and Frederic Remington similar and different? And how might each, if alive today, illustrate future space exploration?

- Analysis: the ability to take apart and understand the interrelationships and structure of the whole. Name one thing that you could delete from this painting that would not alter the artist's intent. What does this object tell us about the artist's attitude toward war?

- Elaboration: the ability to expand and embellish ideas with intensive detail. Select two or more musical pieces to accompany this object. Pretend you are

a character in this painting and tell us as much as you can about your life. Describe the events of the day leading up to and following Mr. Brady taking this picture of President Lincoln and General Grant. Describe any technical problems Mr. Brady might have had in taking these photographs.

- Fluency: the ability to produce a quantity of possibilities, ideas, consequences, or products. Describe all of the feelings you derive from this object. What other formats for expression are necessary in order to represent those feelings? If you were to paint two panels that would be placed on either side of this portrait of General Washington, what would you illustrate and why?

- Originality: the ability to produce unusual, unique, or highly personal responses, ideas, or solutions. If this object could fly, where would it go? If the paintings in this gallery were viewed as a storyboard, what would be the content of a play or movie that might result? How would your interaction with the objects of this museum change if they were electronically displayed through multimedia and accessed as a "virtual museum" collection?

- Evaluation: the ability to draw conclusions by interpreting data and appraising alternatives. If you could select one object to take home with you for display in your house for a year, which would it be and why? Would your parents select the same object or something different? Why? If you could rearrange the manner in which objects are displayed here and add new displays, what changes would you make? Which items should be on permanent display, always available for people to view each day?

- Flexibility: the ability to view something in many different ways with a variety of ideas or products. If this scene was painted to depict different lighting because of time of day or weather conditions, what would differ from the original? This exhibit on the use of the first atomic bomb seems to express one viewpoint, but what other ideas, events, or opinions should be represented? This painting depicts Westward expansion for American in the 1880s. What else does it depict?

Synectics: Where Critical and Creative Mix

"Synectics" is derived from the Greek word synecticos, meaning "understanding together that which is apparently different." Synectics is a process that uses group creative processes to create new insights-a creative group energized without restrictions and results in synergy. The synectics process was first widely employed about forty years ago by groups of individuals responsible for developing new products. Think tanks thrive in this process as members often play out "what if" scenerios.

From synectics have come several techniques useful for the stimulation of creative thinking. Mary Alice Gunter, Thomas H. Estes, and Jan Schwab describe these techniques in their text Instruction: A Models Approach. The assumption is made that the human mind is not able to understand something new unless the new concept is associated with something that is already familiar to the learner.

In synectics, "metaphor" is broadly defined to include all figures of speech such as simile, personification, and oxymoron. These join together different and apparently irrelevant elements through the use of analogy. Three forms are stressed in the synectic model:

- Direct Analogy: a direct comparison between two objects, ideas, or concepts. How is a classroom like an anthill? How is math like a crowded bus? Within such questions is an implied metaphor or an analogy by metaphor. Students, with guided practice and comparison of ideas, are usually able to eventually give elaborate responses beyond the obvious.
- Personal Analogy: an invitation to students to become part of the problem to

be solved. How would you feel if you were a tree attacked by acid rain? The goal here is empathy.
- Symbolic Analogy: a compressed conflict involving descriptions that appear to be contradictory. When is silence deafening? How can love nurture and smother? When is duty both ennobling and unkind?

Detached observation and analysis are essential to solving problems, but the ability to use empathy, imagination, and feelings are equally essential, perhaps most important in presenting a proposed solution to others and gaining acceptance. The flashes of insight and creativity that come from nonrational thinking create unique and extraordinary images and solutions. The critical thinker will center on quantitative measures for precise comparisons. The creative thinker will concentrate on elaborations through qualitative measures based on case studies in order to find the contrasting perspectives. One offers concise arguments while the other offers elaborations and detail.

Gunter, Estes, and Schwab offer this outline for the steps in the Synectics Excursion to problem solving through the search for new solutions:

- Present the Problem. Select and then present to the class an interesting and challenging problem.
- Provide Expert Information. Provide the class with as much expert information as possible. (Of course, we would want to add to this step that students should seek as much expert information as possible with the guidance of the school library media specialist.)
- Question Obvious Solutions and Purge. Lead the class in an exploration of the most obvious solutions and purge those that are not feasible.
- Generate Individual Problem Statements. Have each student write a statement regarding the problem by giving his or her interpretation or focus.
- Choose One Problem Statement for Focus. The problem statements are read aloud and one is selected by the class for focus.

- Question through the Use of Analogies. Present analogies to the class stated in the form of evocative questions.
- Force Analogies to Fit the Problem. Return to the original problem and ask the students to force the analogies to fit the problem.
- Determine a Solution from New Viewpoints. Look at the problem from a new viewpoint and ask students to determine a solution.
- Evaluate. Develop a process for determining if the techniques are becoming effective, habitual, and more natural for students to employ as they face other problems.

Creating Meaning through Story and Reflection

Creative thinking also provides the narrative, the description, or the story necessary to express meaning for the emotions that compose our lives. Howard Gardner's recent study of eleven world leaders suggests that what they had in common was the fact that they arrived at a story that worked for them and, ultimately, for others as well. They told stories-in so many words-about themselves and their groups, about where they were coming from and where they were headed, about what was to be feared, struggled against, and dreamed about. They created meaning.

Gardner's study of leading creative minds tells us that individuals can differ enormously in terms of energy. What struck Gardner about his subjects was that they were each productive every day. Eliot may not have written poetry each day, but he wrote hundreds of reviews, edited major publications, and issued books on a wide range of subjects. Gandhi's literary output fills ninety volumes. Einstein worked on questions of physics until the last years of his life. Picasso may have made a thousand paintings over a five-year period, but in his own mind one or two of them were far more important than the others. Freud may have written a dozen papers a year, though he could be repetitive in these essays, and he stressed his own need to search actively for new ideas.

Each found meaning through revision and elaboration-reflection based on various perspectives imagined at different stages in their personal intellectual growth and development.

For Further Reading

Coleman, Connie, Jeff King and Mary Helen Ruth. "Developing Higher-Order Thinking Skills Through the Use of Technology." ERIC Document ED459702, 2001.

Chaffee, John. Thinking Critically. 5th ed. Boston: Houghton Mifflin, 1997.

Gardner, Howard. Creating Minds: An Anatomy of Creativity Seen through the Lives of Freud, Einstein, Picasso, Stravinsky, Eliot, Graham, and Gandhi. New York: Basic Books, 1993.

Gardner, Howard. Extraordinary Minds: Portraits of Exceptional Individuals and an Examination of Our Extraordinariness. New York: Basic Books, 1997.

Gardner, Howard. Leading Minds: An Anatomy of Leadership. New York: Basic Books, 1995.

Gartenhaus, Alan Reid. Minds in Motion: Using Museums to Expand Creative Thinking. Caddo Gap, 1997.

Gordon, William J. Synectics: The Development of Creative Capacity. New York: Harper and Row, 1961.

Gunter, Mary Alice, Thomas H. Estes, and Jan Schwab. Instruction: A Models Approach. 2nd ed. Boston: Allyn and Bacon, 1995.

Junion-Metz, Gail. "The Art of Evaluation." School Library Journal (May 1998): 57.

Starko, Alane Jordan, Jared Chrislip, and David Jernigan. Creativity in the Classroom: Schools of Curious Delight. Lawrence Erlbaum, 2000.

Swartz, Robert J. "Teaching for Thinking: A Developmental Model for the Infusion of Thinking Skills into Mainstream Instruction." In <u>Teaching Thinking Skills</u>, edited by Joan Boykoff Baron and Robert J. Sternberg, 106-126. New York: W. H. Freeman, 1987.

Key Words
Critical Literacy

Advocates of critical literacy emphasize the empowering role that literacy can and should play in reshaping the environment in which one lives and works. Through mastering the skills of critical literacy, students apply the inquiry process and knowledge gained as a means for political action. By gathering appropriate information, organizing, and defining specific objectives, literacy serves as a method to change the status quo. More than an academic exercise, critical literacy is not complete unless change is proposed, contested, debated and ultimately determined by the power of evidence and argument.

More than seeking meaning through the selection and use of information, critical literacy is the process for seeking self. The student who has reached mature levels in critical literacy will challenge, de-construct, and re-construct information in terms of arguments to justify social and political reform. Through this process, the student defines himself or herself. In authentic application, critical literacy is the strongest form of due process and judicial review in a democratic society.

Patrick Shannon, Professor of Education at Pennsylvania State University relates critical literacy to the public education setting. He writes in response to Kathleen Jongsma, column editor, in The Reading Teacher:

> Critical literacy education pushes the definition of literacy beyond the traditional decoding or encoding of words in order to reproduce the meaning of text and society until it becomes a means for understanding one's own history and culture and their connections for fostering an activism toward equal participation for all [in] the decisions that effect and control our lives. This type of education has a distinguished history in America. When led by teachers who demonstrate the power of critical literacy, students of all ages have learned to read and write both the word and the world as perceived through multiple-symbol systems.
>
> For example,...intermediate grade children in Chicago at the turn of the [last] century were able to read why technological change in industry always causes new social problems. In McDonald County around 1920, children were able to read about typhoid problems of local farmers and to write a plan for a community health cooperative. During the 1920s and the 1930s, at the Work Peoples College in Duluth, Minnesota, workers were reading about the advantages of organized labor and writing a union of the Farmer and Labor Parties. Throughout the southeastern United States in the late 1950s and early 1960s, disenfranchised blacks were learning to read the Constitution in Citizenship Schools and were writing an end to apartheid in America. (p. 518)

Critical literacy has a rich history in development of education settings. From John Dewey to Lev Vygotsky to Paulo Freire, progressive education has been based on providing students not merely with functional skills, but with the conceptual tools necessary to critique and engage society along with its inequalities and injustices. Horace Mann, known as the Father of the Common School and free public education, challenged his students to, "Be ashamed to die until you have won some victory for humanity."

Other proponents of critical education agree that this approach can begin only by breaking down traditional teacher/student roles, and focusing on talking, reading, and writing learners' histories and experiences, background knowledge, and world views. To do so, teachers have to become learners of students' cultures and teachers have to reposition students as teachers of their own knowledge. Such learning environments depend on teacher leadership and effective learning exercises based on feedback, guidance, and scaffolding to provide increased responsibilities for all learners. Through critical literacy, the teacher of the information literacy processes will guide the student to make sense of self in today's society.

Discussion and Debate

As with other literacy applications, critical literacy can be found in poems, essays, dramatic narratives, documentaries, and even autobiographical or biographical texts. Such often rely on emotion as well as reason and may be tied to historical contexts that reflect some social or political injustice. The most common form of critical literacy, however, rests in informal and formal formats for discussion and debate. Formulations of proposals for change, based on evidence and argument, require the student who practices critical literacy to gain expertise in selection of evidence to support a targeted cause. Critical literacy asks the student to consider the politics of the authors or evidence read and to decide on which side of the debate the student is as he or she communicates or presents responses.

Critical debate asks students to make the strongest possible case for a position that is diametrically opposed to their own. It's the kind of exercise, according to Stephen Brookfield and Stephen Preskill, that may help them strengthen their own argument by anticipating the claims of opponents, or it may cause them to look at the issue in a new light and bring about a shift in their point of view.

Here's how critical debate works:

1. Find a contentious issue on which opinion is divided among participants. Frame the issue as a debate motion.
2. Propose the motion to participants. Ask people to volunteer by a show of hands to work on a team that is preparing arguments to support a motion or one that is preparing arguments to oppose it.
3. Announce that everyone will be assigned to the team opposite the one for which they volunteered.
4. Conduct the debate. Each team chooses one person to present the arguments. After initial presentations, the teams reconvene to draft rebuttal arguments. A different person presents these.
5. Debrief the debate. Discuss with participants their experience of this exercise. Focus on how it felt to argue against positions to which you were committed. What new ways of thinking about the issue were opened? Did participants come to new understandings? Did they change their positions on this issue at all?
6. Ask participants to write a follow-up reflection paper on the debate. Students should address the following questions:

What assumptions about the issue were clarified or confirmed for you by the debate?

Which of these assumptions surprised you during the debate?

Were you made aware of assumptions that you didn't know you held?

How could you check the validity of these assumptions?

What sources of evidence would you consult? In what ways, if any, were your existing assumptions challenged or changed by the debate?

Formal Debate

Formal debate follows three styles.

Lincoln-Douglas Debate. This style is modeled after the famous debates between Abraham Lincoln and Stephen Douglas. This type of debate is also known as "values" debate. Debaters focus on competing values inherent in the proposition and are expected to argue on the basis of the underlying principles of their side of the resolution or motion. For example, an affirmative argues that "Government ought to provide for the needs of the poor," and would make a broad philosophical case for this government obligation. The affirmative would not have to prove the effectiveness of any particular government program. In general, Lincoln-Douglas Debate centers on the ideas, values, and spirit governing the political, economic, social, moral, and aesthetic positions held.

Parliamentary Debate. This style is modeled on the British House of Parliament. One team represents the Government and the other the Loyal Opposition. A Speaker of the House officiates and judges. A specific resolution is offered with a definition of terms. Usually two debaters represent each opposing side and debate may center on specific practical approaches to solve a problem or change the status quo. Audience members are free to interject opinions, insights, questions, or even provide a good heckle.

Policy Debate. The focus is on a specific plan to meet a resolution. Such may be statements as "Government should provide public works jobs for the unemployed" or "Government should ban all tobacco advertising." Each term of the resolution must be defined, a series of needs to justify change must be introduced and defended, and a plan to resolve the issues must be detailed. While the affirmative must provide evidence for such change, the negative side will seek to show that there is no real need for change and that the affirmative team's plan may actually cause more problems than it solves. Specific time limitations are placed on each speaker. Often time is set aside for face-to-face cross examination. Usually a single judge determines the winner with feedback provided on value of the arguments presented and the merits of the evidence offered.

Debaters mature in their abilities to apply argument to social action and find that the true information search is not so much for a gathering of impressions and descriptions, but for hard evidence that supports or rejects specific arguments and plans. Further, they learn the use and meaning of the following terms:

Ad hominem: attacking your opponent personally rather than his/her argument; fallacious argumentation.

Argument: a conclusion supported by proof that may consist of analysis, reasoning, and evidence.

Assertion: an unsupported statement or claim.

Burden of Proof: the obligation to prove the need for change and establish a prima facie case.

Causal Link: analysis that is based on cause and effect; the affirmative must identify and remove the causes of the supposed problem without creating a new set of significant problems.

Counter Plan: accepting there is a need for change, the affirmative's plan may be rejected in favor of a different approach to solve the problem which may not be as costly or disruptive to the status quo.

Operational Definition: beyond what is offered in the dictionary or expert opinion, but defining terms as they specifically relate to how things operate or will be managed in a proposed plan for change.

Prima facie Case: a case that would convince the average reasonable and prudent person that a proposal for change is warranted.

Refutation and Rebuttal: counter argument to a proposal, opinion, evidence, or need for change based on reasoning and a line of argument with its own set of evidence to justify its merits.

Jurisprudential Inquiry

Bruce Joyce and Marsha Weil outline jurisprudential inquiry as a key instructional method for learning to think about social policy.

Participants should be versed in three competency areas:

Familiarity with the values of the American creed. Understanding of principles embedded in the Constitution and the Declaration of Independence. These principles form the values framework or basis for judging public issues and making legal decisions.

Skills for clarifying and resolving issues. This will involve coming to terms with value differences, clarification of facts, and definition of key terms of any proposal or resolution.

Knowledge of contemporary political and public issues. Although a broad understanding of the history, nature, and scope of contemporary issues is important, in the jurisprudential inquiry model, students explore issues in terms of a specific legal case rather than in terms of a general study of values.

Introduction of this critical education method often rests with the use of Socratic dialogue. In the Socratic style, the teacher asks the students to take a position on an issue or to make a value judgment, and then he or she challenges the assumptions underlying the stand by exposing its implications. For example, according to Joyce and Weil, if a student argues for freedom in some situation, the teacher will test whether the argument is meant to apply to all situations. The function of the teacher is to probe the students' positions by questioning the relevance, consistency, specificity, and clarity of the students' ideas until they become clearer. Practice in this method should help both teacher and student to become skillful in the following:

- pose worthwhile questions;
- evaluate the adequacy of an argument;
- recognize facts, inferences, and opinions and use each appropriately;
- deal with quandaries and ill-formed problems that have no pat or unique solutions;
- give and receive criticism constructively;
- agree or disagree in degrees (based on common definition of terms, students may find they do not totally disagree but will find portions of issues on which there is common ground);

- extend a line of thought beyond the range of first impressions; and
- articulate a complex position without adding to its complexity, but begin to understand a wider range of opinions.

For Further Reading and Viewing

Brookfield, Stephen D., and Stephen Preskill. Discussion as a Way of Teaching. San Francisco: Jossey-Bass, 1999.

Jongsma, Kathleen Stumpf. "Questions and Answers: Critical Literacy." The Reading Teacher 44, no. 7 (1991): 518-519.

Joyce, Bruce, and Marsha Weil. Models of Teaching. 6th ed. Boston: Allyn and Bacon, 2000.

Know It All: Saying It Another Way. Program 5. 20 min. Great Plains National in collaboration with the American Association of School Librarians, 1997. Videocassette.

Langford, Linda. "Critical Literacy: A Building Block Towards the Information Literate School Community." Teacher Librarian 28:5 (2001); 18-21.

Lewis, Barbara A., Pamela Espeland, and Caryn Pernu. The Kid's Guide to social Action: How to Solve the social problems You Choose - And Turn Creative Thinking into Positive Action. Free Spirit Publishing, 1998.

Shannon, Patrick. The Struggle to Continue: Progressive Reading Instruction in the United States. Portsmouth, NH: Heinemann, 1990.

Sheingold, Karen. "Keeping Children's Knowledge Alive through Inquiry." School Library Media Quarterly 15, no. 2 (1987): 80-85.

Shor, Ira, and Caroline Pari, eds. Critical Literacy in Action. Portsmouth, NH: Heinemann. 1999.

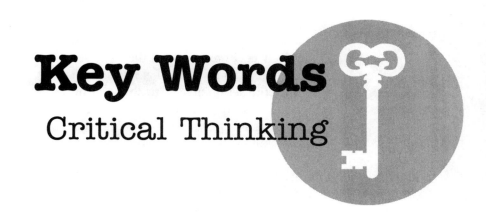

Key Words
Critical Thinking

John Chaffee, director of the Center for Critical Thinking and Language Learning at the City University of New York offers two useful and contrasting definitions.

- Thinking critically is the cognitive process we use to carefully examine our thinking (and the thinking of others) in order to clarify and improve our understanding.
- Thinking creatively is the cognitive process we use to develop ideas that are unique, useful, and worthy of further elaboration.

Related term descriptors from the Educational Resource Information Clearinghouse (ERIC) serve to provide additional notions for contrasting critical and creative thinking.

- Both critical and creative thinking are subsets of cognitive processes.
- Critical thinking is associated with the more narrow terms convergent thinking and evaluative thinking, while creative thinking is associated with the more narrow terms divergent thinking and productive thinking. Critical thinkers seek the best or most reasonable solution from available options to solving a problem. Creative thinkers raise alternatives that lead to new or unique solutions.
- Critical thinking is related to citizenship education, consciousness raising, controversial issues, decision making, heuristics, inferences, problem solving, and logic. Creative thinking is related to concept formation, discovery processes, heuristics, imagination, improvisation, intuition, inventions, problem solving, and visualization. Thus, there are areas of overlap as well as contrast.

Chaffee concludes that thinking critically enables humans to identify and accept the problem. When humans generate alternatives for solving the problem, they are using creative thinking abilities. When they evaluate the various alternatives and select one or more to pursue, humans are thinking critically. Developing ideas for implementing solutions and alternative approaches, if necessary, involves thinking creatively. Constructing a practical plan of action and evaluating the results depends on thinking critically.

Critical thinking will be discussed here in relation to modern instructional programs and information literacy with some comparison to creative thinking. In a future column, the outline and discussion will be inverted and highlight creative thinking with some comparison to critical thinking.

Goals in the Critical Thinking Curriculum

Robert H. Ennis, whose work for the University of Illinois Critical Thinking Project during the 1980s provided much of the initial critical skill identification, argued that critical thinking is influenced by five key ideas: practical, reflective, reasonable, belief, and action. These ideas combine, according to Ennis, for the working definition: critical thinking is reasonable reflective thinking that is focused on deciding what to believe or do. Influenced by Bloom's taxonomy of educational objectives, Ennis outlined the basic student dispositions and abilities that must be evident in the critical thinking curriculum. He did not equate such student actions with higher order thinking skills, but was satisfied to state that these skills represent the more cognitive material to be acquired in school than banks of memorized and soon-to-be-forgotten facts. Selected items from the Ennis curriculum, many relevant to information literacy skills, are as follows.

Student Dispositions
- Seek a clear statement of the thesis or question.
- Try to be well informed.
- Use and mention credible sources.
- Take into account the total situation.
- Look for alternatives and seriously consider other points of view.
- Withhold judgment when the evidence and reasons are insufficient.
- Take a position and change a position when the evidence and reasons are sufficient to do so.
- Seek as much precision as the subject permits.
- Deal in an orderly manner with the parts of a complex whole.
- Be sensitive to the feelings, level of knowledge, and degree of sophistication of others.

Student Abilities
- Focus on a question: formulate a question and criteria for judging possible answers.
- Analyze arguments: identify arguments, stated and unstated reasons, and handle irrelevance.
- Ask and answer questions for clarification and/or to challenge: Why? What is your main point? Please give me a specific example. What difference would that make? What are the facts? Would you say more about that?
- Judge the credibility of a source including expertise, lack of conflict of interest,

agreement among sources, and reputation.
- Judge observation reports or witnesses, testing with corroboration.
- Make correct application of either deductive or inductive logic.
- Infer conclusions and hypotheses.
- Determine an action to address the problem.
- Interact with others through presentation of a position, oral or written.

A Newer List of Critical Thinking Skills

In 1995, the National Center for Education Statistics published a study in which the perceptions of selected undergraduate instructors and managers that hire college graduates at entry level professional positions were compared. The following is a list of student abilities highly rated by those from either academic or employer ranks and provides more precision of student actions than the Ennis guide from the previous decade.

More refined description of critical thinking skills can lead to more precise measurement of student performance. While this list describes critical thinking abilities of college graduates, lower level scope and sequence skills can be extracted and reworded for K-12 levels. Academic faculty, business managers, and policy makers agreed it is extremely important that the college student be able to demonstrate adequate performance of each of the following critical thinking skills.

Student Disposition
- Be curious and inquire about how and why things work.
- Persevere and persist at a complex task willingly.
- Be flexible and creative in seeking solutions.
- Be inclined to arrive at a reasonable decision in situations where there is more than one plausible solution.
- Exhibit honesty in facing up to prejudices, biases, or tendency to consider a problem solely from one's personal

viewpoint.

- Find ways to collaborate with others to reach consensus on a problem or issue.

Interpretation Skills

- Formulate categories, distinctions, or frameworks to organize information in order to aid comprehension.
- Translate information from one medium to another to aid comprehension without altering the intended meaning.
- Make comparisons: note similarities and differences between or among informational items.
- Classify and group data, findings, and opinions on the basis of attributes of a given criterion.
- Detect the use of leading questions that are biased towards eliciting a preferred response.
- Recognize the use of misleading language, such as language that exaggerates or downplays the importance of an issue or neutralizes a controversial topic.
- Detect instances where irrelevant topics or considerations are brought into an argument that divert attention from the original issue.
- Recognize the use of slanted definitions or comparisons that express a bias for or against a position.
- Recognize confusing, vague, or ambiguous language that requires clarification to increase comprehension.
- Ask relevant and penetrating questions to clarify facts, concepts, and relationships.
- Identify and seek additional resources, such as resources in print, that can help clarify communication.
- Develop analogies and other forms of comparisons to clarify meaning.
- Provide an example that helps explain something or removes a troublesome ambiguity.

Analysis Skills

- Identify the ideas presented and assess the interests, attitudes, or views con-

tained in those ideas.
- Identify the background information provided to explain reasons that support a conclusion.
- Identify the unstated assumptions of an argument.

Evaluation Skills

- Assess the importance of an argument and determine if it merits attention.
- Evaluate the credibility, accuracy, and reliability of sources of information.
- Determine if an argument rests on false, biased, or doubtful assumptions.
- Assess statistical information used as evidence to support an argument.

Inference Skills

- Determine what is the most significant aspect of a problem or issue that needs to be addressed, prior to collecting evidence.
- Formulate a plan for locating information to aid in determining if a given opinion is more or less reasonable than a competing opinion.
- Combine disparate pieces of information whose connection is not obvious, but when combined offers insight into a problem or issue.
- Judge what background information would be useful to have when attempting to develop a persuasive argument in support of one's opinion.
- Determine if one has sufficient evidence to form a conclusion.
- Seek the opinion of others in identifying and considering alternatives.
- Seek evidence to confirm or disconfirm alternatives.
- Assess the risks and benefits of each alternative in deciding between them.
- After evaluating the alternatives generated, develop, when appropriate, a new alternative that combines the best qualities and avoids the disadvantages of previous alternatives.
- Use multiple strategies in solving problems including means-ends analysis, working backward, analogies, brain

storming, and trial and error.

- Seek various independent sources of evidence, rather than a single source of evidence to provide support for a conclusion.
- Note uniformities or regularities in a given set of facts, and construct a generalization that would apply to these and similar instances.
- Employ graphs, diagrams, hierarchical trees, matrices, and models as solution aids.

Presenting Arguments Skills

- Present supporting reasons and evidence for conclusion(s) that address the concerns of the audience.
- Negotiate fairly and persuasively.
- Present an argument succinctly so as to convey the critical point of an issue.
- Cite relevant evidence and experiences to support a position.
- Formulate accurately and consider alternative positions and opposing points of view, noting and evaluating evidence and key assumptions on both sides.

A skill rated as important by most evaluators, but for which there was considerable disagreement as to the degree of importance (faculty ranked it higher than employers) is:

- Illustrate control concepts with significant examples and show how these concepts and examples apply in real situations.

Reflection Skills

- Apply the skills of self-analysis and evaluation to arguments and confirm and/or correct reasoning and conclusions.
- Make revisions in arguments and findings when self-examination reveals inadequacies.

Application across the Curriculum

Critical thinking skills are best employed in learning situations if:

- they are modeled by teachers, especially teachers of information literacy;
- they are not taught as a separate or special set of skills, but taught as normal expectations integrated in many areas of the curriculum;
- they are practiced and refined based on shared reflections among learners and teachers;
- they are linked to real life situations as well as the demands of academic exercises.

While each of the critical thinking skills given above may seem impossible for the average student and far beyond the usual performance of most students in the K-12 setting, these statements should serve as descriptions of behaviors for which all learners and teachers strive. Application of these statements can result in evaluation stages or rubric measures of student performance. Consideration for these levels and discussion between learner and teacher about the meaning of such performance can set the stage for increasing the proportion of college students and other secondary school graduates who are knowledgeable in the practice of critical thinking.

Mel Levine, founder of All Kinds of Minds Institute, has outlines his steps for parents to engage their children in critical thinking and problem-solving (p. 204-205). His philosophy is based on the assumption that children at all levels can engage in these steps with some guidance.

Step 1 - Enumerating the Facts. Report the facts as known, objectively.

Step 2 - Uncovering the Author's or Creator's Point of View. Help the child determine the point of view, intention, or motive behind the information.

Step 3 - Establish What the Child Thinks. What are the child's feelings and thoughts and how do they relate to the facts? What are the options to explore

Step 4 - Searching for Errors and Exaggerations. Evaluate, with the child, to find false claims and misleading information.

Step 5 - Get Outside Help. Search for and explore lots of related outside resources. Get guidance from the local public or school librarian and explore information resources.

Step 6 - Weighing the Evidence. Pull together what you have found and consider the additional facts and opinions as objectively as possible.

Step 7 - Communicating. Once an evaluation of the evidence is concluded, the child should be guided in framing and stating a conclusion. The child will learn from communicating what new information they have learned and identifying new questions or areas they have discovered which will need more information to address.

For Further Reading

Browne, M. Neil, and Stuart M. Keeley. Asking the Right Questions: A Guide to Critical Thinking. 3rd ed. Englewood Cliffs, NJ: Prentice Hall, 1990.

Callison, Daniel. "Expanding the Evaluation Role in the Critical-Thinking Curriculum." In Assessment and the School Library Media Center, edited by Carol Collier Kuhlthau, 43-57. Englewood, CO: Libraries Unlimited, 1994.

Chaffee, John. Thinking Critically. 5th ed. Boston: Houghton Mifflin, 1997.

Elder, Linda and Richard Paul. "Critical Thinking: Distinguishing Between Inferences and Assumptions." Journal of Developmental Education 25, no. 3 (2002), 34-36.

Embry, Robyn L. "Critical Thinking Skills in the High School Science Classroom." Hoosier Science Teacher 26, no. 3 (2001), 77-82.

Ennis, Robert H. "A Taxonomy of Critical Thinking Dispositions and Abilities." In Teaching Thinking Skills, edited by Joan Boykoff Baron and Robert J. Sternberg, 9-29. New York: W. H. Freeman, 1987.

Gunter, Mary Alice, Thomas H. Estes, and Jan Schwab. Instruction: A Models Approach. 2nd ed. Boston: Allyn and Bacon, 1995.

Levine, Mel. A Mind at a Time. New York: Simon & Schuster. 2002.

National Center for Education Statistics. National Assessment of College Student Learning: Identifying College Graduates' Essential Skills in Writing, Speech and Listening, and Critical Thinking. Washington, DC: U. S. Government Printing Office and Superintendent of Documents, 1995. U. S. Department of Education NCES 95-001.

"Teaching Critical Thinking Online." Journal of Instructional Psychology 29, no. 2 (2002), 53-77.

Key Words
Current Resources

Current: occurring in or belonging to present time; most recent.

Why is this an instructional term? Key to becoming effective users of information is learning the importance and relevancy associated with the age of information that has been located, the copyright date of a book or other resource, deciphering the true date of a Web site, and determining data that is the most recent. Although teachers of information literacy have always alluded to the currency of information as one strand in the test for authoritativeness, practice in the selection and use of truly current data has become an extremely critical Information Age skill.

School library media collections that have become out-of-date because of lack of weeding and limited expenditures for new materials confound the selection of current and timely information. Often such situations only reinforce the false notion that the only place to find really up-to-date information is through the computer or television. While we know that such electronic telecommunication systems are essential for tracking current events, they also may be misleading at times. Teachers of information literacy strive to establish current collections so that situations can be created in which students learn the value and context of currentness as well as gain a level of trust that current information can be found through the school library media center.

Aging Collections

If you have served as a school library media specialist for over twenty years in the same building and have been the only one to evaluate the age of your collection, there is a good chance that nearly half of your nonfiction collection is out-of-date and of little use in the modern school information laboratory. Extensive weeding, which includes collaboration with selected teachers who want and know updated resources, is essential.

New library media specialists entering a school that has been under the direction of the same person for twenty or more years will likely find that a top priority for the first years of their service will be to manage a systematic revitalization of the collection through extensive weeding. Numbers gathered for the 1994 survey for the U. S. National Commission on Libraries and Information Science illustrate some aspects of the currency problem:

- One in four elementary school library media centers did not have a world atlas with a copyright of 1990 or more recent.
- In most elementary and secondary school library media centers, the average copyright date for books dealing with health and medicine was between 1970 and 1984.
- In over a third of the elementary and secondary school library media centers, the average copyright date of books dealing with space exploration was between 1960 and 1979.
- A third of the school library media specialists rated their collections in science and technology as "poor," 44% rated their collections in health as "poor," 70% rated their collections in mathematics as "poor," and nearly 75% rated their collections in careers, foreign language, and English as a second language as "poor."

In several individual state surveys taken between 1990 and 1995, the following trends seemed to be consistent from one area of the country to another:

- One third of the nonfiction books on the shelves of school library media centers are over twenty-five years old.
- One fourth of the audiovisual materials (mostly filmstrips) held in school library media centers are over twenty-five years old.
- Over half of the nonfiction books in areas of physics, chemistry, geography, and travel are over twenty-five years old.
- Over a third of the nonfiction books in areas of civil rights, space travel, health education, evolution, and astronomy are over twenty-five years of age.

What's Missing in the Old Stuff

Think of the descriptions of the Soviet Union or China in filmstrips, atlases, and travel books published twenty-five to thirty years ago. Go to your school library media center shelves in areas such as world politics, space exploration, medicine, or environmental studies, and the following content will be missing in most of the books that deal in general with any of those topic areas:

- very little pressure on South Africa to end apartheid.
- modern Strategic Arms Limitation Talks have yet to begin.
- scientists have yet to build the first continuous-wave laser.
- scientists have yet to discover the process by which RNA code is transcribed on DNA.
- first black hole discovery has not been made.
- first transplants of human eye, heart, or lung have yet to be performed.
- first pocket calculator has yet to be sold.

Common content provided in older publications includes:

- you have to be twenty-one to vote.
- asbestos and DDT are recommended as safe.
- benefits of smoking cigarettes include healthy relaxation.

The concern may not be so much that children accept the information as fact in such dated books, but we must be concerned by the poor impression made on those students who want the most recent and relevant information possible. For those students who can discriminate in the selection of current information, their out-of-date school library media center is an embarrassment. For those who can't or don't discriminate, an out-of-date collection is fundamentally harmful to their intellectual health.

Students May Lack Age Sensitivity

Issues related to student misuse of dated resources were flagged over fifteen years ago in studies conducted by Jacqueline C. Mancall and M. Carl Drott at Drexel University. They examined papers written by several thousand secondary school students and concluded that students show relatively little sensitivity to age when selecting materials. They observed that insensitivity to age seems to be more of an oversight rather than a conscious selection strategy. The average age of the books cited by students who wrote science reports was several years older than the average age of books used for papers in the humanities or social sciences.

One conclusion from the researchers was that some use of the older material may reflect what was available in the collections to which students had access. Clearly, even then, school collections in the science areas were dated. It may be that science book collections do not receive the attention necessary to update them because few library media specialists have expertise in the science field. Most have academic backgrounds in humanities and history. However, it may also be the case that science book collections age with little attention given to evaluation because science teachers and students will tend to seek out current information from periodicals, newspapers, journals, and, most recently, the Internet.

The Mancall and Drott study raised the need for more education of students so that they might demonstrate a greater sensitivity to the age of materials used. Practice in critical analysis of the content of science texts and trade books may help students form a sense for demanding and expecting the most timely information possible. Practice in critical comparison of the content found in various formats and in similar publications that are revised and updated over time would help to acquaint the student with how dramatically the world has changed, especially in such areas as environmental studies, health education, medical practices, and applied technologies.

Take Any Old Science Book

A reasonable recommendation often made in cases where there has been extensive weeding of the science collection is that these books be removed from the educational environment. They should be destroyed and classrooms should not become salvage yards for old science texts and trade books. That recommendation probably has a great deal of merit, though it may be difficult for some to even consider that out-of-date books be eliminated completely and removed from the reach of teachers and students.

However, there may be some useful instructional exercises that can be developed from a few selected titles held from those weeded. Consider students role playing as "textbook publishers" or "editors for revised editions" and determining what needs to be done to bring a given "oldie" up-to-date. Depending on the content of the old titles and the subject matter of the class, students might be directed to work in teams to revise a chapter or a set of titles. With access to a wide range of current science materials, including an array of science journals and open use of the Internet, their task might include at least some of the following challenges:

- Terms. Identify and define important key terms essential to this field of science today, but not included in the vocabulary when the older text was written.
- Illustrations. Correct illustrations not only for content, but also experiment with more current means of generating illustrations, such as animation, time-lapse photography, or computer graphics.
- Names. Are the people who were named as prominent in the field during the writing of the older text still prominent today? What new names have come on the scene and why should they be added or take the place of some previous personalities?
- Events. What have been the key events in this field over the past two or three decades that influence the tone or overall message to be conveyed in a revised text as compared to the older text?
- Diagrams, Charts, and Tables. Update statistical information, but show a progression over time whenever possible. Display such numbers so that the reader can see change and evolution or constant patterns.
- Research. Find key research conclusions over the past decade and relate them to findings reported in the old text so you can discuss findings that are no longer considered valid and earlier findings that have been substantiated by current investigations. Establish a context for currentness.

For Further Reading

Callison, Daniel, and Rebecca Knuth. "The AIME Statewide Survey of School Library Media Centers: Expenditures and Collections." Indiana Media Journal (Spring 1994); 103-162. ERIC Document #374824.

Lynch, Mary Jo, Pamela Kramer, and Ann Weeks. Public School Library Media Centers in Twelve States: Report of the NCLIS/ALA Survey. Washington, DC: U. S. National Commission on Libraries and Information Science, 1994.

Mancall, Jacqueline C., and M. Carl Drott.
<u>Measuring Student Information Use</u>. Littleton,
CO: Libraries Unlimited, 1983.

Key Words
Facilitator

The term "facilitator" is generally not recognized as a standard instructional term, but it is often related to such actions as "intervention," "planning," "guidance," and "mediation." The term has gained popularity over the past decade with increased agreement that teachers should act more as facilitators of learning and less as the sole fountain of knowledge.

Just as facilitation of managerial responsibilities requires actions at the stages of planning, implementation, and evaluation, specific actions are also necessary at the same three stages of facilitation of instruction. Knowledge in how to collaborate in planning, intervene and mediate during instructional implementation, and constructively give feedback for purposes of evaluation are essential for today's teacher of information literacy.

Intermediary Process

Kathy Brock has suggested a model to depict the actions of the teacher-librarian involved in the information search and use (ISU) process. In her model, facilitating occurs through six phases of the student's information search and use experience:

- Defining the Problem: the library media specialist helps students select topics, suggests sources for topic overview, and consults as students develop authentic topics and research questions.
- Developing Information-Seeking Strategies: the library media specialist suggests specific resources and explains strategies that lead to a variety of information formats.
- Locating Information: the library media specialist helps students become independent in locating resources and may provide guidance and personal contact in helping students obtain resources beyond the library media center.
- Gathering and Assessing Information: the library media specialist helps students make decisions in evaluating, assimilating, selecting, and rejecting information and become independent in making and recording such decisions.
- Synthesizing Information: the library media specialist helps students become independent in organizing information selected for presentation.
- Evaluating and Refining Results: the library media specialist provides constructive feedback concerning the product or presentation and gives suggestions for revision.

Prompting for Elaboration

Much of the current research related to reading-to-write/writing-to-read implies the importance of the role of the teacher as facilitator for extending the student's consideration of a topic or argument through prompts. This technique places the facilitator in the position of asking the student to consider options. The teacher of library media can adopt such prompting as well. Normally the library media specialist raises options by asking if the student has considered other resources. Beyond resources, however, are prompts that the library media specialist should employ to facilitate with other teachers greater student consideration of the content to be synthesized and eventually incorporated into the student's paper or presentation.

Michael Zellermayer has outlined two categories for prompting. The first is prompting for increased quantity of facts, opinions, and ideas. The second is prompting for quality or better consideration of the evidence or opinions located in order to establish linkages among evidence and to derive conclusions.

- Quantity
  Facts: Could you add more details?
  Thoughts: Do you have further thoughts on this issue?
- Quality
  Evidence: What evidence do you have? From whom, where, how recent?
  Personal View: What is your opinion?
  Deduction: What are your conclusions?
  Hypothesis: What would happen if...?
  Explanation for Clarity: What exactly do you mean when you say...?
  Relation: Why is this important or more important than other facts, evidence, or issues? Why is this point relevant and how does it relate to others?
  Cohesion: How does this relate and enhance what you said before?
  Judgmental: Why is this interesting to you? Why would this be interesting to your audience?
  Creative: Tell me a story or analogy based on this information.
  Audience Analysis: How would you revise this information to make it more meaningful for your intended audience?

When the library media specialist moves from the limited role of facilitating resource options and access and into the cooperative facilitation role with other teachers of prompting selection and use of evidence, the librarian becomes a true teacher.

Conversations in the Constructivist Role

Kuhlthau tells us that library media specialists and other teachers play a central role in facilitating learning in the constructivist approach. Based on her research, it is clear that while transmission of information may rely on textbooks and packaged materials (including multiple resources through libraries and the Internet), guiding the learning process through construction calls for expertise that only skillful sensitive professionals can provide.

Skilled facilitators know not only how to intervene in order to prompt and guide, but know when to do so. Kuhlthau refers us to the Russian psychologist, Vygotsky, and his concept of the zone of proximal development. The zone of intervention, and best time for facilitating learning, is when the learner can use guidance and assistance in what he or she cannot do alone. She tells us that help within this zone moves the student along in the information search process. Intervention on both sides of the zone is inefficient and unnecessary, and attempts to facilitate become meaningless or overwhelming. Timely intervention within this zone is efficient and enabling. How does the facilitator determine the best time to intervene? Kuhlthau's list of coaching strategies help the skilled facilitator place the student in situations where the student voices, writes, or performs in some manner in order to give the facilitator clues leading to identification of student needs in the information search and use processes.

- Collaborating: students move from isolated information searching and use to sharing the effort with other students, and in the mix of seeking and selecting information together, voice to the group and the teachers their successes and frustrations; often students become facilitators themselves as they teach each other.
- Continuing: voicing when there is or is not enough information; to move out of the exploration stage of the information search and into an area of focus with assurance that there is enough information to continue the process.

- Conversing: describing the information search and use experiences with everyone who will listen and provide feedback; other teachers and sometimes even parents can facilitate, but usually the mere act of verbalizing the needs and progress along with the intended direction of the project helps the student focus.
- Charting: providing a visual representation of the search process to date and organizing the evidence located helps to convey what has and has not been accomplished; diagrams, categorizing note cards, outlining, or sequencing the task in some visual manner helps the facilitator identify both gaps and areas that seem near completion.
- Composing: journals and logs help the student record actions and thoughts about those actions; pre-writes or pre-speaks may help the student formulate pieces which eventually are linked for the product and they also provide tangible items to which the facilitator can provide feedback.

For Further Reading

Brock, Kathy Thomas. "Developing Information Literacy through the Information Intermediary Process." Emergency Librarian 22, no. 1 (September-October 1994): 16-20.

Callison, Daniel. "Expanding the Evaluation Role in the Critical Thinking Curriculum." In Information for a New Age: Redefining the Librarian. 153-170. Englewood, CO: Libraries Unlimited, 1995.

Kuhlthau, Carol Collier. "Learning in Digital Libraries: An Information Search Process Approach." Library Trends 45, no. 4 (Spring 1997): 708-724.

Zellermayer, Michael. "The Development of Elaborative Skills: Teaching Basic Writing Students to Make the Commitment to Audience and Topic." Linguistics and Education 3, no. 4 (1991): 359-383.

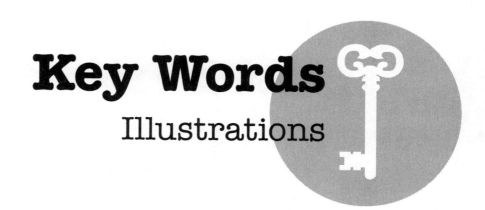

Key Words
Illustrations

Illustrations are visual techniques intended to help increase the portion of the audience who will understand a message. The purpose of illustration is to make clear through comparison, a more tangible example, or a less complex perspective. Illustrations are usually drawings or photographs, but also may include dramatic presentations, computer graphics, gestures, and even images in the mind.

Cartoons helped to convey the depth of corruption of the Boss Tweed political machine in New York City during a time when most city citizens could not read the newspaper without the assistance of illustrations. Artists during the Middle Ages crafted murals and stained glass scenes to tell the Christian story. Illustrations helped to communicate across a wider audience as well as give emphasis and drama to the narrative details available to those who had mastered reading and writing.

Across our information literacy curriculum today, those who teach and model such skills know that the cliché "a picture is worth a thousand words" is only part of the story. Students consume thousands of words, orally and visually, and they need a variety of communication methods to summarize their own sharing of information and knowledge. Illustrations serve to aid the student researcher who wants to grow and mature in communication skills through the use of graphics that enhance, condense, quicken, direct, heighten, or inspire the message.

Edward R. Tufte, as an opening to his classic The Visual Display of Quantitative Information, writes:

Excellence in statistical graphics consists of complex ideas communicated with clarity, precision, and efficiency. Graphical displays should:

* show the data;
* induce the reviewer to think about the substance rather than about methodology, graphic design, the technology of graphic production, or something else;
* avoid distorting what the data have to say;
* make large data sets coherent;
* encourage the eye to compare different pieces of data;
* reveal the data at several levels of detail, from a broad overview to the fine structure;
* serve a reasonable clear purpose: description, exploration, tabulation, or decoration;
* be closely integrated with the statistical and verbal descriptions of a data set.

Visual Literacy

David Considine and Gail Haley have conducted many workshops and written extensively on the use of visual messages in instruction. "Visual literacy" is the ability to comprehend and create information that is carried and conveyed through imagery. Exercises leading to greater student comprehension through the use of visuals include seeking patterns, matching, and categorizing images in both creative and critical ways so that students learn to analyze messages.

The student grows in his or her information literacy status by learning how to read images or hidden meanings, or to elaborate on a story based on the illustrations. Students also use images to convey their own ideas through creation of cartoons, advertisements, and multimedia programming. Students may be challenged to "think visually" in situations where they are to consider images in their own mind that might represent how history would be different had certain events not happened, or to recreate a classic story based on their internal imagery of new central characters.

Overlapping the skills of media literacy, visual literacy may involve an understanding that illustrations are models of reality and have their limitations as well as advantages. Maps are one common example. Mark Monmonier of Syracuse University argues that not only is it easy to lie with maps, it is essential. To portray meaningful relationships for a complex, three-dimensional world on a flat sheet of paper or a video screen, a map must distort reality. To avoid hiding critical information in a fog of detail, the map must offer a selective, incomplete view of reality. Monmonier concludes there is no escape from the cartographic paradox: to present a useful and truthful picture, an accurate map must tell white lies. What a fascinating area for young minds to explore as they question human devices and technologies designed to convey information in strategic ways!

Illustrating the Term Paper

Sue Baugh is one of the few authors of the typical guide to writing a term paper to devote a great deal of attention to the value of illustrations that can be employed by students in nearly any academic setting. Her guide pertains to undergraduate students, but her points have application across all grade levels, K-college.

Baugh states that the art of using charts, tables, or other graphic material effectively is based on two principles:

- Illustrations should be essential to the report and not used to conceal a lack of content.

- Illustrations must support and clarify the text, not stand in place of it.

When does the student need to use illustrations? Baugh offers this criteria:

- The student is describing complex technical or physical processes. For example, how does cocaine affect the human body? In this case, one picture may be truly worth several thousand words. The student can include a diagram that traces the effects of this drug from the time it is ingested until the remaining amount is eliminated from the body. The student can number or letter the stages and refer to them throughout the narrative.

- The student has complex numerical or statistical data to convey. A summary in table format may save space when there is a great deal of data to show. Selected data presented in graph may serve to give special emphasis to enhance a line of persuasion.

- The student is describing a particular event or subject such as a battle, city plan, or interior of a building. A map, blueprint, or other illustration can orient the reader and give a visual reference as the text continues the story or details of the report. Schematics are nearly essential in any paper dealing with computer systems, auto mechanics, or strategies that must be conveyed to a team for common understanding.

- The student wants to present information to the reader and increase the chances that the reader will remember it. Illustrations can make a "lasting impression" if they provide a relevant symbolic icon, summarize a few points in a pattern matching the reader's previous experiences, or are selected for dramatic impact. In more complex situations, the illustrations need to convey clear explanatory elements that the reader can assimilate with both his knowledge base and that of the surrounding text.

Baugh concludes with these guidelines for using illustrations in term papers:

- Use a minimum number of graphics; be selective.
- Use the smallest-sized graphic that conveys the information; illustrations should complement the text, not overwhelm it.
- Make sure all graphics are designed so that words, lines, scales, and other elements are the same size.
- Be sure that the terms used in the graphic are the same terms used in the text.
- Cite or place the graphic in the text as close to the relevant information as possible; text and illustration are more likely to help the reader and to be used together when given on the same page.

Understanding the Visual Display of Information

Virginia Rankin has provided the teacher of information literacy a collection of useful strategies and ideas in her book The Thoughtful Researcher: Teaching the Research Process to Middle School Students. In a key chapter, she addresses information found in visual formats. Her references range from charts and tables that illustrate data of business and society in USA Today and Wall Street Journal to the summary box scores used increasingly in sports telecasting and webcasting. Students placed in situations where they are encouraged to collect visuals (photos, maps, charts, graphs, etc.) along with quotations and paraphrased descriptions will find that development of reports based on the ever-expanding Web and video hypertext formats are more exciting and rewarding.

Rankin identifies these useful visual formats:

- Maps: Students should analyze professionally prepared maps. Rankin states that before students design a map to display data, they must have a reason for doing it; they must have a story they wish to tell. Maps can instantly clarify regional patterns for such matters as poverty, unemployment, or crime rates.
- Graphs: Line graphs may support a very specific point to be made in illustrating a conclusion. Bar graphs may be used to highlight comparisons.
- Tables: May be needed to illustrate a more comprehensive story and show the spread and variance in the data.
- Time Lines: Provide a chronological summary of key events.
- Pictorial Representations: Rankin states that pictures supplemented with a few well-chosen words produce concrete and memorable explanations that tie together a number of related factors. These factors and their relationships can easily become lost in the long narrative, but captured for impact on one page with the use of illustrations.
- Text Itself as Visual: Use boxed phrases or quotations to give emphasis to key points through the use of summary or highlight boxes. This technique is often used in professional trade magazines and is a standard tool on professional Web pages.

Most valuable is Rankin's clear explanation of "teaching the visual display of information" through discussion, examples, and modeling. Rankin's message that library media specialists must provide instruction in the midst of research and not just as an introduction to research is one that all teachers of information literacy should adopt. She encourages teachers of information literacy to show tables, ask students to extract information from charts, and to discuss openly the possibilities of how to visualize the text. The mature or reflective researcher soon will understand that narrative outlining and visual storyboarding are essential companions in the design of information presentation.

Illustrations that Instruct

Richard E. Mayer, at the University of California, Santa Barbara, has based his examination of illustrations over the past two decades on one deceptively simple question,

"How can one teach in ways that result in meaningful learning?" Mayer's work has concentrated on illustrations found in typical science textbooks. His research has moved past the "traditional approach" or simple tests of greater or lesser information retention when illustrations contain color or are placed in a certain area of the page. Mayer has attempted to consider the impact of illustrations through the "cognitive approach" or to what extent does an illustration link to the learner's cognitive system? His work has direct implications for those designing illustrations for Web-based tutorials and interactive computer-assisted instruction.

Under the cognitive approach, illustrations are tested to determine their value to learners who bring to the illustration and text different knowledge backgrounds and abilities. According to Mayer, three major memory stores relevant to a cognitive model of learning from text and illustrations are sensory memory, short-term memory, and long-term memory.

The four cognitive processes most relevant to a cognitive model of learning from text and illustrations are selecting, organizing, integrating, and encoding.

- Selecting: Paying attention to relevant pieces of information in the instructional materials.
- Organizing: The process of building internal connections among pieces of information that are attended to.
- Integrating: The process of building external connections between incoming information and knowledge already in long-term memory.
- Encoding: The process of placing the knowledge constructed in long-term memory for permanent storage and retrieval.

Mayer has classified illustrations into four types:

- Decorative: Fill space on the page, but do not enhance the message of the text. Hence, they do not affect the reader's cognitive processing of the text. Mayer estimates about 25 percent of science text illustrations fall into this category.

- Representational: Portray a single element and serve to direct the reader's attention. Mayer places about 60 percent of illustrations found in typical middle school science texts in this category.
- Organizational: Depict the structural relations among two or more elements. About 5 percent of the illustrations in science texts are organizational.
- Explanative: Explain how some system or process works by showing the principle-based relationships among state changes in the major elements of the system. A principle-based relation is a specific cause-and-effect connection between two events. These illustrations represent approximately 10 percent of those found in typical science textbooks.

So when do illustrations work? According to Mayer, there are four conditions for effective explanative illustrations. First, the text must be explanative rather than narrative and descriptive. Second, the illustration must be explanative rather than decorative, representational, or organizational. Third, the learners must be appropriate; for example, learners who lack knowledge of mechanics would be more likely to benefit from explanative illustrations of how a mechanical system works than learners who possess mechanical knowledge. Fourth, to evaluate the effectiveness of explanative illustrations, the performance test must be appropriate for measuring conceptual retention, nonconceptual retention, and problem-solving transfer, rather than measuring only the overall amount learned.

Mayer contends that explanative illustrations are generally underused or misused. They are, however, a powerful vehicle for instruction. He reports that explanative illustrations improve conceptual retention and problem-solving transfer when presented clearly, within relevant text, and are age or ability-level appropriate. These are clearly the same criteria for all forms of effective instructional oral and visual communication.

For Further Reading:

Bazeli, Marilyn. Visual Productions and Student Learning. ERIC Document ED408969, 1997.

Baugh, L. Sue. How to Write Term Papers and Reports. Lincolnwood, IL: VGM Career Horizons and NTC Publishing, 1993.

Considine, David M., and Gail E. Haley. Visual Messages: Integrating Imagery into Instruction. Englewood, CO: Teacher Ideas Press, 1992.

Mayer, Richard E. "Illustrations that Instruct." In Advances in Instructional Psychology, edited by Robert Glaser. Vol. 4. Hillsdale, NJ: Lawrence Erlbaum Associates, 1993: 253-284.

Monmonier, Mark. How to Lie with Maps. Chicago: University of Chicago Press, 1991.

Mosenthal, Peter B., and Irwin S. Kirsch. "Understanding Documents: Understanding Graphs and Charts." Parts I and II. Reading Journal (February 1990): 371-373; (March 1990): 454-457.

Rankin, Virginia. The Thoughtful Researcher: Teaching the Research Process to Middle School Students. Englewood, CO: Libraries Unlimited, 1999.

Key Words
Inquiry

Inquiry is the reason instructional library media centers exist as learning laboratories. Inquiry is the important process that supports the mission to assure that teachers, including instructional media specialists, and students learn to become effective users of information. Inquiry is the encompassing term that includes subsets, such as critical and creative thinking, and other skill sets related to modern constructivist curriculum. These literacy skill sets are related to understanding mass media, seeking meaning through information resource-based research, and intelligent application of emerging technologies.

Inquiry can be viewed on four levels, each with greater freedom for the student as he or she matures in the inquiry process:

- **Controlled Inquiry** involves practice of many skills, such as raising questions, seeking factual information from a variety of sources, and conducting an interview. The topics for inquiry are usually identified by the teacher with assurance from the library media specialist that enough resources are on hand to support all students involved.

- **Guided Inquiry** combines the research skills into a more natural flow of question raising and information seeking. Students often work in small groups and the topic for exploration is common across the class as all students are generally expected to deal with the same amount of information and eventually make a similar presentation. Final reports will be of similar length and content and assessed on the same rubric.

- **Modeled Inquiry** moves the student to a higher level of investigation as he or she comes under the guidance of someone who has engaged in a great deal of previous inquiry. Through a more independent process, the student is an apprentice in the research process, but has more freedom of choice in research questions and methods. Modeled Inquiry tends to work best when teachers involved have been successful themselves in completing inquiry projects and will engage in research alongside the students.

- **Free Inquiry** is the highest level of independent investigation. The student has ownership of the process from raising questions and identification of key issues to completion of the final report and justification of presentation mode. Access to information, analysis of data, and synthesis for presentation are fully the responsibility of the student inquirer. The student has gained experience and practice in the inquiry process and has matured to the level that he or she knows how to build on these previous experiences to create a truly unique project.

Inquiry is certainly not new. It has many roots in Socratic questioning and scientific methodology. Recently, however, inquiry has been presented in more exciting ways as shifts in emphasis toward student-centered learning combined with the expanding electronic information base open new venues for students and teachers to explore and share ideas. The modern teacher of school media adopts the principles of inquiry to create a learning environment rich in resources and collaboration.

Today we have the theory, techniques, and technologies that can lead us to progressive, social curricula based on information inquiry.

The New Emphasis

The California School Library Association has been one of the leading states in development of activities on the concepts of inquiry and information literacy. Their comparison of past and current emphasis areas, constructed on similar models from Colorado, Minnesota, and Washington, provide a framework for understanding the shifts taking place across the nation. In each example it should be understood that a shift in emphasis does not mean a discarding of the past.

A shift means that more time and energy are given to the new additional layer in order for the student inquirer to find information that will result in a greater possibility that he or she will find understanding and meaning in the information.

- Past: Teacher-identified research topics or projects.
- New: Student collaboration in identifying relevant issues.

An important foundational skill in the inquiry process is the ability to identify issues. Teachers of information literacy need to model this, and guide the student in practice of this skill. The ability to identify key issues for oneself can be the key to continuing the inquiry process in future situations and may be the most effective motivational aspect involved in research. Raising, testing, and grappling with the frustrations of finding meaningful areas for investigation lead to excitement and student ownership of the process.

While some practice exercises may be managed more efficiently when topics are predetermined by teachers to match specific resources available, true inquiry does not take place until students come to grips with potential areas for investigation on their own terms. Even more important is the opportunity for students to model and assist other students in the practice of determining what is really worthwhile to research. Conversations about inquiry success and frustrations are the basis for a social curriculum.

- Past: Locating information.
- New: Evaluating and using/applying information.

Instructional media specialists have contributed only a small portion of their potential role when guidance to resources is the sum of their contribution to the learning experience. All too often the information advisory role stops at directing other teachers and students to the tools of information. Extracting specific data, comparing information and authorities, and considering relevancy and currency all play a part in moving from library skills to research skills. To limit the library skills program to location of information makes the library media center little more than a giant textbook.

Creating situations in which the teacher and library media specialist immerse themselves with the students to compare and contrast information and to discuss the implications of what is and is not found moves the environment into an information laboratory setting. Skilled teachers of information inquiry give more time and more value to the discussion of the meaning of information than time given to overall orientation to reference tools and catalogs. Creating a context for information meaning drives the need to learn location skills. Too often we have let location practice fail to evolve into meaningful information analysis and synthesis discussions.

Instructional school library media specialists differ from colleagues in the public library and academic ranks in two ways. First, school library media specialists should be skilled not only in the use of various information formats, but also should have and practice skills in the production of a variety of information formats including such areas as web mastering, video production, and multimedia presentations. Second, the primary task of the school library media specialist is to teach and thus provide service to patrons. The primary task of other information specialists and librarians is to serve and assist based on the patron's described needs and requests. The school library media specialist teaches and guides the student through collaborative interactions that give value to the student's interests while also teaching information access, use, and analysis. The school library media specialist will show the student possible new options for investigation and presentation. Both roles are extremely demanding and require multi-talented individuals who also seek to teach these same skills to and with collaborating teachers.

- Past: Printed material.
- New: All sources of information.

Of course, school libraries that have become media centers housing multiple formats of information and access points to varied resources is not a new concept. However, the scope of such varied resources has increased and the understanding of how to best apply these resources is maturing. Students are not assigned projects in which they have to use nonprint resources just for the purpose of using that format even if the information contained is not relevant. Assignments that require five sources, two of which must be other than a book, are counterproductive if the topic at hand really requires no exploration beyond secondary or tertiary resources.

Inquiry is open to data from all possible resources and depending on the questions and issues, may result in greater use of human interviews, current unpublished Web sites, and even popular television programming. The objective is to determine the most relevant and authoritative information possible-not to belabor the experience just to be sure the student has used every form of media immediately available.

- Past: Secondary sources.
- New: Primary sources.

Basic reference tools remain important for obtaining some facts and providing the student with the means to gain some general background and definition of terms. Reference tools help the student to explore possible issues and determine the range for possible focus. However, such basic resources too often are allowed to dictate the inquiry assignment. Encyclopedic assignments that do not demand more than a general overview of a state, animal, event, or disease will result in an encyclopedic product.

Placed in a situation in which the student deals with questions that are of personal or local interest, the student begins to do what most two-years-olds do best: asking "why?" constantly. What makes the student inquirer different is the opportunity to mature in terms of timing and filtering so that primary resources can help to localize and personalize the responses. Interviews with experts or subjects with special experiences take place after some general background allows specific questions to emerge. Contact with museums and historical societies may lead to primary artifacts and expert interpretations that meet the more personal and customized questions. Access to local insurance agents, tax advisors, or loan officers may lead to more recent and relevant data that changes the meaning of general information previously gathered by the student researcher on finance issues.

- Past: Established authority of reference sources; single perspective.
- New: Questioning and identifying point of view; multiple perspectives.

Because it is in print does not make it true. Because Dan Rather reports it does not make it true. Because the President says it does not make it true. The mature inquirer knows that "truth" often shifts with the situation, the context of the discussion, the recency of the facts known, and even the definition of terms. While many accepted authoritative sources remain the initial starting point for gathering some facts, the student inquirer seeks out other evidence to corroborate or counter the first. The advanced inquirer will not stop short on this process and remain satisfied with the journalist's or lawyer's second source or second opinion. The advanced inquirer knows that authority may shift over time and that questioning the "facts" and "opinions" never stops.

Often we hear that "the truth" lies someplace among the various perspectives. Seeking out and considering a wide range of perspectives is a demanding task for all involved in the inquiry process. A common general dictionary definition of "inquiry" is "a close examination of a matter for information or truth." Information and truth can often be different things, and the mature inquirer has learned how to detect the difference.

- Past: Product usually is a paper.
- New: Thinking and problem solving of the search process and application allow for a variety of communication formats.

Writing is the foundation for efficient and effective communication. We organize our thoughts and group them in symbols common enough to share with another audience. As important as this skill is, communication options for sharing findings in the inquiry process and presentation should not be restricted to written documents only, nor should the written document be restricted to the "typical" student research report.

Written documents can include journals, lab reports, consumer summaries, survey results, video and play scripts, or outlines for discussion and debate, to name a few. Marilyn Joyce and Julie Tallman have provided a useful guide that demonstrates that regardless of the format for the final product, an important companion piece to be written by the student inquirer is a discussion of the inquiry process. From reading such process summaries, teachers of information inquiry can learn which resources and information access points proved to be most useful at least in the opinion of the student, and can provide valuable information for adjusting future inquiry projects. Reading I-Search papers, viewing student presentations, and taking an active role in student discussions as topics evolve can provide valuable information for collection development as well.

Of course the array of presentation modes is vast and growing with emerging technologies. Students can present through video, multi-media, plays, and posters. A key evaluation question that should always be addressed, however, is: Does the presentation mode fit the process? Does the presentation mode allow for the findings or message to be conveyed best in terms of being persuasive and most likely to be understood by the intended audience? A set of data about teenage suicide may be precise in table format, but a student-produced play may create more emotion.

The dynamics of critical and creative thinking must be considered by students and teachers. Expecting the student to present findings to different audiences may result in different products. Mature student inquirers learn to adjust through the use of strategic intelligence-finding the best fit for the data to meet the needs and interests of the audience addressed.

Inquiry and Standards for the English Language Arts

The National Council of Teachers of English (NCTE) defines "inquiry" as "a mode of research driven by the learner's desire to look deeply into a question or an idea that interests him or her." Several of the twelve standards outlined in 1996 relate directly to the inquiry process. NCTE released these statements in order to encourage the development of curriculum and instruction that make productive use of the emerging literacy abilities that children bring to school. The standards provide ample room for the innovation and creativity essential to teaching and learning. They are not prescriptions for particular curriculum or instruction. A few statements most relevant to inquiry are given:

4) Students adjust their use of spoken, written, and visual language to communicate effectively with a variety of audiences and for different purposes.
5) Students employ a wide range of strategies as they write and use different writing elements appropriately to communicate with different audiences for a variety of purposes.
6) Students apply knowledge of language structure, language conventions, media techniques, figurative language, and genre to create and discuss print and nonprint texts.
7) Students conduct research on issues and interests by generating ideas and questions, and by posing problems. They gather, evaluate, and synthesize

data from a variety of sources (e.g., print and nonprint texts, artifacts, people) to communicate their discoveries in ways that suit their purpose and audience.

8) Students use a variety of technological and informational resources (e.g., libraries, databases, computer networks, video) to gather and synthesize information and to create and communicate knowledge.

11) Students participate as knowledgeable, reflective, creative, and critical members of a variety of literacy communities.

12) Students use spoken, written, and visual language to accomplish their own purposes (e.g., for learning, enjoyment, persuasion, and the exchange of information).

The Information Laboratory and Science Education

Over two decades ago, Edward Victor listed the elements of inquiry learning for science education. These elements help us define information inquiry in our expanding technological age.

Element One: Inquiry lessons are carefully planned. Inquiry is not a wide open free lance approach to curriculum. It is a demanding process, requiring a great deal of collaborative planning as well as experience in practicing the inquiry process personally by teacher and media specialist.

Element Two: Inquiry lessons follow a general pattern. While the process may have some common stages, students follow this general pattern with various degrees of concentration depending on their information needs and abilities. Journals, peer conferences, and open discussion of information needs and successful uses of information help to move all inquirers along the general and recurring patterns of question identification, general reading for context and meaning, gathering information for evidence, constructing arguments or solutions through analysis and synthesis, and proposing a thesis or final set of findings.

Element Three: Inquiry learning is highly process-oriented. The process is assessed and evaluated as much as the product. Students share information and assist each other in practice of the stages of the process as well as the presentation of the product.

Element Four: Teaching and learning are question-oriented. Students come to the library media center and resources not only for answers, but to help raise more questions. The mature student inquirer learns that some questions can be answered to a high degree of satisfaction, other questions lead to only partial answers, and some questions will continue to puzzle for a lifetime.

Element Five: The teacher is the director of learning. As a facilitator, the teacher of information inquiry models the process and engages in it along with students. Teacher and library media specialist share in the excitement of discovery. They advocate, promote, and reward inquiry in the same manner that librarians have rewarded extensive reading. Yes, bulletin boards celebrate information discovery with displays of student work. Information discussion groups based on what students have researched and presented lead to pizza parties too.

Element Six: Time is not of prime importance, but timing is. Inquiry projects that truly engage students in the process need more than the usual two weeks. The library media specialist introduces some reference and index tools on the first day, often before students have any understanding of possible topics. Students are then set free for several days to locate the required number of resources and are expected to complete the paper within the next week or so.

Timing includes monitoring student actions so that skills can be taught at the time of need and application has a greater chance of being assimilated for future use. Students move on projects for concentrated periods of several days, but also pull back in order to reflect and rethink what they have or have not accomplished. Flexible scheduling at elementary levels and block scheduling or extended class periods in secondary schools help to make the best use of time and timing.

Element Seven: Students are teachers too. Peer and self-evaluation have value along with evaluations from the teachers of information inquiry.

Element Eight: Peer interaction is necessary during and following the experience. Working as part of a research team is one method to create peer interaction. Even more effective, however, is the development of electronic bulletin boards or listservs through which students express information needs and are rewarded for finding and providing information leads and specific evidence to support classmates. Even without e-mail, students can post information needs on a regular bulletin board in the classroom or the library media center and helpful responses received can be noted by the student in his or her journal.

Element Nine: The end product is shared with others. The final audience extends beyond the teacher and includes peers, parents, community members, and others who will appreciate or critically review student presentations. Documents that reflect process and presentation should be gathered for student portfolios and comments from various audiences can become part of the assessment record.

Element Ten: Some students and teachers may demonstrate the desire to learn more. Inquiry does not stop with the presentation. If students have been encouraged to develop topics of personal interest, questions will continue to evolve and the investigation should continue over several grade levels or across several discipline areas as the mature student inquirer seeks answers to various aspects of the original question or problem set.

For Further Reading

Beach, Richard, and Jamie Myers. <u>Inquiry-Based English Instruction: Engaging Students in Life and Literature</u>. Teachers College Press, 2001.

California School Library Association. <u>From Library Skills to Information Literacy</u>. San Jose, CA: Hi Willow Research and Publishing, 1997.

Callison, Daniel. "School Library Media Programs and Free Inquiry Learning." <u>School Library Journal</u> 32, no. 6 (1986): 20-24.

Callison, Daniel, Joy H. McGregor, and Ruth V. Small, eds. <u>Instructional Intervention for Information Use: Research Papers of the Sixth Treasure Mountain Research Retreat for School Library Media Programs</u>. San Jose, CA: Hi Willow Research and Publishing, 1998. *See the Minnesota Inquiry plan described by Mary S. Dalbotten, "Inquiry in the National Content Standards" on pages 30-82.*

Joyce, Marilyn Z., and Julie I. Tallman. <u>Making the Writing and Research Connections with the I-Search Process</u>. New York: Neal-Schuman Publishers, 1997.

Kuhlthau, Carol. "An Emerging Theory of Library Instruction." <u>School Library Media Quarterly</u> 16 (1987): 23-28.

Kuhlthau, Carol. "Implementing a Process Approach to Information Skills: A Study Identifying Indicators of Success in Library Media Programs." <u>School Library Media Quarterly</u> 22 (Fall 1993): 11-18.

National Council of Teachers of English. Standards of the English Language Arts. Urbana, IL: NCTE, 1996.

Victor, Edward. "The Inquiry Approach to Teaching and Learning." <u>Science and Children</u> (October 1974): 23-26.

Recommended Websites

Colorado's Plan for Information Literacy. http://cde.state. co.us/infolitg.htm

Washington's Plan for Information Skill Scope and Sequence. http://www.wlma.org/literacy/eslintro.htm

A Questioning Toolkit by Jamie McKenzie. http://www. fromnowon.org/

Key Words
Integrated Instruction

When teachers of library media and information literacy speak of "course integrated library instruction," they usually are describing library use or information seeking instruction given as a part of a course in a subject area. Certain information skills have been identified to help the student complete a multiple resource task that has been assigned by his or her classroom teacher.

Integrated activities involve a systematic organization of units or lessons presented in a meaningful pattern. That pattern may represent a scaffold or progression of building from less difficult tasks to more complex ideas and applications. That pattern may be shown in parallel to the progression of skills outlined for other subjects across the curriculum. While science, math, social studies, and language arts curricula often are mapped across the grades or in relation to the normal expected intellectual development of most students, so too are information skills. An integrated curriculum will show these progressive patterns together on the same pages and clearly linked to specific skills. For example, if students are expected to demonstrate their abilities in knowing the difference between fact and fiction, this information skill shows in areas of language arts curricula where it will be introduced, reinforced, and mastered. Sample lessons that depend on multiple resources for the skills also are suggested.

Integrated instruction, however, is only one aspect of teaching library and information use at the "point of need." Often identified as an essential element of the collaborative teaching process, integrated instruction is accepted as a powerful technique to show immediate and meaningful application of information skills to students as they will find the application of such skills necessary to meet the subject-based assignment. Understanding integrated instruction becomes more clear if one also understands the aspects of isolated instruction and independent instruction in relation to the teaching role of the library media specialist.

History of Course-Related Integrated Instruction

Patricia Knapp was an academic librarian and educator who focused on two major topics: the fusion of academic librarianship with academic instruction and the role of the undergraduate library within universities. Her work, conducted mostly at Wayne State and Monteith College in the 1960s, has a great deal of importance in the concept of integrated instruction for not only the college setting, but also elementary and secondary schools. Knapp's experimental library-centered learning efforts promoted the view that a college education should consist of a series of exercises in independent discoveries of the systems of ways and patterns in which knowledge is organized. This is the more meaningful path to preparation for lifelong learning, rather than the usual accumulation of facts through lectures, assigned readings, and tests.

Knapp argued that competence in library use, like competence in reading, is clearly not a skill to be acquired once and for all at any one given level in any one given course, but is a complex knowledge set composed of skills and attitudes that must be developed over a period of time through repeated and varied experiences in the use of library resources. The same principles apply to educational experiences prior to college..

Knapp maintained that course-relatedness in library instruction is not enough. The faculty member must communicate, and even model for students, the value of library competence. Library instruction must be an integral part of the curriculum so that such instruction secures a place in the academic setting regardless of the preferences or assignments that might vary among instructors. The intent was that as new instructors came into the college, they were expected to come on board accepting the broader resource-based curriculum. The curriculum, thus, would change not only students, but also faculty. Her experiment was not widely adopted nor did it continue even within her own institution for more than a few years. However, her efforts and documentation of her program changed the way many librarians viewed library instruction programs and gave birth to much of what we refer to today as course-related instruction.

Implementing a similar model more than anyone else in the decades following Knapp, Evan Farber, at Earlham College, insisted that the college library existed to support the learning and teaching process. Library or bibliographic instruction has only one main purpose, to prepare the student to be successful in completion of academic assignments. This was based on the understanding, however, that librarian and professor work together to establish meaningful assignments and that the librarian has not only the responsibility to meet the objectives of the instructor, but also to introduce and promote library and information use as primary learning goals as well.

Ideally, according to Farber, both the teacher's objectives and the librarian's objectives are not only achieved, but are mutually reinforced-the teacher's objectives being those that help students attain a better understanding of the course's subject matter, and the librarian's objectives being those that enhance the students' ability to find and evaluate information.

As has become true in public school settings, Farber has concluded that teaching faculty have become increasingly aware of the educational challenge posed by the Internet.

Teachers also are aware that they do not have the time nor the expertise to keep up with the continual changes and improvements. They know that while they can provide some guidance in helping students find and evaluate information, they will have to depend on library media specialists to really do the job. Modern information technologies, therefore, have ushered in a new era for both course-integrated information instruction and more extended follow-up sessions to meet individual needs.

Thomas Kirk, who has followed Farber as Director of the Earlham Libraries, believes technology has shifted the instructional role, content, and context to the extent that today one of the instruction librarian's most important responsibilities is helping students understand the differences among information resources and how to make judgments about the value and appropriateness of the information found. The diversity of search engine designs has complicated information instruction as well. Analysis of search results has become an important portion of both formal instructional sessions and individual reference interactions.

Isolated and Individual Instruction

Isolated instruction is currently viewed as not productive and a danger sign that the library media center is not an accepted part of the learning environment. Isolated instruction may take the form of introduction of library skills to elementary school students left at the library media center once a week while the teacher is free to gain some planning time away from the class. The library media specialist may introduce basic organization and search skills, but these are not tied to specific academic assignments and therefore, it is assumed, are lost, not used, and fade in importance once the student is placed back in class. In such situations, everyone seems to lose. The library media specialist is trapped with a class of students who don't really care and communication between the library media specialist and the teacher is lost, perhaps even discouraged from ever taking place in the rush from one class to the next.

Even when valuable chains of library and information skills have been introduced, they are ignored and treated as time-fillers and not as experiences that merit assessment of student performance nor the attention of the teacher for future lessons.

Isolated instruction also has been used to describe the standard library orientation. In secondary schools and colleges, the one-credit course provided to students to acquaint them with the library and basic resources, also is viewed as somewhat useful, but unless clearly linked to an immediate need, one that fades from the students' mental list of survival skills. Thus, isolated instruction has become synonymous with wasted efforts and indications that library information services are separate from true academic experiences.

Many of the labor intensive efforts to create effective orientations have given way to online tutorials with graphics and situations that tend to maintain attention and teach more than the live one-hour tour of the library. Such tutorials, in addition to providing more interactive learning options, also can be accessed nearly any time and can be repeated as often as needed. Sophisticated design allows for entry level skills or a profile of the student to be gathered by the computer in order to determine the degree of difficulty or depth of the tutorial. Some programs provide a series of questions during or at the end of the orientation in order to adjust and compile the content of a review tutorial that will address what the student seems not to understand. A growing list of useful interactive tutorials can be located through the Association of College and Research Libraries Instruction Round Table website (http://diogenes.baylor.edu/Library/LIRT/lirtproj.html).

Yet we know there is value in teaching basic information skills even though it requires repetition in different settings and at different times in order for most students to comprehend them and apply them effectively. In some cases, introduction to the library media center and links to its many in-house and electronically-extended resources provides awareness that was not present before.

Isolated instruction has little value when the lesson does not match the task. Individualized instruction, however, implies that the lesson or conversation between library media specialist and student has been refined purposefully in order to meet a current information need. Individualized instruction also may be framed to address additional needs that are most likely to become a part of what the student will need to address very shortly. Thus the school library media specialist, as readers' advisory and reference librarian, may find that teachable moments occur as they assist the student in the process of identifying information questions, resource options, search processes, and information selection.

Isolation from academic assignment should not mean basic information skills are not introduced and taught when other opportunities present themselves. Personal information needs outside of academic requirements often lead to some of the most powerful teaching opportunities. Conversations concerning more precise search terms or the quality of a located website should not be reserved only for times when the student is beginning work on a term paper or class report. Just as reading advisory leads students to materials for academic and pleasurable purposes, so to does information advisory.

"Information advisory," in an instructional sense, means not only helping the student determine a good resource, but also reinforcing basic skills (linked to an assignment or not):

- Read general background materials that will help you identify useful terms and names to use in more specific, advanced information searching.
- Browsing, either print or electronic sources, will help you explore options and expand your thoughts.
- Examine parts of resources by using the table of contents or index, and look to confirm search terms and locate new ones.
- As key terms become clear, use them to be more precise as you search for very specific information to answer your need.

INTEGRATED INSTRUCTION

- Talk with others-friends, teachers, parents, and your school library media specialist-to express your current thoughts and interests so they may be "on the lookout" for information sources that will help you. Talking about a topic also helps you refine your need and expand the relevant information vocabulary.
- Question validity and authority. Just because this document is from a source in the library or on the Internet does not mean it is the best item to select for the information need or that it is reliable.

Integrated More Powerful than Parallel

Carol-Ann Haycock, President of the Human Resources Development Group, has stressed the importance of moving collaborative planning from a parallel model to an integrated effort in order for meaningful planning partnerships to evolve. Her work with the Norman, Oklahoma, Schools in the early 1990s was based on the following interactive planning discussion between school library media specialist and other teachers. In this process, the library media specialist often takes the lead in the interview to pose the questions, and thus define the learning environment to increase the chances of student success.

- What are the characteristics of the learners? Determine readiness factors such as prior learning experiences, learning styles, reading abilities and interests, information skill levels, knowledge base, and conceptual understandings of the content area prior to the resource-based project.
- Why are we doing this? What is the tie to the curriculum and what are the goals for the project? Do goals of the library media specialist and other involved teachers interact in some manner to create new goals for all involved?
- What specifically is the student to learn? What are the objectives for student performance that are observable and measurable? What are the best techniques for instruction to meet these objectives? Can the current teaching team provide those techniques or should additional team members be recruited?
- How will the student gather the information needed? Have the instructors tested for the potential and problems of the project? Have they examined the information possibilities, pre-selected some key resources, determined strategies for information access both within the current environment and beyond the school, and considered how students can effectively apply information search skills?
- How will the student extract information? What is necessary to assure that the student will obtain relevant information and apply it to their information needs?
- How will the student process and organize information? To what extent will the students be able to apply an intellectual process resulting in categorizing, synthesizing, and analyzing information to solve problems? Will there be time, resources, and adequate instructional support to assure these processes are possible?
- How will the student produce and present findings? Will the student have options to say, draw, write, do, or otherwise present a product that displays their work for others?
- How will the performance be evaluated? What are the most important elements for formative evaluation of the process, summative evaluation of the product, and self-evaluation by the learner?

This is a complex and invigorating co-planning process. Close interaction is important here, and Haycock warns that such will not take place in a simple parallel process. In parallel planning, the school library media specialist and other teachers agree on a theme, topic, or exercise, but conduct their roles separately. The classroom teacher determines objectives for the student tasks in the classroom along with instructional strategies and learning activities there. The library media specialist prepares support materials and engages students who come to the library media center in a manner parallel to the teacher, but never collaborates in specific details for student performance and evaluation.

While there may be some instructional activities for which such parallel actions are adequate, quality and depth in the information inquiry process are not likely to take place without integrated partnerships.

Does it make a difference for information skills instruction to be course-integrated? A few limited studies suggest students improve their information search skills to solve specific problems within the subject context. Ross Todd, of the University of Technology in Sydney, Australia, found this to be true among a small number of high school students tested. Others have suggested that students are more likely to pursue search questions in more depth and to do a better job of assessing and using library resources. The greater benefit may come from the increased instructional conversations between teacher and library media specialist. Through course-integrated instruction, both become more aware of the other's instructional intents and come closer to working together as a team of instructional specialists, both ready to teach students how to solve information problems.

While the desirability of integrating information skills instruction with a subject area and specific assignment, there is little documented research to support this view or to support the different approaches offered to effect integrated instruction in elementary and secondary schools. Michael Eisenberg and Michael Brown, in a review conducted at Syracuse University, found this to be true in 1992, and very little has been added to the literature since.

An exception to this is the documentation recently released concerning the lessons from the national Library Power Project sponsored by DeWitt Wallace and the Reader's Digest Fund. Prior to the implementation of the project, library media specialists collaborated with under one-fourth of their fellow teachers. Teacher involvement in developing collections and selection of resources to support information instruction was unheard of in nearly three-fourths of the schools involved. Funding to support flexible scheduling and full-time library media specialists at each building, and to update aging collections reversed these findings of isolated actions and resulted in broad changes to integrate school library media programs as an essential ingredient for quality education.

Adam Stoll, the Evaluation Officer for Library Power, concluded:

This vision of integrated practice changes the expectations for practice. As we can see in the years since the vision was articulated through its implementation in Library Power, it is no longer acceptable to think of a school library program as a stand-alone entity that supplements classroom teaching and learning. Under the integrated practice envisioned in Information Power, high performing school library programs are fully integrated into the schools' instructional and curricular activities.

Marilyn Miller and Marilyn Shontz have found that an important characteristic of high-performance school library media programs is the amount of co-planning with teachers for integrated instruction. In high-service school library media programs in the 1990s, at nearly twice the frequency over lesser-service programs, the library media specialist:

- offers curriculum-integrated skills instruction;
- conducts workshops for teachers;
- assists curriculum committees with recommendations;
- helps teachers develop, implement, and evaluate learning;
- coordinates in-school production activities;
- coordinates computer networks and cable television access;
- communicates proactively and frequently with the principal; and
- gives substantial time to co-planning with other teachers.

The recent study concerning the impact of

school library programs and information literacy in Pennsylvania schools released in February 2000 concludes:

Higher and lower scoring elementary schools are distinguished by the amount of time school library staff spend in teaching students and teachers how to access and use print and electronic information resources. At higher achieving schools, library staff spend three days on such activities for every two by lower achieving schools. [Even small additional] investments of time in key activities pay off. At higher achieving schools at all grade levels, library staff are involved in committees to provide in-service training to teachers. Library staff at lower achieving schools usually do not engage in these activities at all.

Independent Inquiry

The information literacy standards for student learning contained in the 1998 Library Power guidelines includes standards for independent learning. Indicators for student performance usually relate to personal information needs rather than to academic activities as in the other standards. Such is probably understandable as the independent performance of information literacy is most likely to indicate that the student is maturing as a "lifelong learner."

The independent learning standards include:

- The student pursues information related to personal interests-career interests, personal well-being, community involvement, health matters, recreational pursuits, etc.
- The student appreciates literature and other creative expressions of information-a self-motivated reader derives useful personal information from a variety of formats and can communicate through a variety of formats.
- The student strives for excellence in information seeking and knowledge generation -can assess independently the value of information processes and products, and can devise and implement strategies for revising and updating self-generated knowledge.

These are extremely high-level skills. While they may be developed through integrated instructional activities and refined through guidance of the library media specialist and other teachers, independent information literacy moves beyond the typical course-integrated approach. Opportunities for the independent learner are needed at all age levels, K-college, even though the more mature actions we often associate with such independence may not be found except in a few of the more talented students during their late years of secondary school.

It also should be clear that "teaching how to use the library" as an isolated set of skills or as a fill-in subject weakens the potential for full instructional applications, except in cases of personal information advisory where point of need is identified and the library media specialist provides such instruction. It also should be assumed that inquiry as an instructional method is best explored and refined through exercises that are interesting, challenging, and academically relevant for the student. There is, however, a level of independent inquiry beyond the course-integrated approach.

This level requires independent performance on the part of the instructional library media specialist and other teachers. It moves beyond the norm and into analysis of personal need and motivation of student performance that may come to the attention of teachers of information literacy only a few times each year. Sensitivity to and understanding of this level, however, will result in creating a learning environment that will increase the number of independent learners as they become aware that such behavior is acceptable and valued.

In the early 1970s, Frank Ryan, of the University of California, and Arthur Ellis, of the University of Minnesota, saw the independence in inquiry as a behavior that evolves through the degree of teacher direction. Ryan and Ellis expect a progression from teacher-directed to teacher-independent implementation as students undertake succeeding inquiry experiences. They have diagramed this process as shown. (Fig. 1)

Nature of Inquiry Model Implementations	Teacher-directed	Teacher-guided	Teacher-independent	Fig. 1
Approximate Grade Levels	K-4	3-7	6-12	

The main point of the diagram is that a continuum of strategies may be used for each grade level (indeed, even for each lesson), with an overall progression from teacher-directed to teacher-independent implementation. The specific grade-level designations should be viewed as examples, not as prescriptions.

Independent inquiry projects involve the same basic tasks as course-integrated resource-based projects:

- stating the problem;
- selecting data sources;
- gathering data;
- processing data; and
- making inferences.

What will change from course-integrated instruction will be:

- time periods for investigations are more likely to be extended and re-occurring over several years if the student has persistent interest in the topic;
- greater self-motivation as the student is engaged in the inquiry to meet clear personal needs, and no letter grade will be involved unless the project becomes an academic independent study;
- a desire to either keep the investigation private and personal or other students may seek the opportunity to share discoveries and need assistance in displaying results and finding an audience;
- instead of one product, a series of products with each representing a progression in understanding of the issues and problems; and
- a greater degree of exploring the subject through reading widely, although the library media specialist still may need to place before even the most independent inquirer materials that broaden his or her perspectives.

Inquiry and the Learning Academy

While "learning about the library" is not a context for a "stand-alone course," the inquiry process is. This is not to imply that a course for secondary school students, college-bound or not, would be isolated from other areas of the curriculum. The process and practice of inquiry, including the information search process and elements of information literacy, are so critical to the development of mature learners that such experiences should not stop at just course-integrated programming.

In true collaboration, teacher teams composed of subject area specialists and school library media specialists can become even more effective as teams of information specialists, each versed in the master level teaching techniques for information inquiry. Courses that are centered on the information use processes and then extend into investigation areas of importance and interest to the learning agenda of students can result in new course offerings. These experiences are not tagged just as elective credits or alternative projects. They are formal courses and successful completion of such should be required for graduation.

Components of such courses may include the following, in addition to the now traditional information literacy skills:

- understanding of discourse in a variety of subject areas-science, history, literature, journalism;
- knowledge and practice of critical literacy to effect change-debate, community service, local legislation;
- use of primary resources not normally available because of limitations of time and typical school resource projects;
- gathering and sharing of original data through electronic communication-a

true community of student scientists who share and critique arguments and evidence, and help each other gain insights and inferences; and

- presentation of investigations that have matured over time, multiple products developed with several student teams-a portfolio of academic achievement based on application of progressive and advanced inquiry experiences.

This author made such proposals in the late 1980s. Many in the school library media field rejected such as an isolated curriculum. Many in the composition, social studies, and science education fields accepted such as movement toward development of an essential curricular component, expansion to a social curriculum to engage in the human conversation. Perhaps the discussions and models for information literacy have expanded and refined enough over this past decade to now fully embrace inquiry and we will see signs of new experimentation based on the philosophy we have inherited from Patricia Knapp. Can we immerse ourselves, our teachers, and our students in a new "learning academy?"

Immersion

Johanna Olson Alexander, of California State University, Bakersfield, recently took integrated planning to the level of full immersion. The context for her study was greater use of information technology (IT) systems. Integrated information technology immersion allows students to learn and master a wide variety of information technologies as computer tools and resources are used, that is, as students are immersed in information technology through exploratory learning.

Information technology literacy is best achieved when information skills are taught as an integral part of the curriculum. IT immersion provides for individual student needs and knowledge levels by offering instruction and consultation as needed, with a variety of tools, in a distributed learning environment. Much of the success in this approach is dependent on application of constructivist theory and asynchronous communication so that there is room for attention to individual entry skills and experiences and the student can become immersed in application of the technologies to meet problems relevant to his or her needs.

Challenges for Change

Donna Peterson, Director of Library Media Services at the award-winning Library Power Lincoln Public School District, Nebraska, reminds us that the challenges that face library media specialists who wish to improve student learning through collaboration and integration are significant because they involve change. The essence of change is that deeply-ingrained behaviors must be altered. Change automatically means resistance, especially in the field, where the basic behaviors of teaching have not changed much in 100 years.

Peterson draws from previous educators to summarize the barriers:

- Changes in methods of instruction are more difficult than changes in curriculum or administration. It is easier to use a new text than to teach in a different way.
- If a change requires teachers to abandon an existing instructional practice, it is in danger of defeat. Teachers don't want to give up what is comfortable and known.
- If retraining is required, success is threatened unless strong incentives are provided. Training is hard work and failure is always a possibility. Motivation is important to any change in behavior.
- Efforts to change curriculum by integrating or correlating the content are resisted and are especially at risk. Big changes require big efforts, and it is just easier not to do it unless it is required.
- The cost of the change is a significant factor in determining the permanence of the the change. If the change puts a strain on school personnel, or if it requires a substantial investment in learning new facts and procedures, it is not likely to persist. Hard work in this circumstance means that the sooner it can be discarded, the easier life will be.

For Additional Reading and Viewing

American Association of School Librarians and the Association for Educational Communications and Technology. <u>Information Power: Building Partnerships for Learning</u>. Chicago: American Library Association, 1998.

Alexander, Johanna Olson. "Collaborative Design, Constructivist Learning, Information Technology Immersion, and Electronic Communities." <u>Interpersonal Computing and Technology</u> 7, nos. 1-2 (October 1999). http://jan.ucc.nau.edu/~ipct-j/1999/n1-2/alexander.html

Brodeur, Doris R. "Thematic Teaching: Integrating Cognitive and Affective Outcomes in Elementary Classrooms." <u>Educational Technology</u> 38, no. 6 (1998), 37-43.

Eisenberg, Michael B., and Michael K. Brown. "Current Themes Regarding Library and Information Skills Instruction." <u>School Library Media Quarterly</u> 20, no. 2 (1992). http://www.ala.org/aasl/SLMR.slmr_resources/select_eisenberg.html

Farber, Evan. "Faculty Librarian Cooperation." <u>Reference Services Review</u> 27, no. 3 (1999): 229-234.

Guthrie, John T., Allan Wigfied, and Claire VonSecker. "Effects of Integrated Instruction on Motivation and Strategy Use in Reading." <u>Journal of Educational Psychology</u> 92, No. 2 (2000), 331-41.

Kirk, Thomas G., Jr. "Course-related Bibliographic Instruction in the 1990s." <u>Reference Services Review</u> 27, no. 3 (1999): 235-241.

Lance, Keith Curry, Marcia J. Rodney, and Christine Hamilton-Pennell. <u>Measuring Up to Standards: The Impact of School Library Programs and Information Literacy in Pennsylvania Schools</u>. Pennsylvania Department of Education, Office of Commonwealth Libraries, February 2000.

Miller, Marilyn L., and Marilyn L. Shontz. "More Services, More Staff, More Money: A Portrait of High-Service Library Media Centers." <u>School Library Journal</u> (May 1998).

Orlosky, Donald E., and B. Othanel Smith. "Educational Change: Its Origins and Characteristics." <u>Phi Delta Kappan</u> 53, no. 7 (1972): 413-14.

<u>Partners for Quality Education with Carol-Ann Haycock</u>. A video series in three parts. Vancouver, BC: Vision Resources, 1991.

Peterson, Donna L. "Collaboration in Teaching and Learning." In <u>Learning and Libraries in an Information Age</u>, edited by Barbara K. Stripling. Englewood, CO: Libraries Unlimited, 1999.

Ryan, Frank L., and Arthur K. Ellis. <u>Instructional Implications of Inquiry</u>. Englewood Cliffs, NJ: Prentice-Hall, 1974.

Todd, Ross J. "Integrated Information Skills Instruction: Does It Make a Difference?" <u>School Library Media Quarterly</u> 23, no. 2 (1995). http://www.ala.org/aasl/SLMR/slmr_resources/select_todd.html

Worrell, Diane. "The Work of Patricia Knapp: Relevance for the Electronic Age." <u>The Katharine Sharp Review</u>, no. 3 (Summer 1996). http://edfu.lis.uiuc.edu/review/summer1996/worrell.html

Zweizig, Douglas L., and Dianne McAfee Hopkins. <u>Lessons from Library Power: Enriching Teaching and Learning</u>. Englewood, CO: Libraries Unlimited, 1999.

Key Words
Interview

The interview can be a valuable skill used in the inquiry process to gain primary information that will help to clarify and add meaning. The information literate student who has gained a mature sense for seeking evidence will use the personal interview in order to:

- Verify evidence from written sources. It is not uncommon to find, as one discusses issues based on what is written in popular magazines and newspapers, that some facts may depend on specific situations or no longer be true and relevant at all. An interview with a person of expertise related to the issue can add weight to the evidence or explain how new knowledge counters what is "conventional wisdom."
- Add color and story. Personal interviews can often lead to testimonials, descriptions of life experiences, and even embellishments of extreme opinion. Interviews can give context to the information that the student takes to the interview. The interviewee may give detail to events so that the student begins to understand various situations over time or in different cultures.
- Extend a line of inquiry. Interviews can make the topic more local and personal and, while doing so, lead to new questions for further exploration.

Techniques for successful interviews must be practiced and refined just as with other skills involved in information searching and application. Knowing when to seek an interview, with whom, what questions to pose and how, and how to listen for the most relevant information are elements that are not easy to master. The mature information literate student will seek out interviews often and even return to the same source to get further explanation and elaboration, just as he or she might return to re-reading basic reference materials on a topic. Teachers of information literacy skills will find that interventions for modeling such skills will be important, and should realize that the school library media program has as much an obligation to provide an environment that encourages use of human resources as it does provision of print and electronic materials.

Encouraging the use of interviews means thinking of such events as being as much a part of the center's collection as books, magazines, and the Internet. Teachers of information literacy may maintain a list of good resource people in the community who are willing to be interviewed and who are authoritative, but also able to communicate with students. Such a list may correspond to the typical controversial issues many students research concerning drug abuse, peer pressures, capital punishment, or the environment. Interviewing can take the shape of individual face-to-face questioning or e-mail and written correspondence.

Afraid to Make the Most of Interviewing

Ken Metzler, a journalism teacher, has written extensively about student fears of interviewing and such anxiety is at the core of what Metzler calls "unseen problems":

- An aversion to asking questions for fear of being shown up as ignorant. Metzler notes that a natural, childlike curiosity unfortunately seems to go out of style as people reach a certain age-the teens, perhaps. He reminds us of a Chinese proverb, "He who asks is a fool for five minutes; he who does not is a fool forever."

- Failure to define clearly and state the purpose of the interview, or general lack of preparation. Ability to define purpose is not likely to come early in the student's inquiry process, but later as they begin to gain focus. There should be a need for the interview, and if one can not be stated, then using the expert's time for specific answers should wait until unique questions can be identified.

- A lack of enthusiasm and natural curiosity about people and the world at large. Lack of interest on the part of the interviewer lessens the likelihood of an enthusiastic responder and increases the likelihood that answers will be short and without the rich details that can make an interview a key source of information.

- Failure to listen. Elements of a professional listener include getting ready to listen, giving attention and eye contact, avoiding prejudgment of people, listening for major points and supporting evidence, and evaluating what is said and not said or only half-articulated. Interviewers who are more secure in their craft will offer encouragement and direction and show that they are listening through interview etiquette, which may even include dressing in proper attire to demonstrate that the interviewer is serious about the situation.

- Failure to probe, vagueness, and convoluted or overdefined questions. Opening questions should set the interviewee at ease and allow them to demonstrate what they know or believe. Follow-up questions help the interviewee to further define and give specific examples or illustrate their thoughts in some manner. The mature interviewer knows that this is not the time to

demonstrate all of his or her knowledge about a subject through expansive questions, but to demonstrate enough knowledge to be credible and yet curious for more information.

Interviews for Inquiry

Interviewing is a skill that can be introduced very early in the student's academic experience. Some would agree that most two-year-olds are natural interviewers and that their first experience in school, unfortunately, is to learn not to ask too many questions.

Paula Rogovin, an elementary school teacher at the Manhattan New School, believes in and practices inquiry through interviews as the foundation for her curriculum. Based on her experiences growing up in a family life rich with conversations around the dinner table, field trips to museums and art galleys, and open debate concerning the progressive issues of the day, Rogovin has drawn from those experiences to create a classroom full of questions.

Working with students from five to seven years of age, Rogovin has constructed a learning environment around children who interview their parents and other relatives, local neighborhood workers and personalities, and even a celebrity from time to time. But the emphasis is on learning from people with whom we live and see. Learning about different cultures and careers is driven by interviewing, listening, reflecting, and asking again and again. Insightful information, as well as moments to learn correct spelling and grammar, are facilitated through her guidance of thirty young inquiring minds. Interviews may involve several guests each week along with field trips.

Interviews usually take place first thing in the morning, when students are fresh and alert. Writing accompanies the interviewing as students use personal journals to write what they have heard and what they think about what they have heard. Pages of notes eventually evolve into class-produced books that are accumulated for reading and story time during other parts of the day. Parents, grandparents, and others who have had their thirty minutes in the interviewee's seat often autograph the book compiled and illustrated by the children.

Rogovin has perfected several strategies for successful interviewing over years of experimentation and hundreds of contacts in her community:

- Acknowledge prior knowledge. Just as students bring knowledge to any other situation, so they have prior knowledge they bring to an interview situation. By creating a context for the interview prior to the person being present, students can share such knowledge and thus can help to form and practice question building. Prior knowledge may come from knowing the person to be interviewed, having read or heard stories relevant to the occupation of the interviewee, or remembering similar information from previous interviewing experiences.
- Help guests feel at ease. For some adults, the thought of being interviewed by children is scary. Rogovin leads her class in a friendly and polite "good morning" and emphasizes that sometimes the most significant issues of the interview come from informal discussions to help the guest relax. While being prepared is essential, being flexible and alert to comments that may have special interest to the children is important for successful facilitating of the interview.
- Focus the interview in questions about facts and feelings. What kind of work do you do? How did you learn to do that job? How did you feel when the customer was rude to you?
- Model the questions and the sequence. While children will have many questions, the interview bears more fruit if children see from the teacher that questions should be open-ended at first and then move to the specifics as the discussion progresses. Often questions are rehearsed or practiced and students may role play prior to and even during an interview.
- The teacher serves as an interpreter and

one who helps to link information to help the students find meaning. Constantly alert for the "teachable moment," Rogovin will capitalize on new words, emotions, and surprise comments in order to explain the spelling of a new term, location of a different country, or ask students to think or write about how they might feel in a similar situation just described by the interviewee. Interviews also open the opportunity to make connections with literature and music as a rich collection of cultural heritage is available in this metropolitan neighborhood.

Rogovin does not elude to a school librarian or media specialist. Hopefully there are many helpers who supply additional learning resources and collaborate on ideas. Her classroom is filled with books, records, maps, and illustrations. Resource "cubbies" house books, illustrations, toys, and artifacts gathered by the children. These resource shelves are labeled by the children in terms that they use to describe the careers or other topics being explored. These collections of items therefore serve on a continuing basis for linking interviews together, both in reference to previous interviews and in preparation for the next. Interviewing becomes not only a method to extract information, but an experience for exploring the world.

For Further Reading

Metzler, Ken. Creative Interviewing: The Writer's Guide to Gathering Information and Asking Questions. 2nd ed. Englewood Cliffs, NJ: Prentice Hall, 1989.

Rogovin, Paula. Classroom Interviews: A World of Learning. Portsmouth, NH: Heinemann, 1998. *With companion 50-minute video on vhs from Heinemann Videos.*

Key Words
Learning Laboratory

One of the principles given to describe the modern school library media center in the 1960 AASL Standards is:

The library is a laboratory for research and study where students learn to work alone and in groups under the guidance of librarians and teachers. Thus it contributes to the growth and development of youth in independent thinking, in abilities to study effectively, and in desirable attitudes toward reading, toward other media of communication, and toward all learning and research. (p. 15)

Much has changed during the four decades since this principle was used to illustrate one of the functions of a modern school library media center. The laboratory analogy still holds merit today, especially in relation to modern technologies for information search and presentation as well as learning environments that promote constructivist and open inquiry methods.

Marjorie L. Pappas and Anne E. Tepe have provided a useful illustration of the array of paths and combination of possible skills involved as a student moves through information exploration processes. Their illustration shows how choices expand and fan out as the student, with guidance from the instructional media specialist and other teachers, faces choices for information search, interpretation, communication, and evaluation.

Kuhlthau has documented how important the exploration stage is in the Information Search Process (IPS). Time and support for useful exploration may be the most critical aspect of IPS. Exploration often is restricted by educators who insist that they provide their students with a research focus so that the task can be completed in an efficient manner. And yet, exploration is a stage that can be associated closely with the laboratory analogy. The opportunity to explore, to think about, and to talk about what is possible are at the heart of laboratory environments. Kuhlthau described this when she wrote:

Exploration in learning is not necessarily linear. Nor are students simply solving an information problem as they formulate new ideas. The inquiry approach develops skills that are fundamental to learning in an information-rich environment. Students develop competence beyond location and use strategies in their ability to interpret, understand, and learn from information-and that is information literacy. They learn to incorporate reading strategies, such as using prior knowledge, asking questions, and drawing inferences. They learn that the research process is not an end in itself, but an avenue of discovery as they are building a knowledge base. (p. 15)

Inquiry Theory and Practice

Donald A. Schon of the Massachusetts Institute of Technology, has described several aspects of the theory of inquiry:

From the perspective of designing as learning and learning as designing, the teaching/learning process could be seen, at its best, as a collaborative, communicative process of design and discovery. We would see it...as a dialogue within which teachers and students would be designers in several aspects. ...[T]hey would seek to design a way of framing the situation that opens up paths to solution. ...[T]hey would face a problem of communicating across divergent design and problem-solving worlds; their task here would be to create and sustain a community of design inquiry. This is the meaning I would like to reserve for the term "reflective teaching" (p. 133).

Kathy G. Short, Professor at the University of Arizona, collaborates with many elementary school teachers to implement the principles of inquiry or discovery learning as they convert the typical classroom into a learning laboratory. Over several years of experimentation, inquiry has become the curriculum, not just a teaching technique. Their approach is to assure that students become problem-posers as well as problem-solvers.

We saw that in our classrooms we [teachers] were the problem-posers; our students were forced to become the problem-solvers, answering our [teacher] questions. We realized that problem-solving and research are empty processes when the question is not one that really matters in the life of the inquirer. While there are many research strategies that support our lives as inquirers, focusing on learning those strategies is a waste of time if we don't first take time to find a significant question. Even then, we may not find a specific question, but an interest, an issue, or a general wondering that we want to pursue further. As we work through inquiry, we do not usually end with one answer or even a set of answers. Inquiry does not narrow our perspective; it gives us more understandings, questions, and possibilities than when we started. Inquiry isn't just asking and answering a question. It involves searching for significant questions and figuring out how to explore those questions from many perspectives. (p. 8)

Questions drive the activities of the typical library media center. A systematic method applied to display, examine, extend, and reflect on those questions as well as explore a variety of means to address questions and present possible solutions will establish the library media center as a learning laboratory.

The Scientist in the Laboratory

While some of these skills have been mentioned here, the seven process skills of science are usually listed as:

- Observing-watching carefully, taking notes, comparing and contrasting.
- Questioning-asking questions about observations; asking questions that can lead to investigations.
- Hypothesizing-providing explanations consistent with available observations.
- Predicting-suggesting an event in the future, based on observations.
- Investigating-planning, conducting, measuring, gathering data, controlling variables.
- Communicating-informing others in a variety of means: oral, written, representational.

Science is a way of thinking and acting. It is a process of inquiry, resulting in a body of systematized knowledge. The essence of science is not in simple statements of principles or accepted laws, but rather the struggle to find out about the material world. Can children do what scientists do? Perhaps not with results on the systematic levels commonly associated with scientific method, but children, the younger the better, have universal traits such as curiosity, wonder, excitement, and, usually, a willingness to share. More often it is the teacher who must find the child's level for effective information investigations rather than the child adapting to the adult.

Principles that guide much of today's thinking as to the best learning practices are designed to bring the teacher into closer communication with an understanding of their students before lessons are implemented or student performance is evaluated. Steve Zemelman and his colleagues at the Center for City Schools, National-Louis University, have determined that these principles include:

- Student-Centered-The best starting point for schooling is young people's real interests; all across the curriculum, investigating students' own questions

210 ....

KEY WORDS

should always take precedence over study of arbitrarily and distantly selected content.

- Experiential-Active, hands-on, concrete experience is the most powerful and natural form of learning. Students should be immersed in the most direct possible experience of the content of every subject.
- Holistic-Children learn best when they encounter whole ideas, events, and materials in purposeful contexts, not by studying sub-parts isolated from actual use.
- Authentic-Real, rich, complex ideas and materials are at the heart of the curriculum. Lessons or textbooks that water-down, control, or oversimplify content ultimately disempower students.
- Expressive-To fully engage ideas, construct meaning, and remember information, students must regularly employ the whole range of communicative media-speech, writing, drawing, poetry, dance, drama, music, movement, and visual arts.
- Reflective-Balancing the immersion in experience and expression must be opportunities for learners to reflect, debrief, and abstract from their experiences what they have felt and thought and learned.
- Social-Learning is always socially constructed and often interactional; teachers need to create classroom interactions that "scaffold" learning.
- Collaborative-Cooperative learning activities tap the social power of learning better than competitive and individualistic approaches.
- Democratic-The classroom is a model community; students learn what they live as citizens of the school.
- Cognitive-The most powerful learning comes when children develop true understanding of concepts through higher-order thinking associated with various fields of inquiry and through self-monitoring of their thinking.
- Developmental-Children grow through

a series of definable but not rigid stages, and schooling should fit its activities to the developmental level of students.
- Constructivist-Children do not just receive content; in a very real sense, they re-create and reinvent every cognitive system they encounter, including language, literacy, and mathematics.
- Challenging-Students learn best when faced with genuine challenges, choices, and responsibility in their own learning. (p. 8)

The Information Scientist

A recent comparison of seven scientists who are challenging our world, written by Ted Anton, suggests that a new interdisciplinary approach has given rise to a new fundamental approach to science, with most of its innovations coming from researchers outside the envelope of their fields. Investigative methods familiar to information science and use of computer technologies to gather, analyze, and disseminate ideas have become attributes of the new "bold science."

Gary Marchionini, Boshamer Professor of Information Science at the University of North Carolina, writes:

Information science is emerging as an interdisciplinary subject that draws theories and principles from many fields and has begun to expand from its traditional application base of libraries to offices, museums, schools, and homes. Documentation writers, linguists, archivists and curators, Web site designers, instructional designers, computer scientists, and educators are making valuable contributions to this growing field and we can expect new penetration of information science topics into the undergraduate and K-12 curriculums in the years ahead. (p. 24)

What does the information scientist do? Are such actions relevant to the information process and information literacy skills that have been introduced by many school library media specialists and college instructional librarians across the nation? The following activities define the business of information scientists:

- Classification Theory-In what manner can knowledge or information be represented so effective and efficient retrieval can take place? In what manner should such representation change to meet different discourse, discipline, or information format variables?
- Information Use Behavior-In what manner do humans seek and use information or not? What information do they find useful or not? How do diverse cultures and media formats affect behaviors?
- Knowledge Creation and Dissemination-In what manner can information be best communicated or transferred to meet needs of different groups? How is knowledge communicated, validated, valued, and assimilated? What use patterns can be documented? What do the use patterns tell us?
- Social Informatics-What is the role of information in the social and cultural milieu? Issues studied may involve information equity, information security, political or economic values of information, and intellectual property rights.
- Interaction Studies (Marchionini, p. 24)-Also termed "information architecture" or "information design," this area draws from studies related to human-computer interaction. Scientists seek to determine the processes which influence and are influenced by human use of information systems. Scientists strive to determine ways that interactive experiences can be well structured and properly positioned within the wider or global electronic information infrastructure.

Information science is a complex discipline. Does application to a K-12 setting still apply? Yes, although student activities, processes, and products will need to be scaled to meet their abilities and needs. There is value in students attempting to address (test, discuss, and document) the following types of questions:

- What were the most effective search terms used to locate information on your topic? Answers can involve several combinations across different databases and different aspects of information need. How did your research questions evolve over the information search process? Illustrate how the questions clustered into groups, became more detailed, specific, or sophisticated as you explored more background information. Were there questions for which search commands were not really possible or useful? What were they? Questions, along with successful search term combinations, can be compiled, organized, and illustrated graphically on a bulletin board near computer terminal centers for other students to examine and learn from as they consider their own search strategies.
- What specific resources from different general formats (print, electronic, human, video, periodical, book, computer) did you find most useful for your project and why? Compilation of these sources with abstracts under specific research questions compiled on a website can provide tangible leads for other students as they enter a similar research project.
- Based on the resources the members of the class found to be most useful, what patterns emerge as to information formats or information location? Are there some useful indicators your class can extract from this to help predict search strategies in similar future information need situations? Do patterns point to specific indexes or that the local public library has as much or more to offer than the school library media center?
- Of the websites explored by the class, which are most authoritative and which should not be considered authoritative at all? What criteria are most useful to make these decisions? Students may debate this in class and later display homepage print-outs on a bulletin board near search terminals or create a

website with links to sites that illustrate the criteria.

- Of the resources located by this class in the study of a given environmental issue, what few key items (books, journal articles, speeches, documentaries, etc.) or authors have had the most social or political influence? Why? This discussion can be a companion piece to each student's research report.

- In what manner can your group's report be best presented to the rest of the class? To parents? To a younger student group? How can you determine if you have communicated the message and conclusions you want to express? Do you modify the presentation and the evaluation of your communication in some manner for each audience? Why? How?

- In what manner can pieces of relevant information be linked to provide evidence for a logical argument? What information is lacking to make the argument more convincing and how would you go about gathering original data or other information to fill that gap? From previous experiences, is such information likely to be available or within your means to produce? How may the constructed argument be accepted or rejected by different political groups or cultures, based on biases or other strongly held opinions and traditions?

Note that most of these questions are associated closely with the processes of locating, evaluating, and using information. As illustrated by Marilyn Joyce and Julie Tallman in their application of the I-Search Process and by Carol Kuhlthau in Library Research Process, mapping, charting, and journaling portions of the information search process allow for student reflection and sharing of their successes and frustrations. Each process becomes a product to be open for either self-evaluation or teacher assessment of student progress. These process pieces are products, or process-products, open for discussion and evaluation during

the inquiry experience. These process-products contain a heavy dose of what information science is about, and they are the experimental exercises of the learning laboratory.

The Information Learning Laboratory

What might the Information Learning Laboratory look like and how might it be different from the current typical school library media center? What might be different from the usual vision that one conjures with the term "laboratory" for language study or computer skills?

An innovative outreach program at the Denver Public Library has arranged computer carrels around the perimeter of their "Library Laboratory" to allow teachers to move freely among students. Oral explanations, demonstrations, and lots of hands-on experimentation are reinforced with written handouts. The emphasis of these practice sessions held at the public library for school children of all ages is on strategy and critical thinking.

The Information Laboratory includes practice exercises and free movement among computerized student workstations. Actions, attitudes, and means for sharing process-products are attributes as well. The list that follows may provide some visionary possibilities and many of these exist in current school media programs to some degree.

Actions and Attitudes of Instructional Media Specialists and Other Teachers:

- Model and engage in research with students by selecting questions they will explore along with the rest of the class.
- Value and reinforce the processes of research over the product as everyone needs time and support to explore.
- Provide access to a wide variety of resources at different levels of sophistication and authority so that students grapple with determining value levels.
- Listen to, observe, and reflect on student information needs, performance, and revisions to improve inquiry engagements and environments.

- Intervene and discuss alternatives at point of need to help students hypothesize and test their assumptions.
- Give time to inquiry process tasks and issues as well as to products and presentations.

Actions and Attitudes of Students:
- Work in and be rewarded for team and cooperative efforts, but ultimately display individual initiative to continue similar investigations beyond that given as the academic exercise.
- Plan and demonstrate ways to verify, extend, organize, and/or discard ideas, information, and resources.
- Express ideas in a variety of ways: journals, talking or reporting, drawing, graphing, charting.
- Link information into evidence and share information and leads to information with classmates. Express appreciation to those who help, and acknowledge them in final products.
- Communicate the level of understanding of concepts that they have developed to date.
- Use questions that lead to investigations that generate and redefine further questions and ideas.
- Observe carefully and make connections to previously held ideas.
- Accept, create, and use quality indicators to assess their work; reflect on their work with peers and teacher-mentors.
- Predict search strategies and resources that are most likely to be relevant in other information-need situations.

Displays, Bulletin Boards, Wall Charts, Websites:
- Maintained by students who display individual and group work on the information search and use processes.
- Show student products and describe the actions taken to produce the product, including information selection, contacts with experts, and scripting the final presentation.
- Archived for future student researchers to examine and thus provide a jump-start on ideas and directions.
- Display student work in the library media center, across the curriculum, and in spaces provided in hallways and classrooms to illustrate student research projects.
- Readily available to parents at any time, but clearly on display at parent visitations and school open house events.
- Viewed and examined by many instructional media specialists and peer teachers for ideas and information literacy lesson sharing.
- Part of the annual review process for evaluation of school library media services and instructional library media specialist performance.

Furniture, Space, Computers and Other Tools:
- Allow for space so inquirers may spread out resources, paper materials, and plans for outlines or storyboards as well as access to terminals networked to a variety of design tools and information databases.
- Connections are provided to databases and resources beyond those held by the school.
- Connections to human resources is facilitated through telecommunications and a resource guide maintained by the instructional media center staff.
- Portals are created so students may view and critique peer work on drafts and test sites and can share information leads or specific evidence; quick electronic "cut-and-paste" can be used to experiment with a variety of ways to display information and data, but used less and less often to copy materials as the inquirers mature in their process skills.
- Production and presentation areas available so students can experiment across all stages of the information search and use processes; audiences have access to student projects at process and product levels.

For Further Reading

American Association of School Librarians. Standards for School Library Programs. Chicago: American Library Association, 1960.

Anton, Ted. Bold Science: Seven Scientists Who Are Changing Our World. New York: W. H. Freeman, 2000.

Callison, Daniel. "Comparison of Teacher and Student Ratings of Microcomputer Software." Computers in the Schools 6, nos. 1 & 2 (1989): 97-108.

Callison, Daniel. "Inquiry." School Library Media Activities Monthly 15, no. 6 (February 1999): 38-42.

Callison, Daniel. "Methods for Measuring Student Use of Databases and Interlibrary Loan Materials." School Library Media Quarterly 16, no. 2 (Winter 1988): 138-142.

Callison, Daniel. "Reflection." School Library Media Activities Monthly 16, no. 2 (October 1999): 31-34.

Callison, Daniel. "Schema and Problem-Solving." School Library Media Activities Monthly 14, no. 9 (May 1998): 43-45

Callison, Daniel. "Student-Talk." School Library Media Activities Monthly 14, no. 10 (June 1998): 38-41.

Doris, Ellen. Doing What Scientists Do: Children Learn to Investigate Their World. Portsmouth, NH: Heinemann, 1991.

Inquiry: Thoughts, Views, and Strategies for the K-5 Classroom. Foundations Vol. 2. Washington, D. C.: National Science Foundation. 2000. *Available free through the Exploratorium and Institute for Inquiry* http://www.exploratorium.edu/IFI/index.html. *Search also for "Inquiry Based Science: What does it look like?"*

Joyce, Marilyn Z., and Julie I. Tallman. *Making the Writing and Research Connection with the I-Search Process.* New York: Neal-Schuman, 1997.

Kuhlthau, Carol C. "Literacy and Learning for the Information Age." In Learning and Libraries in an Information Age: Principles and Practice, edited by Barbara K. Stripling, 3-21. Englewood, CO: Libraries Unlimited, 1999.

Kuhlthau, Carol C. Teaching the Library Research Process. 2nd ed. Metuchen, NJ: Scarecrow Press, 1994.

Marchionini, Gary. "Educating Responsible Citizens in the Information Society." Educational Technology 39, no. 2 (March-April 1999): 17-26.

Pappas, Marjorie L. "Pathways to Inquiry." School Library Media Activities Monthly 16, no. 9 (May 2000): 23-27.

Pappas, Marjorie and Anne E. Tepe. Pathways to Knowledge and Inquiry. Libraries Unlimited, 2002.

Schon, Donald A. "The Theory of Inquiry: Dewey's Legacy to Education." Curriculum Inquiry 22, no. 2 (1992): 119-139.

Short, Kathy G., and others. Learning Together through Inquiry. York, ME: Stenhouse, 1996.

Zemelman, Steven, Harvey Daniels, and Arthur Hyde. Best Practice: New Standards for Teaching and Learning in America's Schools. 2nd ed. Portsmouth, NH: Heinemann, 1998.

Key Words
Lesson Plan

A "lesson plan" may be either an informal or formal set of actions taken by a teacher or a group of teachers to determine what their students are to learn, how the teaching activity will be implemented, and how the acquisition of new skills or knowledge may be demonstrated and evaluated. This process is illustrated in three basic questions from the lesson plan outline provided through AskERIC.

Each teacher should ask and answer:

> Where are my students going?
> How are they going to get there?
> How will I know when they have arrived?

Collaborative lesson planning among the instructional media specialist and other teachers can involve more complex questions in order to move through a systematic method for shared teaching roles. As with most processes, the lesson plan will reach higher levels of effectiveness when communication channels are open for interactive input among the educators. Although often illustrated in a linear fashion, the spark to initiate the plan or to elaborate on new potential areas for the plan may come at any juncture of the elements that are discussed here.

The Instructional Consultant Role

Patricia Pickard's study of the instructional consultant role for school library media specialists in DeKalb County provides insight on the classic issues faced over the past four decades concerning the potential for leadership from library media specialists in lesson planning and curriculum development. Her survey is based on an extensive literature review to establish these key points:

Actions for the library media specialist to play a key role in curriculum development include:

- Be aware of the total instructional program in the school.
- Visit and participate in classes as much as possible.
- Know current trends in successful teaching methods.
- Become involved in curriculum planning, not just responding to the established curriculum.
- Conduct in-service for teachers. Teach teachers whenever possible.
- Establish, read, and promote a current collection of professional materials, including texts and quality websites.
- Join and participate as a member of instructional teams. Create the instructional plan and act as leader when beneficial to the project.

Depending on the situation, the library media specialist may take active or proactive steps to engage in the lesson planning and curriculum development processes. At the highest levels, interactive steps are taken so that the library media specialist acts as co-educator, listens to and evaluates ideas and input from other teachers, and provides his or her own insights. Such input moves beyond "knowing resources" to knowledge of teaching and evaluation methods. Callison wrote in 1987:

"The [instructional] media specialist acts, not only as a leader, but also begins to examine the educational system in terms of evaluating its successes and failures. The [instructional] media specialist becomes an important force for curriculum development. This impact involves not only integrating information skills into all areas of the curriculum, but working to revise lessons and activities to the degree that such lessons require the use of [resource-based education] through the media center and guided by the [instructional] media specialist." (p. 24)

Several studies conducted since 1970 suggest that administrators and teachers see the potential for instructional involvement of the school library media specialist, and often more so than do media specialists themselves. Among many other leaders in school media education, Eisenberg has concluded that the activities associated with curriculum support and instructional design have not been fully realized, exemplifying the gap between literature and practice. More than a decade after his observation, and nearly two decades after Craver's extensive review of the library media specialist's instructional role, the primary challenge remains: to narrow the gap between theory and practice and between internal and external perceptions and expectations.

In the early 1990s, Pickard found, as continues to be true across the nation, a small portion (10%) of the practicing library media specialists perceived their instructional role to be important. When accepted at all, it was in a supporting role and seldom in a leadership position. Tasks that involved the library media specialist in evaluation of student performance were viewed as too time-consuming and reserved for the teacher, even though such responsibilities move the library media specialist into a stronger co-educator role. Such engagement with student performance also provides essential feedback concerning the effectiveness of bibliographic instruction and the degree to which students may effectively select and use information. Without such evaluation, the library media specialist continues on a blind track in faltering attempts to teach information literacy.

How Teachers "Plan"

Linda Lachance Wolcott, from the Instructional Technology Department of Utah State University, has made the case that a greater understanding on the part of library media specialists as to how teachers plan or don't plan will strengthen instructional partnerships. Certification programs in many states are moving beyond basic teacher certification for library media specialist to require successful classroom teaching experience as well. Evidence of successful teaching practice is now seen in many position announcements for new media specialists. Knowledge of technology and resources as they can be applied to instruction, along with management of information access and control, have become more common job descriptors than ten years ago.

Wolcott noted that when planning does take place between library media specialist and classroom teacher, it is seldom formal. Often spur-of-the-moment plans take place because of lack of time, lack of awareness for the need of collaborative participation, or because the "library lesson" may be seen as peripheral to the major learning task. Certainly, some library media specialists are in familiar territory with teachers who have worked with them before and there are tasks that are quick and routine to plug in. Formal planning, however, can increase interaction and effectiveness in the long run. Formal planning is more likely to lead to integration of information literacy skills for units that support inquiry learning.

Wolcott describes two types of planning. "Incremental planning" is characterized by a short problem-solving stage, brief unit planning, and reliance on trying activities in the classroom. "Comprehensive planning" gives more attention to the unit as a whole and attempts to specify plans thoroughly prior to teaching. Her review of the research on teacher planning practices indicates:

- Planning is a mental activity. Very little of what teachers plan is committed to paper. Teachers form a "mental image" of the lesson and activities often based on routines or sets of procedures. Objectives often are conveyed verbally, if at all. This practice increases the chance of the students misunderstanding the intent of a lesson especially when written statements are not available, explained, or practiced.
- Planning in practice is nonlinear. Ideas or lessons may originate from several of the stages often described in a more formal model. Textbook outlines, schedules, and personal interests may influence the origin of the lesson more than any reflective thoughts on evaluation or analysis of student learning needs.
- Planning is influenced by published curriculum. Although teachers may not tend to write their own plans, those which have been written for them through state, district, or textbook guides often are employed. Tailoring curriculum to meet local needs and custom design of lessons based on predetermined entry level skills for the specific students at hand usually is not attempted.

To engage teachers in the planning process, Wolcott identifies several strategies. These are based on the assumption that the library media specialist will be in tune with the normal planning habits of the teachers and thus engagements may be more likely after the teacher is into a unit, rather than pre-planning a unit far in advance. Wolcott's suggestions are paraphrased and elaborated on here:

- Seek occasions to talk with teachers about what they are teaching and enjoy teaching. Informal moments may arise concerning specific resources the teacher is seeking for today's or this week's lesson. A quick follow-up with the teacher may open possible collaborative teaching when the lesson is presented again.

- Involve teachers in weeding of resources as well as selection and purchase of resources. Often through the weeding process, teachers can see gaps in the resource collection and conversations can begin as to how these might be filled, along with resource-based units in the future.
- Think of planning as a series of increasingly broader-reaching centric circles radiating out from a central focus. From the instructional task at hand, what stages might evolve, over time, that will move the activity into a more resource-based experience? Build from where the teacher is and together modify as the teacher learns of more resource options and the library media specialist learns of the specific instructional objectives intended.
- Accommodate various types and styles of planning. Often planning and teaching is a solitary activity. Teachers need to be offered teaming approaches that will prove to be not only more successful for the students, but also save time and concentrate on objectives the teacher finds meaningful. While the library media specialist will introduce additional information literacy skills to a lesson, these should be seen as integrated with the other skills and not simply add-ons. Some teachers just may not be open to teaming and success may be limited to showing the teacher information skills they can incorporate on their own. On other occasions, success may be finding a teacher who becomes a team player for the first time.
- Provide leadership. Often scheduling, resource management, and consolidation of ideas and objectives must be completed by one team member who has a vision of where the lesson can go in the future as a unit to involve different areas of the curriculum and several teachers. Instructional media specialists are at their best when they take this leadership role.

Models for Formal Planning

While it is reasonable to become acquainted with common teacher planning practices, analysis of local teacher planning behaviors and needs is critical. Just because most teachers push aside planning methods as cumbersome jargon, the conclusion should not be that haphazard lessons are successful ones. The instructional media specialist also will want to become well-versed in the elements of more formal planning. These elements, while not always used in a linear or sequential manner, still provide the context for the questions, ideas, and conversations (informal or formal) to engage teachers in the possibilities. More important, these models serve as a map to make more meaningful lesson planning a reality.

If we stay in a world of fragmented solitary planning, with no communication of objectives, or verbal communication only, and curriculum guided by forces outside of the creativity of our best local teachers, we remain in a very narrow, textbook-dominated educational environment. We waste the reason why we exist, regardless of how much principals, teachers, and other library media specialists may not realize the protential of our instructional role. Much depends on attitude as well as expertise. Without the desire to make a difference in the educational structure, time for planning and meaningful conversations don't stand a chance.

Multi-Disciplinary Planning: Elements of the Instructional Resource Plan (IRP)

Movement from a basic lesson to a series of activities coordinated with several teachers takes instruction into a full unit of study. Talents of the teachers involved must be organized and managed, just as resources are, by the instructional media specialist. There is a fundamental difference between the reactive levels of the library media specialist and the interactive levels of the instructional media specialist. Management of ideas, talents, expertise, methods, analysis of needs, and evaluation are as important, if not more important, than man-

agement of access to resources.

The fourteen elements listed and discussed here are based on my twenty-five years of teaching the development of Instructional Resource Plans (IRP) at Indiana University and other schools, as well as seven years of experience as a high school instructional media specialist. Nearly all of these elements I have learned from others, practicing library media specialists and other teachers. Not all of the elements must be in place for a unit to be successful, nor would the planning process always follow the order in which the elements are listed.

Each element can tie to many others. The spark for a more formal unit plan can come within any element as noted several times in the following detailed description.

- IRP Objectives. Objectives, clearly stated in observable terms to direct student performance and evaluation, are essential. These may be drawn from proven local classroom objectives, district or state guides, or national standards. Information Power provides not only nine standards for student performance in information literacy, but also specific objectives or indicators along with statements that illustrate levels of proficiency and relevance to different areas of the curriculum.

Are there entry-level skills that need to be mastered prior to introducing these objectives? Are these objectives reflected in lessons, activities, and other elements of the plan that follow? New standards can and should spark new ideas for lessons and units as well as bring together previous successful lessons that stood alone, but gain strength as skills can be connected through a full unit.

- IRP Context. Think about and discuss the context for the unit. What interests and excites the students, you, and other teachers? Do you know critical characteristics about the students to be involved? Are they more or less creative than previous groups? Do some important skills seem in need of reinforcement? Are there teachers who have interests and expertise along with a willingness to experiment with a teaming unit? Have they demonstrated in the past the willingness to commit to a project and share ideas?

For the first attempts at such units, a small team of two to four will be plenty. Do not force all areas of the curriculum to be represented in the unit or project. Select those that seem most likely to cooperate, and plan to add more teachers as the unit matures through several intervals of implementation. Extensive units that place the instructional media specialist in a lead role are likely not to number more than three or four for a given semester even in the hands of the most skilled and efficient specialist. First timers may want to begin with one such unit for the first year or two.

- IRP Time Frame. Schedule the important events that come to mind for brainstorming, resource considerations, lesson planning, implementation, and evaluation. Through e-mail communication or on a calendar posted in the teachers' lounge for all to see, block and reserve times. Common lunch periods and evenings will come into play. Some school corporations pay for additional summer days for in-depth planning.

- IRP Lessons and Roles. Usually a full unit of study will involve several lessons and activities. Determine which teacher takes the lead for each lesson and what joint roles, if any, other team members will play. In some cases, this will mean individual teachers will facilitate different groups of students on either different skills to meet different ability levels or to provide for small group interaction. In other cases, one teacher may take the lead for full- or large-group presentations. In such cases, other teachers may have time to work on other elements of the unit. In all cases, the instructional media specialist and other teachers may find that teaching in tandem is beneficial. This does not mean one teaches while the other sits. It means both or several have presentation roles in the lesson and all engage the

learners. In hands-on skills practice, for example, one teacher may present the steps and methods to the entire group while other teachers serve as "rovers" to work with individual students and their specific problems.

Sample lessons should be sketched out with individual objectives and necessary resources noted. Different orders of the deliveries of these lessons may depend on scaffolding of objectives and skills. Although never exact, some attention should be given to how practice of some skills is necessary and must be mastered before moving on to higher or more complex skills.

- IRP Questions. As a teaching team, brainstorm the questions you would expect the average student to be able to answer following their participation in the unit. Do these questions represent all of the key content? If the list becomes very long, determine the five or ten most critical questions. These should tie back to the objectives and standards. In some cases, these questions may create new objectives, lessons, and activities. The brainstorming involved in generating these questions may serve as a model for one of the early exercises in any unit with students, to engage them in the generation of questions they want to explore over the coming unit. Who, What, and How questions are often the first to be raised. Remember, for strong inquiry units, there should be lots of Why questions.

- IRP Resources. This element includes the traditional role the library media specialist has played in the tie with instruction. What resources are available to support the unit? What access is possible to additional materials through other schools, the public library, or other libraries in the area? Are there good Internet resources suitable for the age group involved? Are there new materials on the market that should be considered, or previewed, and ordered?

The less traditional use of resources, but more important in the plan development, involves idea generation. What have you read or seen that gives you good ideas for this unit? This is similar to the exploration stage in the Kuhlthau Information Search Process-read, view, and discuss widely in search of ideas. Reading a good book or magazine article or ideas from viewing that PBS special last week often spark further unit planning. In some cases, that special resource is the seed of the idea for beginning the planning for the possible unit, so stage one might be right here. In other cases, immersion in unit planning triggers a more sensitive awareness of potential resources. This may happen even without a great deal of systematic searching as newspaper articles, television news, or discussions with friends will suddenly include notice of items that would have been ignored before.

- IRP Search. A more systematic search for additional resources may be necessary. Time invested under the management of the instructional media specialist may include examination of both resource guides used to locate library media materials as well as journals and guides used by classroom teachers for resources. These are not the same, and both should be explored as there is often little duplication and both will contain potentially useful materials. Examination or preview of additional resources available at other schools and libraries should be a task for a team member or two.

- IRP Packaging. Gathering the resources and materials for the unit can involve most of the team members, although, again this is a traditional role often played by the library media specialist. It should not be the only role, nor should it be one isolated for the library media specialist alone. Arrangements to alert the local public library of the up-coming unit can be a responsibility of a classroom teacher on the team. The local children's or youth public librarian may be willing to serve as a community member on the team and provide read-

ers with advisory and reference services specifically in support of the unit.

For some units, special resource corners in the library media center that highlight the unit serve to not only provide a central place to gather the resources in a convenient location, but bring attention to the unit and publicize such multi-disciplinary collaboration. Packaging also may involve composing a webography along with the usual bibliography so that primary sites can be located quickly and provide a jump start for students. Some instructional media specialists construct a WebQuest, an online package of resources to support many elements of the plan as well as instructional activity links. Human resources who are willing to be interviewed by students or come as guest speakers may be included in this packaging. At the end of the unit, a compilation of quality resources should be available in a local resource kit, ready for use the next time the unit is implemented, and available for loan to other schools. The objective is to manage information resources for efficient access and to help learners move quickly beyond the location stage and into the information use stages.

- IRP Common Piece of Literature. Many resource-based lessons, and eventually units, spring from a strong and emotional piece of young adult literature. This can serve as a common base for all involved in the unit, teachers and students. From this piece can come strands for a broader theme and ties to other relevant literature pieces to promote. Centered on this piece can be teacher and student read-alouds in class, and often serves as the basis for dramatic outlets to student products in stories, essays, plays, and multimedia. Students who have not had the desire to read before often are engaged when this one title drives an exciting unit. Although not always the case, and not required for a resource-based unit to be successful, a good young adult novel can stimulate a great many themes for learning. A classroom set or a copy for all students involved often is provided if the budget will allow.

Clusters of children's books, a major motion picture, or even a classic nonfiction book are all candidates for a common base of information from which grows the purpose for the unit. If the materials are of quality and engage learners in thoughtful questions, the tie to many of the standards is natural. While the usual approach is to identify the learning objectives first, some young adult titles are so powerful that they deserve not only promotion for reading for pleasure but have a place in driving the curriculum as well.

- IRP Community. Community involvement is high on the list of most school districts, but such ties should be considered not just because of the insistence of the administration. Community experts can provide valuable information on some topics as guest speakers or by responding to student questions over e-mail. Parents may help with field trips and some may play the role of tutor. Depending on the theme of the unit, local businesses and organizations may have resources to contribute. Recruiting such community support should be based on a clear vision as to how it will enhance students' learning.
- IRP Evaluation. At least two types of evaluation should be considered, with the first being the task of evaluating student performance. Specific criteria should come from the standards and objectives. A checklist or a rubric of criteria with levels of performance may be useful. Clear understanding on the part of the teaching team and the students as to what will be evaluated and by whom is important to convey. Student performance in such a unit should be reported within the context of how students are graded for the given school. Often multi-disciplinary units allow for evaluation of multiple skills. Some students who struggle with initial phases of the unit will shine at the performance and presentation stages. A com-

posite of the evaluations based on different skills from different evaluators should generate a comprehensive judgment of the learner's accomplishments.

The second type, evaluation of the unit and its lessons and activities, is essential. Depending on the length of the unit, there may need to be a mid-point, formal evaluation by the team. Adjustments are thus made for the next implementation with emphasis on identification of new resources that will support the unit in the future. Should roles be combined, eliminated, or expanded in some manner? Are there new areas for future student evaluation, and who will develop the evaluation method and take the lead?

- IRP Budget. While it may seem very much out of place in lesson planning, there can be expenses that stand in the way of moving an otherwise strong resource-based unit into action-expenses for materials, duplication, field trips, guest speakers, and classroom sets of common literature pieces. While the library media center budget and departmental budgets may cover some of these expenses, a well-organized unit plan will attract dollars from the principal's budget, and from the local parent/teacher associations as well.

The elements addressed in this Instructional Resource Plan are the common elements normally required to detail in a formal grant application. Practice in development of the IRP can lead directly to seeking additional funds through school district and state agencies.

- IRP Celebration. A resource-based unit that involves several teachers and dozens of students in a special theme deserves celebration. Often a special evening or open house in the library media center will provide the opportunity for students to display what they have accomplished. Other classes in school may visit during the day and parents and friends in the evening. Often students remain with their displays to explain and talk about what they learned, similar to the science fair format.

- IRP Modeling Inquiry. These multi-disciplinary units provide the opportunity for the instructional media specialist and other teachers to model how they learn. Create segments in which teachers raise questions they want to explore. They should ask and talk through information problems and how they plan to find solutions as clear examples for the students. They should explore and participate in the projects as much as the students and share their successes and frustrations. Instructional media specialists and other teachers become co-investigators in inquiry projects. They explore and reflect as well as facilitate and evaluate.

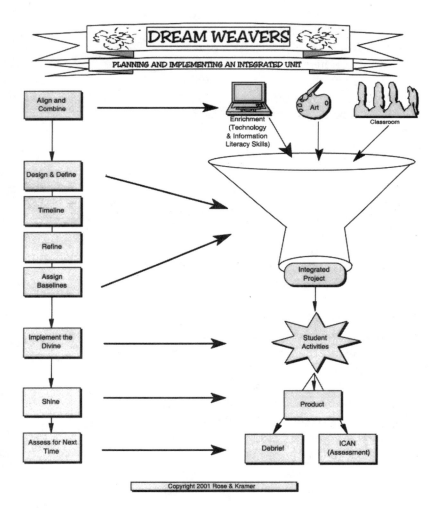

Copyright 2001 Rose & Kramer

The Dream Weavers Model

The Dream Weavers are composed of a group of eleven teachers in the Pike Township School Corporation of Indianapolis. Led by a cadre of specialists in library/media, art, music, and enrichment, these educators base their planning at the Fishback Creek Public Academy on the ICAN learning philosophy-learning through multiple skills. ICAN is a state experimental program that provides a computerized interdisciplinary curriculum to developmental benchmarks and allows the compilation and analysis of individual student records. As a part of the mission of this academy, all learners are involved in meaningful activities that address their strengths and provide opportunities for growth.

The Dream Weavers Model has been illustrated (see Figure) and outlined by Kym Kramer, library media specialist, and Nicole Rose, art teacher.

- Align and Combine. Begin with classroom curriculum. Brainstorm and align additional areas. Approximately eight to twelve weeks prior to the next grading period, the Dream Weaver Team meets to share what they have planned in their classroom. A list is made of key lessons and activities. The specialist cadre members chime in and list from their areas ideas for providing common learning threads based on media, literature, stories, art, and music projects.
- Design and Define. Core planners design the project, weaving the curriculum together. Define each area's responsibilities.
- Timeline. Create calendars and a linear flow chart. Show responsibilities. List benchmarks and critical due dates of the project. These are provided for all to see so that, at any point, team members can easily see what is going on in any room. Due dates make team weavers accountable to others.
- Refine. Meet with the team, review calendars, and make final changes just a few weeks prior to implementation.
- Assign Baselines. Discuss what will be

graded. Decide who will be responsible for grading specific skills. Set due dates.

- Implement the Divine! Just Do It! But communicate frequently to be sure things are on track! The specialists weave their activities among the classes to support, enhance, and extend the classroom activities.
- Shine! Celebrate! After weeks of work, give children and teachers the chance to shine and enjoy the products of their learning efforts.
- Assess for Next Time. Debrief as a team on how program goals were met or not. Did the weaving activities strengthen classroom activities and support learning objectives?
- No Confines! Continue to weave. Projects are never ending-poetry, book-making, insect kits, play and story creation, multimedia, and storytelling festivals with the kids as stars!

For Further Reading and Viewing

AskERIC Education Information. "Lesson Plan." http://ericir.syr.edu/Virtual/Lessons/Guide.shtml

Callison, Daniel. "Evaluator and Educator: The School Media Specialist." Tech Trends 32, no. 5 (October 1987): 24-29.

Callison, Daniel. "The Twentieth Century School Library Media Research Record." In The Encyclopedia of Library and Information Science, edited by Allen Kent. Vol. 71. New York: Marcel Dekker, 2002. 339-368.

Craver, Kathleen W. "The Changing Role of the High School Library Media Specialist: 1950-1984." School Library Media Quarterly 14, no. 4 (1986): 183-191.

Haycock, Carol-Ann. "Developing the School Resource Center Program: A Systematic Approach." Emergency Librarian 12 (September/October 1984): 9-16.

Libraries Are for Conversations. Distributed by Heinemann Publications, 1994. Videocassette: 30 min.

Pickard, Patricia W. "Current Research: The Instructional Consultant Role of the School Library Media Specialist." School Library Media Quarterly 21, no. 2 (1993). http://www.ala.org/aasl/SLMR/slmr_resources/select_ pickard.html

Turner, Philip M. Helping Teachers Teach. 2nd ed. Englewood, CO: Libraries Unlimited, 1993.

Turner, Philip M. "Information Skills and Instructional Consulting: A Synergy." School Library Media Quarterly 20, no. 1 (1991): 13-18.

Wolcott, Linda Lachance. "Understanding How Teachers Plan: Strategies for Successful Instructional Partnerships." School Library Media Quarterly 22, no. 3 (1994). http://www.ala.org/aasl/SLMR/slmr_resources/select_wolcott.html

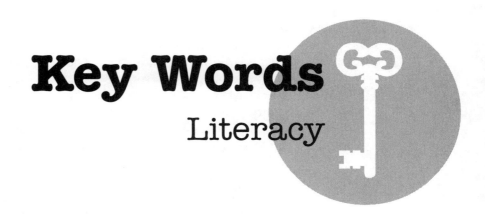

Key Words
Literacy

Modern applied research and educational theory have combined to broaden the meaning of literacy as we should view it today. A true understanding of literacy is certainly more than basic reading and writing. The dynamics of literacy across learning environments also is much more than what has been sparked by the technologies of the Information Age. Literacy has several rather traditional aspects that are now emerging in new ways as we gain a greater understanding of interactive learning.

Shirley Brice Heath, Professor of Anthropology, English, and Education at Stanford, voiced several aspects of the new literacy during a recent interview at Indiana University. Heath places her definition in the more powerful learning contexts outside of the school room. Literacy is knowing how to get information that is needed in order to get around within your environment and to get things done. Literacy is knowing how to select, reject, or revise information from a variety of access points for use in a host of different communication channels. Literacy is a dynamic skill requiring fluency in a variety of decoding situations.

"Information fluency" would counter the common core of national cultural literacy described in 1987 by E. D. Hirsch, Jr. In addition to an understanding of a common series of names, events, facts, values, and ideas, information fluency involves the ability to move from one community of literacy to another. The maturing, information-fluent student sees value in the differences and relationships from the literacy of one environment to another. That student applies the process skills to become productive and communicative across a variety of audiences. This does not necessarily mean the student is "multilingual" but that the information-fluent student is "multiliterate" and understands the information search, analysis, and synthesis necessary within and across a variety of settings.

Heath says that today's youth would scoff at limited definitions of literacy based only on a common set of reading and writing mechanical skills. Literacy is both fluid across disciplines and ever-changing with the growth and maturation of the learner. Therefore, what is a strong measure of "being literate" will change and evolve with the learning content, physical and mental growth of the learner, and the variety of audiences and contexts with which the learner must deal, especially in the workforce or "real world." Schools continue to do students the disservice of limiting the scope of literacy skills and regimenting learning experiences to the point that such environments are not authentic, but isolated from critical thinking that really matters for survival and success.

Beyond the ability to read the modern codes and icons of the electronic age, students may begin to reach new levels of literacy when literature is presented in a more challenging and dynamic manner. According to Heath, literature response and text interactions should mean that literature never says the same thing twice. The growing and changing literate student moves from the common meaning given in text to adding his or her own personal meaning. Each time one returns to text, even the same text, one has changed and holds new experiences ready to trigger new meaning. The mark of a quality or classic literary writer is that he or she has layered within the text the figures of speech and nuances necessary for the reader to discover new thoughts with each revisit. Critical thinking in this context involves not only problem solving but the insight to find richer linkages to historical and contemporary issues through literature. Quality text is not stagnant, but turns on the reader, and actually interacts with the maturation of the learner.

Heath concludes that literacy is not acquired in a vacuum. Nor does it spring fully formed from our minds, like Athena from the head of Zeus. It is an evolutionary process changing from generation to generation and from life to life.

Emergent Literacy

Stuart McNaughton, Professor of Education at University of Auckland, has written of the socialization model of emergent literacy and argues that child development should be seen as occurring through complex and dynamic exchanges between its parts. The parts are, on the one hand, children and their actions to make sense out of their world (their constructions); and, on the other hand, the social and cultural process in everyday activities, such as what guidance is given, and how that guidance is given. All factors are dependent on each other as well as a part of each other, hence the term "co-construction."

According to McNaughton, one of the central functions of the family is to socialize children into the ways of thinking and acting that are appropriate for the community of which the family is a member. His model involves ambient, joint, and personal activities to engage the child in the expertise and relationships of literacy. Jean M. Casey has summarized these elements in more tangible terms as the basic ingredients for early literacy:

- a positive attitude toward writing and reading what they have written,
- listening to adults reading to them, and
- being surrounded by interesting books.

The Multitude of Literacies

The new Literacy Dictionary defines "literacy" as the minimal ability to read and write in a designated language, as well as a mindset or way of thinking about the use of reading and writing in everyday life. It differs from simple reading and writing in its assumption of an understanding of the appropriate use of these abilities within a print-based society. Literacy, therefore, requires active, autonomous engagement with print and stresses the role of the individual in generating, as well as receiving and assigning, independent interpretations to messages.

In current usage, the term implies an interaction between social demands and individual competence. Thus, the levels of literacy required for social functioning can and have varied across cultures and across time within the same culture. Today literacy is understood as a continuum, anchored at the bottom by illiteracy. Of equal importance to illiteracy, however, is aliteracy-the unwillingness to use literacy even though the capability is present.

Representative Types of Literacy

Adult literacy: A level of literacy that enables a person in or about to enter the workforce to function effectively both as an individual and as a member of society.

Autonomous literacy: Independent literacy; the individual's ability to make independent judgments of meanings in text.

Community literacy: Reading, other than that done in school, associated with participation in neighborhood activities, local government, church, and social organizations.

Computer literacy: Possession of the skills and knowledge necessary for operating a computer. Generally thought of as familiarity with the personal computer and the ability to create and manipulate documents and data via word processing, spreadsheets, databases, and other software. Understanding of the importance and implementation of electronic technologies to communication and learning.

Craft literacy: Knowledge of the skills, tools, and procedures for meeting the standards of a given craft.

Critical literacy: The use of language in all of

its forms, as in thinking, solving problems, and communicating solutions; the ability to participate in challenging and changing power structures.

Family literacy: Literacy efforts or activities that involve more than one generation; activities may range from study skills to reading aloud to foster appreciation for literature.

Functional literacy: A level of reading and writing sufficient for everyday life but not for completely autonomous activity.

Information literacy: The ability to identify an information need or question; the ability to find, evaluate, and use information effectively in personal and professional situations; the ability to locate, analyze, evaluate, synthesize, and selectively use information from different sources regardless of format and to effectively communicate or present results to relevant audiences.

Intergenerational literacy: The efforts of second- and third-generation adults in a family, usually an extended family, to help themselves or others in the family learn to read and write.

Media literacy: The ability of a citizen to access, analyze, and produce information for specific outcomes. Those who advocate media literacy recognize the influence that television, motion pictures, recorded music, and other mass media have on people daily. The media literacy movement also recognizes the fact that educators have traditionally spent a preponderance of time teaching reading, and little time focusing on decoding media. Education aims to increase students' understanding and enjoyment of how media work, how they (media) produce meaning, how they are organized, and how they construct their own reality.

Network literacy: Awareness of the range and uses of global, networked information resources and services; understanding by which networked information is generated and managed; ability to retrieve specific information from a data network by using a range of information mining or discovery tools.

Quantitative literacy: Fluency in reading and writing computational data; numeracy.

Real-world literacy: The literacy and numeracy skills needed to survive in the nonacademic world.

Survival literacy: Minimal reading, writing, and often numeracy skills needed to get by in everyday life in the target or local community language.

Technology literacy: A complex, integrated process that involves people, procedures, ideas, devices, and organization for analyzing problems and devising, implementing, evaluating, and managing solutions to those problems, involved in all aspects of learning.

Television literacy: Competence in using television to enhance daily life and to acquire social power; competence in interpreting the successive patterns, or mosaics, of television stimuli that are characterized by low visual orientation and high involvement with maximal interplay of all the senses; teleliteracy.

Vernacular literacy: The ability to read, write, and sometimes speak the common language of a speech community; popular literacy.

Visual literacy: The ability to understand and use images, including the ability to think, learn, and express oneself in terms of images; the ability to interpret and communicate with respect to visual symbols in nonprint media, as visual literacy in viewing television, art, and nature.

Workplace literacy: Literacy that focuses attention on individuals in relation to the societal and economic concerns of a nation; on a more local application, knowledge and command of the communication tasks to be successful on the job.

For Further Reading

Callison, Daniel, and Carol L. Tilley. "Information and Media Literacies: Towards a Common Core." In Instructional Intervention for Information Use, edited by Daniel Callison, Joy H. McGregor, and Ruth V. Small, 110-116. San Jose: Hi Willow Research and Publishing, 1998.

Casey, Jean M. Early Literacy: The Empowerment of Technology. Englewood: CO: Libraries Unlimited, 1997.

Harris, Theodore L., and Richard E. Hodges, eds. The Literacy Dictionary. Newark, DE:

International Reading Association, 1995.

Heath, Shirley Brice. <u>Children of Promise:</u> <u>Literate Activity in Linguistically and</u> <u>Culturally Diverse Classrooms</u>. Washington, D.C.: NEA Professional Library, 1991.

Heath, Shirley Brice. <u>Truths to Tell: Youth and</u> <u>Newspaper Reading: How Youth View, Read,</u> <u>and Hope to Change Newspapers</u>. St. Petersburg: Poynter Institute of Media Studies, 1997.

Heath, Shirley Brice. <u>Ways with Words:</u> <u>Language, Life, and Work in Communities</u> <u>and Classrooms</u>. Cambridge: Cambridge University Press, 1996.

Heath, Shirley Brice, and Diane Lapp. <u>Handbook of Research on Teaching Literacy</u> <u>through the Communicative and Visual Arts</u>. New York: Macmillan Library Reference, 1997.

Hirsch, E. D. <u>Cultural Literacy: What Every</u> <u>American Needs to Know</u>. Boston: Houghton Mifflin, 1987.

McNaughton, Stuart. <u>Patterns of Emergent</u> <u>Literacy: Processes of Development and</u> <u>Transition</u>. Oxford: Oxford University Press, 1995.

Pappas, Marjorie L., and Ann E. Tepe. "Media, Visual Technology, and Information: A Comparison of Literacies." In <u>Instructional</u> <u>Intervention for Information Use</u>, edited by Daniel Callison, Joy H. McGregor, and Ruth V. Small, 97-109. San Jose: Hi Willow Research and Publishing, 1998.

Spitzer, Kathleen L., Michael B. Eisenberg, and Carrie A. Lowe. <u>Information Literacy:</u> <u>Essential Skills for the Information Age</u>. Syracuse, NY: ERIC Clearinghouse on Information & Technology, 1998.

Tyner, Kathleen. <u>Literacy in a Digital World:</u> <u>Teaching and Learning in the Age of</u> <u>Information</u>. Mahwah, NJ: Lawrence Erlbaum Associates, 1998.

Wolf, Anne Shelby, and Shirley Brice Heath. <u>The Braid of Literature: Children's Worlds of</u> <u>Reading</u>. Cambridge: Harvard University Press, 1992.

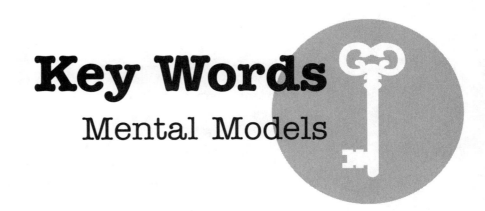

Key Words
Mental Models

The term "mental models" must rest in jargon vocabulary at the current time because the term is not recognized in the vocabularies of educational indexes and databases. Acceptable related terms are "mental representation" and "cognitive mapping." The most common related term is "schemata" which concerns mental images and concepts that provide a cognitive framework by which the individual perceives, understands, and responds to stimuli. There is a growing interest in the process, intuitive and guided, that learners employ to construct meaning. "Mental modeling" has been the term of choice in recent discussions concerning student abilities to visualize or comprehend the demands of the information research process.

Evolution of Perspectives on Learning

Over the past fifty years, there has been a clear evolution in the perspectives held by most leading educators concerning "how we learn." This evolution is simplified in the outline below.

Behaviorist Perspective

In the mid-1950s there was a shift from research on communication stimulus to learner response to stimuli. Behaviorists, such as B. F. Skinner, were interested in voluntary behavior rather than in reflexive behavior. Behavior could be modified, based on reinforcement theory, through reinforcing [learning] and leading the learner through a series of specific instructional steps.

Behaviorists refuse to speculate on what goes on internally when learning takes place. They rely solely on observable behaviors. As a result, they are more comfortable explaining relatively simple learning tasks. Information processing is too complex to be limited to this single perspective.

Cognitivist Perspective

Cognitivists make their contributions to learning theory and instructional design by creating models of how information is received, processed, and manipulated by learners. Cognitivists create a mental model of short-term and long-term memory. New information is stored in short-term memory where it is considered, rehearsed, and examined relevant to held knowledge until it is ready to be stored in long-term memory, in relation to previous knowledge. If the information is not rehearsed it is not likely to be retained. Learners then combine the information and skills in long-term memory to develop cognitive strategies for dealing with complex tasks.

Jean Piaget identifies three concepts for such mental development:

- Schemata: mental structures by which learners organize their perceived environment.
- Assimilation: process by which the learner integrates new information and experiences with existing schemata.

- Accommodation: the process of modifying or creating new schemata. Experienced learners have a broader network of schemata, refined over time as the learner progresses through natural maturation.

Constructivist Perspective

This current movement extends beyond the usual stages of ability, to the advocation of engaging students (regardless of age) in meaningful experiences that will accelerate and enhance the construction of schemata. The shift is from passive transfer of information to active problem solving. Constructivists emphasize that learners create their own interpretations of the world of information. The constructivist will argue that the student situates the learning experience within his or her own experience and that the goal of instruction is not to teach information, but to create situations so that students can interpret information for their own understanding. Learning is a search for meaning.

The constructivist believes that learning occurs most effectively when the student is engaged in authentic tasks that relate to meaningful contexts. The ultimate measure of learning is based therefore on the ability of the student to use knowledge to facilitate thinking in real life. The ultimate role of the teacher is to facilitate situations in which the student finds relevance and constructs meaning through observation, interviewing, debate, conversations, evidence selection, and other skills that are practiced in an authentic context.

Applications to Interactive Technology

Early use of the term "mental models," over fifty years ago, was often connected to the thesis that advocated that humans construct internal models of the environment around them, and from these models humans reason and predict outcome of events. Just as an engineer may build a scale model of a building so as to see the effects of applying various stresses prior to building the real thing, humans build models that enable us to make predictions about an external event before carrying out an action. Mental models are considered essentially as internal constructions of some aspect of the external world that can be manipulated, enabling predictions and inferences to be made. Various applications of mental modeling have evolved and today the term is used in reference to applied problems of human-computer interaction (HCI) and human-machine systems (HMS), and a variety of planning sequences for development of interactive information systems (IIS).

Defined within the interactive software development world, a mental model is a conceptual cognitive structure within a specific domain that a student develops and uses to explain and confront novel situations and problems. Different forms of mental models have been derived from the three levels of knowledge used to represent domain specific skills required for success in use of computer programs. These three discrete knowledge levels are:

- Declarative: information is described as factual information;
- Procedural: information is the compilation of declarative knowledge into functional units; and
- Conditional: knowledge is described as the understanding of when and where to employ procedures.

The knowledge levels have been applied to use of a CD-ROM encyclopedia, and mental models describing development of knowledge levels have been formulated by Ron Oliver. The three mental model descriptions corresponding to the discrete knowledge levels are:

- Management. This mental model describes the user's understanding of the control and guidance of a program. It influences the decisions and choices made by the user in interacting with the software to display specific information. It represents the user's construction of the protocols and procedures of the CD-ROM encyclopedia interface.
- Navigation. The navigation mental model describes users' constructions

and schemata of moving within the information base between discrete elements and nodes. This mental model differs from management in that it pertains to users' understanding and concepts of information access, rather than simple interactions with the interface.

- Organization. This mental model describes users' understanding of the manner is which the information is organized within the CD-ROM encyclopedia. This mental model is dependent on users' information skills and mental constructions of the information base. It differs from navigation in that it is less specific to an individual CD-ROM, and represents broad and transferable skills and knowledge.

Mental modeling is useful in attempting to address the most common problems in design and development of interactive information systems:

- Disorientation: difficulty knowing where one is in the product.
- Navigation: difficulty moving from one point to another.
- Cognitive Overload: exposure to information that vastly exceeds that required to answer a given question.

Student Information Decision Making

The concepts related to mental models have been used to attempt to address the question: When students are seeking and using information, why do they make the decisions they make? Limited research is attempted to determine answers to these related questions:

- What prior learning do students have (established mental models) that influences the decisions they make while seeking and using information?
- How is that prior learning the same as or different from what students need to address their information task?
- If differences exist between what students need to know and what they do know, how do they cope?

One proposed notion in response to these questions is that a student will bring several mental models to a problem or project and will rely on those models he or she has developed and practiced in the past to apply to the new situation. In terms of meeting information problems, the student has two options. First, the student may hold a previous mental model based on facts, concepts, and opinions about the subject-matter content that may be closely related to the new problem. (What do I know about other historical events that will help me address the questions I need to answer about a new historical event?) A second model involves information access skills. (How have I accessed information on previous topics which I can now apply to finding necessary information on this new topic?)

In one recent study, conducted by Judy Pitts at Florida State University, concerning senior high school science students assigned the task of producing video programs on a variety of subjects, the researcher concluded that incomplete subject-matter mental models led to incomplete identification of information need. The analysis of the students' information-seeking activities showed that most were driven by very general information needs. When asked what kind of information they were seeking, students frequently responded by restating their topic or with a shrug and phrases such as "I don't know," "Anything we can put on the video," and "Whatever."

Pitts went on to speculate that it is probably true that most people who begin a new research project are at first novices in the subject matter involved. If those people have expert information-seeking-and-use understandings, however, they know how to use the information skills to strengthen the subject understandings. They might, for example, know how to find general, overview information as a first step and thus obtain the expertise necessary to identify clearly the information needs. This idea can be expressed in the following equation: novice subject understandings + expert information skills = students who may use information skills to find information necessary to strengthen subject understandings.

In the opposite case (people with expert subject understandings but novice information skills), students know enough about their topics to articulate their information needs clearly to an information professional. This situation can be represented by another equation: expert subject understandings + novice information skills = students who may articulate information needs clearly to those who can help them.

But, concludes Pitts, if both subject understandings and information skills are weak (as was the case with most students in her study), students have little chance of being able to progress on either [mental model] strand. One strand cannot support the other. A third equation represents this dilemma: novice subject understandings + novice information skills = students who are not likely to make progress on either strand.

A second study, conducted by Joy H. McGregor, concluded that most students do not make intuitive shifts from one mental model to another, or stated in another way, students do not instinctively operate in a metacognitive manner. McGregor made the following recommendations for practice:

- A metacognitive environment in which thinking strategies are discussed, modeled, monitored, and evaluated in a supportive atmosphere could help students as they learn to think about using information more effectively.
- In order to monitor thinking processes, it is necessary for students to have a vocabulary they can use to talk about such processes.
- The process of doing a library research paper provides many opportunities for practice in analyzing, synthesizing, and evaluating information and practice in mental model construction and mental model transfer.

For Further Reading

Collis, B. "The Evolution of Electronic Books." Educational and Training Technology International 28, no. 4 (1991): 355-363.

Fasick, Adele M. "What Research Tells Us about Children's Use of Information Media." Canadian Library Journal, February 1992: 51-54.

Jin, H., and T. Reeves. "Mental Models: A Research Focus for Interactive Learning Systems." Journal of Education Training Research and Development 40, no. 3 (1992): 39-53.

Jonassen, David H. and Phillip Henning. "Mental Models: Knowledge in the Head and Knowledge in the World." Educational Technology 39, no. 3 (1999), 37-42.

Kuhn, Deanna. "The Development of Cognitive Skills to Support Inquiry Learning." Cognition & Instruction 18, no. 4 (2000), 495-523.

McGregor, Joy H. "Cognitive Processes and the Use of Information." In School Library Media Annual 1994, edited by Carol Collier Kuhlthau, M. Elspeth Goodin and Mary Jane McNally. Englewood, CO: Libraries Unlimited: 124-133.

Oliver, Ron. "Interactive Information Systems: Information Access and Retrieval." The Electronic Library 13, no. 3 (1995): 187-193.

Pitts, Judy (edited by Joy H. McGregor and Barbara K. Stripling). "Mental Models of Information." In School Library Media Annual 1995, edited by Betty J. Morris, Judith L. McQuiston and Cecile L. Saretsky. Englewood, CO: Libraries Unlimited: 187-200.

Pratt, Chris, and Alison F. Garton, eds. Systems of Representation in Children. New York: John Wiley & Sons, 1993.

Rankin, Virginia. "Pre-Search: Intellectual Access to Information." <u>School Library Journal</u>, March 1992: 168-170.

Rogers, Yvonne, Andrew Rutherford, and Peter A. Bibby. <u>Models in the Mind</u>. New York: Academic Press, 1992.

Vandergrift, Kay E. <u>Power Teaching</u>. Chicago: American Library Association, 1994.

Key Words
Metacognition

"Metacognition" is a term that gained acceptance in educational research and instructional design circles in the 1980s. In a narrow sense, the term refers to meditation or reflection on what one thinks. In a broader sense, metacognition involves all of the cognitive processes and places emphasis on the process of learning more than the products the student generates to display what he or she has learned. Metacognition is thinking about thinking; knowing what we know and what we don't know.

Understanding metacognition is essential for those teachers who want to facilitate effectively the creation of learning environments in which the student learns how to learn and extends much of that learning activity primarily through the student's abilities to instruct himself. This term is key to lifelong learning.

Strategies

Several studies have suggested that increases in learning have resulted from direct practice of metacognitive strategies. Elaine Blakey and Sheila Spence have outlined several strategies for developing metacognitive behavior, in a publication for the U.S. Office of Educational Research and Improvement:

- Baseline Knowledge. At the beginning of a research activity, students need to make conscious decisions about their knowledge. It is useful to write or voice "what you know" and "what you want to learn."
- Talking about Thinking. Students need a thinking vocabulary. During planning and problem-solving situations, teachers should model and talk through the process so students can follow demonstrated thinking procedures. Teachers can facilitate student thinking by labeling thinking processes and telling students when they are effectively employing them.
- Paired Problem Solving. Peers, parents, and others can help to extend the process by listening as the student talks through the problem and potential options for solutions. Students can take turns establishing and refining questions and gaining focus by eliminating information that is not relevant.
- Keeping a Thinking Journal. This is now widely accepted in situations where the student is expected to monitor his or her thoughts over a lengthy time span based on what the student reads, hears, and writes in a formal manner. The journal provides a concrete record of student reflection for all to review at various steps in the thinking experience.
- Planning and Self-Regulation. Assuming that such responsibilities are modeled correctly by the teacher, the students should be expected to assume increasing responsibility for regulating their learning. Students can be taught to make plans for learning activities that include estimating time requirements, organizing materials, and scheduling procedures necessary to complete an activity.
- Debriefing the Thinking Process. A three-step method is useful. First, the teacher guides

students to review the activity, gathering impressions on thinking and feelings. Then, the group classifies related ideas, identifying the thinking strategies used and the strengths and weaknesses of each as related to the recent information research (or other learning) activity. Finally, students and the teacher evaluate their success, discard inappropriate strategies, and discuss application of the best strategies for future applications.

- Self-Evaluation. Guided self-evaluation can be introduced through individual conferences and checklists that focus on the thinking processes. As students begin to recognize that some learning activities in different disciplines are similar, they will begin to transfer self-guided learning strategies.

Educating Students to Think

In 1985, a select group of educators was called together by the National Commission on Libraries and Information Science. A concept paper evolved from those discussions and the ideas expressed by the authors (Mancall, Aaron, and Walker) are foundational to the models which have evolved over the past decade concerning the instruction of information literacy skills across our nation. "Educating Students to Think" is an essay every teacher of school library media should read and reflect on frequently.

Citing several learning and information theorists, the authors of this concept essay describe concerns related to the novice-expert dimension. Elizabeth Robinson is quoted, "Novices at any task not only lack the skills needed to perform it efficiently, but are also deficient in self-conscious participation and intelligent self-regulation of their actions." (p. 19) If instruction based on metacognition theory is to be effective, two conditions must be met. First, the student must be developmentally ready to learn the skill. Second, the student must realize that use of the skill will be effective in solving a personal cognitive problem.

The teacher of literacy information is a critical player in facilitating the "learning to think" environment. Unless able and willing to model, council, and evaluate the student's information selection and use process, moving the student from the child novice levels to higher order thinking skills will falter. National guidelines for school library media programs now call for library media specialists to adopt such a teaching role, but it remains to be seen how widely such a role will be accepted. Future national guidelines may define specific information skills at progressive cognitive development levels for learners and hold the teachers of library media information literacy responsible for student performance.

Implications for Information Skills

Linda H. Bertland conducted an extensive review of research in cognitive psychology. Her report was key to the essay mentioned above. Bertland's insightful conclusions help us understand some of the implications for the timing and structure related to teaching information skills:

- Research in comprehension indicates that greater attention needs to be paid to the level at which children are processing information. Shallow processing of information will probably lead to rote copying from sources without any perceived need to evaluate and relate the material into a meaningful whole.
- More attention must be paid to the way children perceive the task parameters of reading and viewing. Children in early grades do not seem to be aware of the various goals of reading, nor of strategies appropriate to the realization of those goals.
- Children who perceive little need to invest mental effort in television viewing may be learning less from instructional audiovisual material than would be anticipated, regarding it more as a source of amusement rather than instruction.
- Metacognitive strategies that apply to information skills instruction include the need to teach students question

analysis, practice careful definition of the topic, manage the consideration of time and task parameters, and gain practice and feedback leading to the most effective strategies for use of resources in order to gain meaningful evidence.

For Further Reading

Ana, Gil, Nilma Osiecki, and Alberto Juarez. "Students Reflecting on What They Know." ERIC Document ED457222, 2001.

Bertland, Linda H. "An Overview of Research in Metacognition: Implications for Information Skills Instruction." School Library Media Quarterly 15, no. 2 (Winter 1986): 96-99.

Blakey, Elaine, and Sheila Spence. Developing Metacognition. Washington, DC: Office of Educational Research and Improvement, 1990.

Bondy, Elizabeth. "Thinking about Thinking." Childhood Education 60, no. 4 (March/April 1984): 234-238.

Mancall, Jacqueline C., Shirley L. Aaron, and Sue A. Walker. "Educating Students to Think: The Role of the School Library Media Program." School Library Media Quarterly 15, no. 1 (Fall 1986): 18-27.

Manning, Brenda H. Self-Talk for Teachers and Students: Metacognitive Strategies for Personal and Classroom Use. Boston: Allyn and Bacon, 1996.

Peterson, Donna and Carol VanDerWege. "Guiding Children to be Strategic Readers." Phi Delta Kappan 83, no. 6 (2002), 437-9.

Robinson, Elizabeth. "Metacognitive Development." In Developing Thinking, edited by Sara Meadows, 106-141. London: Metheun, 1983.

Sanacore, Joseph. "Metacognition and the Improvement of Reading: Some Important Links." Journal of Reading 27, no. 8 (May 1984): 706-712.

Scruggs, Thomas K. "Maximizing What Gifted Students Can Learn." Gifted Child Quarterly 29, no. 4 (Fall 1985): 181-185.

Key Words
Motivation

Students are learning all the time. It is not possible to stop them from learning. An important task for the teacher of information literacy is not so much to teach students how to learn, but to motivate them to learn at times that may not seem immediately rewarding to the student.

Motivation helps to increase the chances that students will learn what is needed even when they may initially classify the activity as being overly demanding or of no interest. Motivation approaches are varied and in many ways common sense, but often left out or given little attention as teachers concentrate on academic goals to meet cognitive performances. Attitudinal performances toward the learning situation are just as important to consider.

Characteristics of Motivation

Wilbert McKeachie, former President of the American Association for Higher Education and Director of the Center for Research on Learning at the University of Michigan, has classified his observations on motivation in the following categories:

- Curiosity. People are naturally curious. They seek new experiences; they enjoy learning new things. Although derived at different levels and various formats, humans find satisfaction in solving puzzles, perfecting skills, and developing competence. Asking students questions, rather than presenting statements of fact, not only improves learning, but increases interest in learning more about the topic in discussion.

- Competence. In addition to natural curiosity, another intrinsic motive for learning is competence or self-efficacy. Students will receive pleasure from doing things well and knowing they have done things well. Teachers may need to link success with the perception that the success was due to the student's own ability and effort. For students who lack a sense of efficacy, teachers must not only provide situations where success occurs, but to prove that they have themselves mastered the task without special help.

- Affiliation. Most students want to be accepted and liked. Approval from the teacher may be an important reward, but may also lead to being ostracized as the "over achiever." In addition, motivation may be complicated by conflicting needs for independence and dependence. While students are likely to resent the teacher who directs their activities too closely, they are also likely to be anxious when given independence. McKeachie suggests that the solution is to find ways to simultaneously satisfy both needs.

- Grades. In most educational environments, this is the most tangible and, for many, the most important motivation. Grades represent an expert's appraisal of performance and such are recorded for others to see and consider for future advancement or rejection. Because grades are important to them, most students will learn whatever is necessary to get the grades they desire. If instructors base grades on memorization of details, students will memorize the facts or even the text as given. If the student believes grades are based upon the ability to integrate and apply principles, he or she will attempt to do this.

Too often, however, tasks related to the selection and use of information are not demanding enough and adequate grades can be achieved with location of a minimum number of required resources without reward for making wise choices and discarding poor information. In such cases, the grade is unwisely based on quantity and not quality. Getting the citation format correct is not motivating. Expressing why a source is "the best that can be located" can be motivating.

- Achievement. Some research suggests that students with high achievement motivation are more likely to remain highly motivated in highly competitive environments where their chances of success are about fifty-fifty. Some tests have shown that in such environments the students not only excelled, but reported greater interest in school work. The conflict remains today on the advantages and disadvantages for individual students or the common good as decisions are made concerning tracking or inclusion. The latter approach may present more motivational challenges.
- Modeling. Perhaps the key source of stimulation for motivation, or the major controlling agent for motivation factors, is the teacher. McKeachie stresses the obvious, but as teachers of information literacy, we should never forget that our own enthusiasm and values have much to do with our students' interest in the subject matter. Nonverbal as well as verbal methods are used to communicate such attitudes. Smiles and vocal intensity may be as important as the words we choose.

Legendary Teachers

Playing strongly on techniques used by successful coaches, David Scheidecker and William Freeman, both successful public school teachers, have recently summarized how "legendary teachers" bring out the best in their students. Their approaches to motivating high student achievement include:

- Convey Enjoyment. Even on the worst days, motivational teachers convey to their students that they enjoy being with the students and having them in class.
- Take the "We" Approach. The teacher does not separate him or herself from the student when failure occurs, but finds a way to partner with the student to determine what went wrong and to help guide the student to improve for better results.
- Build Safety Nets. It seems more and more students face conflicts and failures within their home environments. Students who are willing to take the risk to achieve at school should find safety in celebration of victories. Scheidecker and Freeman also recommend such systemic safety nets as ungraded pretests for practice prior to exams, mandatory make-up exams for below average performance, and additional review sessions for those testing below average. Motivation grows from legendary teachers who are available when needed and provide the time and guidance for students to correct mistakes.

Motivation in the Multigenre Research Paper

Margaret Moulton, a high school teacher, reports that she has found the multigenre research paper to lead to greater interest by her seniors in the process to gather and present information. Defining her approach closely in terms of the I-Search model, Moulton's students were encouraged to select a topic of their choice and also to select multiple ways to present their findings.

Seniors presented a portfolio of artifacts that represented different aspects of their information research. Encouraging alternative presentation modes, usually formats other than paper (such as video), is not new to teachers of information literacy. However these seniors were expected to express themselves in multiple genres to match varied emotions and communication levels. Thus, a portfolio might include original sheet music, a eulogy, a wedding invitation, a list of trivia facts and quotations, journal entries, a student-designed poster (wanted poster, playbill, concert, movie, etc.), or student-created newspaper tabloid front page. A variety of artifacts are selected and created that best reflect the theme or character chosen and may range from a few to more than a dozen. Students were motivated through choice and variety.

One of Moulton's students reported, "Throughout doing all these multigenres I realized that I learned more than doing a regular research paper. I really got to know the person I had to write about and at some point the person I had to be. I enjoyed this assignment. The only thing that I did not like was all the typing because I wrote more than a regular research paper and because of that my wrists hurt. Besides that, this was the best and most educational report I have ever had to do. To think about it, it is kinda sad to know a senior did a great report only once."

Reading Motivation

Our literature is filled with useful methods designed to motivate students to read. An Indiana collaborative team representing the classroom, the school library media center, and the local public library has elaborated on the "original recipe" to motivate reading in the middle schools. Programming is designed around a theme and includes:

- A Design Team. School teachers, school library media specialists, and public librarians plan, read, discuss, and support each other.
- Quality Book Selection. Multiple copies of well-written books with genuine dialogue and strong characters, with heavy investment in paperbacks.
- Funding. Encourage community groups to donate to the cause so that there is a local investment in the activity.
- Food. Tie the eats to the theme and the content of the key books selected for the theme. This age group, grades six to ten, will come into the activity if they have a role in food selection too.

- Publicity. Enthusiasm is contagious! Excited students can create more excitement if they are engaged in the promotional activities.
- Connections. Attempt to make thematic connections with the local environment including historical sites, community organizations, and colorful personalities.
- Mood. Re-create a mood that is built on the key elements of the novels selected to support the theme.
- Facilitators. Kids are more motivated to read and communicate if facilitators are good listeners rather than constantly offering a critique of what the kids have to offer.

Motivation and Information Skills Instruction

Ruth V. Small, Professor at Syracuse University, has initiated a series of studies to explore motivational strategies used by school library media specialists during information skills instruction. She has based her work on the ARCS Model of Motivational Design.

- Attention. Perceptual Arousal, Inquiry Arousal, and Variability.
  Gaining and sustaining Attention to the instruction by stimulating curiosity and interest.
- Relevance. Goal Orientation, Motive Matching, and Familiarity.
  Providing the Relevance, importance, and value to learning.
- Confidence. Learning Requirements, Success Opportunities, and Personal Control.
  Building learner's Confidence in their abilities to succeed at the task.
- Satisfaction. Natural Consequences, Positive Consequences, and Equity.

Promoting the potential for learning Satisfaction.

Small has found that school library media specialists tend to use attention motivational strategies more than three times as often as relevance, confidence, and satisfaction strategies combined. At least among the actions of the elementary and middle school library media specialists that Small documented, most of the attention strategies could be classified as inquiry arousal or questioning and problem-posing strategies to spark curiosity. Small also reported that her test group used significantly more rewards than punishments. Analysis of extrinsic motivators revealed that ninety percent were informational in nature, "Great! You seem to really remember how to do a bibliography."

For Further Reading

Buckley, Shannon, and Julie Wilkinson. "Improving Student Motivation by Increasing Student and Parental Awareness of Academic Achievement." ERIC Document ED455462, 2001.

Closter, Kathryn, Karen L. Sipes, and Vickie Thomas. Fiction, Food, and Fun: The Original Recipe for the Read 'n' Feed Program. Englewood, CO: Libraries Unlimited, 1998.

Guthrie, John T., Susan Alverson, and Carol Poundstone. "Engaging Students in Reading." Knowledge Quest 27, no. 4 (March/April 1999): 8-16.

Joyce, Marilyn Z., and Julie I. Tallman. Making the Writing and Research Connection with the I-Search Process. New York: Neal-Schuman Publishers, 1997.

Kariotakis, Constantine, Karen Kelly-Moutvic, and Cathy Roberts. "Teaching Strategies to Improve Student Motivation." ERIC Document ED446819, 2000.

Kohn, Alfie. Punished by Rewards: The Trouble with Gold Stars, Incentive Plans, A's, Praise, and Other Bribes. Houghton Mifflin, 1999.

Kuhlthau, Carol Collier. Teaching the Library Research Process. Lanham, MD: Scarecrow Press, 1994.

McKeachie, Wilbert J. Teaching Tips: A Guidebook for the Beginning College Teacher. Lexington, MA: D. C. Heath and Company, 1978.

Moulton, Margaret R. "The Multigenre Paper: Increasing Interest, Motivation, and Functionality in Research." Journal of Adolescent & Adult Literacy 42, no. 7 (April 1999): 528-539.

Scheidecker, David, and William Freeman. Bringing Out the Best in Students: How Legendary Teachers Motivate Kids. Thousand Oaks, CA: Corwin Press and Sage Publications, 1999.

Small, Ruth V. "Designing Motivation into Library and Information Skills Instruction." School Library Media Quarterly Online, 1998. http://www.ala.org/aasl/SLMQ/small.html.

Small, Ruth V. "An Exploration of Motivational Strategies Used by Library Media Specialists during Library and Information Skills Instruction." School Library Media Research, 1999. http://www.ala.org/aasl/SLMR/motive.html.

Small, Ruth V., and Marilyn P. Arnone. Turning Kids on to Research: The Power of Motivation. Libraries Unlimited, 2000.

Key Words
Nonfiction

Have you seen a presentation by Beverly Kobrin when she shows you the multitude of possibilities for engaging kids with nonfiction? It is an eye-opener! She defines nonfiction to include newspapers, magazines, cookbooks, small appliance manuals, phone books, and much more. The most important message from Kobrin is that nonfiction can be just as engaging and emotional as fiction.

Nonfiction plays a dominant role in the wide range of signs and signals that kids must handle in order to make meaning of their world. A child's decoding starts from the very beginning of his or her life. Parents, Kobrin insists, should be the first and foremost guides for their children as both parent and child discover that practical nonfiction can be both fascinating and enlightening.

Betty Carter, associate professor at Texas Woman's University, tells us that high interest in nonfiction crosses ability levels and grows and expands as the child moves into adolescence and young adulthood. Teenage boys read more nonfiction than teenage girls. Much of the nonfiction read by young adults is read for pleasure, diversion, and entertainment.

According to Carter, knowing books translates into reading books. There's a strong tendency for librarians and teachers to equate reading books with reading fiction. Textbooks on young adult literature heavily favor fiction, the content of young adult literature courses typically stresses fiction, lists of teen-favored books contain fiction, and awards traditionally go to fictional works. Many teachers and librarians are drawn to their particular profession because they themselves enjoy fiction. Yet, the undisputed fact remains that young adults read nonfiction. And since teachers and librarians accept the charge to help young adults grow into mature readers, they must read widely in all areas of literature-in the multiple genres of fiction as well as poetry, drama, information books, and biography.

Many school library media center collections reflect the strong selection of qualify fiction and the lack of useful nonfiction. Surveys in twelve key states in the mid-1990s by the Amer-ican Library Association showed both elementary and secondary collections to be adequate to excellent in fiction, but poor and out-of-date in nonfiction areas such as mathematics, multicultural education, science, technology, geography, fine arts, and careers.

New Collections and Radical Change

The computer technologies that now bring reams of nonfiction information to students through the Internet also have led to a revolution in the design and printing of thousands of new nonfiction titles for children and young adults over the past two decades. This explosion of quality nonfiction, often graphically illustrated, creates new opportunities for school library book collections to be revitalized. If funded and managed properly, the adventure to weed out the old and to select the new leads to exciting collaborative planning in thematic lessons and information literacy education. Dianne McAffe Hopkins, from the University of Wisconsin, found this to be true through the recent evaluation of the national Library Power project. She reported that in situations where collections were updated based on collection mapping that targeted selected areas of the curriculum:

- New collection development practices led to improved collections and expanded use of collections in instruction.
- Changes in collection development practices were well regarded by librarians, teachers, and principals.
- Strong connections were established between library collections and instruction.
- Up-to-date collections selected by both teachers and librarians represented the basis for most collaborations between librarians and teachers. The wide availability of appropriate resources was clearly the first basis for collabortion efforts.

Eliza Dresang, Professor at Florida State University, has illustrated how nonfiction books for young adults are undergoing radical change. Hypertext and digital design are enhancing nonfiction in ways that make engagement with text more exciting than ever. Students may rewrite text or story to suit different audiences, move text and compare facts, or skim and highlight with electronic key term searching. These changes in literature for children and young adults will open new discourse levels on social and political issues as access to data will be more extensive and placed within richer contexts that include interviews and motion illustrations. Formats will become more interactive as well as

- nonsequential in organization and format;
- and interlaced with multiple layers of meaning.

Research on Reading Related to Nonfiction

The research on reading education and skill development has provided several new insights that also pertain to how a student makes meaning from information. The teacher of information literacy processes should give attention to the following findings from studies completed over the last twenty years.

- Children who engage in daily discussions about what they read are more likely to become critical readers and learners.

Students' discussions in classrooms are important to their learning. Research shows that students' verbal exchanges about content improve learning and increase their level of thinking. The social nature of learning implies that, because each context is different, participants must always evaluate what to say, when and how, consider options, and make choices. Learning rests in taking these actions. Discussion concerning information needs, quality and relevance of information located, and optional leads to more information are activities that teachers of information literacy skills can lead, model, and support to increase critical thinking at any grade level.

Given the importance of discussion for effective learning, effective teaching involves providing students with ample opportunities to engage in daily discussions with one another. Small-group and peer-to-peer interactions are valuable in promoting academic and social learning. Some researchers have concluded that children who rely on each other for help learn more than children who work alone.

- Expert readers have strategies that they use to construct meaning before, during, and after reading.

As students become proficient readers, they develop a set of plans or strategies for solving problems they encounter in their reading experiences. These strategies include:

- Inferencing: The process of reaching conclusions based on information within the text and the cornerstone of constructing meaning. Inferencing includes making predictions by using prior knowledge combined with information available from text.
- Identifying important information: The process of finding critical facts and

details in narrative (story) or expository (informational, nonfiction) text. The tasks may differ from narrative (plot, character, theme) to expository (background facts, arguments, warrants a thesis or prediction, evidence, and conclusions), but both will include identification of key text items. The student will mature in his or her information fluency through both seeking more demanding reading experiences and an increased sophistication in accessing information.

- Monitoring: A metacognitive or self-awareness process that expert constructors of meaning use to help themselves overcome problems as they read. For example, when good readers have difficulty understanding a paragraph, they become aware of the problem and stop immediately to fix it by employing a technique such as rereading, and in some cases, rereading prior paragraphs for context, not just the problematic paragraph.
- Summarizing: Process that involves pulling together important information gathered from a long passage of text.
- Question generating: Involves readers asking themselves questions they want answered from reading that require them to integrate information while they read.
- Children's reading and writing abilities develop together.

Both reading and writing are constructive processes. Current research also suggests that a similar, if not the same, level of intellectual activity underlies both reading and writing: interactions between the reader/writer and text lead to new knowledge and interpretations of text. Just as thoughtful readers read for a specific purpose by activating prior knowledge about the topic at hand, writers activate prior knowledge that relates to the topic and has a purpose for writing-to impart meaning to a reader.

While reading, readers reread and modify meaning accordingly. While writing, writers think about the topic and the more they think, the better developed their writing becomes. They also think about what they've written, reread it, and make revisions to improve it. This process of reading and writing not only unfold in similar ways, they tend to be used together. It remains to be shown if those who manage access to more information and learn how to identify pertinent information efficiently may accelerate the reading and writing processes more than those who rely on a few common knowledge information resources (i.e., those who never move past basic encyclopedia sets and popular news magazines). Effective management of multiple sources of information depends on growth and maturation beyond basic reading and writing skills.

- Children increase their ability to use language by becoming involved with language that is somewhat more mature than what they currently use.

Canadian educators Terry Johnson and Daphne Louis contend that children need to be introduced to literacy through somewhat simplified language, but they believe the unconscious simplification used in creating stories and poems the young mind can appreciate to be infinitely preferable to the conscious mechanical simplification that comes from word counts and sound/symbol regularities. Where the Wild Things Are will serve children better than demanding that they "see Dan run" or that they get their mouths around "ack," "ile," "ump," or "og." Engaging in story opens more meaning than simply engaging in sound.

The introduction to information resources is also, at times, too remedial. Treasure hunts may provide practice in searching, but are more effective if used as tools to open discussions about what the found information means:

Are there other ways to find the same information?

How might you use this information to solve a problem?

Are there similar sources of information available at other libraries or likely to be found at home?

Students at any age should be challenged to apply information, not just hunt for unrelated facts. Students at any age should be encouraged to talk aloud about their perception of the potential usefulness of several information resources. Voicing meaning from text provides the practice and opens the opportunity for feedback. As the student gains confidence, he or she will move to more challenging resources. Discourse about information findings leads to meaningful conversations concerning information seeking and information application.

- The most valuable form of reading assessment reflects our current understanding about the reading process and stimulates authentic reading tasks.

Until very recently, reading assessment focused on measuring students' performance on a hierarchy of isolated skills that, when put together, were thought to compose "reading." Now it is known that the whole act of reading is greater than the sum of its parts (i.e., isolated skills). Moreover, these parts are interrelated within a literacy context and do not always develop in a hierarchical way.

The same should be extracted for the information search and use processes. Growth in the students' abilities to access and process multiple nonfiction texts and to derive meaning through the process is recursive, interactive, or a dynamic evolution, not just a step-by-step skill sequence. Information as evidence may change in meaning and value depending on its context with other data, additional primary and secondary sources explored, considering how to present to different audiences, and frequent conversations with others (peers, parents, library media specialist, and other teachers) to verify it. Reflection at any point in the information search and library research process may send the student back to rethink previous experiences before moving forward.

Teaching Students to Read Nonfiction

Virginia Rankin's collection of practiced and refined strategies for teaching the research process in middle schools, The Thoughtful Researcher, is a must-read and reread for anyone who strives to implement an effective information literacy instructional program. Many of her activities can be used by classroom teachers. Rankin recommends that most of her lessons will have even more impact in raising student interest, and perhaps student performance, when the library media specialist presents them in conjunction with an actual research project. The following portion of questions from her handouts illustrate key questions that students must address as they gain practice and grow in becoming mature users of nonfiction text information.

Judging Suitability of the Information Resource

Is there confusing vocabulary? If only a word or so, work on finding an understandable definition. If many difficult words, move on to another source.

Does it contain references to persons, places, or things with which I'm familiar? Skim it for a quick overview to seek new information which may relate to your current knowledge.

Does it assume I already know too many things? Skim to look for new information or it may be an item which will have more meaning later after you have read other resources.

Understanding and Comprehending Information

Is a concept confusing? Try to tell it in your own words to someone or see if you can write a summary without a great deal of rereading the text.

Can I sum up the main point? Look at the introduction, conclusion, topic sentences, and section headings.

Evaluating and Extracting Information

Do I know what I want from this source?

Does this relate to my research questions? Make value judgments-this is an important piece of information to record; this is not. Make comparisons with what you read to what you already know.

Does this expand my idea?

Does this make a complete new point I have not yet considered?

Does this disagree with something I thought I knew or with a previous source?

Following Up or Linking to Other Information

Has the author mentioned other authorities on my topic? Should I try to find material by them?

Is there a bibliography that might give me ideas for further reading? Which seem interesting, most relevant, most likely to be accessible?

After completing some reading on this topic, I seem to be more sensitive to it and note items on television, in the newspaper, and even in conversations with peers and parents; which of these information leads should I follow up and how?

Are there some new questions I have as a result of this reading?

For Further Reading

Baxter, Kathleen A., and Marcia Agness Kochel. Gotcha! Nonfiction Booktalks to Get Kids Excited about Reading. Englewood, CO: Libraries Unlimited, 1999.

Carter, Betty, and Richard F. Abrahamson. Nonfiction for Young Adults from Delight to Wisdom. Phoenix: Oryx Press, 1990.

Cazden, C. Classroom Discourse: The Language of Teaching and Learning. Portsmouth, NH: Heinemann, 1988.

Cianciolo, Patricia J. Informational Picture Books for Children. Chicago: ALA, 2000.
Colman, Penny. "Nonfiction Is Literature, Too." The New Adovate 12, no. 3 (1999): 215-223.

Dresang, Eliza T. Radical Change: Books for Youth in a Digital Age. New York: H. W. Wilson, 1999.

Hansen, Jane, and Donald H. Graves. "The Language Arts Interact." In Handbook of Research in English Language Arts, edited by J. Flood, J. M. Jensen, D. Lapp, and J. Squire. New York: Macmillan, 1991.

Hopkins, Dianne McAfee. "The School Library Collection: An Essential Building Block to Teaching and Learning." School Libraries Worldwide 5, no. 2 (1999): 1-15.

Kobrin, Beverly. Eye-openers: How to Choose and Use Children's Books about Real People, Places, and Things. New York: Penguin, 1988.

Langer, J. A. "Reading, Writing, and Understanding: An Analysis of the Construction of Meaning." Written Communication 3, no. 2 (1986): 219-267.

Loertscher, David V. Collection Mapping in the LMC. San Jose, CA: Hi Willow Research and Publishing, 1996.

Lynch, Mary Jo, Pamela Kramer, and Ann Weeks. Public School Library Media Centers in 12 States: Report of the NCLIS/ALA Survey. Washington, DC.: U. S. Commission on Libraries and Information Science, 1994.

Rankin, Virginia. The Thoughtful Researcher. Englewood, CO: Libraries Unlimited, 1999.

Saul, E. Wendy, ed. Nonfiction for the Classroom. New York: Teachers College Press, 1994.

Stiggins, R. J., and N. F. Conklin. In Teacher's Hands: Investigating the Practices of Classroom Assessment. Albany, NY: State University of New York Press, 1992.

Sweet, Anne P. "State of the Art: Transforming Ideas for Teaching and Learning to Read." Indiana Media Journal 17, no. 4 (1995): 128-142.

Key Words
Organizers

"Organizers" are tools or techniques that provide identification and classification along with possible relationships or connections among ideas, concepts, and issues. Organizers are useful to the learner when given in advance of instruction and often serve as clues to ideas that the instructor plans to introduce. Such organizers seem to have a positive influence on the learner's ability to focus on new information and may increase the portion that is eventually assimilated as new knowledge for the student.

Organizers also may help to illustrate potential student research topics that derive from brainstorming a given theme. When student ideas are connected through some graphic means, the organization of these often random thoughts may show how eventual student projects will relate and support each other. Such visual mapping of concepts and questions also can illustrate the need for students to be more open and cooperative in the research process as they discover facts and resources that overlap with the information needs of others in the class.

In addition to serving as primers, objectives, outlines, and mental maps, organizers also may prove useful to enhance summaries and conclusions. Here, ranking and rating may enter the process more strongly than in the planning stages as the learner displays new knowledge in the form of conclusions and findings. The learner may have gained enough entry-level expertise not only to organize information, but also to make decisions as to which findings are more important or more relevant than others. Organizing such thoughts in order of importance is one sign that the maturing information literate student is becoming a critical thinker.

Advance Organizers

David Ausubel's research and ideas concerning organizers given in advance of lessons have become fundamental aspects for modern discussions of learning theory. He defined "teaching" as the deliberate guidance of learning processes for the purpose of enhancing learning outcomes. To enhance the instructor's guidance toward meaningful information, Ausubel offered the following proposal as to the power of an effective advance organizer:

> If an organizer can first delineate clearly, precisely, and explicitly, the principal similarities and differences between the ideas in a new learning passage on the one hand, and existing related concepts in [the student's] cognitive structure on the other, it seems reasonable to postulate that the more detailed ideas and information in the learning task would be grasped with fewer ambiguities, fewer competing meanings, and fewer misconceptions suggested by the learner's prior knowledge of the related concepts; and that as these clearer, less confused new meanings interact with analogous established meanings during the retention interval, they would be more likely to retain their identity. (p. 2)

Bruce Joyce and Marsha Weil, co-authors of the classic educational text Models of Teaching, provide one of the more clear descriptions of Ausubel's work and application of his ideas to instructional practice. Joyce and Weil compare and contrast a wide variety of approaches to instruction.

The strongest advance organizers are those that provide a conceptual framework through which students, with some variety in backgrounds and experiences, each may connect and construct an intellectual scaffold. Through the use of specific models, examples, and analogies, the teacher helps students identify elements of a new concept in concrete ways. The organizer is broad, however, and conceptual in nature so that it provides a large umbrella under which many more specific items can be identified, discussed, and related. The organizer must be new to the audience if learning is to take place. The advance organizer sets a stage for a new experience-one that can be linked to experiences brought to the situation by the students. The effective teacher, in Ausubel's view, directs such linkage. A growing body of modern constructivist theory would suggest, however, that such linkage becomes stronger and more likely to be retained when the students are emerged in a social environment among themselves and the resources in order to build additional linkages for themselves.

The Implications of Ausubel's Theory

Joyce and Weil have summarized implications to educational structures that derive from Ausubel's work.
Curriculum:
- Progressive differentiation. The most general ideas of the discipline are presented first, followed by a gradual increase in detail and specificity.
- Integrative reconciliation. New ideas should be consciously related to previously learned content.
Teaching:
- Expository organizer. Provides a general model for introduction of new facts or ideas, but broad enough to move the learner up a notch or so on the complexities of the material to be learned. Ausubel recommended this type of

organizer for completely unfamiliar learning material in which it is necessary to furnish an expository organizer consisting of more inclusive or superordinate ideas that could subsume or provide anchorage for the new material.
- Comparative organizer. Provides a more specific model closer to that which is already familiar and very similar to concepts just mastered. Ausubel recommended this approach for introduction of relatively familiar learning material, organized along parallel lines to that already held by the learner, but designed to increase discriminability between new and existing ideas, to refine differences with precision and detail.

Webbing: Organizing Information and Ideas

Organizing techniques have always been effective for teachers who want to bring meaning out of information overflow and sort out misinformation and irrelevant information. Kay Vandergrift, professor of library and information science at Rutger's, gives attention to a specific technique,"webbing," in her guide to the teaching role of the school library media specialist. A web may be a visual representation of different subsets of names, events, concepts, or questions related to a more general topic or theme. A web may serve as a visual representation of characters, events, conflicts, and new vocabulary with a novel serving as the center for the web and one result being identification of additional similar books to spark young reader interest. The web may have been constructed by professional educators as a guide to illustrate the wide choice of topics possible for a given theme. For student research topics, exploration of basic classification systems such as Dewey Decimal and Library of Congress can provide, to some degree, the "lay of the land" for organized information. Textbook outlines, tables of contents, and glossaries sometimes provide the same initial, but expertly formal, approach.

The more effective approach, supported by

Vandergrift, is to use webbing as an engaging technique to bring students into the creation of the research agenda. Students brainstorm expressions of experiences, events, and questions, and place these ideas on a large board or overhead. No initial judgment is made as to value or relevance, although as items are clustered and related, students begin to see that some subtopics offer more potential depth than others. Some see webbing as a free-flowing outline that allows ideas to be expressed and captured without the constraints of an ordered progression. Webbing seems to work best with groups of students as they are encouraged to express ideas for themselves and for peers to learn of the variety of possibilities for their classmates. Formal outlining, however, will eventually have its place in the research process, especially in the presentation stage that requires judgment and order.

Vandergrift reminds us that large-group semantic webbing is a triggering device that will need to be followed by continued background reading and likely a series of webs created by the individual student before he or she gains focus for the project. "They reconsider what they already know, identify what they want to find out, and formulate specific research questions or hypotheses. Even if a teacher has assigned the broad topic, this activity can help students see possibilities within that topic, encourage their personal ownership and involvement with the assigned task and, most importantly, get them excited both about what they already know and what is yet to be known."

The KWL Table, created by Donna Ogle and illustrated by James Bellanca in his collection of graphic organizers for cooperative thinking, has become a common tool for students to individually map their research agenda. By using this simple three-column structure, the students list what they Know, Want to learn, and have Learned. The visual organizer again helps students see relationships, but also helps learners see personal progress and initiates self-evaluation.

K	W	L

Graphic Organizers

Leticia Ekhaml, professor of research at State University of West Georgia, has described how graphic organizers have recently evolved from traditional charts and tables to specific designs associated with different tasks in problem-solving and critical thinking. Some of the benefits of such organizers listed by Ekhaml include:

- see connections, patterns, and relationships
- facilitate recalling or retelling of literature
- rank ideas
- list causes and effects
- improve comprehension skills and strategies

Ekhaml, based on Bellanca's cooperative think tank ideas, illustrates four basic patterns for graphic organizers: sequential, conceptual, hierarchical, and cyclical. Although each of these organizers is likely to be more formal than the less structured brainstorming, such as webbing, each represents an effective visualization of showing steps, decision points, relationships, and rankings. Creating visuals that personalize such organizers may well be a new trend in summaries and visual presentations we will expect from students as they demonstrate their information literacy skills. Visual organizers can convey the core of the essential or critical message that student researchers are expected to discover.

Basic Patterns of Graphic Organizers

Conceptual

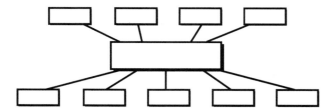

Sequential

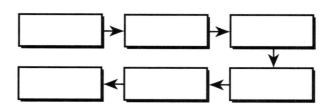

Cyclical

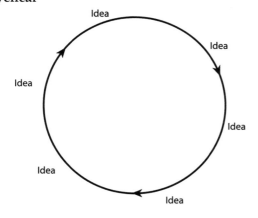

Hierarchial

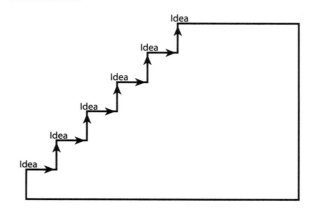

For Further Reading

Ausubel, David P. Learning Theory and Classroom Practice. Bulletin No. 1. The Ontario Institute for Studies in Education, 1967.

Bellanca, James. The Cooperative Think Tank: Graphic Organizers to Teach Thinking in the Cooperative Classroom. Palantine, IL: Skylight Publishing, 1990.

Bellanca, James. The Cooperative Think Tank II: Graphic Organizers to Teach Thinking in the Cooperative Classroom. Palantine, IL: Skylight Publishing, 1992.

Carroll, Lynda and Susan Leander. "Improving Student Motivation through the Use of Active Learning." ERIC Document, ED455961, 2001.

Clarke, John H. "Using Visual Organizers to Focus on Thinking." Journal of Reading 34, no. 7: 526-534.

Cramr, Cynthia, Joan Fate, and Kristin Lueders. "Improving Reading Achievement through the Implementation of Reading Strategies." ERIC Document ED454503, 2001.

Dunston, Pamela J. "A Critique of Graphic Organizer Research." Reading Research and Instruction 31, no. 2: 57-65.

Ekhaml, Leticia. "Graphic Organizers: Outlets for Your Thoughts." School Library Media Activities Monthly 14, no. 5 (January 1998): 29-33.

Fisher, Andrea L. "Implementing Graphic Organizer Notebooks: The Art and Science of Teaching Content." Reading Teacher 55, no. 2 (2001), 116-20.

Hobbs, Renee. "Improving Reading Comprehension by Using Media Literacy Activities." Voices from the Middle 8, no. 4 (2001), 44-50.

Hoyt, Linda. Revisit, Reflect, Retell: Strategies for Improving Reading Comprehension. Portsmouth, NH: Heinemann, 1999.

Johnson, Linda Lee. "Learning Across the Curriculum with Creative Graphing." Journal of Reading 32, no. 6 (March 1989): 509-519.

Joyce, Bruce, and Marsha Weil. Models of Teaching. Englewood Cliffs, NJ: Prentice-Hall, 1980.

Lepine, Simone. "Grab a Graphic Organizer!" Mailbox Intermediate Edition 23, no. 1 (2001), 4-11.

Mathena, Traci Johnson. "Prompting Kids to Write." American Educator 24, no. 3 (2000), 16-21.

Tomlinson, Carol Ann. How to Differentiate Instruction in Mixed-Ability Classrooms. Alexandria, VA: Association for Supervision and Curriculum Development. 2001.

Vandergrift, Kay E. Power Teaching: A Primary Role for the School Library Media Specialist. Chicago: American Library Association, 1994.

Westwater, Anne and Pat Wolfe. "The Brain-Compatible Curriculum." Educational Leadership 48, no. 3 (2000), 49-52.

Key Words
Portfolio

A portfolio is a collection of a student's work. The intent is to provide a more complete and richer display of a student's abilities to deal with complex problems. The portfolio is one answer to those who feel that the traditional evaluation of student performance, limited to letter grades or points for academic work and behavior, is too narrow to depict other possible student talents. While grades seem cold and conclusive, portfolio collections often can open constructive conversations among teacher, parent, and student about the processes that have brought the student to the conclusion of the most recent product and raise plans for future possibilities.

Portfolios can, if gathered and maintained in a systematic manner, provide a record that:
- has been compiled with the participation of the student through self-reflection and selection of the pieces to represent his or her record;
- is tangible and can be compared to others in the class and to previous work by the student to clearly show areas of progress or need for attention;
- leads to a progressively more complex and demanding set of academic requirements, tailored to the student's individual talents and needs.

Portfolios can, if not valued as a valid means for evaluation and if not regularly groomed and up-dated, become space-consuming clutter, vulnerable to those who are quick to criticize educational fads.

The means for evaluation and the potential content for the student portfolio have been given reasonable attention over the past decade. Implementation of portfolio assessment is still at the experimental stage, but some schools are making progress. Composition and science seem to be the frontline curricular areas to adopt this approach. Progressions in student grammar, spelling, sentence structure, and communication of meaning are clearly composition elements that can be demonstrated and compared from one year to the next. Defining terms, practice in basic experiments, documenting observations in narrative and numeric methods, and drawing conclusions or making predictions offer scope and sequence that can be reflected in science portfolios.

The portfolio approach opens evaluation to richer descriptive records. Reading performance, for example, becomes more than a number of titles read or reading ability at, below, or above a specific grade level. Reading teachers and library media specialists can comment on the student's ability to make reading selections and the student's growth in discussion about the content of what has been read. The portfolio record may even document the student's reflections on what he or she has selected and favored over the years and can define a goal for reading more in terms of questions to be explored and personal interests rather than just mastering basic phonetic skills. The same may be true for portfolios in information literacy. Will they be used to document basic steps or to illustrate critical thoughts?

The Portfolio and Information Literacy

What is the potential for use of portfolios to document the information literacy performance of students? Should this be a record compiled by classroom teachers, by library media specialists, or both? Can such records be realistically gathered and maintained in a timely, efficient, and understandable manner? These are demanding and largely unexplored questions for the school library media field. Library media specialists who have established information skills instruction integrated at the point of need with specific assignments, collaboratively planned and implemented with the classroom teacher, are clearly on the cutting edge for instruction today. They may feel that there is no need to expand this instructional role into the evaluation of student performance through portfolio records. Some schools have adopted a scope and sequence curriculum that includes identification of specific information skills; however most have not coordinated such efforts so that information literacy is a performance to be evaluated in a variety of curricular settings across the student's academic career.

Without such a curricular framework it is difficult to illustrate the degree of proficiency of a student's information selection and use skills. To add an evaluation process that requires documentation of student work; conversations with student, teachers, and parents; and writing a constructive judgment may be asking too much of the library media specialist. And yet, we must speculate on the possibilities if the teaching role is to be implemented fully.

Conducting evaluation completes the teaching cycle. Evaluation can take many forms, including the assessment of student information needs through reference interviews, determining reading options through reader's advisory, and feedback to classroom teachers for purposes of revising collaborative lessons. Evaluation of student performance, however, is the key to becoming a full player in the information literacy educational process. Such evaluation can tell us much about what students really select as valid information, when and how they make those judgments, and what library media specialists and other teachers should do to encourage or correct various information use or misuse behaviors.

It seems that the most reasonable approach for introducing the potential for portfolio assessment in the information literacy curriculum is to further expand the basic principles that provide the foundation for the collaborative instructional activities. Information literacy becomes a component of the assessment criteria for the portfolio, and this component can appear in a record related to any area of the curriculum. The criteria, however, remain the same across the curriculum. These criteria can be introduced to teachers with the hope that they will adopt them as part of the established evaluation process, or these evaluation criteria can become an extension of the collaborative teaching role now seen as key to ensuring that students are effective users of information.

The Colorado Model

Work in development of information literacy rubrics in Colorado has led to identification of some of the evaluation criteria measures that should be applied in portfolio assessment for information skills.

A rubric is a descriptive measurement, given on a progressive scale. Often the rubric defines in a set of related statements what the learner should know and be able to demonstrate for self-evaluation or evaluation by others. The progressive scale usually ranges from basic skills to advanced skills relative to the age group being measured. Target indicators are used to show the skills to be considered. Measures range from entry-level actions such as "in the process of making progress toward this skill" to "showing signs of being proficient in this area" to "demonstrating advanced, creative, exceptional performance compared to peer group."

The Colorado Information Literacy Rubric provides one of the first systematic frameworks for documenting the ability of every student in how he or she:

•constructs meaning from information;

- creates a quality product;
- learns independently;
- participates as a group member;
- uses information and information technologies responsibly and ethically.

As with any pioneering document, there is still room for refinement and greater specificity, but the Colorado instrument goes a long way in introducing some skill development strands which can be converted to evaluation criteria applicable to student portfolios of information use, composition, and critical thinking. One rubric strand is illustrated below.

Target Indicator: The student acquires information.

Progressive, observable actions for the student to reflect on and for others to consider in evaluation of performance:

a. In Progress: "Someone helps me extract details from information."

b. Essential: "I can extract details and concepts from one type of information resource."

c. Proficient: "I extract details and concepts from different types of resources."

d. Advanced: "I extract details and concepts from all types of resources."

Taking this one example from the Colorado plan, in isolation, does not illustrate the full range of information literacy skills contained in their proposed rubric framework. However, this one sequence, as others from the rubric, can give rise to ideas concerning evidence necessary for the components in a portfolio that would represent information literacy. Examples from the student's work would be sought to indicate that the student:

a. Follows specific steps concerning what to read and what information to look for to answer a given question. Guidance may be given by the library media specialist, classroom teacher, parent, or other student. A worksheet with pre-stated questions and specific examples for guidance may be evidence of the practice of this first-level skill.

b. Knows the difference between fact and concept. Along with this, the student can demonstrate how to extract facts and concepts from an information source which is commonly accepted as a resource for the student's ability level: an almanac table and summary, an encyclopedia article, a magazine article. Exercises in practice of fact and concept identification from an information source may serve as evidence of this ability.

c. Examines several resources for identification of related information, similar or conflicting, from several sources and links these pieces together to construct aspects of an argument, to expand perspective by listing several related issues, or to describe in detail an event or phenomenon. This is a jump to sophisticated skills. Demonstration of the ability to move through a variety of information sources for such purposes may be difficult to document. One option is a collection of note cards that contains both direct quotations and paraphrasing of information extracted by the student. In addition, the student needs to show evidence from a variety of sources and to document which sources were most useful and why. Therefore, notes should include room for the student to document judgments concerning the adequacy of the source and information extracted.

d. Can determine which resources are most likely to provide the information necessary to confirm, contradict, and therefore expand a line of argument; provide association and clustering of issues; or enrich a description of an event. Evidence at this point is more than simply showing that the student can extract information from a personal interview, a self-conducted survey, a televised debate of experts, a primary source, or any other type of resource we might identify. Extracting information from any one resource is basic and doesn't change the skill level, even through the student may now be able to demonstrate how to extract information from an almanac, a journal, and a personal interview. Evidence that the student has used three different sources is simply one skill times three-a repetition of level one-unless newly introduced sources require a different set of skills for extracting information. Assignments in which the student has been required to use three sources, whether necessary or not for the completion of the report, do no more to document advanced skills than do basic worksheets for practice use of one source. Knowing why other sources are necessary and best in predicting where, when, and how to approach those sources for gathering the potential evidence to meet a specific information need are the advanced skills to be documented. While these may be reflected in a student's product, such as a report based on use of multiple resources, these advanced skills are best documented by a reflection paper or a critical discussion by the student in which he or she explains why certain resources were selected and what limitations as well as merits each resource provided in helping the student accomplish his or her desired communication goal.

The Colorado Information Literacy Rubric does not get into the details for specific student products for portfolios, nor does it expand on each indicator suggested above. It is, however, an invaluable collection of potential evaluation categories from which can be extracted checklists, questions, and evaluation criteria for student portfolio review. Moving from this given rubric to information literacy portfolio evaluation criteria will result in additional consideration as to what critical skills are worth the time and effort to document.

The Evaluator's Rubric

Getting started in the complexities of information literacy portfolio construction and review may require some consideration of a rubric that illustrates the roles and actions of those involved. Division of time and effort among other tasks is certainly a key factor that will delay full implementation of portfolio review for information literacy skills; however, the potential is enormous if the review process is established in relation with successful portfolio programs for student composition, reading, and critical analysis skills across the curriculum.

Target Indicator: The School Library Media Specialist as Evaluator of Student Information Literacy Performance

In Progress: The teacher of school library media collaborates with the classroom teachers to integrate information literacy with various assignments requiring the use of multiple resources. Specific student performance skills for information use have been identified and organized in a scope and sequence across the academic program for typical, special need, and gifted students K-12.

Essential: The school library media specialist and the classroom teacher collaborate to present, facilitate, and coach students as they develop skills in the selection, analysis, synthesis, and application of information to solve problems. Both the school library media specialist and other teachers feel comfortable in conversing with students about their information needs, interpretation of information content, and alternatives for further information. Exercises in information use are evaluated by both teachers from the library media center and from the classroom. Student information literacy performance has an influence on the overall evaluation of the student.

Proficient: Evaluation of the student's product includes evaluation of the information selection and use process. Criteria for this evaluation have been established and provided to the student prior to the beginning of the process, and the application of the criteria has been modeled by the school library media specialist and the other teachers. Application of the criteria for evaluation includes student self-evaluation as well as feedback from the library media specialist and other teachers.

Advanced: Examples of communication products, including those electronically recorded with narrative and visuals, are gathered to reflect the progression in information literacy by the student. A record of the evaluation of student performance by the library media specialist, other teachers, student peers, and the student are contained in checklists and descriptive notes. The student's progress is mapped against the scope and sequence measures for the school's information literacy curriculum.

For Further Reading

Callison, Daniel. "Evaluator and Educator: The School Library Media Specialist." Tech Trends 32 (1987): 24-29.

Callison, Daniel. "The Potential for Portfolio Assessment." In School Library Media Annual 1993 , Vol. 11, edited by Carol C. Kuhlthau. Littleton, CO: Libraries Unlimited, 1993: 30-39.

Chang, Chi-Cheng. "Construction and Evaluation of a Web-based Learning Portfolio System: An Electronic Assessment Tool." Innovations in Education and Teaching International 38, no. 2 (2001), 144-55.

Chatel, Regina G. "Portfolio Development: Some Considerations." ERIC Document ED459437, 2001.

Clemmons, Joan. Portfolios in the Classroom: A Teacher's Sourcebook. New York: Scholastic Professional Books. 1993.

Colorado Department of Education and Colorado Educational Media Association. "Rubrics for the Assessment of Information Literacy." Indiana Media Journal 18 (1996): 50-61.

Rousculp, Edwin E., and Gearld H. Maring. "Portfolios for a Community of Learners." Journal of Reading 35 (1992): 378-385.

Valencia, Sheila W., and Scott G. Paris. "Portfolio Assessment for Young Readers." Reading Teacher 44 (1991): 680-682.

Key Words
Questioning

Probably the most frequently-stated reason for using a library, besides finding a good book, is to "find an answer." I accept both of those, but I want you to give some additional thought to "the library media center is the best place for students to raise questions."

The ability to question is the ability to see beyond the facts and opinions placed before you. The ability to see that most answers are only partial solutions and there are many more questions to explore, is a sign of a lifelong learner (whether aged 2 or 92).

Conversations with parents at home, in the evening around dinner, may include such statements as "I got an A on my history paper" or "I answered 90 of 100 math questions correctly today." Good bragging rights, no doubt. But the conversation could also be sparked by Johnny telling his parents what he has read about ancient Egypt and all the questions he now has about mummies. Why did they preserve bodies so well? Who got selected and why? What modern preservation methods do we use today that are the same as 3,000 years ago?

Not good dinner conversation, you say? Anything with questions, leading to more reading, or more net-surfing, or for Mom and Dad to join in the exploration is the best chatter of all.

While interesting questions can lead to interesting discussions, mastering the formulation of questions in a manner that leads to organizing how information is to be searched, retrieved, and sorted is the primary step leading to critical thinking. Questions, voiced or written, can reveal thoughts and help organize thinking.

Types of Questions

Questions can be limited to recall of factual responses. Questions may also involve processes (critical thinking):
- How are these alike or different?
- Which is best and why?
- Which path do we take? Why?
- What are the advantages and disadvantages?

Questions may stimulate imagination (creative thinking):
- What if you could change things?
- What will things be like in the future?
- What is your plan for action?

When to question and when not to question, that is the question

When students learn and practice effective questions, most of the following actions take place:
- They have the opportunity to hear for themselves what they want to know; to express to other students what they think is important to know; and to see how their questions are

simliar to the concerns of many others and yet discover those questions they have that might be different or even insightful.

- Questions voiced by students help them identify issues, frame parameters for argument, and determine points that must be explored further for more convincing evidence.
- Student ownership of the questioning process leads to students becoming content experts if they continue to question, probe, and explore. An expert discovers the questions that are "central to the issue;" questions that are of more interest currently; questions that have "haunted humankind for ages."
- Renovated and revised quesions, documented in journals, voiced on a regular basis, will give the library media specialist one important indication of the student's progress through the information selection, analysis, and synthesis processes.

Look for evidence that the questions evolve in detail and complexity, but questions should not end there. Detail and complexity show that new informatin is driving the thoughts. Simplicity and clarity show that these questions have been reconsidered in order to construct a focus for all further investigation.

Look for new questions that have come from reading, viewing, internetting, and discussion-questions that were not possible for the students to consider before such activities. Are there new questions now being asked by the student that show that new information is needed, that the student has consumed the materials immediately available, and that new questions can only be addressed with access to resources and people beyond the school library media center?

The school library media program moves into higher levels of service when such questions become the driving force for further student inquiry.

- Questioning and talking reduce the prewriting tension related to not knowing what to write about. Brainstorming ideas, constructing topic webs, or basic outlining of the topics related to a given theme can help the student get a better grasp on what may eventually be the focus of his or her work. Library media specialists and other teachers should encourage students to state questions related to each new topic as it is placed before the class for consideration.

Instructional media specialists, as teachers of information processing, should practice the following actions related to questioning:

- Model questioning. As reference materials are introduced, the library media specialist should state questions that might be addressed by these tools, and state questions that will not be. This gives you a chance to link to other reference tools and show a pattern of question raising and possible question answering.
- Engage students in sharing questions and resources. Ask students to describe sources (reference materials, magazine articles, a web site) in terms of what questions might be answered from the source. This is an important way to help the student practice synthesizing what the document has to offer in his or her own words and to determine why the document is or is not useful.
- Look for a variety of questions which demonstrate various levels of thinking. Do not, however, expect questions to build in a progressively more complex and precise manner. Even though we might look for such examples to determine maturity in the questioning process, questions (just as thinking) usually scatter and jump about without immediate linkage to other questions. Thus, students need to keep track of questioning thoughts. The teacher is an important coach to help them cluster, organize, map, and associate these questions in order to move along on finding meaning.

Information comes from text. Meaning comes from questions organized within a context. Who, what, where, when, why, and how give a start toward construction of this context.

- Reward questioning. Tell students when you hear a good question and why the question is good. Use questions to stimulate conversations by asking the students questions for which you know they can deliver the answer and then lead them into new questions, many for which the students and library media specialist may not know complete responses.
- Display questioning. Often bulletin boards display a "general idea" but do not really raise new questions. A rewarding and interactive method to display questioning is to allow students to post their questions on bulletin boards (traditional or electronic) and expect peers and teachers to respond.

Often library media specialists will give guided practice in reference skills by posting a weekly list of questions that can be answered with facts located in the general reference collection by students. Allow such given questions to be extended by students and let the challenge begin.

- Organize by questions. Signs over various book shelves often give the classification number and the general topic. Could questions be added to these signs? Government: How are laws written? Sociology: What is special about how other people live? Biology: What animals live in the Wetlands? Such question-displays help elementary school students understand the meaning of the more general categories. They may be encouraged to compose such questions for display over the course of the school year.

Promote Reading with Questions

Bibliographies and pathfinders can often be organized under question-headings. What general books will give me an overview of this topic? What materials in addition to the book collection will help me? What local people in the community are willing to tell me more about this topic?

- Promote reading with questions. Many good booktalks end with questions that invite the audience to read the book being promoted. Questions can be used to head a book list or a poster that lists several books that help answer questions such as "What will be the best job for me when I am twenty-five? or "How can I start my own business?"

The most effective use of questions to promote reading, however, is again related to student-generated questioning. Students at all levels (and teachers, too, but that really leads to another instructional term to define at a later date) should read on a regular basis, sustained through time and reading collections provided by the school. But even with a library of 20,000 titles before many students, the haunting question comes, "So, what shall I read?"

Book lists and recommendations from fellow students help. A major item that will jump-start reading is a list of questions I want to find answers to (not an answer, but answers). From five to ten stated questions will come a plan for reading and viewing for the semester. Materials should vary in format, and much nonfiction will begin to show in the form of magazines and newspapers. The reading record (once "a list of books I have read this year") is compiled to show the materials used to answer the first set of questions and material that spun new questions.

In closing, there are two actions that library media specialists and teachers should not take in the questioning process:

- Do not ask all the questions. The more student-centered, student-generated the questions and information discussions, the more powerful the learning process.
- Do not expect immediate answers nor immediate questions every time. Wait time is probably the most abused segment of the academic day. It is difficult to wait thirty seconds before a response

comes from the class. It is very frustrating to wait several days before students, often struggling with information on a given subject for the first time, begin to identify questions of merit. Getting focus takes time, and often after several failed attempts.

While many of our best questions, from students and teachers, come in almost a natural way, the rest of our best come from reading, writing, listening, debating, and interacting with each other and information texts.

For Further Reading and Viewing

Brown, M. Neil and Keeley, Stuart M. <u>Asking the Right Questions: A Guide to Critical Thinking</u>. Englewood Cliffs: Prentice Hall, 1990.

Christenbury, Leila and Kelly, Patricia P. <u>Questioning: A Path to Critical Thinking</u>. Urbana: National Council of Teachers of English, 1993.

<u>How to Improve Your Questioning Techniques</u>. Video. 15 minutes. Association for Supervision and Curriculum Development, 1998.

Rubin, Donald L. and Dodd, William M. <u>Talking into Writing</u>. Urbana: National Council of Teachers of English, 1987.

Key Words
Reflection

Reflection is key to both the student process for learning effective use of information and for the teacher who wants to evaluate his or her own techniques for instruction in information literacy. To be reflective is to consider options and to make a judgment. For the emerging information literate student, this may involve selective use of evidence, knowledgeable use of authority, experimentation with the plausibility of an argument, and self-evaluation of final selection of information for presentation. For the teacher, reflection involves the questions and attempts to gain answers to revise and correct approaches that guide students in the information literacy process.

At the highest levels of reflection, the mature information literate student will demonstrate these actions:

- The student draws extensively on evidence from multiple resources (human, print, nonprint) to support conclusions and the conclusions clearly show a coherent use of the evidence.
- The student has significant recognition of authority and has shown some attempt to investigate and document the authority's credibility or point of view.
- The student recognizes all sides of an issue, is able to weigh the pros and cons of all sides, and recognizes the strengths and limitations of each position in taking a stand.

Reflection has a powerful impact on student learning when implemented as part of the process of dealing with ill-structured problems, i.e., those situations in which there is no clear right or wrong set of answers or conclusions.

The Elementary Levels for Student Reflection

Linda Hoyt, an elementary school teacher and curriculum specialist, has provided a recent guide to strategies for improving reading comprehension through reflection and application of skills for elementary students to revisit, reflect, and retell. Her list of questions for students to ask each other about books are also questions that elementary level students should ask as they engage with new information and attempt to assimilate that information with previous knowledge and experiences:

- What did you notice?
- What did you like?
- What is your opinion?
- What did you wonder?
- What does this mean?
- What did you learn?
- How did it make you feel?
- What parts of the story seemed especially important to you?
- As you read, were there any places where you thought of yourself, people you know, or

experiences you have had?
- What did you read that gives you new ideas?
- What do you know now that you did not know before?

Hoyt's strategies to engage young learners in conversations about books and to manage personal and social exploration of meaning have applications for placing elementary students on tasks to become selective and critical of information from nonfiction materials as well. Students must select the key or most important elements which summarize the message of a story. "Two-Word Strategy," for example, asks each student to select and justify just two words that reflect their understanding, feeling, or related experience to a thought-provoking selection from a story, newspaper article, or passage from a resource book. As students share their selections, Hoyt notes that a rich tapestry of various understandings, visions, and feelings emerge.

Other strategies place young readers in the position to rank characters and events from a story or news happening. They demonstrate the ability to concentrate on the most important issues. Such skills eventually lead to the ability to center on the key arguments so that limited time and resources can be directed to address these while minor characters, events, or nonmeaningful evidence can be discarded. Her use of "book commercials," similar to "booktalking," places the student on the task of gleaning for the most interesting or intriguing elements in order to provide excitement as they sell the story through a variety of formats, similar to advertising in mass media.

Retelling expository text is a practiced skill that will build to more mature critical analysis of documents at higher grade levels. For the elementary school student, Hoyt poses these questions for student reflection on information documents such as magazine articles, encyclopedia articles, or newspaper features:
- What is the topic?
- What are the most important ideas to remember?
- What did you learn that you did not already know?

- What is the setting for this information?
- What did you notice about visuals such as graphs, charts, and pictures?
- Can you summarize or retell what you learned?
- What do you think was the author's purpose for writing this article?

Her recommended techniques also place younger learners in situations to practice paraphrasing or claiming the key message in their own words after they have identified important information clusters:
READ only as much as your hand can cover.
COVER the words with your hand.
REMEMBER what you have just read. (It is okay to take another look.)
RETELL what you just read inside your head or to a partner.

Reflection on Process for Older Learners

Carol Collier Kuhlthau's steps to the library research process culminate in application of self-evaluation techniques designed to cause the high school student to reflect on the research experience. Two important areas for reflection are "use of time" and "use of sources." The mature student researcher learns to pace him(her)self and through the use of a timeline or diary can visualize actions that took more time than necessary and the need to allow for more time in critical areas. These critical areas may include time to compare and contract evidence in a variety of ways before launching into the writing or preparing to present tasks. More time may be necessary to acquire materials from distance loan or to establish a useful interview with an expert in the community. Knowledge of their own limitations in management of time and correcting for such helps the maturing information literature student to both conserve and concentrate time and energies in order to arrive efficiently at the focus of their research. Testing and confirming focus is crucial to eventual development of presentation of meaningful findings. Kuhlthau's recommended techniques are:
- Timeline. Plotting the stages initiated

and completed during library research and recalling when focus seemed to emerge.

- Flow Chart. Decision boxes show the linkages and recursiveness through the process and may highlight "ah-ha" experiences when key ideas and key resources emerged.
- Conferences. Debriefing sessions involving the student or small groups of students along with the library media specialist and other teachers can lead to recall of key decision and inspiration points. These conversations can help identify important times for interventions by the library media specialist and other teachers in future research assignments.
- Writing a Summary Statement. A clear abstract of the process and product can help the student convey to himself and others the focus or meaning of the research experience. In this technique, as in the others, students should be expected to be critical as they select and summarize their best ideas and resources.

Reflection in the I-Search Process

Marilyn Joyce and Julie Tallman have placed reflection at several strategic points within the I-Search process. Their approach is to create intervention experiences along the research path so that teachers and students are constantly raising questions about decisions and actions so that research topics become manageable as well as personal.

Students are expected to journal and or vocally state their reflections on such questions as:

- What are some of the research projects you have completed prior to this?
- From these previous experiences, what does "research" mean to you?
- Describe one of your research successes. Why was the experience positive?
- Describe one of your research failures or frustrations. Why was the experience negative?

Small group and individual conferences are held to help generate, expand, and clarify research question formation. Students generate potential areas to explore based on interest and resource availability and pre-notetaking reflection can serve to gain an initial focus so that eventual information selection and gathering becomes more targeted and meaningful. Joyce and Tallman recommend that students address the following kinds of questions as they reflect on pre-notetaking and background reading:

- Describe how the pre-notetaking sheet helped you find both a focus for your topic and research questions to investigate.
- Summarize what happened during your conference. What problems or obstacles did you identify during your conference? Whatstrategies will you use to overcome them?

In true application of the I-Search process, the student may demonstrate emerging information literacy skills by composing a report or paper on the research process itself. This may serve as a companion piece to the final research product and becomes a document that should be read and evaluated by both the library media specialist and collaborating teacher. Sample questions given below could be used in peer or teacher evaluation of the student product as well as self-assessment by the student as they report on their experiences.

Presearch
- Has the student chosen a personally meaningful topic?
- Did the student create original and demanding research questions that move the need for evidence beyond simply fact gathering and into evaluation of evidence in terms of relevance, authority, and display of various perspectives?
- Did the student show organizational strengths through an ability to prioritize potential topics, clarify search questions with key terms for more precision, make quality resource choices, and consider alternative solutions to problems

through extensive background reading?

Search
- Did the student examine a sufficient variety of relevant sources including interviews and use of electronic documents?
- Did the student show the ability to apply relevant evidence and to discard irrelevant sources or misleading evidence?

Presentation
- Is the presentation organized and based on the key issues relevant to the audience addressed?
- Is the presentation based on relevant information and the use of multiple resources and multiple perspectives where necessary?
- Can the student articulate a likely personal information search and selection strategy to be used in similar future assignments?

The Reflective Teacher

Kathleen Blake Yancey of the University of North Carolina at Charlotte states:

"If we want students to be reflective, we [teachers] will have to invite them to be so, [and] may need to reflect with them. Reflection, like language itself, is social as well as individual. Through reflection, we tell our stories of learning; in the writing classroom, our stories of writing and of having written and of [what we] will write tomorrow.... I suppose I think this reflection is so important because without it, we live the stories others have scripted for us, in a most unreflective, unhealthy way. And I think the stories we make-whether inside the classroom or out, whether externalized or not-construct us, one by one by one. Cumulatively. So I think it's important to tell lots of stories where we get to construct many selves...."

Yancey's statement is important in at least two ways. First, reflection on writing and research processes helps the student to construct a personal identity derived from the choices made, questions fashioned, presentations scripted, and assimilations to previous personal experiences. Student reflection on these actions is essential to the growth and maturation of the information literature student.

Second, the teacher of information literacy needs to participate in reflection as well, not only as a coach or model of the reflection process, but to be one who reflects on teaching style, purpose, and actions. "Reflective teaching" has become a generic term referring to a range of efforts intended to prepare teachers to be more thoughtful. Some advocates hope to engage teachers in becoming more thoughtful about the educational/cultural context, with the assumption that teachers are or should be agents of social change. Others wish to focus teachers' thoughts on the art of teaching, in the hope that through inspection, introspection, and analysis, teaching can be enhanced.

The reflective teacher monitors, invites peers to monitor with him or her, and may even journal thoughts in response to questions such as:
- How do I interact with students?
- How do I respond when they ask questions?
- What kind of classroom atmosphere do I create?
- What kinds of questions do I ask?
- Is my classroom spontaneous or is it predictable?
- Are my students involved?
- Why didn't a lesson go over well?
- Why did a lesson work?

More precise areas for reflection have been identified by the National Council of Teachers of Mathematics, but these apply across the curriculum including those who teach library research processes and information literacy:

Nature of Task
- Is the task a problem or an exercise for my students?
- Is it possible to make the problem realistic and grounded in real-world experiences?
- Is it possible to represent and respond

to the problem concretely, pictorially, and abstractly on several levels of learning and intelligence?

Teacher's Communication
- Am I determining what the students "know" or bring to a situation?
- What kinds of questions do I ask?
  - Genuine questions for which I do not know the answers?
  - Testing questions to find out what my students know or have learned?
  - Focusing questions that encourage students to think about some idea, to explain, to justify, to hypothesize or predict?
- Am I using wait time before and after I receive responses to questions?
- Am I exploring alternative strategies posed by different students?
- Am I using various forms of communication-reading, writing, listening, speaking?
- Am I modeling creative and critical thinking?

Students' Communication
- What kind of questions are my students asking?
- Are my students talking to each other constructively-disagreeing, challenging, debating?
- Are my students willing to take risks?
- Are my students listening to each other?
- Are my students taking time to think about problems fully?
- Are my students able to explain their ideas clearly and precisely?
- Are my students able to reflect on the experience and identify that which was hard or easy for them, what worked and what didn't, and what they liked and disliked?

Tools that Enhance Discourse
- Am I making use of the technology available?
- Are meaningful and representational models for process and product available for my students?

- Do I encourage and reward by using various tools to communicate ideas?

For Further Reading

Cruickshank, D. Reflective Teaching: The Preparation of Students of Teaching. Reston, VA: Association of Teacher Educators, 1987.

Hoyt, Linda. Revisit, Reflect, Retell: Strategies for Improving Reading Comprehension. Portsmouth, NH: Heinemann, 1999.

Joyce, Marilyn Z., and Julie I. Tallman. Making the Writing and Research Connection with the I-Search Process. New York: Neal-Schuman, 1997.

Kuhlthau, Carol Collier. Teaching the Library Research Process. 2nd ed. Lanham, MD: Scarecrow Press, 1994.

National Council of Teachers of Mathematics. Curriculum and Evaluation Standards for School Mathematics. Reston, VA: NCTM, 1989.

Tallman, Julie I., and Lyn Henderson. "Constructing Mental Model Paradigms for Teaching Electronic Resources." School Library Media Research. 1999. http://www.ala.org/aasl/SLMR/mental.html

Walkington, Jackie, Hans Peter Christensen, and Hanne Kock. "Developing Critical Reflection as Part of Teaching Training and Teaching Practice." European Journal of Engineering Education 26, no. 4 (2001), 343-50.

Yancey, Kathleen Blake. Reflection in the Writing Classroom. Logan, UT: Utah State University Press, 1998.

Key Words
Rubrics

The rubric strategy is one of several assessment methods recommended in the student performance assessment section of Information Power. A "rubric" is a set of scaled criteria, usually ranging from performance that is considered unacceptable to minimal through progressive stages which eventually defines that which is observable superior performance. Language is used, in terms that both the student and teacher understand, so that precise actions are defined for what the student must do to demonstrate a skill or proficiency at a certain level.

Grant Wiggins, director of programs for the Center on Learning, Assessment, and School Structure, proposes that rubrics should answer the following questions:

- By what criteria should performance be judged?
- Where should we look and what should we look for to judge performance success?
- What does the range in the quality of performance look like?
- How do we determine validly, reliably, and fairly what score should be given and what that score means (so that a score means the same from one similar task performed by a similar group to another but evaluated by different instructors, or the same instructor, over time)?
- How should the different levels of quality be described and distinguished from one another?

Some rubric models allow for points at each level so the point totals can be translated into standard grades, if necessary. Some rubric models show a relationship between the percentage or degree of proficiency and the action demonstrated. In these cases, lower performance may be at the 50% level implying that the student has demonstrated only half of the skills in the given area evaluated, or that the student is below the norm in this area. The percentage gradually increases until, at the highest level, the student has demonstrated 95-100% proficiency. Such numeric guides, however, should not take away from the purpose and value of rubrics: to write in clear statements those performances that are not acceptable and those that are acceptable as measured against the expected standard performance for the task and age group. Rubrics provide phrases to translate for the student, teacher, and parent why the student has failed, needs more practice, has performed in a satisfactory range, or has excelled.

Classification of Performance

Rubrics may provide classification of performances in several ways. Usually the rubric is constructed on a grid with the evaluation skill levels or target indicators listed down the left-hand side and the levels of performance classified across the top of the grid. The skill levels may range from "basic knowledge," followed by "analysis skills," and then "synthesis skills." Or, the skills may simply be clustered in such categories as "written," "oral," and "social." Some evaluators cluster the skills by Gardner's multiple intelligence categories which include linguistic, logical, spatial, musical, kinesthetic, intrapersonal, and interpersonal. Obviously, not all seven are always listed and synonyms often are found for elementary and middle grade students to understand.

Some rubric designers cluster skills by those which reflect critical thinking and those which match more to creative thinking. Thus the student may be evaluated on his or her skills in selecting the best information to prove a point in a logical manner and be evaluated again on the ability to create a plan that will address the given problem. Still other rubric designs allow for skills that are essential or required and allow space for elective skills. This is similar to judgments made in some Olympic competitions in which the performance is compared very closely to others in the required elements, but there is room for judgment of individual initiative as well.

The rubric also will display the progression or range of quality of performance in terms of "novice" to "apprentice" to "expert." Other terms used to classify the progression are "beginning," "developing," "accomplished," and "exemplary." Usually no fewer than three levels are given and often room is provided for notes from the teacher and student that describe actions to be taken to improve future performance.

In cases where students are truly involved in self-evaluation, space is provided on the grid in both the list of skills and columns for levels of criteria so students may add their own expectations beyond those listed as common for the entire class.

Rubrics can be constructed for any area of the curriculum, across all grade levels and entry ability levels. Thus, a given rubric should be labeled as an evaluation instrument for a specific set of learners and for a specific lesson or task. It also is useful to provide a list of entry level skills, those the student should have mastered prior to this lesson. Also useful, and likely to be similar to the proficient level for the instructional performance indicators, will be exit objectives, the minimum basic skills the student will demonstrate during and as a result of the given lesson.

The rubric method is most useful when applied to a lesson that will require multiple skills to be demonstrated over time and during which the student will be evaluated on both process and product. Checklist methods help to keep the student on track and to make certain all tasks are completed, but little evaluation really takes place. Conference and journal methods allow for more extensive intervention and teacher direction, and as outlets for self-reflection.

Rubrics, therefore, take objectives for student performance and provide an evaluation grid or map so the learner knows what is expected and what will be valued. The rubrics for a given lesson should be provided as an opening organizer for the lesson, a midpoint check or evaluation so adjustments in performance are possible, and serve as a menu, guide, or agenda for the final evaluation or exit conference concerning student performance among several groups that may include student, library media specialist, other teachers, and parents.

Advantages and Frustrations

Rubrics allow for evaluation of academic and social skills. As Jean Donham at the University of Iowa suggests, one rubric set can be applied to one task and result in an examination of a portion of a performance set, or rubrics compiled over time and across several lessons will lead to a more complex or holistic view of the student's progression in skill mastery. For rubrics to work effectively, especially applied to student self-assessment, there are, according to Donham, three critical attributes:
Explicit criteria. The criteria provide enough description that students know what successful performance looks like.
Structured feedback. The criteria are ordered to show students how close to excellence they are. Feedback is not hit-or-miss-all students get feedback.
Front-end information. The criteria for success are provided as the student begins the work, not at the end.

The advantages of rubrics in assessment are:
- Assessment is more likely to be reasonably objective and consistent from les-

son to lesson and from student to student, especially useful in team teaching situations that involve collaboration among the library media specialist and other teachers.

- Teachers focus on the essential criteria and performances.
- Students have a more clear visual of their progress and what is necessary to achieve a higher rating than is reflected in simple letter grades.
- Feedback is easy to convey and can provide a benchmark from one lesson to the next. Communication with parents is often more constructive.
- If applied correctly, rubrics come close to assuring that inadequate, satisfactory, and excellent mean the same thing on the same skill set from one group of students to a similar group regardless of who makes the evaluation.

Frustrations of rubrics include:
- Construction of good rubric statements takes time and practice. There is still a great deal of room for experimentation.
- Although the rubric instrument as an assessment innovation has been given a great deal of attention, letter grades remain the standard. Even the best rubric matrix eventually melts back to A, B, C, D, or F, unless the school district is committed to archiving portfolios.
- Although consistency can be provided within a lesson, the more teachers, grade levels, and subjects involved, the wider the range and definitions of acceptable performance criteria, and evaluation suddenly becomes very complex and confusing.
- When rubrics do define a standard performance, such is often resisted and viewed as taking true evaluation out of the hands of the individual teacher.
- Poorly constructed rubrics give emphasis to quantity rather than quality; the student does something more times rather than doing something better.

Process and Product

The Minnesota Department of Children, Families, and Learning has developed a set of evaluation rubric guides for application across the curriculum and at all grade levels. Sample exercises are provided on their website along with possible evaluation criteria. Two key elements are present in many of these state recommended examples:
- Both teacher and student identify where they believe the learner stands on a given performance level.
- Elements of the process are listed for evaluation as well as elements of the final product or final performance.

Thus the student makes judgments along with the teachers of information literacy and inquiry on such process stages as:
- Research questions are relevant to the topic and are adequate to lead to sufficient and appropriate kinds of data.
- The investigation plan allows for adequate and feasible collection of data.
- Data chart/matrix/note cards include bibliographic information.
- The interview questions are designed to get the needed information, clearly relate to research questions, and lead to responses that are complete and detailed. The interviewer is adequately prepared to ask additional questions for clarification.

Midpoint evaluations, or multiple checkpoints, in the progress of the student toward completion of a complex research project can be guided by the process portion of the evaluation rubric. Often teachers of information literacy and inquiry can guide a student who is off track back to a focus and direction if inadequate preparation is discovered during these debriefings.

Types of Rubrics

Despite the variety of rubric formations that have been described here, Germaine Taggert and Marilyn Wood of Fort Hays State

University have summarized three rubric types:

Holistic. Holistic rubrics are criterion-referenced, which show what a student knows, understands, or can do in relation to specific performance objectives of the instructional program. How does one perform overall?

Analytic. Criterion-referenced analytic rubrics assess summative or formative performance along several different important dimensions. How does one perform on several individual tasks?

Primary trait. These define the essential traits that must be observed for successful performance. How does one perform on the specific essential elements for success in this lesson or activity?

Although the current literature generally agrees that the rubric approach is clearly criterion-referenced and must be tied to a standard for acceptable performance, room also should be given for objective evaluation of personal growth. Within the series of evaluation conversations, students and teachers need to consider progress that is evident and reward such progress in order to motivate more constructive action. Some students will not achieve at the adequate or excellent level on most criteria, but rubrics that allow for a wide enough range to show some progress will serve to encourage a wider spectrum of students. Movement for some from "inadequate" to the basic "in need of improvement" or "emerging" levels will prove helpful in some performance phases.

Any evaluation rubric should allow space for additional comments that will address individual traits and special characteristics of the learner so that such information is not lost in rigid standards. These additional principles should be kept in mind:

- Rubrics are texts that are visible signs of agreed-upon values. They cannot contain all the nuances of the evaluation community's values, but they do contain the central expressions of those values.
- Rubrics need to grow out of and be accompanied by discussion. A core set of rubrics should be available to the learner from the beginning, but options for additional criteria should be present as the activity unfolds.
- Rubrics provide a map and guide for student assessment. More importantly, a record of the discussion concerning student performance should be included in the student portfolio to show areas of progress over time.

Rubrics for Information Literacy

Several creative groups, under the guidance of the Colorado Department of Education in 1996, provided some excellent examples of rubrics in information literacy. Two are illustrated here:

Target Indicator: Student is a self-directed learner.

In progress: I have trouble choosing my own resources and I like someone to tell me the answer.

Essential: I might know what I want, but need to ask for help in solving information problems.

Proficient: I choose my own resources and like being independent in my information searches.

Advanced: I like to choose my own information resources. I am comfortable in situations where there are multiple answers as well as those with no answers.

Target Indicator: Student as a group contributor.

In progress: I need support to work in a group. I have trouble taking responsibility to help the group.

Essential: I usually participate with the group. I offer opinions and ideas, but cannot always defend them. I rely on others to make group decisions.

Proficient: I participate effectively as a group member. I help the group process, and evaluate and use information with the group.

Advanced: I am comfortable leading, facilitating, negotiating, or participating in a group. I work with others to create a product that fairly represents consensus of the group.

A Rubric for Rubrics

Given the trends in current development of the rubric strategy for evaluation of student performance, one can consider this rubric to help test the degree to which new instructional rubrics have been constructed for effective use:

Target Indicator: Write a meaningful rubric statement set.

In progress: Statements are not clearly tied to a standard for student performance and fail to provide a reasonable range to reflect progress in student performance.

Essential: Statements are tied to a common standard, but define student progress only in terms of increased quantity and not in terms of quality.

Proficient: Statements are clearly relevant to several accepted standards for student performance and are illustrated in terms of a progressive criteria for increased quality of student performance.

Advanced: Statements illustrate a broad range of tasks to demonstrate student performance measured against acceptable standards in terms of appropriate quantity and/or quality, and allow for the learner to explore additional criteria for evaluation if both student and teacher see merit in such options.

For Further Reading

Arter, Judith A. and Joy McTighe. Scoring Rubrics in the Classroom: Using Performance Criteria for Assessing and Improving Student Performance. Corwin Press, 2001.

Chatel, Regina G. "Portfolio Development: Some Considerations." ERIC Document ED459437, 2001.

Colorado Department of Education. "Rubrics for the Assessment of Information Literacy." Indiana Media Journal 18, no. 4 (Summer 1996): 50-71.

Donham, Jean. "Assessment of Student Work." In Enhancing Teaching and Learning: A Leadership Guide for School Library Media Specialists. New York: Neal-Schuman Publishers, 1998.

Farmer, Leslie. "Information Literacy: A Whole School Reform Approach." ERIC Document ED459716, 2001.

Fiderer, Adele. 40 Rubrics & Checklists to Assess Reading and Writing (Grades 3-6). Scholastic Professional Books, 1999.

Kist, Bill. "Using Rubrics Teacher to Teacher." ERIC Document ED458392, 2001.

Minnesota Department of Children, Families and Learning. Minnesota Electronic Curriculum Repository. http://mecr.state.mn.us/home

Repman, Judi. "Information Literacy and Assessment: Web Resources Too Good to Miss." Library Talk 15, no. 2 (2002), 12-14.

"Student Performance Assessment." Appendix E. In Information Power: Building Partnerships for Learning. Chicago: ALA, 1998.

Taggart, Germaine, ed. Rubrics: A Handbook for Construction and Use. Lancaster, PA: Technomic, 1998.

Wiggins, Grant. Educative Assessment: Designing Assessments to Inform and Improve Student Performance. San Francisco: Jossey-Bass Publications, 1998.

Recommended Websites

Rubrics for Web Lessons
edweb.sdsu.edu/webquest/rubrics/weblessons.htm
www.rubrics.com

Rona's Teacher Tools - Rubrics
www.rubrics4teachers.com

University of Northern Iowa Professional Development
www.uni.edu/profdev/rubrics.html

Region 20 Education Center
www.esc20.net/etprojects/rubrics/Default.htm

Project Based Learning - Checklists
www.4teachers.org/projectbased/checklist.shtml

RubiStar
rubistar.4teachers.org

MidLink Magazine
www.ncsu.edu/midlink/ho.html

Evaluation Rubrics for Websites
www.siec.k12.in.us/~west/online/eval.htm

Schrock, Kathy. Assessment Rubrics.
http://school.discovery.com/schrockguide/assess
.html

Key Words
Scaffolding

"Scaffolding" is a term that has gained popular use as a metaphor for support, reinforcement, learning sequence, and similar phrases which infer that learning is constructed. Similar to a building under construction, student learning is constructed based on a sequence of skills with meaningful activities that are presented by a teacher to help the student climb to the desired educational goal or behavior.

Scaffolding is most commonly associated with Jerome Bruner and his colleagues in the 1970s and 1980s as they attempted to describe the role of the tutoring process in problem solving. Used most often in the preschool and elementary school setting, scaffolding is a useful concept for describing nearly any situation in which a novice and an expert are engaged in the learning process. Just as scaffolding is a temporary device in construction or building repair and eventually removed when the desired work is accomplished, so too in the learning construction-the expert fades from the learning situation as the novice masters the necessary skills and takes on the scaffolding as a new set of mental models.

Laura E. Berk, Distinguished Professor at Illinois State University, and Adam Winsler, Assistant Professor at Alabama University, have provided an excellent guide to understanding the scaffolding metaphor in their book Scaffolding Children's Learning, written for the National Association for the Education of Young Children. Their definition of "scaffolding" is:

A changing quality of support over a teaching session, in which a more skilled partner adjusts the assistance he or she provides to fit the child's current level of performance. More support is offered when a task is new; less is provided as the child's competence increases, thereby fostering the child's autonomy and independent mastery.

The Scaffolding Analogy

A more detailed discussion and diagram of scaffolding moves the metaphor into an analogy as additional similarities between construction of learning and construction of buildings become apparent. (see figure 1)

The purpose of the scaffolding is to help the

Figure 1

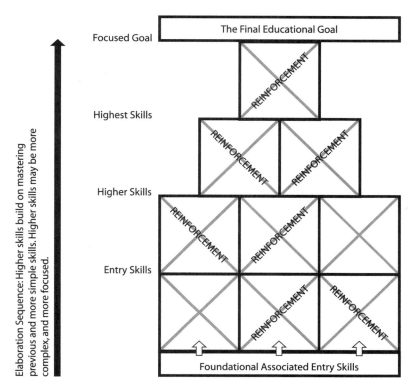

learner or builder reach higher tasks than can be performed at just the base level. The base level is extremely important, however, as a firm, secure, and well-tested foundation is desirable for both learner and builder.

The base may be composed of several associated skills to give it a broad foundation upon which to build higher skills sets. Strength is derived from linking these foundational or entry level skills together and through practice. Success is reinforced by the teacher and by the learner's growing awareness when the task has been achieved. Reinforcements tie the task together and often help to link to other tasks.

Scaffolding can be deconstructed as well as constructed. In some cases, this would imply changing unacceptable behavior or modifying out-dated information, changing the mental model through assimilation of new knowledge leading to a different understanding. Scaffolding also can be thought of as deconstructed so that similar parts can be moved, or transferred, to new learning situations. Hopefully the learner, as he or she matures in the learning process, begins to recognize how portions of the previous scaffold apply to a new learning task and may move forward with self-construction of much of the scaffold without the assistance of the expert. Practice in and observation of likely transfer of learning is an important part of movement toward what many describe as "lifelong learning skills."

Setting up scaffolding in either learning or building construction is hard work, often messy and repetitious. The final result just as often can be frustrating as rewarding, and both can be exhausting.

As the scaffolding is built higher, the skill set may become both more complex and more refined or precise. A focus often will take place so the learner can meet the final educational goal. The focus may change from one situation to another and, therefore, the scaffolding structure or design may change to meet those different needs.

Elaboration Theory

Charles Reigeluth of Indiana University is a leader among many instructional designers who believe elaborations of content in courses of study are based on concepts, principles, and procedures. Sequencing of lessons are best designed when based on the simple and then move toward the more complex. The first lesson, the epitome, is followed by successive layers of complexity and associated lessons that provide illustration and practice. Within the lesson design, easiest or most familiar organizing concepts are presented first.

Summaries are important as a means to provide content review. Summaries may serve to reinforce demonstrated performance as the teacher explains what has been achieved by the student. The student may signal his or her readiness to move on to the next level by the ability to summarize or synthesize for him or herself. Increased learner control of the learning situation is desirable. More confident learners are more likely to move to the highest levels.

A sequence of skills, or elaboration sequence, as noted in Figure 1, is based on moving to higher and more complex skills only after mastering of the basic or more simple ones. The difficult role for the teacher is to find the balance between moving the learner through this sequence too slowly and creating boredom, or moving too quickly and creating anxiety.

Effective use of scaffolding is more than just breaking down a task into substeps offered by the adult or expert to the novice. Such a limited approach reduces the novice or child to a passive recipient of the adult's didactic efforts. Scaffolding should involve a series of social communication efforts, likely to become more complex and detailed just as the elaboration of the skill set content grows. Elaboration may, therefore, be best described as interaction as both parties involved need to communicate for purposes of testing out examples, analogies, predictions, and possible solutions depending on the task at hand. Reaching the desired levels of performance, however, will bring on a dramatic reduction in such communication as the novice-become-expert may begin to dominate the conversations. Such is a strong cue to the teacher to fade from the learned lesson.

Other Elements of Scaffolding

Berk and Winsler identify several additional elements that should be present in an effective scaffolding process. These have only slight concrete ties to the construction analogy.

Joint problem solving. Scaffolding will have more chance of being on a firm foundation if the learner is engaged in a culturally relevant problem that has meaning to him or her.

Intersubjectivity. This is when two people begin a task with a different understanding and arrive at a shared understanding. The final goal must be clear for both novice and expert. Different methods and different perspectives can be adjusted as the two learn to communicate, but the goal or final learning objective should be common to both.

Warmth and responsiveness. Engagement of the novice will be more likely when the expert displays attitudes that are pleasant, warm, and responsive to the learner.

Promoting self-regulation. Encourage the learner to take the role more and more to regulate the information intake. This will provide indications that the learner is growing in his or her understanding of how he or she learns and matures in the knowledge of his or her limits. While the expert continues to find ways to challenge, the healthiest approach includes an increased role on the part of the learner to recognize his or her own abilities.

Keeping the Learner in the ZPD

Although it is unlikely Lev Vygotsky ever used the scaffolding metaphor or the analogies that could be derived from the building or construction tasks, scaffolding is often associated with his notion of the Zone of Proximal Development (ZPD). Vygotsky viewed education as leading development-placing learning within the zone just beyond the learner's proven skills so that the challenge to grow and move forward was always present until the learner had reached full mastery of the skill. As shown in Figure 2, Sequence Performance in ZPD, the novice moves, ideally, with the help of the expert, closer and closer to the final performance goal over a sequence of practice ses-

sions, with each employing strategies to move the learner higher. In a social learning environment, through collaboration and interaction with teachers, parents, and other children, the child actively constructs new cognitive abilities.

According to Berk and Winsler, Vygotsky originally introduced the ZPD in the context of arguing against standard intelligence and achievement testing procedures and against the view of development and education that emerges from the use of such tests. He regarded the traditional tests of intellectual functioning of his time as extremely limited because they only assessed static or fossilized abilities, leaving out the dynamic and every-changing quality of human cognition. Vygotsky suggested that what we should be measuring is not what children can do by themselves or already know, but rather what they can do with the help of another person and have the potential to learn.

Therefore, he defined the ZPD as the distance between the actual developmental level as determined by independent problem solving and the level of potential development as determined through problem solving under adult guidance or in collaboration with more capable peers. Moving the learner into the ZPD and supporting the learner to move beyond it is an essential part of scaffolding.

Figure 2

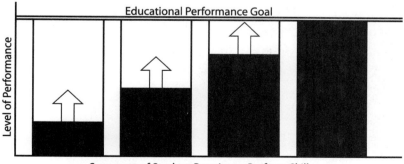

Sequence of Student Practice to Perform Skill

⬆ = Zone of Proximal Development, in which expert helps novice move higher

■ = Area of mastered skills, when complete expert fades.

Inner Speech and External Speech

Vygotsky also saw a developmental relationship between thought and language. His observations of preschool children convinced Vygotsky that children use private speech to bring new concepts into their minds; they move their mouths to do so. Inner speech, sentences spoken silently, help the child formulate the thought as his own. Eventually the child will use external speech to test his or her thought. Inner speech is often both more concise and more complex than external speech. The mind knows cues, images, and relationships that may be difficult or impossible to be expressed to others. With time, the child, or novice, finds ways to elaborate on communications so that thoughts become more expressive and relevant to a growing spectrum of social events.

This process follows the scaffolding pattern just as many other skill sets. In the information search and information use processes, the novice may need to be encouraged to externalize his or her thoughts. Composing visual search strategies with different key terms helps the school library media specialist and other teachers mediate the need to expand, refine, or combine in some other fashion the terms that may lead to the most useful information. Students need to read materials, internalize the major points, and verbalize them before moving on to an external paraphrasing or linkage of the new information to other information gathered. Verbalization of evidence and arguments in small group discussions and even formal debates will help the student reinforce or strengthen the mental model that has been framed through the scaffolding of the information search and selection processes.

For Further Reading

Berk, Laura E., and Adam Winsler. Scaffolding Children's Learning: Vygotsky and Early Childhood Education. Washington, DC: National Association for the Education of Young Children, 1995.

Holliday, William G. "Scaffolding in Science." Science Scope 25, no. 1 (2001), 68, 70-71.

Larkin, Martha J. "Providing Support for Student Independence through Scaffolded Instruction." Teaching Exceptional Children 34, no. 1 (2001), 30-34.

Leong, Deborah J., and Elena Bodrova. Tools of the Mind: The Vygotskian Approach to Early Childhood Education. New York: Merrill Prentice Hall, 1996.

Reigeluth, Charles M. Instructional Design Theories and Models: An Overview of Their Current Status. Hillsdale, NJ: Erlbaum, 1983.

Thomas, Nancy Pickering. Information Literacy and Information Skills Instruction. Englewood, CO: Libraries Unlimited, 1999.

Wray, David. "Developing Factual Writing: An Approach through Scaffolding." ERIC Document ED454534, 2001.

Key Words
Schema and Problem-Solving

Learning theorists have offered various definitions of "schema." Definitions differ according to learning situations and by what is ultimately accepted as evidence that learning has taken place.

Over the past two decades, schemas have been defined as data structures for representing the generic concepts stored in memory. They exist for generalized concepts underlying objects, situations, events, sequences of events, actions, and sequences of actions.

Generally, it is agreed that schemas are not atomic, isolated fragments. Recent theorists often argue that schema contains, as part of its specification, the network of interrelations that is believed to generally hold among the constituents of the concept in question. Therefore, a schema is not simply a list of features, but rather is a collection whose parts are linked together.

Further, schemas are flexible and may change to accommodate a new experience. Schemas develop for those situations, events, or patterns that occur over and over again. At times when events do not fit an established schema, those events (or situations or patterns) may be altered. Such modification is called "assimilation."

A New Basic Definition

Sandra P. Marshall of San Diego State University, has proposed a revised working definition of schema based on her review of the current research:

A schema is a vehicle of memory, allowing organization of an individual's similar experiences in such a way that the individual:

- can easily recognize additional experiences that are also similar, discriminating between these and ones that are dissimilar;
- can access a generic framework that contains the essential elements of all of these similar experiences, including verbal and nonverbal components;
- can draw inferences, make estimates, create goals, and develop plans by using the framework; and
- can utilize skills, procedures, or rules as needed when faced with a problem for which this particular framework is relevant.

Marshall's research about schema formation provides evidence that individuals have and use four types of knowledge.

- Identification Knowledge: the central function is pattern recognition; initial identification of a situation, event, or experience.
- Elaboration Knowledge: identification of the main features of a situation or event; both verbal and visual information is retained enabling the individual to create a mental model about the current problem.
- Planning Knowledge: the way in which the schema can be used to identify expectations and establish goals; acquired from experience and updated with each successive use.

- Execution Knowledge: allows the individual to carry out the steps of the plans and consists of techniques that lead to action.

Issues in Schema Theory

Marshall has translated key issues related to schema theory that were raised by Marvin Minsky in the 1970s. She summarizes these issues in the form of questions:

How is a schema selected?

Schema selection occurs as the result of pattern matching that uses the individual's identification knowledge. Once the basic situation is recognized, the individual then accesses the necessary elaboration knowledge for additional details.

How are additional schemas called on?

As plans are created, the elements within them become themselves the inputs to other schemas. This may occur by direct access to any knowledge component or by additional pattern matching.

How are schemas modified?

Two kinds of modifications must be considered: enlarging schema with new information and changing information that is already part of it. In the first case, the modification occurs as the result of repetition, although the precise amount of repetition remains unknown. The second type has not yet been addressed by researchers.

How are schemas created?

The schema development observed in experimental subjects progresses from a few details of examples to full abstract characterizations and strong mental models.

How does the memory store change as a result of learning?

Perhaps the most important change resulting from schema development is the increased connectivity among schema elements. This suggests that as learning occurs, connectivity strengthens.

Problem-Solving

A schema develops because it is a useful and efficient mechanism for solving problems. If there is no problem to be solved, there is no need to give attention to the processing of information and, consequently, little need to establish memory links among features of the current experience.

To solve a problem, the individual must ask several questions:
- What exactly is the problem?
- Do I have a frame of reference for it?
- Is it unique?
- Have I solved any problems that are similar to it?
- Have I noticed all of its critical features?
- What will I do first to lead to a solution?
- Do I know how to solve it?
- How will I know when I have found a good solution?
- Are there alternative solutions?
- How might I solve similar problems more efficiently next time?
- Does this process apply to other problems I could not solve adequately before?

Information Problem-Solving

During a video interview at the 1994 National Conference of the American Association for School Librarians in Indianapolis, Bob Berkowitz defined "instruction" as a series of information problems that teachers and library media specialists design collaboratively to engage students in learning.

Over the past decade, Berkowitz and Mike Eisenberg have promoted a useful approach to engage students in solving information problems. Their method parallels much of the current thought in schema theory. The foundational similarity-task definition-is often overlooked by those who plan and teach information skills. Eisenberg and Berkowitz tell us:
- Information problem-solving begins with a clear understanding of the problem at hand from an information point of view. In order to solve an informa-

tion problem, students need to determine the range and nature of tasks to be accomplished. Students need to determine the information aspects of the problem: what are the questions to be answered, what kinds of information do they need in order to tackle the problem.

- When students are involved in the process of recognizing that they have an information problem to solve or a decision to make that is dependent on information, they are involved in task definition. Task definition includes stating the parameters of the problem from an information-needs perspective.

Task definition is such an important fundamental element that information problem-solving exercises must include not only those problems designed by teachers of information literacy, but must place students in the position of identifying their own information problems-and doing so in a variety of settings.

This means that teachers of information literacy should invest less time in constructing academic exercises only to be certain that students use all the indexes, reference tools, periodicals, and phone interviews possible, necessary or not. Too often information problem assignments are designed within a limited time frame and are often unchallenging, irrelevant, and lack real world application. It means that more time should be invested in listening to students and observing their individual information needs.

How many inquiry units are limited by teachers of information literacy determining the amount of resources available first and the possible areas for exploration second?

How many information instruction units have started with a general orientation to "all the resources you'll need to know right here in the library media center" because the task has been defined for the student?

How many units give time, long before the introduction of a wide variety of resources, to the process of raising and framing the questions that are most important to the students, by the students? How often is task definition

revisited in the information problem-solving process in order to help students determine if they are on track or not?

Schemas are enhanced through practice activities that engage the learner in taking more and more responsibility for knowledge acquisition with each new experience. Knowing the ability and interest levels at which the student enters the activity is the first key reading of the situation to be taken by the teacher of information literacy. From that point, experiences for assimilation and accommodation are offered and monitored with the student taking an active role in application of the skills from task to evaluation and recycling whenever necessary.

For Further Reading

Eisenberg, Michael B. and Robert E. Berkowitz. Curriculum Initiative. Norwood, NJ: Ablex Publishing, 1988.

Eisenberg, Michael B. and Robert E. Berkowitz. Information Problem-Solving. Norwood, NJ: Ablex Publishing, 1990.

Marshall, Sandra P. Schemas in Problem Solving. New York: Cambridge University Press, 1995.

Minsky, Marvin. "A Framework for Representing Knowledge." In The Psychology of Computer Vision, edited by P. Winston. New York: McGraw-Hill, 1975.

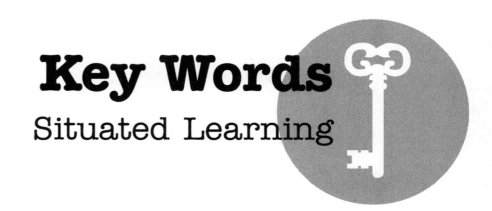

Key Words
Situated Learning

"Situated learning" takes as its focus the relationship between learning and the social situations in which learning occurs. Jean Lave, an anthropologist at the University of California, Berkeley, and Etienne Wenger, computer scientist at the Institute for Research and Learning, Palo Alto, situate learning in certain forms of social co-participation rather than defining learning as the acquisition of propositional knowledge.

Understanding and creative application of the concepts related to situated learning can lead to profound changes in how teachers of information literacy construct learning experiences. Although the impact can be across the curriculum, including vocational and technical preparation, information skills for multiple source lab reports and multimedia productions will be the primary examples of situated learning activities referenced here.

William F. Hanks, from the University of Chicago, writes in his forward to Lave and Wenger's book Situated Learning, "On the one hand, [situated learning] implies a highly interactive and productive role for the skills that are acquired through the learning process. The individual learner is not gaining a discrete body of abstract knowledge which (s)he will then transport and reapply in latter contexts. Instead, (s)he acquires the skill to perform by actually engaging in the process, under the attenuated conditions of legitimate peripheral participation. In other words, students will be engaged as apprentices in authentic activities under the guidance of those who have master-level skills and experiences."

Students, described as "newcomers" to the social context of a discipline, profession, or occupation, are placed in situations in which they learn from models and on a progressive series of scaffolded skills until they become part of the social structure and find their own niche among the "old-timers" or journeyfolk. Learning is a process that takes place in a participation framework, not in an individual mind. In the situated learning approach this means, among other things, that learning is mediated by the differences of perspective among the co-participants: novice, journeyman, and master.

Tools

Lave and Wenger rightly question the idea that verbal explanation is a uniquely effective mode of instruction, somehow superior to direct demonstration. If learning is about increased access to performance, then the way to maximize learning is to perform, not to talk about it. Speaking, reading, computing, and writing are tools which, when practiced in demanding situations involving analysis of message and audience, allow for refinement of meaning and become a technique for acting on the world.

It is quite possible to acquire a tool but be unable to use it. People who use tools actively, rather than just acquire them, by contrast, build an increasingly rich understanding of the world in which they use the tools and of the tools themselves. This understanding, both of the world and of the tool, continually changes as a result of social interactions and negotiations that help the learner reflect and assimilate experiences. Learning and acting are indistinct. Learning being a continuous, life-long process resulting from acting on situations.

The ways schools use dictionaries, math formulae, or historical analysis are very different from the ways practitioners use them. Thus, students may pass examinations, a distinctive part of school cultures, but still not be able to use a domain's conceptual tools in authentic practice.

Critical Characteristics

Initial summaries of the key components of the situated learning model have included apprenticeship, collaboration, reflection, coaching, multiple practice, and articulation. A more recent and refined list of the critical characteristics of situated learning relevant to multimedia instructional design from Jan Herrington and Ron Oliver of Edith Cowan University follows:

- Authentic Context. Provide an authentic context that reflects the way the knowledge will be obtained and used in real-life. Try to preserve full context of the situation without fragmentation and decomposition.
- Authentic Activities. Activities are ill-defined so that students must find problems as well as attempt to solve them. In real-world situations, the solution is seldom neat and seldom a single path, but often will vary given the abilities and resources available to those who must address the situation.
- Expert Performance. Situated learning environments provide access to expert performance-masters who model useful processes and may provide guidance and feedback.
- Multiple Roles and Perspectives. Move away from linear instructional formats that contain a clear beginning and given steps leading to possible solutions. Students should be able to enter the situation at several points and gain various perspectives from a spectrum of resources and several experts. Students

should experience the situation from the perspective of different roles that "newcomers" may play in entering the situation.

Criticisms

While situated learning has met with interest and some acclaim, limitations have also been identified by several critics. Situated learning requires that learners be exposed to "masters" or experts in practice of their trade. Obvious barriers are present for transferring experts to the classroom or the classroom to the experts unless the situation allows for modern telecommunications and wide access to human resources. In other cases, this barrier may be lessened if the situations employ the true expertise held by some teachers. It means that teachers of composition and teachers of information literacy must hold and model real-world skills from professions such as journalism and communications and model at least these skills for their students: information seeking and analysis, problem solving, message creation, information repackaging, and audience-specific presentation.

Such difficult skills are too often simply placed before students as basic expectations for their performance and many teachers and school library media specialists do not seek and provide the opportunity to model their own skills in critical information review or publication. The typical "library research assignment" has been something for students to do and for library media specialists to assist with in resource location while observing from afar. In many cases, teachers are only involved in evaluation of student product and are not aware of the value of the information research process because they fail to engage in it for themselves or with the students. Modeling means truly being a master of the process. The students as "newcomers" take apprenticeship roles.

When situated learning is the driving force for multi-level multimedia instructional materials, designers of such computer programming often risk the danger of the courseware becoming the learning environment in and of itself and thus not creating an authentic situation. Some problem-solving techniques can be demonstrated through computer-assisted instruction, but real-life problems are seldom identified and solved through use of electronic searching, electronic documents, and electronic discussions alone. Although it is fair to say that telecommunications is playing an increasingly wider role in real-life situations, face-to-face human discussions, experiences in dealing with live audience response, and understanding the value of various information sources regardless of format all serve to bring learning situations closer to real life.

Along the same argument, school library media specialists should not suggest that all information problems can be solved through the library, even as a ploy that leads to over-stating the possibilities in most library media centers. Many successful professionals in the real world don't seek and use information through the traditional library research sense. While it is fair to state that information resources and information guidance available through libraries can certainly enhance the professional's search for and location of information, greater emphasis must be placed on human communication, negotiation of information problem and need, market and audience analysis, the context for information use and levels of information relevancy, and mass media impact in order to come closer to a real-life information literacy skill curriculum. The curriculum can not be limited to "I understand the sources" but must be expanded to include "I understand human behavior, how to identify problems and needs, and how to manipulate information in order to address those needs in a variety of situations."

Some Methods Tested

Nathan Bos and other members of the "Teaching and Learning Group" at the University of Michigan (UM), have explored several methods that take the learning experience in composition of science lab reports a few steps closer to real-world situations for secondary school students. Their work has centered on placing students in various roles

that lead to the creation of purposeful World Wide Web artifacts-original products designed to meet specific problems and to convey information to a specific real audience. A range of instructional supports was developed to help students bridge the gap between themselves and authentic outside audiences. The UM group has experienced various levels of success and surprise with these methods.

- Genre Explanations. In teaching students how to write lab reports on air pollution results, teachers conducted in-class modeling of composition of such reports and explained how the different parts of the model met the information needs of the scientific audience. Teachers explained how the restrictive form of a lab report (introduction, methods, data, results, discussion) serves the needs of the readers because it allows them to find the information in understood forms and in predictable places. A common format for discourse in the real scientific community became the template for composition and design of multimedia artifacts.

- WWW Reviews. It is sometimes difficult for students to anticipate the needs of a scientific reader for things such as proper citation, evidence for claims, and predictable organization structure because these are not things that students necessarily pay attention to when reading scientific material. Students can better understand the needs of a scientific reader if they first assume that role. Bos and other members of the University of Michigan Teaching and Learning Group reported that they attempted to help students take on such a role by having them write and publish critical evaluations of existing scientific resources. In the course of their own research, students were asked to identify a few good scientific resources and write critical reviews, scaffolded by an in-class practice review.

- Audience Surveys. To write effectively for an audience, a writer must have some conception of what the audience already knows, what their misconceptions might be, and what they would be interested in learning. While a professional writer might be able to mentally construct such a map of audience knowledge and use it to guide writing, it is much more difficult for high school writers to do so. Given a specific audience and the results of a brief survey of that audience, students tended to use that information to tailor their artifact design decisions.

- Peer Reviews. Students would gain from feedback on their projects written by peers (fellow classmates) knowledgeable about the project and the artifact design constraints. The UM group found several limitations in this method. Students did not have the knowledge level to critique the content of the artifact although they seemed to have the experience to offer suggestions on web-page design and web-site structure. Students did not want to risk alienating their classmates by writing negative comments. The peer review process came too near the end of the project and was given little time in the rush to complete assignments.

- Outside Readers. The UM group reported that this instructional support holds great promise, but also has some glitches. Technologically, contact with and communication from an expert pool can be managed as electronic mail and the World Wide Web allows for reasonable ease in accessing student artifacts. The real world offered several problems to this situated learning attempt. Professional scientists did not usually find time to respond and give feedback within the one-week window. Outside readers do not know how to write specific comments for high school students. Teacher comments were very specifically tied to the project criteria and were written in such a way that they were easily converted into document revisions. Comments from outside readers, who were, of course, not pro-

fessional high school teachers, were much more difficult to comprehend. According to the UM group, this could be another reason students rarely made changes based on outside feedback received. It may be fair to also speculate that unless the classroom teacher gave a great deal of value to the comments offered by outside reviewers, students may be reluctant to incorporate such comments.

Situated learning holds promise and paradox for those who decide to move information literacy skill instruction closer to the real-world setting. Information use in the academic setting and in the workforce have different goals and probably require different instructional methods. The concepts and principles associated with situated learning processes, however, are worth accepting the challenge to modify current instructional practices and to take steps that place teachers and students close to meaningful learning experiences.

For Further Reading

Bos, Nathan. "Analysis of Feedback from 'Authentic' Outside-the Classroom Audiences on High-School Fiction Writing." International Journal of Educational Telecommunications 3, no. 1 (1997, in press).

Bos, Nathan, Joseph Krajcik, and Elliot Soloway. "Student Publishing in a WWW Digital Library-Goals and Instructional Support." 1997. ERIC Document ED408580.

Brown, John Seely, Allan Collins, and Paul Duguid. "Situated Cognition and the Culture of Learning." Educational Researcher 18, no. 1 (1989): 32-42.

Callison, Daniel. "Expanding the Evaluation Role in the Critical-Thinking Curriculum." In Information for a New Age: Redefining the Librarian. Englewood, CO: Libraries Unlimited, 1995: 153-170.

Herrignton, Jan, and Ron Oliver. "Critical Characteristics of Situated Learning: Implications for Instructional Design of Multimedia." In Learning with Technology, edited by J. Pearce and A. Ellis. Parkville, VIC: University of Melbourne, 1995: 235-262. http://www.cowan. edu.au/lr_sys/edu-cres/article1.html

Herrington, Jan, and Ron Oliver. "Multimedia, Magic, and the Way Students Respond to a Situated Learning Environment." Australian Journal of Educational Technology 13, no. 2 (1997): 127-143. http://cleo.murdoch.edu.au/ajet/ajet13/su97p1 27.html

Herrington, Jan, and Ron Oliver. "Using Situated Learning and Multimedia to Promote Higher-Order Thinking." ERIC Document ED428672, 1998.

Hickman, Larry A., and Thomas Alexander. The Essential Dewey. Bloomington, IN: Indiana University Press, 1998.

Hummel, H. K. "Distance Education and Situated Learning: Paradox and Partnership." Educational Technology 33, no. 12 (1993): 11-22.

Lave, Jean, and Etienne Wenger. Situated Learning: Legitimate Peripheral Participation. Cambridge, UK: Cambridge University Press, 1991.

McLellan, H. "Evaluation in a Situated Learning Environment." Educational Technology 33, no. 3 (1993): 39-45.

McLellan, H. "Virtual Environments and Situated Learning." Multimedia Review 2, no. 3 (1991): 30-37.

Resnick, L. "Learning in School and Out." Educational Researcher 16, no. 9 (1987): 13-20.

Key Words

Story

For over one hundred years, many librarians and classroom teachers have found the art of storytelling to be a useful technique to promote reading. Stories stimulate the imagination. A good storyteller who engages the audience to envision a different time and place also will increase the desire to read more about similar characters and events.

Story is a powerful method, and often more powerful than the medium (voice, actions, illustrations) used. When relevant to the needs of a receptive audience, story can promote, persuade, instruct, soothe, and excite. Story can, with the right mix of interaction, enchant.

From the very beginning of human communication, story has provided a way to document human history, events, and behavior through the oral tradition of family or tribal storytelling. Recent studies on cultures that depend on oral family history suggest that males establish story based on memories of personal mischief and challenge, while females tend to center story on family conflict, change, and personal crisis.

Folktales help us seek within a richer context an understanding of the culture of others and give depth to our own personal culture. Some have found folktale storytelling can be used, in school and group settings by teachers, mental health workers, and other group leaders, as a means of increasing self-awareness and building self-esteem. Promoting enjoyment of stories can include audience acceptance of messages for positive social growth.

On another level, story can be one of the most persuasive tools for leadership. Of the many political skills held by Abraham Lincoln, his ability to express a vision for what should be and to convey that to his audience through story is often listed as his most enduring characteristic. This ability to communicate and lead through story did not seem to be diminished by a rather high and often unpleasant voice. Lincoln, and hundreds of other leaders, have found that strength lies in the content, sincerity, and vision of the message, although such can be enhanced with voice control and other techniques that often appeal to the listener.

Story is necessary when reality for an audience does not exist or is not enough.

Telling Tales

Connie Rochman, a professional storyteller for the past three decades and advocate for librarians to engage children and young adults in story through the oral telling tradition, has offered these tips for those who wish to prepare an effective story:
- Choose stories you sincerely love and have a strong desire to share.
- Allow time to learn a story.
- Visualize the setting and the audience.
- Divide the story logically into parts.
- Master the style of the story.
- Tell the story to yourself several times.
- Timing is crucial to a well-told tale. Include pauses for suspense and dramatic

intensity. Change the pace of your voice as the action dictates.

- Find someone to listen to your story and give you feedback.
- The goal is to connect to the imagination of another.
- Find an audience and tell, and retell, the story again and again.

Do Listeners Learn?

The degree to which story helps to instruct has a mixed record in the research. The National Council of Teachers of English suggests that story should be an important part of the curriculum and teachers' instructional tools. Listeners encounter both familiar and new language patterns through story, according to the NCTE position statement. Students learn new words or new contexts for already familiar words. Perhaps even more powerful, learners who regularly "tell" stories become aware of how an audience affects a telling, and they carry that awareness into their writing.

Some researchers suggest that the concept of story schema offers a framework for the mental organization of a story. Children use this framework, or story structure, to aid in listening comprehension and recall. Retelling a story is a constructive process and requires the use of a story structure as a method for the organization of a story from beginning to end. Story schema expands with age and experience with story, thus storytelling and storylistening from early pre-school age through young adulthood seem to help expand memory and mental organization skills to accept more and more complex visions.

Direct impact on reading, comprehension, and composition skills through the use of story seems to be more positive in the lower grades on those students who are below-average readers. Average to above-average readers tend to be successful regardless of the introduction of story to their learning environment, although they often enjoy the entertaining aspects of storytelling.

Enchanting the Listener's Imagination

Brian Sturm, an assistant professor in children's literature at the University of North Carolina at Chapel Hill, has studied the storylistening trance as it pertains to professional storytellers and members of their adult audience. Many of the actions that seem to trigger enchantment for the adult listener are likely to be similar for listeners at younger ages as well.

He illustrates the elements that lead to the entrancing experience with a model composed of three concentric circles representing the baseline state of consciousness, the transitional period, and the discrete altered state of consciousness. The d-ASC, or storylistening trance, is placed within the baseline state of consciousness. The spokes of the wheel are portals from the baseline to the altered state of consciousness.

Sturm proposes that one element of storytelling has remained nearly unconsidered over recent years while storytelling has flourished. This element is perhaps the most profound part of the communication process-the change in the listener's experience of reality. Through enchantment, the normal, waking state of consciousness changes as the story takes on a new dimension. Listeners seem to experience the story with remarkable immediacy, engaging in the story's plot and with the story's characters, and they may enter an altered state of consciousness-a "storylistening trance." The trance has the following characteristics:

- Realism-the sense that the story environment or characters are real or alive.
- Lack of Awareness-of surroundings or other mental processes.
- Engaged Receptive Channels:
  - visual (both physical watching and mental visualization;
  - auditory (both physical hearing and mental "chatter;"
  - kinesthetic; and
  - emotional.
- Control-of the experience by the listener, or someone or something else.
- "Placeness"-the sense that the listener goes somewhere or into another space.

- Time Distortion-the sense that subjective time moves at a different speed than objective, clock time.

The actions that influence the storylistening trance reflect a list of techniques that are often practiced and perfected by those who seek to use storytelling as a powerful method to convey vision and meaning. Sturm identified these elements based on observations and interviews with adult storylisteners at professional storytelling events. He found the listener to be more likely to move toward entrancement if some of the following were present in the telling/listening interaction:

- Storytelling Style
- Activation of the Listener's Memories
- Sense of Comfort and Safety
- Story Content
- Storyteller's Ability
- Storyteller's Involvement
- Expectations (of enjoying the experience)
- Personal Preferences (matching style between teller and listener)
- (relevance to) Training or Social Roles (of the listener)
- Rapport with the Storyteller
- Novelty and Familiarity (of the story)
- Rhythm
- Humor
- Recency

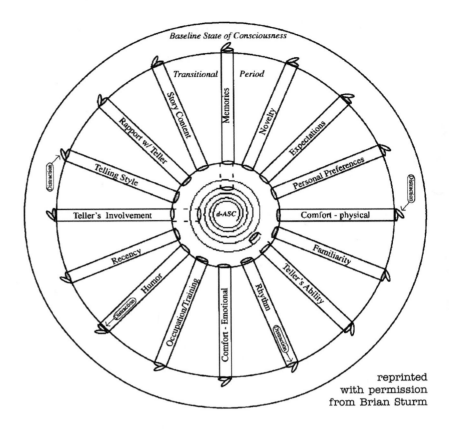

reprinted with permission from Brian Sturm

Do Tellers Teach and Learn?

Use of story seems to be a common teaching technique among those who are successful in engaging their students in more than factual information. They are able to create a mood with verbal illustrations that can transport the student to the intended event. The art, practice, and perfection of storytelling for the classroom may be more of a learning experience for the teller than for the listener. Gathering the information needed for the story and developing the context for the story adjacent to the curriculum are powerful learning experiences for the presenter.

Storytelling for teachers has been shown to be an important and valuable skill in several studies testing different communication methods. Undergraduate teacher preparation curricula, however, seldom provides room for adoption of this method.

Storytelling has often been identified as a key leadership skill for Chief Executive Officers, including school principals and superintendents. One recent study, for example, demonstrated the importance of using storytelling skills to construct and share information in interdistrict magnet schools. Storytelling involved the ability to detail specific events and needs and to illustrate these with stories about relevant individuals involved. Storytelling encouraged constituent participation in the magnet school. Carefully selected words resulted in stories that allowed the leader to market the school and to increase participation of important stakeholders.

Storytelling, thus, is an important option in the menu of methods for student presentation of information for inquiry projects, as well as an entertaining way to pass along culture and heritage.

Story Applied to Inquiry

Jeff Creswell and other teachers who promote the Storyline Method, have applied the principles of story to thematic or discovery learning. Based on a theme (space travel, a hotel, a radio station), elementary school students devote a couple of hours each afternoon to development of characters, plot for events, and design and construction of set. After several weeks of research through the local public library, stories are developed to address specific questions established by both teacher and students.

The Hotel Storyline

[summarized and paraphrased from Creswell, p. 18-19]

Storyline Episodes	Key Questions
1. The Hotel	What is a hotel? Who needs a hotel?
2. The Guests	Who would use a hotel and why? What might draw people to the city at Christmas time? What biographical sketches can be written to describe these people?
3. A Guest Room	What are the necessary features of a hotel guest room? What might a blueprint for the room show? How is it designed and decorated?
4. The Hotel Staff	Who might work at the hotel? Is there a timeline that would tell a story of a typical work day?
5. The Incidents	What could happen to your guests at the hotel?

What stories can be told based on these happenings?

Creswell advocates a learning environment that involves use of multiple resources, creative writing, and hands-on design and construction so his students experience the creation of story. Although not justified through demonstration of stronger performance on standard examinations, Creswell gives justification to the Storyline approach based on strong cooperative learning among students to plan and work together. Many of his projects have been most successful in classrooms with economically and racially diverse students.

Creswell rests this student-centered approach on a "Principle of Story:"

Story is a central part of human experience. Our history, religion, and heritage have all been passed from generation to generation through stories for thousands of years. When we seek to understand the world around us or the culture of a people, we look to stories to enlighten us. Stories provide children with a predictable, linear structure and a meaningful context for learning..." (p. 10).

For Further Reading

Bygrave, Patricia L. "Development of Listening Skills in Students in Special Education Settings." International Journal of Disability, Development, and Education 41, no. 1 (1994): 51-60.

Clark, Rochelle Wallace. "Teachers as Storytellers." Dissertation, Saint Louis University, 2000.

Creswell, Jeff. Creating Worlds, Constructing Meaning: The Scottish Storyline Method. Portsmouth, NH: Heinemann, 1997.

Greene, Ellin. Storytelling: Art and Technique. New Providence, NJ: Bowker, 1996.

Hughes, Catherine. Museum Theatre: Communicating with Visitors through Drama. Heinemann, 1998.

Kempton, Lauren Jayne. "Leaders as Storytellers: An Investigation of Leadership Practices Used in Implementing an Elementary Interdistrict Magnet School for Integration." Dissertation, University of Hartford, 1997.

MacDonald, Margaret R. The Storyteller's Start-Up Book. Little Rock, AR: August House, 1993.

McCormick, Kathleen, and Charles Lipka. Reading Our Histories, Understanding Our Cultures: A Sequenced Approach to Thinking, Reading, and Writing. Allyn & Bacon, 1998.

National Council of Teachers of English. "Position Statement from the Committee on Storytelling." www.ncte.org/positions/story.html

National Storytelling Network. http://www.story.org

Rochman, Connie. "Tell Me a Story." School Library Journal (August 2001): 46-49.

Smith, Patricia Luse. "A Qualitative Investigation into the Educational Benefits of Storytelling: Teaching through Storytelling." Dissertation, Washington State University, 1998.

Rodari, Gianni, Jack Zipes, and Herbert R. Kohl. The Grammar of Fantasy: An Introduction to the Art of Invention Stories. Teachers and Writers, 2000.

Sturm, Brian W. "The Enchanted Imagination: Storytelling's Power to Entrance Listeners." School Library Media Research. Vol 2. ALA, 1999. http://www.ala.org/aasl/SLMR/vol2/imagination.html

Wolfe, Peggy. "Traditional Folktales: Exploring Wants and Needs." School Library Media Activities Monthly 9, no. 9 (May 1995): 29-30.

Key Words

Strategy: Ideas and Composition

Strategies for ideas and composition help the maturing, information-literate student deal with the complexities of the communication process. Idea generation involves not only "what do I want to learn and what do I infer from this new information," but also "what do I want to convey to others and how."

Interwoven from idea to communication are the complexities of information evaluation. Each element of the process is fundamental to the assimilation of new knowledge, both for the learner who gathers and conveys and for the audience which receives. Tasks in the process are not always sequential steps, and they often do not flow easily from one to the other, especially for the novice. Often simple strategies are necessary to solve problems that block progress. These strategies often ask the student to step back and rethink, take a different perspective, relate to previous experiences and thoughts on a concrete basis, or listen to feedback from others. A testing of portions or chunks of the message along the way eventually help to clarify that which finally will be communicated. This is why conversations with others about ideas and information needs are so important during the inquiry process.

In building the message to be communicated, purpose will determine the strategies. Purpose, or goal of the communication, is influenced by learner abilities, previous knowledge of the learner, quality of information available, and the level of learner comprehension. Strategies for communication are influenced by the purpose of the message, the means of communication, and the perceived level of audience reception. The learner will assimilate knowledge for him or herself, but find that such may need to be revised or modified in some manner in order to move a message through different communication channels and to offer it to different audiences. Writing, speaking, use of media, and other formats may alter the message. It is possible during such adjustments to enhance the message for clarity in order to successfully persuade, or to cloud the message resulting in miscommunication.

The format also may influence the continued assimilation of the communicator's knowledge as he or she faces revision tasks to fit the medium. Audience analysis-understanding as best as possible what the audience will understand, accept, or reject-can result in change of both the message and clarity of the communicator's assimilation as well. The goal of employing strategies for idea and composition is to offer a menu of strategies to adjust communication in different ways to meet different needs.

Idea strategies, therefore, imply methods that help the learner to both comprehend and communicate. Ideas help us to move forward, to explore, and to frame questions that are meaningful to us and hopefully to others. Composition strategies can be applied to not only writing for communication, but to a wide array of formats (oral, audio, visual, multimedia), genres, and modes that serve as channels in delivery of the intended message.

Thought Starters

Many college and university writing labs provide guides to strategies that help the novice jump-start the communication process. One of the best is the Owl Online Writing Lab through Purdue University. Among their more useful guides is a list of thought starters based on asking the right questions. These are adapted from Jacqueline Berke, Professor of English Emerita and Director of the Drew University Program from 1965 to 1985.

Definition-What does X mean?

Description-What are the different features of X?

Simple Analysis-What are the component parts of X?

Process Analysis-How is X made or done?

Directional Analysis-How should X be made or done?

Functional Analysis-What is the essential function of X?

Causal Analysis-What are the causes of X, or what are the consequences of X?

Classification-What are the types of X?

Comparison-How is X like or unlike Y, or what is the present status of X compared to previous status?

Interpretation-What is the significance of X?

Reporting-What are the facts (who, what, when, where, and how) about X?

Narration-How did X happen?

Characterization/Profile-What kind of person is X?

Reflection-What is my personal response to X?

Reminiscence-What is my memory of X?

Evaluation-What is the value of X?

Summary-What are the essential major points or features of X?

Persuasion-What case can be made for or against X?

In each case, as the writer matures in information literacy, "why" should be linked to the initial questions. Why is this important? Why did this happen? Why are these causes and consequences relevant to us today? The goal of inquiry is to address or to infer why X seems true, valid, conclusive, or predictable for similar situations. The "what" and "how" questions provide the foundation to assimilate knowledge and to move toward the more demanding questions.

Information Evaluation Phases

The work of Mary Ann Fitzgerald, assistant professor at the University of Georgia, has resulted in some important guidelines and strategies for effective evaluation of information. Fitzgerald reminds us that information is a complex and challenging task. Although it can be assumed that children are more likely to take information at "face value" than most adults, the skills necessary to select information that is authoritative, understandable, and relevant for a given situation requires practice, guidance, and feedback, at any age. Such skill practice should begin in early grade levels and continue through the student's academic career, including graduate school if applicable.

Fitzgerald identifies three phases of information use and strategies for evaluation (selecting or discarding) information at each phase. Some of her original titles and terms have been paraphrased below:

Phase 1: Search and Initial Contact. The student makes selections based on abstracts or key words that indicate likely relevance. The item (article, chapter, book, website, etc.) is noted, retrieved, and copied for further examination and later study. Common evaluation strategies are relevance of key words, author, and title; length of item (too short may be too general, too long may be too specific and overly detailed); and context meets need (opinion, fact, narrative, investigative study).

Phase 2: First Complete Reading. Complete reading may not be reached until the student has skimmed subheadings, and closely examined the lead paragraphs and concluding paragraphs as well as any illustrations, tables, or graphs. The more mature reader also may look for author qualifications and examine the references cited, if any. If the item meets basic tests for quality (clear, focused, interesting, relevant, perhaps contains new information not seen before), it is likely to be selected for specific highlighting of information and taking of notes. Assimilation of the information, or acceptance by the reader, may depend greatly on his or her maturity level in being open to considering both supportive as well as non-supportive content.

Kuhlthau identified the "uncertainty principle" and the idea that the reader may have problems with information that is unfamiliar to him or her is important to remember at this stage. Information that seems to match the knowledge (opinion, bias, basic assumptions) of the reader may be accepted more readily than information that is not familiar. Problems in assimilation may be tied to new terms unknown to the reader as well as opinions or arguments that are not acceptable. The more mature information literate and critical thinker will pause at this point to give as much consideration as possible to new information and may seek additional advice in order to make certain judgments for moving into phase three.

Phase 3: Reconsidering Information. The item has reached the level of thorough examination. Re-reading leads to comparison of information to previous information as well as personal entry level knowledge on the topic. More critical questions are raised to make a final acceptance of the content. Is this evidence trustworthy?

Fitzgerald offers several strategies to help students make judgments concerning information. Although exceptions to these strategies could be noted easily, in general they will help the student make wise decisions. Note that one factor for downgrading or upgrading usually does not lead to a conclusion to reject or accept the information. A combination of factors often will be needed and some negative factors actually may cancel out other positive factors. The combination of factors that lead to a final selection or rejection of the information may differ from one communication situation to another. Audience, learner bias, resource availability, and time limitations all come into play as well. Some of the decision factors Fitzgerald has observed in use among secondary and college students are:

Downgrade information which:
- is blatantly persuasive,
- contains personal attacks,
- contains sarcasm,
- includes vocabulary that does not suit context,
- seems without purpose,
- is not clear,
- is not organized,
- is not current for the issue,
- is essentially an advertisement,
- has errors in grammar or spelling, and/or
- contains inappropriate repetition.

Upgrade information which:
- is organized into tables or clear graphics,
- has clear purpose and audience,
- is supported by other authoritative sources,
- provides fair consideration of other opinions,
- states conclusions based on logic and fact,
- an author who admits and explains personal bias,
- is relevant and current to issues, and/or
- suggests new perspective or new evidence worth considering.

STRATEGY: IDEAS AND COMPOSITION

Strategies in Writing Management

Although many students depend on the last-minute adrenalin rush to complete a composition, those who tend to succeed best are usually those who manage the process over time. Everyone who composes a video script, play, editorial, research paper, or nearly any other kind of communication will find the pressure of the deadline will influence their concentration. Those who have practiced the following strategies, however, will find they have a much richer base to work from when crunch time comes.

Break up writing sessions into small periods. Write portions of the project when an idea is fresh or just budding, even if it may not make it to the final piece. Such parts may be used for either the beginning, middle, or end. Successful writers strive to get things down on paper or into electronic files and worry about fitting the chunk into the whole later. Short writing periods also lead to identification of and time for retrieving additional information. Many of the gaps that otherwise would appear at the deadline will become apparent sooner and can be filled. Writing and reading information feed each other and small steps allow this interaction to take place.

Analyze your audience. Communication will not be complete unless you have a good idea of who will receive your message. Understanding the expectations, biases, and generally held notions of the person or group who will view, hear, or read what is presented is at least half of the communication process. It can greatly influence the other half-seeking, selecting, and composing information.

Define your purpose. Such may evolve, but stating a goal or working thesis from the beginning helps to organize both the information search as well as the writing. As new information is explored, the working thesis likely will change as the final thesis may not become apparent until most of the information from reading, observation, and interviews have been concluded and analyzed.

Outline and organize. Work with guiding questions and subheadings from the beginning. Make these the topics for note cards or for electronic files. As ideas and information are gathered, sort them into these areas and consider new questions and subheadings. The brainstorming exercises that may have helped to identify the branches of an initial topic continue through to the end, but in a more focused manner.

Let it sit for a while. Spend this time on some other tasks that help you relax. Exercise, such as walking, bike riding, or taking a drive, will help to rearrange things in the writer's mind. Letting the draft distill for a couple of days will allow sleep to work its magic as well. New ideas will generate from rest. New ideas also may come from further exploratory reading or discussion of your ideas with peers and mentors. While additional reading and conversations help, an extended stagnant consumption of television programming is more likely to hinder. Short selected viewing, however, can serve as a reward to completion of segments.

Seek a routine. Some writers seek a specific location and setting. Most agree that discipline includes placing yourself in front of the word processor at a regular time each day, and writing something (one thought, one line, one paragraph, or one page) relevant to your topic, whether it is eventually used or not.

Read it out loud. Read it to trusted friends and peers. Free write whenever possible to get something on paper. Seeing some pieces will help generate relationships and ideas that will grow into a full composition. Draw it, if you don't feel at the time you can write it.

Seek help from a qualified editor. Depending on your level of writing, the person who serves as editor will change. The point is that another set of eyes, especially to look for understanding and meaning based on organization of ideas, always will be beneficial. If for no other reason, successful writers find they verbalize thoughts differently in response to questions of the editor. Copy editing is a different process and comes at the final stages of the communication. Concentrate on logic, organization, and clarity of ideas first. Standards of grammar and style come later.

Conference Strategies for Draft and Revision

Intervention strategies are very important as a means for the mentor or peers to help move the writer along when stalled or off track. Good composition teachers seek such interventions and even create conference times to converse with the student about problems. Similar interventions are important for assisting the novice information searcher, user, and presenter.

Randy Bomer has refined these strategies as a middle school and high school teacher. Now codirector of the Teachers Writing Project at Columbia University, Bomer has learned from his students some smart ways to confront composition snags during draft and revision.

Problem: Student has written a beginning and can only imagine the piece going this one way.
Strategy: Write three very different possible beginnings for this same piece.

Problem: Student has written in an order that no longer makes sense to him or her.
Strategy: Outline what has been written and rearrange the chunks.

Problem: Student is having trouble deciding how much background to explain.
Strategy: List what the student assumes the reader knows and what the reader needs to learn.

Problem: Student can't decide what should come next.
Strategy: Ouline four possible options.

Problem: Student's character is really just a name on the page, and the reader hasn't gotten a chance to know the character.
Strategy: Make at least three pages of notes about each character as a person.

Problem: There is no way the reader can imagine the place the student is writing about.
Strategy: Draw the place in detail from different angles, or describe it for two pages.

Problem: The story seems sappy because it only has one simple feeling to it.
Strategy: Write the incident from several different points of view.

Problem: The student hates what he or she has written-the whole thing. It's not saying what he or she means.
Strategy: Write a page of the piece in two other possible genres.

Problem: It's hard to make decisions about what is important because the student is just stringing together entries.
Strategy: Write, "what I want the reader to believe about my topic" at the top of a page and write a half page in response to that.

Problem: What the student is trying to say seems too simple or too obvious.
Strategy: Interview someone who feels differently about the topic. Write down what is said and list new questions.

Problem: The student has blurted out everything he or she has to say in the first two paragraphs and has nothing left to say.
Strategy: Divide a page into three sections, corresponding to sections of the piece, and jot notes about what information to release to the reader and what will remain a mystery for now.

Problem: The student is explaining too much and is having a hard time helping the reader to "see" what he or she is writing.
Strategy: Write a section of the piece as if someone were going to make a movie of it, including directions to designers and dialogue for actors.

Problem: The student feels like he or she doesn't have anything else to say.
Strategy: Read and respond to literature about the topic.

Problem: The student believes his or her writing feels flat and boring, and can't think of how to make it better.
Strategy: Read, copy out good bits, and make notes about the craft of pieces of literature he

STRATEGY: IDEAS AND COMPOSITION

or she admires that is written in the same genre.

Problem: The whole experience is not working; it's hard and boring, and the student hates it and has no energy to write.
Strategy: Write about a time when he or she has written successfully (compared to now), especially if it was a similar kind of piece, and think on paper about what worked before.

Beef Up the Middle

Stephanie Harvey and Anne Goudvis have devised strategies that work to help students extract ideas from text. These ideas, often posted on sticky notes placed directly on the text read, provide the content for detail, extending and connecting thoughts with other texts, or, in short, getting some meat on the bones of the skeleton outline. Although Harvey and Goudvis have refined their exercises for upper elementary students reading nonfiction, these strategies can help the reader make connections and create meaning at any age.
Text-to-Self Connections: Identify information where you connect your life to the text. Think about your past experiences and prior knowledge. Further state words or draw images that represent this connection.
Text-to-Text Connections: Identify information in this text that connects to previous texts (book, movie, article, script, song, or any information that has been formerly composed). Extend this connection in your own words or visuals.
Text-to-World Connections: Using the same techniques as given above, how does the text you have encountered connect to events, people, or issues you know?

Further connections with text become elaborations when the reader can begin to display ideas as a composer in response to challenges such as:
- Write as many new questions as possible that come to mind, organize them, and predict possible solutions or answers.
- Draw your ideas so that you can visual-

ize something that enhances and extends your understanding of the text.
- Synthesize the most important ideas gained from the text and list them in phrases.
- Midway through the text (article, story, play, book), predict the possible conclusions. Infer what the information so far might lead to as a solution or a more difficult problem.

The Intro and the End

How to start and how to conclude seem to remain the two most difficult portions of the composition. Some find that writing a conclusion as one of the first chunks and an introduction as one of the last portions seems to work. Others find assurance in starting in the middle and working in both directions, toward the beginning as well as the end. Still others find comfort in the organization of following the sequence of beginning, middle and end, especially in these days of word processing and the ability to revise and extend easily. Laurence Behrens of the University of California and Leonard J. Rosen of Harvard University promote these proven strategies:
For Introductions-
- Quotation: Use the words of the hero, a victim, the wise person with insight beyond that of the story, or other quotation that can "set the stage."
- Analogy: Similar to quotation use. Suggest something similar to the larger idea of the event to be detailed, but when used as an introduction, an analogy can provide something with which the audience may identify easier.
- Historical review: What are the situations and events that have led to this story?
- Review of a controversy: What are the issues and people who represent the arguments?
- From the general to the specific: What is the greater moral dilemma before specific examples are detailed?
- From specific to general: What specific event illustrates the greater issues to be

discussed?

- Question: The key questions that motivated this investigation are stated early and may serve as an outline for the rest of the composition.
- Statement of thesis: What is the key question tested or to be addressed and what assumptions are made?

For Conclusions-

- Statement of the subject's significance: Conclude with a clear answer to the "so what?" question. Show that this story or study has meaning for others and future situations.
- Call for further research: No investigation is completely conclusive, and pure scientific method begs for replication and further examination beyond any given study. A general statement that more work should be done is not enough. A list of what should be explored is necessary.
- Solution or recommendation: Based on the information and evidence gathered, or based on the experiment conducted, it is logical to conclude the answers or directions for action.
- Anecdote: Is there a brief story, joke, or ironic situation that can either leave the audience with some common insight or raise new questions beyond what has been written or presented?
- Quotation: Just as an insightful statement may entice the reader at the introduction, so may quotations give a more universal ending. Quotations may be remembered when the rest of the essay may not, and often a few memorable lines help to climax emotions.
- Questions: What questions remain? What new questions come from this study or story and are suggested for future compositions, investigations, or dramatic presentation?
- Speculation: Although not a firm conclusion, why do mysteries remain and what seems likely because of this study? What future themes are likely to be explored by the writer or the audience

because of what has been communicated with this piece?

For Further Reading

Behrens, Laurence, and Leonard J. Rosen. Writing and Reading across the Curriculum. 6th ed. New York: Longman, 1997.

Berke, Jacqueline, and Randal Woodland. Twenty Questions for the Writer: A Rhetoric with Readings. 6th ed. Harcourt Brace, 1996.

Bomer, Randy. Time for Meaning: Crafting Literate Lives in Middle and High School. Portsmouth, NH: Heinemann, 1995.

Fitzgerald, Mary Ann. "Critical Thinking 101: The Basics of Evaluating Information." Knowledge Quest 29, no. 2 (2000): 13-24.

Fitzgerald, Mary Ann. "Evaluating Information: An Information Literacy Challenge." School Library Media Research 2 (1999).

Harvey, Stephanie, and Anne Goudvis. Strategies that Work. York, ME: Stenhouse, 2000.

Kuhlthau, Carol C. "Principle of Uncertainty for Information Seeking." Journal of Documentation 49 (1993): 339-355.

Owl Online Writing Lab. Purdue University, West Lafayette, IN. http://owl.english.purdue.edu

Parker, Susan M., Maura C. Quigley, and JoAnn B. Reilly. Improving Student Reading Comprehension through the Use of Literacy Circles. Portsmouth, NH: Heinemann, 1999.

Key Words

Strategy: Search and Comprehension

Strategy is a term often linked with information searching as well as instructional methods. Associated with either search or instruction, "strategy" infers a plan of action, or a systematic way to accomplish a goal and to meet a need. Instructional strategies are overall plans for implementing instructional goals, methods, or techniques. Reading strategies, for example, are methods that can be used or taught to facilitate reading proficiency. Therefore, strategy is also something that can transfer from teacher to learner so that the strategy becomes a skill or process the learner will employ on his or her own as the teacher fades from the situation.

Search strategies are not new to the instructional tasks faced by instructional media specialists and other teachers of information literacy as they attempt to orient the user to the information environment and to establish a framework the student may apply generally to their information search problems. "Search strategy" often is defined as a comprehensive plan for finding information and includes defining the information need, determining the form in which it is needed, if it exists, where it is located, how it is organized, and how to retrieve it. Such a definition has both positive and problematic aspects. It is positive in that it moves search strategy beyond the traditional linear decision-making process that has been used to introduce most students to the library. It is problematic in that the definition assumes a great deal of entry level knowledge on the user's part, and the process still concentrates on location of the source rather than on location of specific information.

In the context of student learning through information literacy, there is a need to give more attention than has been provided previously to the strategies for understanding information and how to use what is extracted in a meaningful and constructive way. This is not to say that search strategies that lead to more efficient ways to locate sources and introduce key resources should not be taught also. It is to state that the information search process does not stop there and the responsibilities of those who teach information literacy are just beginning when the student obtains and is encouraged to question the nature, validity, usefulness, or relevance of the information located.

Purpose Determines Strategy

The intended goal or purpose of the instruction will determine the strategy most suited to accomplish that goal. This can be illustrated by the evolution of library instruction over the past thirty years.

Orientation to Sources and Services. The traditional search strategy concentrates on information tools and services offered within the given library. The student is introduced to a linear progression of information sources and services, not so much to tailor these to meet the students' needs, but to acquaint the students with nearly all the library has to offer. Too often the emphasis is to make the patron fit the collection. Student assignments are often contrived in order to "teach the use of the library" rather than to "teach how to meet information needs." The search strategy is generic and fits the way the institution is organized, and often is not flexible to deal with true inquiry projects.

Thus, the student works from indexes, to reference materials, to general book and periodical collections, to nonprint and electronic sources, to special collections such as local history or government documents. The purpose is to show what is owned, where it is housed, and what must be done to get to the information. The strategy may acquaint the student with the library, but does little to meet his or her specific information needs. Thus, there is frequent use of the reminder, "Ask a librarian."

Awareness of Key Literature. The purpose is to introduce the literature that best supports a given theme or discipline. In school library media center situations, this might involve the best resources for consumer information and students will be introduced to key magazines, annual reports, useful websites, and perhaps how to contact the Better Business Bureau. In the K-12 setting, this approach is often used in those resource-based experiences in which a specific pool of gathered resources allow the student to explore topics related to a theme. The purpose is to read extensively beyond the limits of textbook summaries or classroom discussions. In the academic setting, this strategy is based on a conceptual framework, commonly called a pathfinder. Detailed in theory and practice by Mary Reichel and Mary Ann Ramey, undergraduate and graduate students are introduced to the publication sequences, subject structures, and key reference and index resources as a conceptual framework for information in a field or discipline. The Ohio State University Library Gateway displays examples of such pathfinders (http://www.lib.ohio-state.edu/gateway/subjects.html).

The goal of the framework or pathfinder strategy is for the student to learn key classification numbers, key controlled vocabulary terms, key specific reference materials, core periodicals and textbooks, and the standard or most cited books and people in the discipline at hand. Thus, from knowledge of this central literature, on anthropology for example, the student becomes acquainted with the accepted ideas, trends, and history of a field. This strategy provides the foundation for future exploration, but does not place the student in situations in which he or she must deal with new or unique information problems. Both the source and pathfinder strategies do not typically deal with evaluation of sources or the analysis of information need and do little to teach problem-solving skills.

Critical Thinking and Problem Solving. The strategy best used to meet the information needs at this stage is the process approach. The student, usually selecting from a theme or set of given issues, must determine a topic or problem to explore, determine appropriate resources, extract information, synthesize findings, and present a solution. The process approach is most effective if the student is given time and guidance to read widely about the given theme in order to move beyond the core resources and central issues. While this strategy moves the student through stages of thought and reflection, it is recursive in that movement back to indexes and reference resources will cycle through again and again as the student struggles to find focus.

Inquiry. At this level, the student is challenged with the task to set his or her own research agenda as much as possible. Near mastery of the preceding strategies must be reached as the student faces greater responsibility in formulation of his or her own personal investigation questions. Inquiry is driven by strategies that encourage framing, sharing, and testing ideas. Thus, there is a great deal of reading, discussion, and visualization of thoughts and options. Further, inquiry is driven by evidence. Depending on the nature of the inquiry, evidence can be facts, elaborations, different perspectives, and/or original data. The foundation for evidentual considerations comes from a review of associated literature. Here the student traces citations, both from indexes and from bibliographies of valued initial readings, and critically examines information that has been written by others considering similar issues and problems. Here the student concentrates on what has been examined and reported before he or she moves into investigations, creative writing, or illustrations that are in some manner unique to the student.

In the previous information search process situations, problems and tasks often come pre-defined. At the inquiry level, the student's major task is to identify the problem and associated questions. Strategies must allow for exploration of all possible avenues for ideas and evidence, and these may be outside of standard indexes and literature guides. The goal is for the student to comprehend the value of potential evidence or other pieces of information and determine quality based on relevance and authority specific to the message to be communicated or the argument to be supported.

Search Tactics

Marcia J. Bates, from the University of Washington, defines a "search tactic" as a move to further refine a search. Combinations of these tactics become an important set of techniques that often come to play within the overall search strategy. Bates defined her list of search tactics in 1979 to assist the professional online searcher and secondarily in teaching fledgling searchers how to increase their search sophistication. Although the orientation of her techniques was toward the professional, search technologies have evolved and are somewhat more manageable for the lay person. Nancy Thomas, associate professor at Emporia State University, has taken many of the tactics listed by Bates and refined them as strategies that help student searchers rethink their searches. Intervention and guidance from the teacher of information literacy is usually necessary in order to illustrate these search options. As an apprentice learner, the student must gain an understanding of not only how to employ the tactics, but when and why to apply them.

Bibble-to look for a bibliography already prepared; to see if the search work one plans has already been done in a usable form by someone else; to examine the bibliography of a valued source and select key reference leads.

Record-keep track of trails one has followed and of desirable trails not followed up on or not completed. This can be part of a journal in which the student documents success and frustrations in various search situations. Most modern databases build a search record for the novice to examine and gain understanding of alternatives.

Brainstorming-getting ideas and considering alternative ideas to enrich understanding by talking through the possibilities with others prior and during the search; read widely during the topic formulation stage so terms and ideas flow easily.

Consulting-testing ideas with others, usually mentors or experts who have useful insights to offer, to obtain valuable information and feedback on initial search terms.

Rescuing-being persistent and thorough in order to prevent premature conclusions or bias that may eliminate useful evidence that does not seem to fit preconceived notions.

Wandering-browsing in a variety of resources to stir the imagination and ignite thinking; look for synonyms and antonyms.

Breaching-considering a different subject area or domain, database, or discipline when a given search strategy is exhausted; gaining insight from a different area of discourse.

Reframing-re-examining the question to get rid of distortions or erroneous assumptions.

Jolting-changing the point of view by looking at the question as it has been addressed by different age groups, different cultures, different presentation or communication formats, or different disciplines.

Focusing-narrowing the search or the concept, or looking at only one part of it to give depth and greater meaning.

Dilating-expanding the search to widen the focus or to include larger issues and provide a more meaningful context for the central question.

Neighboring-cluster terms to be located within the text; consider associated terms that help to broaden the context or narrow the focus.

Reflection-stopping at several points in order to determine what else might come to mind; using revision stages to determine if all aspects have been covered.

Parallel-to make the search formulation broad or broader by including synonyms or otherwise conceptually parallel terms.

Contrary-to search for a term logically opposite from that describing the desired information.

Tracing-using the subject tracings that tag relevant citation hits during searching in order to find additional information classified by the database under such terms or subjects; examine information already found in the search in order to find additional terms that can be used to further the search.

Linkage-from the best sources located and read, identify what may be especially valuable such as reoccuring citations to authors, articles, books, or Internet documents. New sources are found through linkage to the referenced documents and tracing of names in indexes or on the internet.

Comprehension to Enhance Understanding

Reading for meaning is key to advancing in the information literacy processes. Useful strategies for reading text critically include first making a photocopy of the pages that seem to contain the most relevant information. Once the pages are copied or printed from the Internet, a highlight pen and a dark lead pencil are used to:

- Highlight or underline key words or sentences.
- Be selective and highlight no more than 20% of the information on the pages; 10% if possible.
- Bracket important passages and write notes near the passages that paraphrase and/or link to items from other sources that have been photocopied or printed.
- Connect related ideas with lines, a number code, or key term code.
- Circle words to be defined further.
- Outline the main ideas in the margin.
- Write brief comments and questions in the margin.
- From these pages, constuct note cards or place information pieces in a database for future sorting, linkage, and summary.
- Always note the correct citation for the records.

One of the most useful publications that contains comprehension strategies based on use of nonfiction literature for children and young adults is Strategies that Work by Stephanie Harvey and Anne Goudvis. The authors define "strategic reading" as thinking about reading in ways that enhance learning and understanding. Strategies that help the student focus on important ideas, drawing inferences, and asking questions can improve the student's overall comprehension of text. It is not enough, however, for the student to simply understand a given strategy. Harvey and Goudvis remind us that students also must understand when and how to use such strategies.

Levels of Comprehension

David Perkins, author of Smart Schools, suggests that learners can be categorized by the following four levels in reading ability. These levels may also apply to information seekers and users:

- Tacit Learner: The student lacks awareness of how to think about what he or she is reading. No association is made between the information being read and information need or associated information need possibilities.
- Aware Learner: The student realizes that meaning has broken down and confusion has set in, but does not have a sufficient set of strategies to remedy the problem. New information is different from or in conflict with that which was expected and the learner may not know how to deal with the content other than to ignore it.
- Strategic Learner: The student understands and applies basic strategies to think about and comprehend what is read. He or she applies systematic methods to assimilate new information and track information gaps, and thus is more likely to identify new information needs and how to address them.
- Reflective Learner: A reader who is strategic about his or her thinking and is able to apply strategies flexibly depending on goals and purpose for

reading. Search and information analysis strategies are transferred easily by the learner to meet new information needs and different information formats so the learner also may be strategic in listening, viewing, speaking, and writing.

Strategies Used by Proficient Readers

Seven strategies that Harvey and Goudvis find key for practice and will result in students becoming more proficient readers:

- Making connections between prior knowledge and the text-Readers naturally bring their prior knowledge and experience to reading, but they comprehend better when they think about the connections they make among the text, their lives, and the larger world.
- Asking questions-Asking questions will keep readers engaged, especially if they discover some answers and raise more questions in a continous learning cycle. When readers ask questions, they clarify understanding and forge ahead to make meaning.
- Visualizing-Active readers create images in their minds based on the words they read in the text. Enhancement of these visions can come from sharing with peers and parents.
- Drawing inferences-Inferring is at the intersection of taking what is known, garnering clues from the text, and thinking ahead to make a judgment, discern a theme, or speculate about what is to come. Inference must occur in order for the teacher to conclude that the student has "used the information."
- Determining important ideas-Thoughtful readers grasp essential ideas and important information when reading. Readers must differentiate between less important ideas and key ideas that are central to the meaning of the text. Such discrimination will help the learner move through large amounts of information by skimming for that

which is most relevant.
- Synthesizing information-Synthesizing involves combining new information with existing knowledge to form an original idea or interpretation. Reviewing, sorting, and sifting important information can lead to new insights that change the way readers think.
- Repairing understanding-If confusion disrupts meaning, readers need to stop and clarify their understanding. Often guidance and support from the teacher are necessary, but students' independent abilities to reflect and clarify come with practice.

Harvey and Goudvis insist that the reading strategies they find worthwhile are most likely to influence learner behavior if these strategies are modeled and clearly practiced by the classroom teacher. Teachers of information literacy also should be model learners and illustrate, vocalize, and share with students how they use strategies to think through information searching, selection, analysis, and application. The information literate teacher is also a strategic, reflective learner.

For Further Reading

Axelrod, Rise B., and Charles R. Cooper. Reading Critically, Writing Well. Boston: Bedford/St. Martin's, 1999.

Bates, Marcia J. "Information Search Tactics." Journal of the American Society for Information Science 30, no. 4 (1979): 205-214.

Bates, Marcia J. "The Design of Browsing and Berrypicking Techniques for the Online Search Interface." Online Review 13, no. 5 (1989): 407-425.

Callison, Daniel, and Ann Daniels. "Introducing End-User Software for Enhancing Student Online Searching." School Library Media Quarterly 16, no. 3 (Spring 1988): 173-181.

Harvey, Stephanie. <u>Nonfiction Matters</u>. York, ME: Stenhouse, 1998.

Harvey, Stephanie, and Anne Goudvis. <u>Strategies that Work: Teaching Comprehension to Enhance Understanding</u>. York, ME: Stenhouse, 2000.

Hirsh, Sandra G. "How Do Children Find Information on Different Types of Tasks?" <u>Library Trends</u> 45, no. 4 (Spring 1997): 725-746.

Kuhlthau, Carol C. "An Emerging Theory of Library Instruction." <u>School Library Media Quarterly</u> 16, no. 1 (Fall 1987): 23-28.

Ohio State University Library Gateway to Information Subject Guides. http://www.lib.ohio-state.edu/gateway/subjects.html

Perkins, David. Smart Schools: <u>Better Thinking and Learning for Every Child</u>. New York: Free Press, 1992.

Reichel, Mary, and Mary Ann Ramey. <u>Conceptual Frameworks for Bibliographic Instruction</u>. Littleton, CO: Libraries Unlimited, 1987.

Thomas, Nancy Pickering. <u>Information Literacy and Information Skills Instruction</u>. Englewood, CO: Libraries Unlimited, 1999.

Tovani, Cris, and Ellin Oliver Keene. <u>I Read It, but I Don't Get It: Comprehension Strategies for Adolescent Readers</u>. York, ME: Stenhouse, 2000.

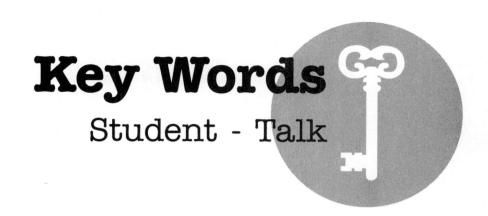

Key Words
Student - Talk

Mary Frances Zilonis, as Director of Library Media Services in Cambridge, Massachusetts, tells viewers in the Kaleidoscope video produced for the American Association of School Librarians that library media specialists and other teachers should give more attention to "student-talk." The implication is that too often student needs and interests are prejudged without a deeper understanding of individual differences. In addition, more student-talk implies a greater responsibility and opportunity placed before the student to take a teaching role themselves-to demonstrate, present, and voice their knowledge. The result should be less dictating of knowledge from the teacher's voice alone, and more teacher facilatation for student self-learning.

While more attention to student-talk does not mean that children create a student-centered curriculum in which they become dictators of the objectives and evaluation, it does imply that teachers listen more to what students have to say about their experiences, interests, and ambitions. Student-talk can lead to important shifts in how children and adolescents can be engaged in learning. It can also lead to dramatic changes in how library media centers provide access to information and to space for student work. Collection development becomes more student-need directed. More work areas for active voices are created in library media centers and classrooms when student-talk is increased.

Social Curriculum

"Student-talk" can be defined as a "social curriculum" in which the student is placed in a variety of problem-solving situations and must express himself or herself in order to gain needed information and to share information. In the social curriculum, students are evaluated on their interactive and interpersonal performances. Their abilities to communicate, negotiate, speculate, and debate verbally and constructively are seen as primary skills.

In the social curriculum, student-talk is at least as valuable as adult-talk. Adults tend to use talk to think aloud, to tentatively explore the beginnings of an idea, to hitchhike on what others have said, to clarify and modify the personal knowledge base, to affirm thoughts to others, and to acknowledge and enable speakers to continue groping for meaning. However, as David Booth and Carol Thornley-Hill suggest in Classroom Talk, children traditionally have been rewarded for using talk in a much more structured, formal way and often only in a question-and-answer pattern where hesitation and change are not rewarded. To observe children engaged in activities that require conversation is to understand the nature of learning. Interactive, voiced problem solving can lead to enhancements for thought and language development and stimulate both intellectual and emotional growth.

Frequent Talking

Students need frequent opportunities to talk. (Yes, you read that sentence correctly.) Establishing situations so that the talk can be constructive and on target takes a great deal of creativity and patience.

The nature and size of groups in the classroom, according to Curt Dudley-Marling of the University of Wisconsin and Dennis Searle of the University of London, can significantly affect students' use of language. The larger the group, the fewer the opportunities that individual students will have to use language. They conclude that whole-class discussions will never be a good way to encourage language use for many students, even though learning to talk in large groups is one of the skills students need to acquire in school. Large-group discussions tend to be dominated by more capable or outgoing students.

One of the best ways to encourage students to engage in discussions is to bring them together in small groups. Students who lack confidence in their verbal abilities may be shy about speaking in front of more fluent classmates. Teachers can provide opportunities for students to use language for different purposes by creating situations that encourage all kinds of talk. Dudley-Marling and Searle remind us that how teachers ask questions is an important factor in how students respond. Open-ended, probing questions, for example, invite students to speculate, imagine, and analyze. In contrast, narrow questions with predictable answers only encourage students to use language to demonstrate factual knowledge without the challenges of elaboration and exploration.

Varied Experiences Increase Vocabularies

Students come to school with a wide range of experiences and backgrounds. In part, these experiences will account for differences in vocabularies for both abilities of expression and reception. Children whose families travel a lot learn words associated with travel ("exit," "motel," "billboard"). Children who enjoy baking with their parents learn words such as "rise," "yeast," and "mix" through direct practice and application. Assume that parents engage their children in conversations during such experiences as the children grow older and the vocabularies should become more precise and more complex.

In general, the more varied people's experiences, the richer and more varied their vocabularies. Some experiences, of course, may not match the normal expectations of teachers. Students' vocabularies, like their experiences, aren't necessarily impoverished, only different. But these differences can interfere with their ability to get along in school.

Talking as You Read

The opportunity to read widely, to read for pleasure, and to share with others what you have read is one of the most powerful techniques to build vocabulary. It may be the best way to enrich experiences so that meaningful discussions can take place through more student-talk. Children have a natural sense of wonder about things and teachers can learn a great deal about how children make sense of their world through careful observation and lots of listening. Construction of meaning can take place through the interactions among a small group of students. This happens when talk is a natural part of their reading and not just the calling-out of words from the printed page.

Children are naturally interested in books. Given time, opportunity, free access to a variety of books, and the security of "discussion buddies," attitudes toward learning improve, depth of discourse gets richer, and those once shy begin to come forward with stories that have expression and meaning.

Storytelling

Most teachers, especially primary teachers, are interested in getting students to construct a good narrative-to relate stories or events in their lives-in a clear and orderly manner. For students to learn how to exploit the narrative function of language, at least two things have to happen. They have to be exposed to regular demonstrations of how narrative works. They need models from older students, parents, teachers, and others who can "tell a good story." And, they have to have frequent opportunities to try out the narrative function themselves. Practice should range from brief and concise descriptions (learning to convey a message in precise terms) to practice in giving detail and colorful elaboration (expression of clarity, wit, opposition, linkage of ideas, and drawing conclusions).

Information Talking

The list of potential oral verbal skills is as extensive, and perhaps more so, as those that can be listed for written communication. Opportunities to practice oral communication skills can be expanded through gathering and considering information. School library media center nonfiction collections and access to World Wide Web sites can certainly enhance many of the following situations:

- Experience Talk: using background experiences, knowledge, and previous information to add to discussions or to assist in problem solving
- Working Talk: giving suggestions, manipulating materials, sharing ideas
- Get Things Done Talk: an organizer, who knows there is a solution or solutions, acts as a motivator for the others in the group
- Asking Questions Talk: asking questions in order to clarify the problem or to gain more precise information
- Exploratory Talk: describing the materials, time, or other variables involved in the problem-solving situation
- Thoughtful Talk: attempting to work things through, and provides initial efforts to solve the problem
- Social Talk: may be counterproductive, but may also provide the means to relax, reflect, release tension with humor, and attack the problem in a new way
- Frustration Talk: can be abrupt short phrases, voiced louder than normal,

and may signal the need for intervention from someone outside the group, or anyone who can mediate talk
- Troubleshooting Talk: informed speculation that leads to solving some problem or aspect of the problem
- Dominating Talk: will continue in any environment until there is full group access to information and passive members gain confidence through opportunities to express themselves

Student-Talk and Collection Development

Mancall has proven to be one of the leading voices in principles of collection development for school library media centers. The relationship between "greater analysis of the user" and "listening more closely to student-talk" is very strong. Mancall recommends that school library media specialists observe more, listen more, and interact more in order to refocus the management of information access and align it more closely with user needs.

To refocus, the developer of the library media center collection must:

- place the users at the center of all considerations;
- define the user's perspective on the problem;
- isolate learner tasks to be accomplished;
- know the learning preferences that may control what access and resources you suggest;
- identify the content that must be accessed and the characteristics of the knowledge required; and
- expand possibilities for retrieval beyond the local collection, especially to meet varied and unique learner needs.

To realign from ownership to access, the collection developer must:

- become an active partner in the teaching/learning process and part of planning teams for curriculum and resource sharing;
- think subject and learner access parameters (abilities, entry skills, time limits

for access and use);

- renegotiate budget lines to relate to the redefined process (change from resource format lines to lines that reflect curricular and information need areas); and
- monitor usage trends so that informed adjustments can be made in collection operation and justification can be based on demonstrated need.

Where to Student-Talk

The locations for practicing constructive student-talk include the library media center as well as the classroom, field trips, and the home. Areas for small group active discussion and verbal communication practice have long been included in library media center facilities. Such "conference rooms" have allowed groups to be isolated and away from disturbing the main area of the library media center reserved for reading and searching for materials.

If student-talk is to be given the opportunity it needs in order to become constructive, observed, and mediated when necessary by library media specialists and other teachers, it may be that the small areas reserved for "conferencing" should be those reserved for "reading and independent study." The wider spaces of the library media center (from the reference areas, to media production spaces, to computer labs, to open areas providing large tables for groups to cluster) should be open for extensive student-talk. An open invitation to students to take a lead in their learning agenda through oral expression makes the school library media center a natural part of a student-centered curriculum.

For Further Reading and Viewing

Allington, Richard L. Celebrate Reading. Glenview, IL: Scott, Foresman, 1993.

Booth, David, and Carol Thornley-Hall. Classroom Talk. Portsmouth, NH: Heinemann, 1991.

Chase, Margaret. "Bridging the Expanse: A Case Study of Literature Discussion with a Cross-Age, Cross-Ability Group of Elementary Students." Ph.D. diss., Indiana University, 1997.

Dudley-Marling, Curt, and Dennis Searle. When Students Have Time to Talk: Creating Contexts for Learning Language. Portsmouth, NH: Heinemann, 1991.

Kaleidoscope: New Visions for School Library Media Programs. 29 min. American Association of School Librarians and Follett Software Co., 1993. Video program.

Kottler, Ellen. Secrets for Secondary School Teachers: How to Succeed in Your First Year. Thousand Oaks, CA: Corwin Press, 1998.

Mancall, Jacqueline C. "Refocusing the Collection Development Process: Collecting, Cooperating, Consulting." Taproot (Spring 1994): 8-13.

Mathematical Association. Math Talk. Portsmouth, NH: Heinemann, 1987.

Pitts, Judy M. Using Kaleidoscope. Chicago: American Association of School Librarians, 1994.

Roth, Kathleen J. Curriculum Materials, Teacher Talk, and Student Learning. East Lansing, MI: Institute for Research on Teaching, 1986.

Rubin, Donald, and William M. Dodd. Talking into Writing. Urbana, IL: National Council of Teachers of English and ERIC, 1987.

Rudder, Michael E. "Eliciting Student-Talk." Forum 37, no. 2 (1999). http://e.usia.gov/forum/

Key Words
Taxonomy

The standard meaning of "taxonomy," when applied to learning, is a systematic classification of what is learned. Classification sorts the kinds of capabilities that the individual acquires or demonstrates as a result of the events of learning.

Various types of learning have been identified over the past fifty years of psychological research. These include classical conditioning, operant learning or simple habit formation, concept learning, problem-solving, and discrimination or perceptual learning. Prominent names, such as Benjamin S. Bloom and David R. Krathwohl in the 1950s and Robert Gagne and Jerome S. Bruner in the 1960s, have been associated with different taxonomies for learning and student performance levels.

Such classifications have been useful to the practical teaching field as they have often served to help identify and construct specific learning objectives and tasks. The taxonomy displays the range, level, and overall hierarchy of possible learning or demonstrations of student abilities through actual performance of tasks. Taxonomies serve to guide curriculum development through scope and sequence plans so educators can visualize the tasks that match maturation levels.

Three domains are standard for many of the taxonomies.

- Cognitive Domain: range of intellectual capabilities from simple recall to creative synthesis and evaluation.
- Affective Domain: an emphasis on feelings and emotions that may be displayed and controlled as the learner matures.
- Psycho-motor Domain: physical tasks requiring practice and refinement through neuromuscular conditioning.

Different taxonomies in learning help us understand learning environments and expectations, and these may differ from one society to another. Much has been written, for example, of the changes in learning expectations placed on humans from the agricultural to the industrial to the current information revolutions. Three waves have caused dramatic changes in the priorities that society places on what students should be able to learn and perform in order to survive and succeed.

Evolution in learning theory has moved much of what we do away from behaviorism and toward constructivism. More time is now invested in knowing the individual learner and providing means for the self-learner to mature as quickly as possible. Much of this is based on the assumption that we do not feel we can predict the stable tasks of the immediate future, and thus, the students who are likely to be most successful are those who learn how to learn, adjust, and analyze problems for themselves.

Scaffolding has an important role in development of meaningful learning activities. One experience builds on the other to advance the learner to the higher order skills. Robert Gagne's theory emphasizes the cumulative nature of learning and the positive transfer of training. Although too rigid for some, his ideas are key to understanding how we grow and mature in our learning and how such can be accelerated somewhat through guided interventions and apprenticeships or modeling. In general, Gagne tells us learning of principles is facilitated by prior learning of concepts, and learning of concepts by prior learning of discriminations. A taxonomy will often help us sort out differences and to link similarities so patterns for instruction can become apparent.

Other Classification Formats

A taxonomy provides one approach to classification and leads to a display of differences, relationships, progression, and hierarchy. Several other formats are useful as well.

- Dichotomy: a division or process of dividing into two mutually exclusive or contradictory groups.
- Rubric: a set of scoring guidelines for evaluation of student work or job performance, usually given in progressive levels that represent stages to be mastered toward excellence.
- Matrix: a new structure that originates from a given framework, showing new dimensions for depth and complexity.
- Discipline: recognized branch or segment of knowledge within a domain of rational learning; holds to some basic standards but most grow and evolve within social contexts in order to be relevant and useful.
- Scope and Sequence: a view, outline, or illustration of the range of skills, tasks, and performances given in an order from basic to exemplary; often tied to specific grade levels and disciplines to show when the basic skill is to be introduced, reinforced, expanded, or mastered.

Learning Taxonomy Applied to Information Literacy

Determined to provide methods to make library research projects in secondary schools exciting, interesting, stimulating, and based on teacher and student interactions resulting in "brainstorms," Stripling and Pitts outlined their own blueprints for the library research process. They designed a taxonomy similar to

Bloom's and tagged it "REACTS" as an acronym to match these levels:

Recalling: student recalls and reports facts discovered.
Explaining: student restates, paraphrases, gives examples.
Analyzing: student shows relationships, cause and effect.
Challenging: student communicates critical judgments.
Transforming: student uses multiple evidence for own conclusion.
Synthesizing: student creates new concepts.

While their definitions differ slightly from Bloom's, their attempt to move the typical research project into a process for thinking and logic was foundational to the current information literacy movement.

Kuhlthau and dozens who have replicated her research have shown an associated affective domain or maturation in attitudes and feelings toward the library research process. Although over time and with experiencing success, the researcher gains self-confidence. However, feelings, for both the novice and experienced researcher, will tend to follow this cycle for each project:

uncertainty
confusion
brief elation upon initial selection
anticipation
doubt
optimism upon forming focus
confidence
increased interest
relief
sometimes satisfaction
sometimes disappointment
sense of accomplishment

Several principles come from Kuhlthau's work and are reflected in the stages often parallel to the growth in complexity of tasks classified by Bloom and others:

- Mastering tasks within a project is best learned by building from one to the next in scaffolded degrees of difficulty.
- The process is as important (perhaps

more important for the novice researcher) than is the product, and stages leading to completion of the product also should be valued and evaluated.

- Much more time must be given to activities that lead to intelligent selection of research topics and search paths. As much thinking and general reading should go into presearch activities as in the analysis and synthesis of evidence for the final product.

Kuhlthau's "reasearch" has changed the role of the school library media specialist and the academic librarian as they today increasingly collaborate with other teachers to help students master information literacy skills.

Learning Taxonomy Applied to Library Media Specialist as Instructor

Perhaps the taxonomy that has influenced thinking more than any other in school media concerning the role of the school library media specialist has been the classification offered by David V. Loertscher. (See Figure 1.) Commonly referenced today as "Loertscher's Taxonomy," it has served to outline the progression toward higher level instructional involvement of the school library media specialist since its introduction in the late 1970s. Key to understanding the implications of The Library Media Specialist's Taxonomy are these concepts:

- The professional strives to improve his or her role in instruction by engaging in activities at higher levels over time and experience. Success is scaffolded similar to a learning progression.
- Lower level aspects are not completely discarded and some may continue to be valid in certain situations. Over time, however, the accomplished library media specialist devotes a greater amount of time to the higher levels of the taxonomy.
- Attitude and vision may be the two most powerful elements in play to move both library media specialist and other teachers up the taxonomy to higher collaborative efforts. Without positive and progressive focus, the small everyday tasks will smother this taxonomy.

- At the highest levels, the school library media specialist engages in curricular planning that not only enhances and helps the teacher, but leads to powerful changes in methods that can result in improved learning environments and greater student academic performance.

Fig. 1

The Library Media Specialist's (Loertscher's) Taxonomy (revised in 2000)

1. *No Involvement*
   The library media center is bypassed entirely.
2. *Smoothly operating information infrastructure*
   Facilities, materials, networks, and information resources are available for the self-starter delivered to the point of need.
3. *Individual reference assistance.*
   The library media specialist serves as the human interface between information systems and the user.
4. *Spontaneous interaction and gathering*
   Networks respond twenty-four hours a day and seven days a week to patron requests, and the library media center facilities can be used by individuals and small groups with no advance notice.
5. *Cursory planning*
   There is informal and brief planning with teachers and students for library media center facilities or network usage, usually done through casual contact in the library media center, in the hall, in the teachers' lounge, in the lunch room, or by email.
6. *Planned gathering*
   Gathering of materials/assess to important digital resources is done in advance of a class project upon teacher or student request.
7. *Evangelistic outreach/advocacy*
   A concerted effort is made to promote the philosophy of the library media center program.
8. *Implementation of the four major programmatic elements: collaboration, reading literacy, enhancing learning through technology, and information literacy.*
   There is concentrated effort for the library media center to achieve its goal of contributing to academic achievement.
9. *The mature library media center program*
   The library media center program reaches the needs of every student and teacher who will accept its offerings.
10. *Curriculum development*
    Along with other educators, the library media specialist contributes to the planning and organization of what will eventually be taught in the school or district.

Loertscher warns against the use of rigidly defined scope and sequence activities that, if poorly implemented, lead back to isolated library skills exercises and little relevance to the academic performance of students. Scope and sequence plans, however, can provide a range of levels to advance information literacy as long as skills reflect checkpoints for student performance and the processes of information literacy reflect constructivist methods or ways of learning and teaching. Integration of information literacy skills can advance and even change the curriculum to the extent that inquiry and other research processes drive what is taught and how it is taught. Constructivist methods must be understood and employed or one will find what Benjamin Bloom discovered, that 95% of demands for student performance remain at the lowest levels-the recall of information.

Margaret E. Chisholm and Donald P. Ely introduced a competency approach to the roles for media personnel in the mid-1970s. They based their "taxonomy" or classification for personnel on several trends that remain true today:

- greater access to information in a variety of formats;
- a greater concern for the individual learner;
- the introduction of new technologies into the process of teaching and learning;
- the emergence of new types of schools; and
- changing goals for education.

To meet these trends, Chisholm and Ely advocated that a team of information media professionals could best address the complex needs of schools that were entering the Information Age. Whether the personnel have professional preparation in librarianship, audiovisual communications, or educational technology, the important factor is that media professionals are resource people and curriculum and instructional developers. They are members of teams of teachers, curriculum specialists, and even administrators. In this ideal situation (now outlined more fully in Information Power 1998), the entire school functions as an information center with the media program providing many of the specific resources.

Based on differing levels of competency in ten function areas, Chisholm and Ely outlined the following personnel classifications:

- Media Aide: serves as the vital link between students and teachers in the day-to-day operation of the library media center. The aide, including adult and student, salaried and volunteer, often performs tasks related to scheduling, inventory, and retrieval of materials and equipment, and may assist in production and training under supervision of professional staff.
- Media Technician: has specialized training and provides essential services that also require general knowledge of the library media program's goals and operations. Based on an associate's degree, the technician may concentrate on such services as production of instructional materials, cataloging of resources, or maintaining electronic information linkages (today's Webmaster) based on guidelines from the professional staff.
- Media Specialist: chosen to specialize in one aspect of the media field, which means that one function will dominate and others will be secondary. Holding a bachelor's degree or higher, emphasis here may be coordination of reference services, production services, media design, or what we see today as distance education. In the context of the times for the Chisholm and Ely job classifications, focus was driven more by information format rather than by subject content, learning styles, instructional modes, or expected learner performance. This level is classified as professional.
- Media Generalist: selected as the leader or manager of the program and directs the functions of other staff to support a defined vision for extensive information media services. Knowledgeable of a wide spectrum of information and

learning theory, application of management skills to program development, and experienced in instructional delivery, this professional will hold a master's degree or higher. This person may hold rank as department chair or district supervisor. This level is professional/administrative.

Of course, much discussion and frustration has come from such personnel classifications. Often seen as too ideal, unrealistic, and/or too expensive, few school districts have actually implemented them. However, the value again in such taxonomies is to illustrate differences and a progression that should be considered in order for instructional programming to advance over time. Without such mapping to illustrate growth potential, the school library media specialist remains one-dimensional, stagnant, and defined only in supplemental roles to the dynamics of the educational process. Within the context of current trends in information literacy, the instructional media specialist as curriculum leader may become the pinnacle for the professional role.

The Taxonomy for Building Partnerships for Learning

For those who believe in the learning principles outlined in Information Power (1998), the 1999 Planning Guide and Assessment Rubric is an essential document. Presented in a rubric format, function areas for the assessment of the school media program and the professional school library media specialist are presented. Important function areas are covered: *Teaching and Learning, Information Access and Delivery, and Program Administration.*

For each, a range of growth, improvement, and evolution are staged in terms of basic, proficient, and exemplary. Designed for the professional to manage self-evaluation, the format also provides a tool for principals to conduct annual reviews and to learn more of the potential for growth in the school library media program. Developed, tested, and revised under the guidance of Barbara Stripling, Carol Kroll, and others, this instrument gives us our most recent classification of the actions of the accomplished school library media specialist. Exemplary actions for indicators of performance in teaching and learning illustrate the future role of the instructional media leader:

- The library media program is a catalyst for intellectual inquiry. Students learn to incorporate information literacy skills into their work and become proactive users of information and resources.
- Teaching is facilitative, collaborative, and creative. Reflection and authentic assessment are built into all instructional units.
- Schoolwide programs enable and encourage students to use their own learning styles, abilities, and needs to solve complex information problems and present their solutions in different formats.
- Inquiry can take place by an individual or in a group. Students determine their own research needs and develop their own research strategies.
- Student learning is assessed through student presentations to peers and adults, by using student- and teacher-produced rubrics. Students also may present to professionals in the field of study.

For Further Reading

American Association of School Librarians. <u>A Planning Guide for Information Power: Building Partnerships for Learning with School Library Media Program Assessment Rubric for the 21st Century</u>. Chicago: ALA, 1999.

Chisholm, Margaret E., and Donald P. Ely. <u>Media Personnel in Education</u>. Englewood Cliffs, NJ: Prentice-Hall, 1976.

Eisenberg, Michael B., and Robert E. Berkowitz. <u>Information Problem-Solving</u>. Norwood, NJ: Ablex, 1990.

Kohn, Alfie. <u>The Schools Our Children Deserve</u>. Boston: Houghton Mifflin, 1999.

Krumme, Gunter. "Major Categories in the Taxonomy of Educational Objectives." http://faculty.washington.edu/krumme/guides/bloom.html. 2000.

Kuhlthau, Carol Collier. Teaching the Library Research Process. 2nd ed. Lanham, MD: Scarecrow Press, 1994.

Loertscher, David V. Taxonomies of the School Library Media Program. 2nd ed. San Jose, CA: Hi Willow Research & Publishing, 2000.

Matthews, Sam. "The Charted Library." The Library Association Record (June 2000): 336-337.

Stripling, Barbara K., and Judy M. Pitts. Brainstorms and Blueprints. Englewood, CO: Libraries Unlimited, 1988.

Washington State Information Skills Curriculum Scope and Sequence." In Information Literacy: Educating Children for the 21st Century, by Patricia Shenn Breivik and J. A. Senn. 2nd ed. Washington, DC: National Education Association, 1998.

Winters, Elaine. "Who Is This Guy, Benjamin Bloom, and Why All the Fuss about His Taxonomy?" http://www.bena.com/ewinters/Bloom.html. 1999.

Key Words
Technology

Heinich, Molenda, Russell, and Smaldino define "technology" in their standard instructional media text as:

1. A process of devising reliable and repeatable solutions to tasks.
2. The hardware and software (i.e., the products) that result from the application of technological processes.
3. A mix of process and product, used in instances where the context refers to the combination of technological processes and resultant products or where the process is inseparable from the product (p. 416).

Healy defines and editorializes a little in her best seller, Failure to Connect: Technology and Power:

> Throughout history, new technologies have altered the existing social order, economy, and power structure. "Technology" is any tool or medium that helps people accomplish tasks or produce products more efficiently, and computers are only the latest in a long line of innovations-going back to axes and fire-that have changed the way humans interact with the world and with each other. Computers, like all technologies that introduce new information or alter the format of information, are changing the balance of power in schools. Increasingly, the "techies" rather than the educators, hold the power to make educational decisions (p. 30-31).

The Association for Educational Communications and Technology released a set of definitions for basic terms in that field in 1977. According to AECT:

> Instructional Technology is a complex, integrated process involving people, procedures, ideas, devices, and organization, for analyzing problems, and devising, implementing, evaluating, and managing solutions to those problems, in situations in which learning is purposive and controlled. [Design of instruction may involve components such as] messages, people, materials, devices, techniques, and settings. Purposive learning is learning in which someone else has determined that learning is to occur within the learner. Further, the purpose of such learning can, and must be, specified in advance [objectives that can be observed and measured]. Controlled learning is learning in which the contingencies of the learner's behavior are determined and managed by someone else [much in step with the principles outlined by B. F. Skinner for the technologies of teaching] (p. 76-77).

Inquiry and Technology

A quarter of a century later, little has changed in defining the purpose of technology in instruction. A great deal, however, has been added to our considerations as to how and by whom technology will be applied to learning. Inquiry includes the guided and purposive learning techniques when some aspects require a training or exercise mode. To hold at that level, though, destroys the potential for the learner to experience self-motivation, self-direction, and to mature as one who can manage the technologies of learning for him or herself.

Therefore, as a tool, technologies can help make some aspects of inquiry more manageable or efficient. Information access can be faster. Information records can be stored easier and sorted or accessed in more combinations. Information communication can be packaged in presentation modes that are designed by the student. While the teacher may master some aspects of instructional design through the latest evolution in hypermedia, the more powerful strategy is the technology in the hands of the learner.

Inquiry can be made more efficient through the application of one of the many models for the information search process or for information problem solving. It is likely, however, to be more effective when there is time given to information exploration, sharing of ideas, and

demonstration of how new information has been assimilated. While technologies are tools that lead to more efficiency, as teachers of information inquiry we also should consider how technology might make learning more effective. Pleasure, motivation, and self-reflection are powerful aspects of a more welcoming learning environment. Perhaps modern technology hardware and software also should be developed to help enhance these behaviors in a positive way.

Curriculum and Technology

A key question is: Where does inquiry enter into the design of learning environments compared to instructional technology? It enters at the foundation. Some would say "inquiry is the curriculum."

Robert Heinich, Professor of Instructional Systems Technology at Indiana University, shifted the educational technology field in 1970 when he moved instructional technology into a planning phase for curriculum development. Thus, instructional media specialists were moved, in his model, to the role of curriculum design rather than reactors to curriculum and simple audiovisual classroom support. In many cases, there was no professional in place in the traditional audiovideo approach. Use of technology in the 1960s, as too often today, was used as an add-on or afterthought. Audiovisual often meant an item that would pass the time faster or relieve the teacher of some talking time.

Programmed instruction in the 1970s was designed to make teaching more efficient, rather than to make learning more effective. The more important agenda was that of the teacher or trainer. Learner needs and entry abilities often were measured only for the purpose of helping the instructional designer. Little consideration was given to the opportunity for the learner to understand his or her own entry abilities and potential.

Heinich moved technology, and it continues to apply today in a world of computers, as tools to help plan and deliver curriculum. The principles of inquiry that place the student at the center of the purpose of curriculum will set the foundation for experiences that are more authentic and meaningful to student needs. This teaching philosophy builds from what the learner brings to the situation, and then applies information-seeking and use models that seem to best fit the situation.

Reflection, the component of inquiry that examines the merits of the process and products of instruction, is important to add in the string of events illustrated in Figure 1. Continuously, technology should be evaluated and modified to serve the curricular and instructional needs of teachers and students. Technology is a tool set that can be reconfigured. The purpose is not just efficiency, but to restructure interactive instructional delivery systems so that the accepted principles of learning can be achieved effectively.

Debbie Abilock, Curriculum Coordinator and Director of Technology and Library at the Nueva School in Hillsborough, California, models this approach in one of several essays gathered by Lebaron and Collier. She "puts technology in its place" as a tool to alter curriculum based on sound learning principles

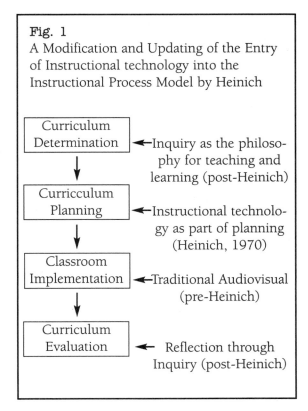

Fig. 1
A Modification and Updating of the Entry of Instructional technology into the Instructional Process Model by Heinich

Curriculum Determination ← Inquiry as the philosophy for teaching and learning (post-Heinich)

Curricculum Planning ← Instructional technology as part of planning (Heinich, 1970)

Classroom Implementation ← Traditional Audiovisual (pre-Heinich)

Curriculum Evaluation ← Reflection through Inquiry (post-Heinich)

that do not change. Abilock coordinates the application of modern information technologies for her school so her students have efficient access to a wide selection of information in electronic, multimedia, and print formats. The information selection tasks remain the same, however, regardless of the technologies employed.

Abilock writes, "The science program at Nueva is hands-on, minds-on, feet-in-the mud, which means that it consists of experiments, simulations, and activities from which students construct an understanding of science concepts" (p. 6).

"In problem-based learning, students are confronted with ill-structured problems that mirror an authentic situation. It is important for them to recognize that just as in real-world problems, there are not simple right and wrong answers. The challenge for students is to understand complex issues, develop an informed and defensible position, locate data supporting [or rejecting] their point of view, recognize information that is relevant, and evaluate the authority of sources."

The Right Questions and Criteria

Healy has generated a list of questions that administrators and teachers should answer prior to investing in the next generation of computers:

- How can computer technology help achieve our educational goals? Are these goals compatible with the interests, abilities, and needs of today's students?
- How and why will this experience [based on the technology to be acquired] improve the quality of learning sufficiently to justify the cost and the time involved?
- What will it have to replace (family activities, silent reading, social playtime, art, music, gym, recess, foreign language) and is the trade-off acceptable?
- Who makes software decisions and on what criteria?
- Are we willing to loosen traditional top-down structures of education and produce students who will think and question?
- What content can be taught, and how do we measure the outcomes? Are computers the best, not just the trendiest, way to do this particular job? (p. 67)

Healy also understands the power of a technological innovation and provides this criteria for methods that will increase the motivation to learn. In the best practices, this motivation is enhanced, allowing the student to explore computers as well as learning specific applications.

- Let the child be an active agent rather than just a button-pusher. Offering the child reasonable choices within limits builds internal controls.
- Avoid programs that give "rewards" for completing tasks, particularly easy ones. Emphasize that pleasure should be found in using one's mind to solve problems and feeling good about success.
- Corrective feedback develops thinking skills and confidence by helping a student understand a mistake and how to

correct it.

- Cultivate the notion that learning is inherently interesting, rather than something so boring that one must be externally rewarded to do it.
- Well-designed hypermedia programs can enhance motivation, especially for youngsters with more visual and kinesthetic learning styles.
- Check whether the program requires only convergent answers or whether it allows the child to do some original thinking. Is it possible to come up with a solution that even the programmer didn't anticipate?
- The depersonalized computer may help uncertain students to take more risks in the service of learning because there is no one there to make fun or criticize.
- Insist that the child take reasonable responsibility. Don't let him or her believe that the computer does the work or blame it for making the mistakes (p. 188-189).

Technology Foundation Standards and Computer Skills

The most recent standards for student performance from the International Society for Technology in Education reflect a multidisciplinary approach. Before computer skills are identified, a clear vision for establishing new learning environments is illustrated.

ISTE advocates technology connections to the curriculum based on a learning environment that prepares students to:

- communicate by using a variety of media and formats.
- access and exchange information in a variety of ways.
- compile, organize, analyze, and synthesize information.
- draw conclusions and make generalizations based on information gathered.
- know content and be able to locate additional information as needed.
- become self-directed learners.
- collaborate and cooperate in team efforts.

- interact with others in ethical and appropriate ways (p. 5).

Doug Johnson, District Media Supervisor for the Mankato, Minnesota Schools, and Mike Eisenberg, Professor at the Information School of the University of Washington, have listed computer skills that they feel reflect each stage of the Eisenberg/Berkewitz Big Six Skills Approach. They identify the following skills for Synthesis (Students must organize and communicate the results of the information problem-solving effort.).

Students will be able to:

- Classify and group information by using a word processor, database, or spreadsheet.
- Use word processing and desktop publishing software to create printed documents.
- Create and use computer-generated graphics and art in different print and electronic presentations.
- Generate charts, tables, and graphs by using electronic spreadsheets and other graphing programs.
- Use presentation software to create electronic slide shows.
- Create hypermedia and multimedia productions with digital video and audio.
- Create World Wide Web pages and sites by using hypertext markup language (HTML).
- Use e-mail, ftp, and other telecommunications capabilities to share [information and ideas].
- Properly cite and credit electronic sources.

Impact of New Technologies on School Library Media Centers

Nearly every current school library media specialist can give examples of how information access has become frequent "uploading or downloading." Electronic searching and full-text access are now common not just in the library media center, but in classrooms and homes. More and more teachers and students are not only users of electronic products, but are the creators of many instructional presentations. Many of the following features suggested by Callison in 1993 are becoming common today:

- electronic continuous access to information, 24/7;
- computers on teachers' desks with software to support grading, student records, professional development programs, and access to the Internet and other electronic databases and libraries worldwide;
- provide for cable and satellite reception in every classroom, with distance education coordinated through the library media center;
- homework hotlines, collaborative writing labs, and immediate contact among school library media centers and local public and academic libraries;
- technologies that have been modified to meet the needs of students with physical and learning disabilities; and
- technologies that extend staff development conferencing throughout the year, including summers.

Instructional Technology Software

Callison and Haycock field-tested early microcomputer software designed for instructional purposes in the 1980s. They found students tended to prefer programs that were simulations with challenging tasks to solve in order to "take a journey" or solve a problem with different possible resolutions. Teachers tended to favor computer software that supported already established curriculum and learning objectives. They tended to look for and approve computer software that reinforced what they were already teaching, and it has not been until the past decade that more and more teachers have been adapting some of the advantages that new technology software has to offer to modify their lessons. Interactivity and student ability options have gained wider acceptance over the two decades since the first computer-assisted instruction packages were introduced.

In the late 1990s, Haughland and Wright provided the foundation for the following guidelines for selection of instructional software for children:

- Is the child in control, an "actor not a reactor"?
- Does the child set the pace of the activity?
- Are instructions clear?
- Does it teach powerful ideas, not just trivia?
- Can the child operate it independently?
- Does it feature discovery learning, not skill drilling?
- Does it capitalize on the child's intrinsic motivation rather than using external rewards?
- Is the process more important than the product?
- Does it reflect the child's experience in the real world?
- Are technical features well-designed-responds quickly, saves child's work, and has uncluttered graphics?
- Does it display gender role equity?

Future Trends in Technology

Ann Barron of the University of South Florida and Gary Orwig of the University of Central Florida have provided an excellent guide to the technology terms and formats of emerging media. Subtitled "a beginners guide," their publication gives excellent outlines for such technologies as CD-ROM, interactive video, digital audio, digital images and video, hypermedia, local area networks, telecommunications, teleconferencing for distance education, and assistive technologies for those with special needs (on-screen keyboards, screen enlargement, braille displays, speech synthesis, text-to-speech conversion).

Through the many editions of the Heinich, Molenda, Russell, and Smaldino text Instructional Media and Technologies for Learning, the authors have attempted to predict future trends in media and technology. These three seem to be most clear:

- Merging of media-away from the 1950s media as separate entities, sometimes combined as multimedia, to the seamless combinations made possible by digitization of print, images, and sound.
- Convergence of telecommunications technologies-high-speed networks for telephone and broadcasting.
- Convergence and disappearance of the computer as we know it today.

Theodore Frick's essay for the Phi Delta Kappa Education Foundation in 1991 gave a vision for future technological systems that will restructure educational settings and result in more community-based learning. Rather than tied to the classroom, students will gain from more direct interaction with cultural, governmental, business, and industrial institutions with technology providing more direct contact with people, events, services, and mentoring. Technology provides two key functions:
- extends the communication and interaction options; and
- makes simulations more realistic and demanding, leading to meaningful learning experiences.

Thus Frick argues that technology will play a large role in restructuring education so that it gains meaning through an environment that consists of the surrounding community and its culture.

One of the most exciting recent discussions concerning future technologies has been written by George Gilder, Senior Fellow at the Discovery Institute. He contends that the computer age is over and a new age of telecommunications, "telecosm," is emerging. Infinite bandwidth will revolutionize our communication and education world again. Delivery of audio and video data will be "instant." Control over what the user wants, when, how often, and at what ability level will be realized as never before. Telecosm entails the domains of technology unleashed by the discovery of the electro-magnetic spectrum and the photon, with fiber optics, cellular telephony, and satellite communications as examples detailed by Gilder.

Under current technologies, both pedagogical techniques and hardware delivery systems, students continue to waste time, according to Gilder, because the educational bureaucracy has yet to provide learning environments that truly meet specific ability levels and support real-world learning experiences, even for the very young. There are signs, however, that the restructuring scenarios described by Frick of Indiana University in 1991 still have a chance to become reality.

For Further Reading

Abilock, Debbie. "Using Technology to Enhance Student Inquiry". In Technology in Its Place, edited by John F. LeBarron and Catherine Collier, 3-15. San Francisco: Jossey-Bass, 2001.

AECT Task Force on Definition and Terminology. Educational Technology: Definition and Glossary of Terms. Washington, DC: AECT, 1977.

Barron, Ann E., and Gary W. Orwig. New Technologies for Education: A Beginner's Guide. Englewood, CO: Libraries Unlimited, 1997.

Callison, Daniel. "The Impact of New Technologies on School Library Media Center Facilities and Instruction." Journal of Youth Services in Libraries 6, no. 4 (Summer 1993): 414-419.

Callison, Daniel, and Gloria Haycock. "A Methodology for Student Evaluation of Educational Microcomputer Software." Educational Technology 28, no. 1 (January 1988): 25-32.

Ely, Donald P. Trends in Educational Technology. Syracuse, NY: Clearinghouse on Information Resources. 1992.

Frick, Theodore W. Restructuring Education through Technology. Fastback #326. Bloomington, IN: Phi Delta Kappa, 1991.

Gilder, George. <u>Telecosm: How Infinite Bandwidth Will Revolutionize Our World</u>. New York: The Free Press, 2000.

Haughland, S. W., and J. L. Wright. <u>Young Children and Technology</u>. Boston: Allyn & Bacon, 1997.

Healy, Jane M. <u>Failure to Connect: How Computers Affect Our Children's Minds and What We Can Do about It</u>. New York: Touchstone, 1998.

Heinich, Robert. <u>Technology and the Management of Instruction</u>. Monograph 4. Washington, D. C.: Association for Educational Communications and Technology, 1970.

Heinich, Robert, Michael Molenda, James D. Russell, and Sharon E. Smaldino. <u>Instructional Media and Technologies for Learning</u>. 5th ed. Englewood Cliffs, NJ: Merrill, 1996.

International Society for Technology in Education. <u>National Educational Technology Standards for Students: Connecting Curriculum and Technology</u>. Eugene, OR: ISTE, 2000. (http://www.iste.org)

Johnson, Doug, and Mike Eisenberg. "Computer Literacy and Information Literacy: A Natural Combination." In <u>Foundations for Effective School Library Media Programs</u>, edited by Ken Haycock, 140-146. Englewood, CO: Libraries Unlimited, 1999.

Norton, Priscilla, and Debra Sprague. <u>Technology for Teaching</u>. Boston: Allyn and Bacon, 2001.

Skinner, B. F. <u>The Technology of Teaching</u>. New York: Appleton-Century-Crofts, 1968.

Key Words
Time on Task

By the time the average American student graduates from high school, he or she will have spent an average of 703,700 minutes or just over 12,000 hours in a classroom. Common-sense notions and some basic research studies lead to the obvious conclusion that students learn more when given more time to learn and when they spend that time actually engaged in academic tasks.

According to the American Association of School Administrators, a "task" is a goal-oriented set of activities specifically intended to produce a particular learning outcome. Next to people, time is the school's most valuable resource. But it is nonrenewable. Once gone, it is gone.

Generally defined for the educational field, "time on task" is that period of time during which a student is actively engaged in a learning activity. Time on task is closely related to other educational terms such as attention, performance, persistence, student behavior, and time management.

A simple conclusion is that time must be efficiently allocated in educational settings, much as time is managed in productive business and industry environments. Application, however, is not always so simple. There are many aspects to timing, integration, association, and level or order of tasks to provide the most effective engaging activities for learning. The product in education is the student who has mastered the process of learning. A wide variety of ability levels, resource support, and adult coaching are just some of the factors that add to the complexities of the business and industry called school.

Time Linked to Learning

Thirty years ago, John B. Carroll of the University of North Carolina outlined the basic factors that influence the distribution of time for learning. The amount of time needed to learn depends on:
- Aptitude-not so much what the student is capable of learning, but the amount of time it takes the student to learn a particular fact or concept.
- Ability-the student's capacity to understand and incorporate the material based on prior learning.
- Quality of Instruction-the effectiveness with which the instruction is presented.

The amount of time actually spent learning depends on:
- Perseverance-the steadfastness with which students devote themselves to learning the material.
- Opportunity-the time the teacher allows for learning and the number of chances the student is given.

Benjamin Bloom, while at the University of Chicago, emphasized that students cannot perform well on a lesson unless they have spent sufficient time mastering the tasks that preceded that lesson. In Bloom's view, quality of instruction depends on four main factors:

- Instructional Cues-particular techniques the teacher uses to convey the content to be learned.
- Reinforcement-time for the attention and praise the teacher gives a student.
- Participation-time for students to become involved in the instruction.
- Feedback and Correctives-the information a teacher gives students to let them know if they are responding appropriately to the learning task.

Inherent in Bloom's approach is the relationship between amount of time spent and when time is spent:
- Timing of Initial Instruction-through formative testing to determine whether students are ready for the task.
- Timing of Correctives-checkpoints in order to determine if actions are needed to get students back on the right track or to intervene with remedial experiences if initial tasks have not been mastered.
- Timing of Guided Practice-which should follow the necessary correctives in order to reinforce learning.
- Timing Student Progress-so that achievements can be related to the next tasks in the progression or scaffold.

Capabilities of teachers that influence the efficient and effective use of time include:
- Planning-detailed specifications and guidelines the teacher develops for the classroom.
- Implementation-the translation of those plans into classroom strategies and activities.
- Inducting-motivating students and increasing their active learning and task involvement.
- Communication Skills-the ability to state instructions and expectations clearly.

Timing and Integration of Information Skills

Two factors that tend to be critical in the effec-tiveness of information skills instruction are:
- Timing the instruction to take place at the time-of-need, and
- Placing the information-use instruction within a meaningful context of personal interest or school subject assignment.

Several other factors noted above are also critical, but these two, timing and integration, seem to need much attention from those who teach school library media skills.

Markel D. Tumlin, from the University of San Diego, has documented some observations of the challenge of introducing new optical discs to the students searching his academic library. These observations have much relevance today to K-12 settings. According to Tumlin, "the skills needed to fully exploit the possibilities of optical products are much more sophisticated than those required to use print sources. Two hour-long class sessions are spent discussing all of the sorts of things that the professional literature on classroom instruction insists are important: Boolean logic, thesauri, database selection, etc. In addition, live demonstrations of actual searches are projected onto a large screen. However, with few exceptions, the students who become the best searchers are those who seek individual assistance after class. Spending some time one-on-one at the workstations helps them develop a better understanding of the systems. The two features of point-of-use [need] instruction most commonly mentioned in the professional literature are that it is useful and that it is time consuming."

Tumlin also reports, "A common criticism of classroom bibliographic instruction is that faculty members schedule them early in the semester, assuming that some students may want to get an 'early start,' however, many students wait to get started on their papers, showing up weeks later having forgotten much of what they heard in the hour that was allotted for them to learn about the library."

Thus, timing is critical in several ways for effective instruction in information access and use, regardless of age level:
- Time is necessary for hands-on practice during, or immediately following, the

introduction of a new search method.

- Timing is key for application of method introduced within a meaningful search problem; for example, tied with the assignment that the student currently faces.
- Students are more likely to see relevance of information skills when there is staging of various steps in the information search and use process to coincide with point of need...as close as possible. In addition, successful teachers of information literacy skills don't frontload everything and expect students to retain and apply over an extended research assignment.
- Time for practice, reinforcement, and presentation of new skills is present throughout the duration of the process.
- Time for debriefing is important as it allows students to express and share the success and failures in their search for resources and information.

Creating the point of need for information skills is often associated with the integration of those skills with the content of a specific assignment from the classroom. Collaboration between the classroom teacher and the teacher of library media skills can enhance that integration and lead to precision in the timing of the presentation of specific search skills necessary and the introduction of resources relevant to the topic at hand. A recent study reported by Ross Todd from Sydney, Australia, demonstrated how such timing in the integration of information skills with science content led to higher student performance scores at all ability levels, especially higher performance by the most academically advanced student group.

Time for the Task

Perhaps the most frustrating discussion for those experienced in the successful application of information skills and reading practice for learning is the struggle to convince teachers and administrators of the need to allot time for such tasks. Sometimes it seems that student learning is hampered most by schedules that simply move students from one room to another, or from one task to another, without time for concentration and reflection.

Evidence presented by Stephen Krashen is very convincing in favor of a simple allocation of time each day for everyone in the school (including teachers, administrators, and all staff) to give twenty to thirty minutes to sustained silent reading. The process works at all grade levels. Kept in place for at least a year or two, this time on task can lead to dramatic increases in reading scores and increased demands for more books for reading pleasure from the school library media center.

While some activities, such as school time allotted to reading for pleasure, can be the easiest to manage, they may be the most difficult to initiate. This simple task does not have the movements and actions associated with student engagement and practice educators can normally observe of students in the science lab, at the computer terminal, or in social issues debates. This task is silent, most effective when sustained, and leads to greater gains in learning when followed by engagement for student sharing of thoughts and reflections. There are situations, therefore, when time on task can be pleasurable as well as educational for all.

For Further Reading

American Association of School Administrators. Time on Task. Arlington, VA: AASA, 1982.

Bloom, Benjamin S. "Time and Learning." American Psychologist 29 (1974): 682-688.

Carroll, John B. "A Model of School Learning." Teachers College Record 64 (1963): 723-733.

Krashen, Stephen. The Power of Reading. Englewood, CO: Libraries Unlimited, 1993.

Levitov, Deborah. "Lincoln Public Schools Guide to Integrated Information Literacy Skills." Nebraska Library Association Quarterly 28 (1997): 19-20.

Todd, Ross J. "Integrated Information Skills Instruction: Does It Make a Difference?" <u>School Library Media Quarterly</u> 23 (1995): 133-138.

Tumlin, Markel D. "Time Management Considerations for Balancing Optical Disc Point-of-Use Instruction with Other Reference Services." <u>Microcomputers for Information Management</u> 10, no. 3 (1993): 215-226.

Part 3
Resources

Reference

Information Literacy: Building Community Partnerships

Compiled by Cheryl McCarthy
Associate Professor, University of Rhode Island

SELECTED WEBLIOGRAPHY ON INFORMATION LITERACY

ACRL Information Literacy
http://www.ala.org/acrl/infolit.html

ACRL Institute for Information Literacy
http://www.ala.org/acrl/nili/nilihp.html

ACRL - Information Literacy Competency Standards for Higher Education
http://www.ala.org/acrl/ilcomstan.html

ACRL California Association of College and Research Libraries (CARL), Draft Recommendations
for Information Literacy Standards. (1997).
http://www.carl-acrl.org/Reports/rectoWASC.html

ACRL/CNI Internet Education Project
http://www.cwru.edu/affil/cni/base/acrlcni.html

ALA Community Partnerships Toolkit
http://library.austin.cc.tx.us/staff/lnavarro/CommunityPartnerships/Toolkit.html

ALA's Internet Resources
http://www.ala.org/ICONN
http://www.ala.org/parentspage/greatsites/amazing.html

ALA Library Instruction Roundtable
http://diogenes.baylor.edu/Library/LIRT/

American Library Association (ALA) Presidential Committee on Information Literacy (1989)
http://www.ala.org/acrl/nili/ilit1st.html

AASL & AECT Information Power: The 9 Information Literacy Standards for Student Learning
http://www.ala.org/aasl/ip_nine.html

The Big 6 Newsletter
http;//www.big6.com

Christine Bruce: Seven Faces of Information Literacy in Higher Education
http://www.fit.qut.edu.au/InfoSys/bruce/inflit/faces/faces1.htm

Classroom Connect's Education Resources
http://www.classroom.com

Colorado's Information Literacy Standards. (1994).
www.cde.state.co.us/download/pdf/infolit.pdf

CSU Information Competence Project
http://www.lib.calpoly.edu/infocomp/project/index.html

Curzon, S. "Information Competence in the CSU." [Online]
http://library.csun.edu/susan.curzon/infocmp.html

Cybertours
http://www.infosearcher.com/cybertours

Directory of Online Resources for Information Literacy
http://www.cas.usf.edu/lis/il

Division of Reference Services, OLIN*Kroch*Uris Libraries, Cornell University Library (September 1997). "Library Research at Cornell: A Hypertext Guide." [Online]
http://www.library.cornell.edu/okuref/research/tutorial.html

Educause Review
http://www.educause.edu/pub/er/erm.html

Eisenberg, M., & Johnson, D. (1996). "Computer Skills for Information Problem-Solving: Learning and Teaching Technology in Context." ERIC DIGEST.
http://ericir.syr.edu/ithome/digests/computerskills.htm

Evaluation Criteria for Good Web-Based Instruction
http://www.lib.vt.edu/istm/WebTutorialsTips.html

Florida International University: Information Literacy on the WWW
http://www.fiu.edu/~library/ili/ilweb.html
Excellent list of websites for all aspects of information literacy.

Florida International University: Programs, Projects, and Initiatives Concerning Information Literacy in Higher Education
http://www.cas.usf.edu/lis/il/academic.html

Florida International University: Programs, Projects, and Initiatives Concerning Information Literacy in Elementary and Secondary Education
http://www.cas.usf.edu/lis/il/school.html

Gateway to Educational Materials
http://www.thegateway.org

Go For The Gold - James Madison University (tutorial)
http://library.jmu.edu/library/gold/modules.htm

Grassian, E., & Clark, S. E. (1999). "Information Literacy Sites." C&RL News. [Online]
http://www.ala.org/acrl/resfeb99.html

Harvard's Educational New Technology Links
http://learnweb.harvard.edu/ent

Information Literacy at Florida international University Home Page
http://www.fiu.edu/~library/ili/

Information Literacy Competency Standards
http://www.fiu.edu/~library/ili/iliweb.html

International Society for Technology in Education (ISTE), National Educational Technology Standards
http://www.education-world.com/standards/national/technology/index.shtml

Internet Resources and Issues for Educators
http://wwwscout.cs.wisc.edu/scout/report

Kathy Schrock's Guide for Educators
http://www.discoveryschool.com/schrockguide

Knowledge Quest: Journal of the American Association of School Librarians
http://www.ala.org/aasl

Lazarra, M., & Heinzel, A. "Information Literacy Adventure." [Online]
http://prwww.ncook.k12.il.us/LearningCenter/infolit/iladventpage/iladvent.html

LOEX Clearinghouse for Library Instruction
http://www.emich.edu/public/loex/loex.html

McKenzie, Jamie. (1997). "A Questioning Toolkit." From Now On: The Educational Technology Journal. 7(3). [Online]
http://www.fromnowon.org/

National Forum on Information Literacy (NFIL). (1990).
http://www.infolit.org/index.html

NFIL. "A Progress Report on Information Literacy: An Update on the American Library Association Presidential Committee on Information Literacy: Final Report." (1998).
http://www.infolit.org/documents/progress.html

net.TUTOR - Ohio State University
http://gateway.lib.ohio-state.edu/tutor/open/courses.html

Oberlin College Library. "Faculty Workshop on Information Literacy." [Online]
http://www.oberlin.edu/~library/services/reference/WT97/

Oberman, C., et al. (1998). "Integrating Information Literacy in the Curriculum: How is your Library Measuring Up?" College and Research Libraries News, 59(9), 347-52.
http://www.ala.org/acrl/nili/integrtg.html

Oberman, C. (1998). "The Institute for Information Literacy." CRL News [Online]
http://www.ala.org/acrl/iiltrain.html

Oberman, C., & Wilson, G L. (1998). "Integrating Information Literacy Into the Curriculum."
C&RL News. [Online]
http://www.ala.org/acrl/nili/integrtg.html

Oberman. C., & Wilson, G. L. (1998). "Information Literacy IQ Test." C&RL News. [Online]
http://www.ala.org/acrl/nili/iqtest.html

Oregon Educational Media Association. "Information Literacy Guidelines: Scientific Inquiry."
[Online]
http://www.teleport.com/~oema/sci.html

Pathways to Knowledge and Inquiry Learning
http://www.fsc.follette.com
http://www.pathwaysmodel.com

Progress Report on Information Literacy
http://www.ala.org/acrl/nili/nili.html

School Library Journal
http://www.slj.com

School Library Media Research
http://www.ala.org/aasl/SLMR

Shapiro, J. J., & Hughes, S. K. "Information Literacy as a Liberal Art: Enlightenment Proposals for a New Curriculum." Educom Review. 31:2. (March/April 1996).
[Online]
http://www.educause.edu/pub/er/review/reviewArticles/31231.html

Smith, R. L. (1997). "Philosophical Shift: Teach the Faculty to Teach Information Literacy."
[Online]
http://www.ala.org/acrl/paperhtm/d38.html

SUNY Information Literacy Initiative
http://olis.sysadm.suny.edu/sunyconnect2/ili/Default.htm

SyllabusMagazine
http://www.syllabus.com

UC Berkeley Teaching Library
http://www.lib.berkeley.edu/TeachingLib

UCSC Net-Trail - University of California, Santa Cruz
http://nettrail.ucsc.edu/nettrail/master/

United States Department of Education. (1994). "Sec. 102: National Education Goals." [Online]
http://www.ed.gov/legislation/GOALS2000/TheAct/sec102.html

University of Arizona Library. (1996). "Information Literacy Project: Project Charge." [Online]
http://dizzy.library.arizona.edu/infolit/CHARGE.HTM

University of Arizona Library. (1996). "Information Literacy Project. Information Literacy Defined"
[Online]
http://dizzy.library.arizona.edu/infolit/DEFINE.HTM

University of Arizona Library. "Descriptions of Information Literacy Efforts at Other Universities."
[Online]
http://dizzy.library.arizona.edu/infolit/DESCRIPT.HTM

University of Louisville Office of Information Literacy. (1998). "Lifelong Learning Through the
Libraries." [Online]
http://www.louisville.edu/infoliteracy/

University of Wisconsin-Parkside Library/Learning Center. (2000). "Welcome to the Information
Literacy Program." [Online]
https://uwp.courses.wisc.edu/public/Infolit2/index.html

Utah State Office of Education - Library Media/Information Literacy Core Curriculum for Utah
Schools.
http://www.usoe.k12.ut.us/curr/library/

UWired Web
http://www.washington.edu/uwired/

Washington's State Information Literacy Standards
http://www.wlma.org/literacy/eslintro.htm

WebLUIS Tutorial - University of Central Florida
http://reach.ucf.edu:8900/public/libtut/

Webquests
http://edweb.sdsu.edu/webquest/webquest.html

Wisconsin Association of Academic Librarians - Information Literacy Ad Hoc Committee
http://facstaff.uww.edu/WAAL/infolit/index.html

Wisconsin's Checklist of Information and Technology Literacy Standards
http://www.rhinelander.k12.wi.us/hodag/educationaltec/index.html

Internet resources verified and updated on October 24, 2000.
JMS

342 ···

REFERENCE

Reference

Information Literacy: Are We There Yet?

Selected References for K-12 Schools

Compiled by Cheryl McCarthy
Associate Professor, University of Rhode Island

ACCESS PENNSYLVANIA Curriculum Guide. (1991). 54p. ED 355 963

Allen, C., & Anderson, M. A., eds. (1999). Skills for Life: Information Literacy for Grades 7-12. 2nd ed. Worthington: Linworth Publishing, Inc.

American Association of School Librarians. (1995). "Information Literacy: A Position Paper on Information Problem Solving." Emergency Librarian. 23(2), 20-23.

American Association of School Librarians. (1999). A Planning Guide for Information Power: Building Partnerships for Learning with School Library Media Program Assessment Rubric for the 21st Century. Chicago: American Library Association.

American Association of School Librarians, & Association for Educational Communications and Technology. (1998). Information Literacy Standards for Student Learning. Chicago: American Library Association.

American Association of School Librarians, & Association for Educational Communications and Technology. (1998). Information Power: Building Partnerships for Learning. Chicago: American Library Association.

American Association of School Librarians, & Association for Educational Communications and Technology. (1988). Information Power: Guidelines for School Library Media Programs. Chicago: American Library Association.

American Library Association Presidential Committee on Information Literacy. (1989). Final Report. Chicago: Author. ED316074

Anderson, M. A. (1999). "Creating the Link: Aligning National and State Standards. Book Report. 17(5), 12-14.

Anderson, M. A. (1999). "The Media Center: Information Power: Because Student Achievement Is The Bottom Line." Multimedia Schools, 6(2), 22-23.

Anderson, M. A. (1996). Teaching Information Literacy Using Electronic Resources for Grades 6-12. Worthington: Linworth Publishing, Inc.

Andronik, C. M. (1999). Information Literacy Skills Grades 7-12. 3rd ed. Worthington: Linworth Publishing, Inc.
Asselin, M. (2000). "Research Instruction." Teacher Librarian. 27(5), 64-65.

Association for College & Research Libraries (ACRL). Information Literacy Competency Standards for Higher Education. [Online] <http://www.ala.org/acrl/ilcomstan.html> April 11, 2001.

Association for Teacher-Librarianship in Canada and the Canadian School Library Association. (1998). "Students' Information Literacy Needs: competencies for Teacher-librarians in the 21st Century." Teacher Librarian. 26(2), 22-25.

Australian Library and Information Association. (1994). Learning for the Future: Developing Information Services in Australian Schools. Australian School Library Association, Goulburn. Carlton, Australia: Curriculum Corp. ED 377 826.

Batz, L., & Rosenberg, H. (1999). "Creating An Information Literate School: Information Literacy in Action." National Association of Secondary School Principals. NASSP Bulletin, 83(605), 68-74.

Bishop, K. & Larimer, N. (1999). "Collaboration: Literacy Through Collaboration. Teacher Librarian. 27(1), 15-20.

Bleakley, A., & Carrigan, J. L. (1995). Resource-Based Learning Activities: Information Literacy for high School Students. Chicago: American Library Association.

Bloom, B. S. (1956). Taxonomy of Educational Objectives: The Classification of Educational Goals: Handbook I: Cognitive Domain. New York: McKay.

Breivik, P. S. (1998.). Student Learning in the Information Age. Phoenix, AZ: Oryx Press.

Breivik, P. S., & Gee, E. G. (1989). Information Literacy. New York: Macmillan Publishing Co.

Breivik, P. S., Hancock, V., & Senn, J. (1998). A Progress Report on Information Literacy: An Update on the American Library Association Presidential Committee on Information Literacy: Final Report. Chicago: ALA, Association of Research Librarians. pp 1-10.

Breivik, P. S., & Senn, J. A. (1993). "Information Literacy: Partnerships for Power." Emergency Librarian. 21(1), 25-28. EJ469 235

Breivik, P. S., & Senn, J. A. (1998). Information Literacy: Educating Children for the 21st Century. 2nd ed. Washington, DC: National Education Association.

Brock, K. (1994). "Developing Information Literacy Through the information Intermediary Process: A Model for Teacher-Librarians and Others." Emergency Librarian. 22(1), 16-20. EJ491 450

Bruce, C. (1997). The Seven Faces of Information Literacy. Adelaide, Australia: Auslib Press.

Bucher, K. T. (2000). "The Importance of Information Literacy Skills in the Middle School Curriculum." The Clearing House, 73(4), 217-220.

Bush, G. (1999). "Creating an Information Literate School: Here and Now." National Association of SecondarySchool Principals. NASSP Bulletin, 83(605), 62-67.

California Department of Education. (1994). Information Literacy Guidelines. Denver, CO: Author.

California Media and Library Educators Association. (1994). From Library Skills to Information Literacy: A Handbook for the 21st Century. Castle Rock, CO: Hi Willow Research and Publishing.

California Media and Library Educators Association. (1997). From Information Skills to Information Literacy: A Handbook for the 21st Century. San Jose, CA: Hi Willow.

Callison, D. (1993). "Expanding the Evaluation Role in the Critical-Thinking Curriculum." School Library Media Annual (SLMA). 11, 78-92. EJ476208

Callison, D., McGregor, J. H., & Small, R. (eds). (1998) "Instructional Intervention for Information Use." Research Papers of the Sixth Treasure Mountain Research Retreat for School Library Media Programs. March 31 - April 1, 1997. San Jose, CA: Hi Willow Research and Publishing.

Carbone, L. (1999). "Leadership for a New Era: Making the Most of Technology in our schools." Schools in the Middle. 9(4), 26-7.

Colorado Department of Education. (1994). Model Information Literacy Guidelines. Denver, CO: ED373 797

Colorado State Department of Education. (1996). Rubrics for the Assessment of Information Literacy. Denver, CO. ED401 899

Craver, K. W. (1997). Teaching Electronic Literacy: A Concepts-Based Approach for School Library Media Specialists. Westport, CT: Greenwood Press.

Donham, Jean. (1999). "Collaboration in the Media Center: Building Partnerships for Learning." National Association of Secondary School Principals. NASSP Bulletin, 83(605), 20-26.

Doyle, C. S. (1994). Information Literacy in an Information Society: A Concept for the Information Age. Syracuse: ERIC Clearinghouse on Information and Technology. ED372 763.

Dreher, M. J. (1995). "Sixth-Grade Researchers: Posing Questions, Finding Information, and Writing a Report." Reading Research Report No. 40 (Summer 1995). 17 p. ED384 014

Dreher, M. J. et al. (1999). "Fourth-grade researchers: Helping children develop strategies for finding and using information. In T. Shanahan & F.V. Rodriguez-Brown, eds. 48th Yearbook of the National Reading Conference. (pp. 311-322). Chicago, IL: National Reading Conference.

Eisenberg, M. B. & Berkowitz, R. E. (2000). The Big6 Collection: The Best of the Big6 Newsletter by Michael B. Eisenberg and Robert E. Berkowitz. Worthington, Ohio: Linworth Publishing.

Eisenberg, M. B., & Berkowitz, R. E. (1988). Curriculum Initiative: An Agenda and Strategy for Library Media Programs. Norwood, NJ: Ablex Publishing Corporation.

Eisenberg, M. B. & Berkowitz, R. E. (1990) Information Problem-Solving: The Big6 Skills Approach to Library & Information Skills Instruction. Norwood, NJ: Ablex Publishing Corporation.

Eisenberg, M. B., & Berkowitz, R.E. (1999). Teaching Information and Technology Skills: the Big 6 in Elementary Schools. Worthington, Ohio: Linworth Publishing.

Eisenberg, M. B., & Brown, M. K. (1992). "Current Themes Regarding Library and Information Skills Instruction: Research Supporting and Research Lacking." School Library Media Quarterly. 20(2), 103-109. EJ441 731

Eisenberg, M. B. & Johnson, D. (1996) "Computer Skills for Information Problem-Solving: Learning and Teaching Technology in Context." ERIC Digest. Syracuse: ERIC Clearinghouse on Information & Technology. ED392 463.

Farmer, L. (1999). "Making Information Literacy a Schoolwide Reform Effort." Book Report. 18(3), 6-8.

Farmer, L. (2001). "Building Information Literacy through a Whole School Regorm Approach." Knowledge Quest. 29(2), 20-24.

Fitzgerald, M. A. (1997). "Misinformation on the Internet: Applying Evaluation Skills to Online Information." Emergency Librarian. (January/February), 9-14.

Giguere, M., And Others. (1995). "Enhancing Information Literacy Skills Across the Curriculum." In Literacy: Traditional, Cultural, Technological. Selected Papers from the Annual Conference of the International Association of School Librarianship. (23rd, Pittsburgh, PA, July 17-22, 1994). ED399 951

Goodin, M. E. (1991). "The Transferability of Library Research Skills from High School to College." School Library Media Quarterly. 20(1), 33-42. EJ436241

Gross, J. & Kientz, S. (1999). "Developing Information Literacy: Collaborating for Authentic Learning." Teacher Librarian. 27(1), 21-5.

Hancock, V. E. (1993). "Information Literacy for Lifelong Learning." ERIC Digest. Syracuse: ERIC Clearinghouse on Information Resources. ED358870

Harada, V., & Donham, J. (1998). "Information Power: Student Achievement is the Bottom Line."Teacher Librarian, 26(1), 14-17.

Harada, V. H., & Nakamura, M. (1994). "Information Searching Across the Curriculum: Literacy Skills for the 90's and Beyond." Catholic Library World. 65(2), 17-19. EJ538020

Haycock, K. (1999). "Fostering Collaboration, Leadership and Information Literacy: Common Behaviors of Uncommon Principals and Faculties." National Association of Secondary School Principals. NASSP Bulletin, 83(605), 82-87.

Haycock, K., ed. (1999). Foundations for Effective School Library Media Programs. Englewood: Libraries Unlimited, Inc.

Haycock , K. (1999). "Information Literacy: Making Effective Use of Resources." National Association of Secondary School Principals. NASSP Bulletin, 83(605), 1-.

Henri, J. & Bonanno, K. ed. (1999). The Information Literate School Community: Best Practice "Topics in Australian Teacher Librarianship. Series." New South Wales: Centre for Information Studies at Charles Stuart University.

Herring, J.E. (1996). Teaching Information Literacy Skills in Schools. London: Library Association Publishing.

Iannuzzi, P., Mangrum, C. T., & Strichart, S. S. (1999). Teaching Information Literacy Skills. Boston: Allyn and Bacon.

"Information Literacy: A Position Paper of Information Problem-Solving." (1995). Emergency Librarian. 23(2), 20-23.

"Information Literacy and Education for the 21st Century: Toward an Agenda for Action." (1989). A symposium sponsored by the U.S. National Commission on Libraries and Information Science and the American Association of School Librarians. Leesburg, Virginia, April 14-16, 1989.

Iowa City Community School District and Langhorne, M. J. ed. (1998). Developing and Information Literacy Program K-12: A How-To-Do-It Manual and CD-ROM Package. New York: Neal-Schuman Publishers, Inc.

Johnson, D. (1999). "Implementing an Information Literacy Curriculum: One District's Story." National Association of Secondary School Principals. NASSP Bulletin, 83(605), 53-61.

Johnson, D. (1997). The Indispensable Librarian- Surviving (and Thriving) in School Media Centers. Worthington: Linworth Publishing, Inc.

Johnson, D., & Eisenberg, M. (1996). "Computer Literacy and Information Literacy: A Natural Combination." Emergency Librarian. 23(5), 12-16. EJ526 333

Joseph, M. (1991). "The Cure for Library Anxiety-It May Not Be What You Think." Catholic Library World. 63(2), 111-114.

Joyce, M. Z. & Tallman, J. (1997). Making the Writing and Research connection with the I-Search Process. Englewood, CO: Libraries Unlimited.

Kansas Association of School Librarians Research Committee. (1999) "Planning and Assessing Learning across the Curriculum." Knowledge Quest 28(1), 10-11, 13-16.

Keenan, N., et al. (1994). The Montana Library and Information Skills Model Curriculum Education Services. 106 p. ED382 216

Kendall, J. S., & Marzano, R. J. (1997). Content Knowledge: A Compendium of Standards and Benchmarks for K-12 Education. 2nd ed. Denver, CO: Midcontinent Research and Evaluation Laboratory.

Kentucky Department of Education. (1995). Online II: Essentials of a Model Library Media Program. Louisville, KY: Author.

Kester, D. D. (1994). "Secondary School Library and Information Skills: Are They Transferred from High School to College?" Reference Librarian. 44, 9-17. EJ488269

Krashen, S. (1993). The Power of Reading. Englewood, CO: Libraries Unlimited.

Kuhlthau, C. C. (1988). "Developing a Model of the Library Search Process: Cognitive and Affective Aspects." RQ 28(2), 232-242.

Kuhlthau, C. C. (1993). "Implementing a Process Approach to Information Skills: A Study Identifying Indicators of Success in Library Media Programs." School Library Media Quarterly. 22(1), 11-18. EJ473063

Kuhlthau, C. C. (1987). Information Skills for an Information Society: A Review of Research. Syracuse: ERIC Clearinghouse on Information Resources. ED297 740

Kuhlthau, C. C. (1993). Seeking Meaning: A Process Approach to Library and Information Services. Norwood, NJ: Ablex.

Kuhlthau, C. C. & et al. (1990). "Validating a Model of the Search Process: A Comparison of Academic, Public and School Library Users." LISR 12, 5-31.

Lance, K. C., Welborn, L., & Hamilton-Pennell, C. (1993). The Impact of School Library Media Centers on Academic Achievement. Castle Rock, CO: Hi Willow Research and Publishing. ED353989

Lance, K.C., Rodney, M.J., & Hamilton-Pennell, C. (2000). How School Librarians Help Kids Achieve Standards: The Second Colorado Study. San Jose, CA: Hi Willow Research & Publishing.

Lance, K.C., Rodney, M.J., & Hamilton-Pennell, C. (2000) Measuring Up to Standards: The Impact of School Library Programs & Information Literacy in Pennsylvania Schools. [Online] <http://www.lrs.org>

Lance, K.C. et al. (2000). Information Empowered: The School Librarian as an Agent of Academic Achievement in Alaska Schools.

Loertscher, D. & Woolls, B. (1999). Information Literacy: A Review of the Research: A Guide For Practitioners and Researchers. San Jose, CA: Hi Willow Research and Publishing.

Logan, D.K. (2000). Information Skills Toolkit: Collaborative Integrated Instruction for the Middle Grades. Worthington, Ohio: Linworth Publishing.

Macrorie, Ken. (1988) The I-Search Paper. Portsmouth, NH: Heinemann.

Mancall, J. C., Aaron, S. L., & Walker, S. A. (1986). "Educating Students to Think: The Role of the Library Media Program - A Concept Paper Written for the National Commission on Libraries and Information Science." School Library Media Quarterly, Journal of the American Association of School Librarians. 15(1), 18-27. EJ344239

Marcoux, B. (1999). "Developing the National Information Literacy Standards for Student Learning." National Association of Secondary School Principals. NASSP Bulletin, 83(605), 13-19.

McCarthy, C. (1997). "A Reality Check: The Challenges of Implementing Information Power in School Library Media Programs." School Library Media Quarterly 25(4), 205-214.

McElmeel, Sharron L. (1997). Research Strategies for Moving Beyond Reporting. Worthington, OH: Linworth Publishing.

McGregor, J. (1999). "Teaching the Research Process: Helping Students Become Lifelong Learners." National Association of Secondary School Principals. NASSP Bulletin, 83(605), 27-34.

McGregor, J. & Strietenbeger. D. (1998). "Do Scribes Learn? Copying and Information Use." School Library Media Quarterly [Online] <http://www.ala.org/aasl/SLMQ/scribes.html> April 11, 2001.

Mendrinos, R. (1994). Building Information Literacy Using high Technology:A Guide for Schools and Libraries. Englewood: Libraries Unlimited, Inc. 190 p. ED375 820

Moyer, S. L. & Small, R. V. "Building a Motivational Toolkit for Teaching Information Literacy." Knowledge Quest. 29(2), 28-32.

Neuman, Delia. (1999). "What Do We Do After the School Has Been Wired?: Providing Intellectual Access to Digital Resources." National Association of Secondary School Principals. NASSP Bulletin, 83(605), 35-43.

Nichols, J. (1999). "Building Bridges: High School and University Partnerships for Information Literacy." National Association of Secondary School Principals. NASSP Bulletin, 83(605), 75-81.

Oregon Educational Media Association. (February 1997) Oregon Information Literacy Guidelines. [Online] <http://www.teleport.com/~oema/infolit.html> Accessed April 11, 2001

O'Sullivan, M., & Scott, T. (2000). "Teaching Internet Information Literacy: A Collaborative Approach." (Part II). Multimedia Schools, 7(3), 34-37.

O'Sullivan, M. and Scott, T. (2000). "Teaching Internet Information Literacy: A Critical Evaluation." (Part I). Multimedia Schools, 7(2), 40-44

Pappas, M. L. (1995). "Information Skills for Electronic Resources." School Library Media Activities Monthly. 11(8), 39-40. EJ499875

Pennell, Victoria, ed. (1997). Information Literacy: An Advocacy Kit for Teacher-Librarians. Canada: Association for Teacher-librarianship in Canada.

Pitts, J., et al. (1995). "Mental Models of Information: The 1993-1994 AASL/Highsmith Research Award Study." School Library Media Quarterly. 23(3), 177-184. EJ503402

Rankin, V. (1999). The Thoughtful Researcher: Teaching the Research Process to Middle School Students. Englewood, CO: Libraries Unlimited.

Reese, J. (2000). "Integrating Information Literacy Skills into the Curriculum." Multimedia Schools 7(5), 46-7.

Salvadore, M. B. (1999). "Developing an Information Literacy Program K-12." School Library Journal, 45(9), 248-249.

Schrock, K. & Frazel, M. Inquiring Educators Want to Know: TeacherQuests for Today's Teachers. Worthington, Ohio: Linworth Publishing.

Secretary's Commission on Achieving Necessary Skills (SCANS). (1991) "What Work Requires of Schools: A SCANS Report for America 2000. Washington, D.C. ED332 054

Small, R. V. & Arnone, M. P. (2000). Turning Kids on to Research: The power of Motivation. Englewood, CO: Libraries Unlimited.

Spitzer, K. L., Eisenberg, M., & Lowe, C. A. (1998). Information Literacy: Essential Skills for the Information Age. Syracuse, NY: ERIC Clearinghouse on Information and Technology.

Steele, S., & Heim, A. (1997). Libraries Enhance Student Learning: A Guidebook of Innovative Library Programs for Youth. Washington, DC: U.S. Department of Education.

Stripling, B. K. (1999). "Expectations for Achievement and Performance: Assessing Student Skills." National Association of Secondary School Principals. NASSP Bulletin, 83(605), 44-52.

Stripling, B. K. (1996). "Quality in School Library Media Programs: Focus on Learning." Library Trends. 14(3), 631-656.

Stripling, B. K. (1995). "Learning-Centered Libraries: Implications from Research." School Library Media Quarterly. 23(3), 163-70.

Stripling, B. K., & Pitts, J. (1988). Brainstorms and Blueprints: Teaching Library Research as a Thinking Process. Littleton, CO: Libraries Unlimited.

Texas Education Agency. (1993). The Library Media Center: A Force for Student Excellence. 96 p. ED366 345

Thomas, N. P., & Montgomery, P. K. (ed.) (1999). Information Literacy and Information Skills Instruction:Applying Research in the School Library Media Center. Englewood, CO: Libraries Unlimited, Inc.

Todd, R. J. (1995). "Integrated Information Skills Instruction: Does It Make a Difference?" School Library Media Quarterly. 23(2), 133-39.

Todd, R. J. et al. (1992). "The Power of Information Literacy: Unity of Education and Resources for the 21st Century." Paper presented at the Annual Meeting of the International Association of School Librarianship (Belfast, Northern Ireland, United Kingdom, July 19-24, 1992). ED 354 916

Todd, R. J. (1999). "Transformational Leadership and Transformation Learning: Information Literacy and the World Wide Web." National Association of Secondary School Principals. NASSP Bulletin, 83(605), 4-12.

Utah State Office of Education.(1991). Elementary and Secondary Core Curriculum Standards. Levels K-12. Library Media. 48 p. ED371720

Walster, D., & Welborn, L. (1996). "Writing and Implementing 'Colorado's Information Literacy Guidelines': The Process Examined." School Library Media Activities Monthly. 12(6), 25-28, 36. EJ516616

Wisconsin Educational Media Association. (1993). Information Literacy: A Position Paper on Information Problem-Solving. 6p. Appleton, WI: Author. ED376 817

Reference

Web Resources on Information Literacy in K-12 Schools

Compiled by Cheryl McCarthy
Associate Professor, University of Rhode Island

American Association of School Librarians/American Library Association. Connecting Learners and Information: ICONNECT. (c)1998-1999. <http://www.ala.org/ICONN> (June 8, 2001).

American Association of School Librarians/American Library Association. Home Page. (c)2000, 2001. <http://www.ala.org/aasl> (June 8, 2001).

American Association of School Librarians/American Library Association & Association for Educational Communications Technology. Information Power: The Nine Information Literacy Standards for Student Learning. August 25, 2000. <http://www.ala.org/aasl/ip_nine.html> (June 8, 2001).

American Association of School Librarians/American Library Association. Knowledge Quest on the Web. (c)2000, 2001. <http:www.ala.org/aasl/kqweb/index.html> (June 8, 2001).

American Association of School Librarians/American Library Association. School Library Media Research. June 8, 2001. <http://www.ala.org/aasl/SLMR> (June 11, 2001).

American Library Association. Great Sites: 700+ Great Sites. January 5, 2001. <http://www.ala.org/parentspage/greatsites/index.html> (June 8, 2001).

Association of College and Research Libraries/Instruction Section/Teaching Methods Committee. Tips for Developing Effective Web-Based Library Instruction. August 11, 2000. <http://www.lib.vt.edu/istm/WebTutorialsTips.html> (June 8, 2001)

Berger, Pam. Infosearcher.com. CyberTours:An Active Learning Strategy. (c)2000. <http://www.infosearcher.com/ctours.htm> (June 8, 2001).

Classroom Connect. (c) 2000. <http://www.classroom.com/login/landing.jhtml> (June 8, 2001).

Colorado Department of Education. Colorado Information Literacy. December 4, 2000. <http://www.cde.state.co.us/cdelib/slinfolitindex.htm> (June 8, 2001).

Dodge, Bernie. The WebQuest Page. November 17, 2000. <http://edweb.sdsu.edu/webquest/webquest.html> (June 11, 2001).

Heinzel, Aimee & Lazarra, Marlene. Information Literacy. April 10, 2000.
<http://prwww.ncook.k12.il.us/LearningCenter/infolit/ilpage.html> (June 11, 2001).

Indiana Standards for Teachers of Library Media
<http://www.in.gov/psb/standards/teacherindex.html>

Indiana Standards for Student Learning: Correlation of the Library Information Literacy Standards.
<http://ideanet.doc.state.in.us/standards/welcome2.html>

International Society for Technology in Education (ISTE). National Educational Technology
Standards Project. April 27, 2001. <http://www.iste.org/standards/index.html> and
<http://www.cnets.iste.org> (June 8, 2001).

Internet Scout Project, Computer Sciences Department, University of Wisconsin-Madison. The
Scout Report. June 1, 2001. <http://wwwscout.cs.wisc.edu/scout/report> (June 8, 2001).

McKenzie, Jamie. "Beyond Technology to Learning and Information Literacy." From Now On:
The Educational Technology Journal. May 2001. <http://www.fno.org> (June 11, 2001).

Oregon Educational Media Association. "Information Literacy Guidelines: Scientific Inquiry."
<http://www.teleport.com/~oema/sci.html> (June 11, 2001).

Reed Elsevier Business Information Publication. School Library Journal Online: For Children's,
Young Adult, and School Librarians. (c)2001. <http://www.slj.com> (June 11, 2001).

Shapiro, Jeremy J., & Hughes, Shelley K. Information Literacy as a Liberal Art: Enlightenment
Proposals for a New Curriculum. Educom Review. 31:2. (March/April 1996).
<http://www.educause.edu/pub/er/review/reviewArticles/31231.html> (June 11, 2001).

Schrock, Kathy. Kathy Schrock's Guide for Educators. June 7, 2001.
<http://discoveryschool.com/schrockguide> (June 8, 2001).

Smith, Drew. Directory of Online Resources for Information Literacy. December 18, 1999.
<http://www.cas.usf.edu/lis/il> (June 8, 2001).

United States Department of Education. (1994). Sec. 102: National Education Goals.
<http://www.ed.gov/legislation/GOALS2000/TheAct/sec102.html> (June 11, 2001).

U.S. Department Education and ERIC Clearinghouse on Information Technology. The Gateway to
Educational Materials. (c)2000. <http://www.thegateway.org> (June 8, 2001).

Utah State Office of Education. Library Media/Information Literacy Core Curriculum for Utah
Schools. May 22, 2001. <http://www.usoe.k12.ut.us/curr/library/core.html> (June 11, 2001).

Washington Library Media Association & Office of Superintendent of Public Instruction, Olympia,
Washington. Essential Skills for Information Literacy. 1996.
<http://www.wlma.org/literacy/eslintro.htm> (June 11, 2001).

Washington Library Media Association. Information Literacy. March 27, 2001.
<http://www.wlma.org/Literacy/infoskil.htm> (June 11, 2001).

Wisconsin, Department of Public Instruction. Wisconsin's Model Academic Standards: Information and Technology Literacy Standards. September 1, 1998. <http://www.dpi.state.wi.us/dltcl/imt/itls.html> (June 11, 2001).

Reference

Web Resources on Information Literacy in Higher Education

Compiled by Cheryl McCarthy
Associate Professor, University of Rhode Island

American Library Association. Community Partnerships Toolkit, January 10, 2000. <http://library.austin.cc.tx.us/staff/lnavarro/CommunityPartnerships/Toolkit.html> (4 April 2001).

American Library Association. Library Instruction Roundtable, January 10, 2001. <http://diogenes.baylor.edu/Library/LIRT/> (4 April 2001).

American Library Association. Presidential Committee on Information Literacy, January 10, 1989. <http://www.ala.org/acrl/nili/ilit1st.html > (4 April 2001).

Association of College and Research Libraries. Information Literacy, February 15, 2001, <http://www.ala.org/acrl/infolit.html > (4 April 2001).

Association of College and Research Libraries. Institute for Information Literacy, August 3, 2000. <http://www.ala.org/acrl/nili/nilihp.html> (4 April 2001).

Association of College and Research Libraries. Information Literacy Competency Standards for Higher Education, April 3, 2001. <http://www.ala.org/acrl/ilcomstan.html> (4 April 2001).

Association of College and Research Libraries. Progress Report on Information Literacy, July 28, 2000, <http://www.ala.org/acrl/nili/nili.html> (1 May 2001).

ACRL Instruction Section Teaching Methods Committee. Rips for Developing Effective Web-Based LibraryInstruction, July 17, 2000. <http://www.lib.vt.edu/istm/WebTutorialsTips.html> (1 May 2001).

Bruce, Christine. Seven Faces of Information Literacy in Higher Education, 1997. <http://www.fit.qut.edu.au/InfoSys/bruce/inflit/faces/faces1.htm> (4 April 2001).

California State University System. CSU Information Competence Project, February 25, 2001. <http://www.lib.calpoly.edu/infocomp/project/index.html> (4 April 2001).

Case Western Reserve University. ACRL/CNI Internet Education Project, March 27, 1998. <http://www.cwru.edu/affil/cni/base/acrlcni.html> (4 April 2001).

Curzon, Susan C. Information Competence in the CSU, January 15, 1998. <http://library.csun.edu/susan.curzon/infocmp.html> (4 April 2001).

Division of Reference Services, OLIN*Kroch*Uris Libraries, Cornell University Library. Library Research at Cornell: A Hypertext Guide, September 9, 1999. <http://www.library.cornell.edu/okuref/research/tutorial.html> (4 April 2001).

Education World, International Society for Technology in Education (ISTE), National Educational Technology Standards, 2000, <http://www.education-world.com/standards/national/technology/index.shtml> (1 May 2001).

Educause. Educause Review, March 2001. <http://www.educause.edu/pub/er/erm.html> (1 May 2001).

Florida International University. Information Literacy on the WWW, February 6, 2001. <http://www.fiu.edu/~library/ili/iliweb.html> (1 May 2001).

Florida International University. Programs, Projects, and Initiatives Concerning Information Literacy in Higher Education, November 27, 1999. <http://www.cas.usf.edu/lis/il/academic.html> (1 May 2001).

Florida International University. Information Literacy at Florida International University Home Page, July 19, 2000. <http://www.fiu.edu/~library/ili/> (1 May 2001).

Grassian, E., & Clark, S. E. Information Literacy Sites, February 1999, C&RL News. <http://www.ala.org/acrl/resfeb99.html> (1 May 2001).

Harvard University. Education with New Technologies: Networked Learning Community, <http://learnweb.harvard.edu/ent> (1 May 2001).

James Madison University. Go For The Gold (tutorial), <http://library.jmu.edu/library/gold/modules.htm> (1 May 2001).

LOEX. LOEX Clearinghouse for Library Instruction, December 3, 2000. <http://www.emich.edu/public/loex/loex.html> (1 May 2001).

National Forum on Information Literacy. The National Forum on Information Literacy - Overview, October 4, 2000, <http://www.infolit.org/index.html> (1 May 2001).

National Forum on Information Literacy. A Progress Report on Information Literacy: An Update on the American Library Association Presidential Committee on Information Literacy: Final Report, March 1998, <http://www.infolit.org/documents/progress.html> (1 May 2001).

Ohio State University Libraries. net.TUTOR, 2001, <http://gateway.lib.ohio-state.edu/tutor/open/courses.html> (1 May 2001).

Oberman, Cerise, Bonnie Gratch Lindauer, and Betsy Wilson. Integrating Information Literacy in the Curriculum: How Is Your Library Measuring Up, College and Research Libraries News, 59(9), 347-52, 1998. <http://www.ala.org/acrl/nili/integrtg.html> (1 May 2001).

Oberman, Cerise. The Institute for Information Literacy, CRL News, 1998, <http://www.ala.org/acrl/iiltrain.html> (1 May 2001).

Oberman. Cerise, & Betsy Wilson. Information Literacy IQ Test, C&RL News, 1998, <http://www.ala.org/acrl/nili/iqtest.html> (1 May 2001).

Smith, Drew. Directory of Online Resources for Information Literacy, December 18, 1999. <http://www.cas.usf.edu/lis/il> (4 April 2001).

Smith, Rise L. Philosophical Shift: Teach the Faculty to Teach Information Literacy, 1997, <http://www.ala.org/acrl/paperhtm/d38.html> (1 May 2001).

State University of New York. SUNY Information Literacy Initiative, October 2, 1997, <http://olis.sysadm.suny.edu/sunyconnect2/ili/Default.htm> (1 May 2001).

Syllabus. SyllabusMagazine, May 2001, <http://www.syllabus.com> (1 May 2001).

Taxas University Information Literacy Tutorial. <tilt.lib.utsystem.edu> (18 September 2002)

University of Arizona Library. Information Literacy Project: Project Charge, 1996, <http://dizzy.library.arizona.edu/infolit/CHARGE.HTM> (1 May 2001).

University of Arizona Library. Information Literacy Defined, 1996, <http://dizzy.library.arizona.edu/infolit/DEFINE.HTM> (1 May 2001).

University of Arizona Library. Descriptions of Information Literacy Efforts at Other Universities, 1996, <http://dizzy.library.arizona.edu/infolit/DESCRIPT.HTM> (1 May 2001).

University of California-Berkeley. The Teaching Library, 1995, <http://www.lib.berkeley.edu/TeachingLib> (1 May 2001).

University of Central Florida. WebLUIS Tutorial, <http://reach.ucf.edu:8900/public/libtut/> (1 May 2001).

University of Louisville. Information Literacy Program, January 22, 2001, <http://www.louisville.edu/infoliteracy/> (1 May 2001).

University of Washington. UWired Web, 2001, <http://www.washington.edu/uwired/> (1 May 2001).

University of Wisconsin-Madison. The Scout Report, April 27, 2001. <http://wwwscout.cs.wisc.edu/scout/report> (1 May 2001).

University of Wisconsin-Parkside Library/Learning Center. Welcome to the Information Literacy Program, Spring 2001, <https://uwp.courses.wisc.edu/public/Infolit2/index.html> (1 may 2001).

Wisconsin Association of Academic Librarians. Information Literacy Ad Hoc Committee, February 1, 2001, <http://facstaff.uww.edu/WAAL/infolit/index.html> (1 May 2001).

Part 4

Index